Inclusion 101

Inclusion 101

How to Teach All Learners

by

Anne M. Bauer, Ed.D.
University of Cincinnati
Cincinnati, Ohio

and

Thomas M. Shea, Ed.D.
Southern Illinois University–Edwardsville
Edwardsville, Illinois

·P A U L·H·
BROOKES
PUBLISHING Cº

Baltimore • London • Toronto • Sydney

Paul H. Brookes Publishing Co.
Post Office Box 10624
Baltimore, Maryland 21285-0624

www.brookespublishing.com

Typeset by Barton Matheson Willse and Worthington, Baltimore, Maryland.
Manufactured in the United States of America by
The Maple Press Company, York, Pennsylvania.

Library of Congress Cataloging-in-Publication Data

Bauer, Anne M.
    Inclusion 101 : how to teach all learners / Anne M. Bauer and
Thomas Michael Shea.
        p.   cm.
    Includes bibliographical references and index.
    ISBN 1-55766-372-6
    1. Inclusive education—United States.   2. Classroom management—United States.
3. School management and organization—United States.   I. Shea, Thomas M., 1934–   .
II. Title.
LC1201.B38   1999
371.102—dc21   98-30328
                                                                                                CIP

British Library Cataloguing in Publication data are available from the British Library.

Contents

15 **Voices from Inclusive Learning Communities**
Karen Matuszek, Linda Phillips, Jan Rich, Regina H. Sapona,

Preface

I have been teaching 5 [or 10, 20, or 25] years, and these children are different. These are not the children I was prepared to teach! I have no two students at the same level in the same subject. Two of the children used to be in special education, one is in foster care, two of them have parents going through a divorce, and three have single parents. Several of these children would go hungry without the breakfast and lunch program at school.

We frequently hear comments such as these from the teachers with whom we work in the community schools. They are correct. Society is different. Schools are different. Students are different. We are aware that we are often unprepared by training and experience to deal with the problems that confront us in today's schools. As Epanchin (1993) suggested, if teachers are to deal effectively with children who come from diverse backgrounds, a new emphasis on content that is not part of most traditional teacher-training programs, including ethics, diversity, communication skills, leadership skills, and group behavior, is essential.

In 1962, Kuhn coined the phrase *paradigm shift* to describe a new way of thinking about or conceptualizing activities, events, and efforts. This phrase has been used to describe what is happening in schools. A new way of thinking has indeed emerged in education. This paradigm shift recognizes that the student produces the educational outcome (i.e., learning) (Lipsky & Gartner, 1991). With the diversity apparent in classrooms, the purpose of schooling is to enable all students to participate actively in their communities so that their peers care enough about them to find ways to include them as part of those communities (Ferguson, Meyer, Jeanchild, Juniper, & Zingo, 1992).

In the new education paradigm, several assumptions emerge. Among these is respect for students and their individual strengths and contributions (Stainback & Stainback, 1991). From this perspective, students themselves are seen not as problems but rather as presenting challenges to their teachers' professional problem-solving abilities. Failure is seen not as a personal failure of the students but as a failure of the school to meet the students' needs (Lipsky & Gartner, 1991).

According to Lipsky and Gartner, within the new paradigm, teachers are enablers of their students' learning who work with other professionals across disciplines as members of a team. As enablers, teachers engage in a variety of interactions with students. Parents are recognized as essential members of the team.

Inclusion 101: How to Teach All Learners recognizes the new paradigm for education and the emerging role of the teacher. In this book, we assume that, in each classroom, there are students who vary significantly from their peers in terms of their interactions, learning styles and rates, and ways in which they gain access to the learning environment. We do not argue for or against inclusion; we simply recognize that it exists—it is in the classrooms in which we work—regardless of whether students have received a label as having disabilities. We celebrate diversity in classrooms and schools as the way to prepare the children and youth in our charge to grow as caring, empathetic, proactive problem solvers and critical thinkers.

In this book, we assume that good teaching matters and that efforts made to meet the needs of students with specific challenges benefit all students. We assume that teachers are scientist practitioners who are able to define, reflect on, design, and evaluate solutions to the challenges that they confront in classrooms and schools. We posit that because teachers are critical thinkers, they do not need a "cookbook" approach to interventions; rather, they need skills to be able to assess situations, develop strategies, and respond to their students' needs. We believe that the parents, caregivers, and significant others in each student's life must be actively engaged in the student's education. The school and the practitioner must seek and support their participation.

In the first section of *Inclusion 101,* the reader is introduced to the concepts of inclusive society, schools, classrooms, and services. Chapter 1 examines ethnic, cultural, and linguistic diversity as well as issues related to gender and disability. The caregiving environment that many children and youth experience because of poverty, divorce, adolescent parenthood, maternal employment, single-parent families, substance abuse, and maltreatment is discussed. Recognition of each student's contribution in terms of empowerment, self-determination, and the need to receive the least intrusive or most natural intervention is explored.

In Chapter 2, the legal foundations for inclusion and government support for education are reviewed. In Chapter 3, the qualities of inclusive schools and classrooms are considered. The chapter includes discussion of the school as a reflection of society and the principles of normalization, fairness, and dignity and respect for the individual. Every child presents a challenge, and these challenges occur on a continuum, thus necessitating a continuum of services. The roles and functions of parents and teachers are presented. Chapter 4 is a discussion of individualized education programming, assessment and diagnosis of problem situations, prescriptive teaching, and services.

Chapter 5 focuses on working as a member of an education team. In this chapter, shared instruction, role release, teacher assistance teams, collaborative consultation, and other issues related to collaboration with colleagues are discussed. In Chapter 6, the reader's attention is turned to the parents' role in the decision-making process shared with practitioners. This chapter includes a discussion of parents' rights and responsibilities with regard to the education of their children. Techniques for increasing parents' participation in the education of their children are reviewed. Chapter 7 contains detailed discussion of assessment and evaluation, including the ecobehavioral interview with teachers, parents, and children; the portfolio; and curriculum-based assessment.

The second half of the book presents a variety of topics and issues related to the management of inclusive classrooms and schools. Chapter 8 discusses the organization and management of inclusive schools and classrooms. The chapter discusses differences in the agenda that students and teachers bring to the classroom as well as the structures for student participation, the physical environment, and natural school supports. Chapter 9 presents information on structuring programs for all learners. In that chapter, consideration is given to rules and routines; explicitness; and the application of scripts and natural, nonintrusive interventions. In Chapter 10, the principles of learning are presented and discussed. Reinforcement, shaping, cuing, modeling, and contingency contracting are reviewed. Chapter 11 focuses on self-management, and Chapters 12 and 13 describe specific group and individual strategies. Chapter 14 provides information on moving learners from restrictive to inclusive classrooms. Chapter 15 provides three case studies of inclusion.

In this book, we have made a conscious effort to model the instruction strategies that we discuss. Each chapter begins with learning objectives and key words and phrases. The learning objectives provide the underlying structure of the chapters. Throughout the chapters, we have included "Your Turn . . ." boxes that allow readers to reflect on the information and integrate it with their experience. Chapters include a variety of figures and tables to support the narrative and end with a Summary, a Self-Evaluation quiz, a Make the Language Your Own exercise, Application Activities, and References.

We hope that you join in our celebration of diversity and affirm with us that you can and will "teach all the children in your classroom."

REFERENCES

Epanchin, B. (1993). *Schools for the twenty-first century: Challenges for teacher preparation* (Proceedings of the Illinois Faculty Summer Institute). Edwardsville: Southern Illinois University Press.

Ferguson, D.L., Meyer, G., Jeanchild, L., Juniper, L., & Zingo, J. (1992). Figuring out what to do with the grownups: How teachers make inclusion "work" for students with disabilities. *Journal of The Association for Persons with Severe Handicaps, 17,* 218–226.

Kuhn, T.K. (Ed.). *The structure of scientific revolutions.* New York: Basic Books.

Lipsky, D.K., & Gartner, A. (1991). Achieving full inclusion: Placing the student at the center of educational reform. In W. Stainback & S. Stainback (Eds.), *Controversial issues confronting special education: Divergent perspectives* (pp. 3–12). Needham Heights, MA: Allyn & Bacon.

Stainback, S., & Stainback, W. (1991). Schools as inclusive communities. In W. Stainback & S. Stainback (Eds.), *Controversial issues confronting special education: Divergent perspectives* (pp. 29–43). Needham Heights, MA: Allyn & Bacon.

A Personal Note from Anne M. Bauer

One of my daughter Sarah's favorite books is *Walk Two Moons* by Sharon Creech, which contains a mysterious message: "Don't judge a man until you've walked two moons in his moccasins." As my husband and I parent five children, each with a unique background and set of experiences, all assembled as a family, I feel that we have indeed "walked two moons" regarding the individualized education programs, accommodations, services, therapy, arguments, breakthroughs, and tears as parents of children who vary from their peers. My husband and I have a college graduate, two children in an inclusive high school that prides itself on its diversity, and two students in an elementary school that has implemented a wide range of accommodations to meet their needs and help them feel successful as students. It is hard to keep wearing the "professional" hat when I am also a parent—it just keeps slipping off. I hope that Tom Shea and I have worn both hats—that of parent and that of professional—throughout this book. Thanks to Demian, Tarie, C.J., Sarah, and Mickey (all of whom are in the photograph above; Mickey is Tom Shea's godson) for helping me "walk two moons."

For Riley, Demian, Tarie, C.J., Sarah, and Mickey

and

Delores, Keith, Kevin, and Jane

Inclusion 101

An Inclusive Society

People expected us to fail. That didn't happen. They realized how powerful we were. We stuck together, we worked together, we drew the line of what was unacceptable. On Friday I was on Welfare. On Monday I was Rehab Director of the State of California.

Ed Roberts (1994, p. 7)

The preceding statement represents one of many changes occurring as American society moves closer to embracing diversity. Although Ed Roberts is describing efforts related to equity for people with disabilities, the same statements could have been made by an individual of color or by a woman. His assertion illustrates changes in the status of diversity in culture, language, ethnicity, style of interaction, learning style and rate, and ways of gaining access to the environment. Just as changes have occurred in rehabilitation services for adults with disabilities, there have been changes in schools. The statement is not included here to suggest that American society has reached full equity of opportunity in education for people who are perceived to vary from their peers. It is included to suggest, however, that classrooms in the late 1990s reflect greater diversity than previous generations of American students experienced.

This book does not argue *for* inclusive classrooms. It contends that inclusive classrooms in which teachers and learners diverge in as many ways as there are participants are a reality. Teaching "to the middle" or "to the average student" is no longer acceptable; indeed, it may be impossible even to determine what *is* the "middle" or the "average" in the contemporary classroom. This chapter discusses many of the variables that contribute to this diversity in classrooms. The intent is not to present a comprehensive survey of human diversity—an impossible goal—but to raise the reader's awareness of the learners whom they serve in classrooms.

LEARNING OBJECTIVES

After completing this chapter, readers will be able to

1. Describe issues related to ethnic, cultural, and linguistic diversity
2. Describe issues related to diversity that individuals experience, including gender and disability
3. Discuss diversity within the caregiving environments that children and youth experience
4. Discuss the emerging issues of empowerment and natural support
5. Explain the premises on which this book is written

KEY WORDS AND PHRASES

African Americans—Americans of African ancestry

Appalachians—Americans with ancestry in the federally defined Appalachian region

Asian Americans—Americans of Asian ancestry

child maltreatment—child abuse and child neglect

constructivism—learning theory that emphasizes development of knowledge as a result of interaction between the individual and his or her social and physical environments

cultural pluralism—mutual appreciation and understanding of the various cultures in society

culture—the covert and overt beliefs, expectations, and values of people and institutions

disability—a limitation that requires support

ethnicity—membership in a group of people who share a unique social and cultural heritage that is transmitted through generations

European Americans—Caucasian Americans of European ancestry

fetal alcohol effects (FAE)—prenatal and postnatal growth retardation and central nervous system involvement caused by prenatal alcohol consumption by the mother

fetal alcohol syndrome (FAS)—a syndrome caused by prenatal alcohol consumption by the mother, which is identified by prenatal and postnatal growth retardation, central nervous system involvement, and common facial characteristics

Hispanic Americans—Americans of all races whose heritage is tied to the Spanish language and Latino culture

migrants—individuals who move frequently to find work

Native Americans—Americans with ancestry in the native populations of North America

substance abuse—the use of any chemical substance that causes physical, mental, emotional, and social harm to an individual or those close to the individual

urban Appalachians—Appalachians who are residents of urban areas outside the Appalachian region

welfare—common term for the federal Temporary Assistance to Needy Families (TANF) program (formerly called Aid to Families with Dependent Children [AFDC])

LEARNING OBJECTIVE 1: To be able to describe issues related to ethnic, cultural, and linguistic diversity

In a discussion of the changing face of American education, Grossman (1992) stated that the U.S. population is rapidly becoming less **European American.** Yates (1987) projected that by 2000, European Americans will represent only one in three Americans. As of 1999, European American students are the minority in the 25 largest school districts in the United States. As a consequence, society's perception of the dominant and minority **cultures** must change. Grossman suggested that teachers maintain prejudicial expectations and anticipate that students who are not European Americans will present more disruptive behavior in the classroom and in school generally than these students' European American peers even in classrooms in which students are not predominantly European Americans.

Although often discussed, *cultural diversity, culture,* and **ethnicity** are rarely defined. This book suggests, as did Spindler and Spindler (1994), that culture is more than a factor in or an influence on people's behavior and is a continuous process in everything that people say, do, and think. Kugelmass

(1993) suggested that culture is the covert and overt beliefs, expectations, and values of people and institutions; culture is that which gives meaning to people's experiences. In multicultural societies such as the United States, individuals' cultural patterns may be based in several cultural traditions; thus, understanding individuals' behavior as an aspect of their culture becomes even more difficult.

Ethnicity is defined as membership in a group of people who share a unique social and cultural heritage that is transmitted from one generation to the next (Mindel & Habenstein, 1981). Race and ethnicity may overlap (e.g., **African Americans, Asian Americans**), or they may be independent of each other (e.g., Hispanics may be members of Caucasian, African, or Native American racial groups, or a combination of all three). Because the terms *dominant culture* and *minority* are relative to the composition of the specific group under consideration, minority groups are those groups that have unequal access to power and are for the most part considered inferior or less worthy of sharing power in some way (Mindel & Habenstein, 1981). The major minority groups in American society according to this definition are African Americans, Asian Americans, **Hispanic Americans**, **Native Americans**, **Appalachians**, **migrants**, females, and people with disabilities.

The cultural assimilation or "melting pot" perspective in American society has been replaced by **cultural pluralism** or a "salad bowl" perception (Kochman, 1991). The melting pot perspective, which was dominant in the late 19th and early 20th centuries, expected immigrants to abandon their native language and culture as soon as possible after entering the United States for a new, homogeneous American language and culture. Instead of creating this harmonious new culture, the melting pot perspective resulted in racism, segregation, poverty, and aggression toward succeeding waves of immigrants. Cultural pluralism began to replace assimilation toward the end of the 20th century. Cultural pluralism involves

> Mutual appreciation and understanding of the various cultures in our society; peaceful co-existence of diverse lifestyles, folkways, manners, language patterns, religious beliefs, and family structures; and autonomy of each group to work out its own social future as long as it does not interfere with the same rights of other groups. (Poplin & Wright, 1983, p. 367)

In addition to an acceptance of pluralism, there is renewed recognition of the variations among individuals within minority groups. Traditional descriptions of characteristics of members of various groups may, in fact, be stereotypes. In response to variations within groups, lists of characteristics are not offered in this chapter; rather, this chapter presents the major issues confronting the education of people within the largest cultural, linguistic, and ethnic groups: African Americans, Hispanic Americans, Native Americans, Asian Americans, Appalachians, and migrants.

African Americans

Since the beginning of the 20th century, the African American population of the United States has remained between 10% and 12% (Allen & Majidi-Ahi, 1989). The lifestyles, values, and experiences of African Americans vary greatly; but, as a group, they share economic isolation, prejudice, and legally reinforced racism (McAdoo, 1978). As a basis of this discussion of African

American learners, this chapter accepts Steward and Logan's (1992) assumption that African American families are not homogeneous; that is, there is no such thing as "the African American family." There is, among African American families, diversity in terms of values, personal characteristics, lifestyles, religious influences, regional influences, socioeconomic status, level of acculturation, family size and structure, and age.

According to Steward and Logan (1992), traditional research on African American family life has perpetuated the notion of a lower-class subculture. The strengths and resilience of African American families, as Taylor and Dorsey-Gaines described in *Growing Up Literate: Learning from Inner-City Families,* suggested that African American families "spent time together, that there was a rhythm to their lives, and that they enjoyed each other's company" (1988, p. 191). Taylor and Dorsey-Gaines reported that parents shared a sense of conviction in their own abilities and were determined to raise healthy children. To the best of their abilities and resources, they provided loving, structured home environments with climates of cooperation and participation. Parents were concerned with the safety and well-being of their children. In their efforts to combat racism, African American parents emphasized the development of achievement motivation, self-confidence, and high self-esteem (Peters, 1981).

With regard to African American communities, Steward and Logan assumed that African American communities and neighborhoods, like the families of which they are composed, are not homogeneous entities. The communities reflect a variety of lifestyles and experiences for their inhabitants based on either the availability or the lack of resources. Cohesiveness in these communities is demonstrated by the tendency to adopt children informally and to incorporate non–family members into the family household. In addition, there is a pervasive assumption that people are doing the best that they can. The African American community is a valuable source of support for children and families.

European American teachers may view the differences in cohesiveness among community members between African American and European American cultures as problems (Hanna, 1988). African American classmates may support each other. When classmates are confronted with a task or a problem, they may work together on it. Some teachers may view this cooperation as cheating. New children in the classroom negotiate interpersonal relationships, and participants probe for common experiences with their peers. Students seek cues in how to act or in what to expect from the teacher, and, when they are unable to acquire adequate information, they turn to their peers for help.

Communication patterns among some African American students may be perceived as inappropriate, resistant, or apathetic by European American teachers. They may converse without constant eye contact (Allen & Majidi-Ahi, 1989), which a European American teacher may interpret as inattention. African American students may be less likely to verbally reinforce one another in conversation (Smith, 1981). African American children may speak in a dual system of a standard English dialect and African American English, carrying a more demanding cognitive burden than individuals who speak in a single language system in which there are fewer translations necessary. Teachers may view communication skills that are valued among African American children, such as verbal dueling and argument, as aggressive and disruptive (Lynch, 1993).

Hispanic Americans

Hispanic Americans are those people of all races whose cultural heritage is tied to the Spanish language and Latino culture (Fradd, Figueroa, & Correa, 1989). Hispanic Americans are among the fastest-growing populations in U.S. society. The poverty rate for Hispanic families was about 2.5 times greater than that of non-Hispanic families in 1986 (Buenning, Tollefson, & Rodriguez, 1992). Hispanic Americans may belong to any of a large number of ethnic groups, including Mexican Americans, Puerto Ricans, Cubans, and groups from other Latin American countries. The largest of these groups are Mexican Americans and Puerto Ricans. This Hispanic American population is concentrated in urban areas and tends to reside in segregated communities, separate in housing and schooling from other ethnic groups (Hyland, 1989). This isolation is said to be related to linguistic skills because Hispanic children are usually placed in classrooms or schools in which most of the children have limited English proficiency.

Approximately 25% of the Mexican American population have earnings below the poverty level, and as many as one third may be considered working poor (Valdivieso, 1990). They often must confront the challenges of illiteracy and lack of facility with English (Ramirez, 1990). The Mexican American family reflects a mixture of traditional and contemporary cultural patterns. Mexican Americans believe in the primacy of the family, and kinship ties are strong. The concept of *machismo* (male dominance) influences the role of men in Mexican American culture. Ramirez (1990) also suggested that the parent–child relationship overshadows the marital relationship. The home may be child centered, with the parents' behavior being passive and indulgent toward their children. There is an emphasis on cooperation and respect for authority. Mexican Americans appear to be oriented more to the here and now and emphasize doing rather than being.

Puerto Ricans in the United States reside primarily in New York City and the Northeast. As American citizens, they have voting privileges and ease of travel between the U.S. mainland and the island of Puerto Rico. As with many other Hispanic ethnic groups, *machismo* is considered a virtue, and personalism calls for the development of inner qualities to attain self-respect and gain the respect of others. Catholicism, with its emphasis on a personal relationship with God, is the predominant religion (Garcia-Preto, 1982). Generational change is apparent among Puerto Ricans. First-generation migrants exhibit traditional values, with barrios serving to recreate and preserve the native culture. Second- and third-generation Puerto Ricans cope with and adapt to the language and values of the dominant culture, often generating feelings of failure and stress because of tensions between the traditional and new cultures (Inclan, 1985).

Hispanic American learners may enter school with a significantly different social, economic, and cultural background than their peers who understand the dominant American culture (Hyland, 1989). For example, Hispanic American students may view "copying" as a legitimate activity. Copying work may be based on home socialization patterns that stress collectivity and social cohesiveness. Rather than representing low ability and lack of motivation, copying may be considered a constructive approach to intellectual exchanges and the acquisition of new knowledge in a social unit composed of peers (Delgado-Gaitan & Trueba, 1985). In addition, the organization of classroom instruction may limit these students' abilities to demonstrate their full range of competence in two languages. Teachers may interpret a lack of English language structural proficiency and a lack of vocabulary in Spanish as a lack of conceptual ability (Commins & Miramontes, 1989).

Native Americans

In the United States, 36 states recognize Native American tribes, and there are 517 federally recognized Native American entities (196 of which are in Alaska). Each of these entities has unique customs, traditions, social organizations, and ecological relationships to the environment (Leap, 1981).

Native Americans share a history of cultural, psychological, and physical genocide. Once estimated at 10 million, the Native American population has been reduced through cultural genocide to fewer than 2 million. As a consequence of efforts first to eliminate them and then to assimilate them, many Native Americans experience a sense of alienation from European Americans (LaFramboise & Low, 1989).

Spindler and Spindler (1994), through their work with the Menominee tribe, described the responses of Native Americans to this sense of alienation. These responses include reaffirmation, withdrawal, constructive marginality, biculturalism, and assimilation. Among the Menominee, reaffirmation was represented by a group of cultural "survivors" from the past and a larger number of younger people who had encountered European American culture in school and at work and were trying to recreate and sustain a recognizable Native American way of life. Another group of Native Americans was so torn by conflict that they could identify with neither the traditional nor the European American cultural symbols or groups and withdrew into self-destruction by engaging in **substance abuse** or by doing nothing.

Spindler and Spindler (1994) described *constructive marginality* as forming a personal culture that was instrumentally productive but was usually constituted of several different segments, some of which were European American. Among those who assimilated, two groups emerged: 1) those who were deemed more respectable than most European Americans and denigrated Native Americans who did not conform and 2) those who were undifferentiated culturally from European Americans but were interested in Native American traditions in a distant way. Bicultural Native Americans were equally at home in traditional and dominant culture contexts. Spindler and Spindler described these strategies as defensive because these individuals' self-esteem was threatened.

Grimm (1992) reported that several issues challenge the identity of Native American learners, such as removal from the family to boarding schools and foster placements, high dropout rates (60% among children attending boarding school), overidentification as special education students, high incidence of alcohol and other drug abuse, high suicide rates, ongoing health problems, and low income.

Perhaps most difficult for Native American learners is the conflict between their traditional cooperative learning styles and the competitive environment of the school. Native American children learn by observing rather than by displaying curiosity and verbal questioning. They prefer cooperation and harmony. In school, such behaviors may be perceived as a general lack of individual competitiveness and an overreliance on peer structure (Brod & McQuiston, 1983).

A Native American philosophy of child development has become the basis for working with learners with special needs (Brendtro, Brokenleg, & Bockern,

1990). The basic premise underlying this Native American philosophy is that, to develop successfully, children must have or feel the spirit of belonging (e.g., trust, attachment, love, friendship), mastery (e.g., success, achievement, motivation, creativity), independence (e.g., autonomy, confidence, responsibility, self-discipline, inner control), and generosity (e.g., self-sacrifice, caring, sharing, loyalty).

The performance of Native American learners in the public schools is influenced by the anxieties, mores, aspirations, and behavior patterns of Native American culture (Pepper, 1976). These children may tend to withdraw in unfamiliar situations. They are taught to listen and await the age at which it is perceived that their years of experience and learning have prepared them to be influential enough to attract listeners. Rather than make an announcement or offer verbal recognition, Native Americans may rely on quiet recognition and silence as expressions of respect. European American teachers may expect verbal affirmation and recognition when addressing their students.

Asian Americans

Since 1970, the Asian American population has doubled, and it continues to increase (Ho, 1992). The Asian American population actually comprises many diverse groups, including Chinese, Japanese, Korean, and Pilipino Americans; immigrants and refugees from Cambodia, Indonesia, Laos, Thailand, and Vietnam; people from Ceylon, India, and Pakistan; and children with one Asian parent. The heterogeneity of this group is exemplified by language, historical, social, and economic differences as well as by differences that are based on generational status (Ho, 1992).

Although cultural values may vary depending on how they are related to language, historical, social, generational, and economic differences, several values may put Asian American learners in contrast to the conventional school behavior of students from the dominant American culture. For example, among Asian American learners, expectations to comply with authority with an uncomplaining attitude may be perceived as complacency or lack of motivation. Subordination to the group may be inconsistent with competitive classrooms. Silence and esteem for "the middle position" may be out of place in a classroom in which the student must request help or materials.

Asian Americans, unlike other cultural, ethnic, and linguistic groups, are stereotyped in a positive way with regard to school achievement. Dao (1991) contended, however, that changes have occurred in the Asian American population and that many of these children are at risk of school failure. Many children are from families with life and educational experiences that are vastly different from those of children from established Asian American families. Recent immigrant or refugee children face the triple burden of learning English and the new school curriculum, adjusting to a new culture, and surviving in an impoverished environment. In addition, recent refugees may have had traumatic experiences, including deaths among relatives, friends, or members of their community; piracy; and extreme violence; and they may not be emotionally ready to benefit from instruction.

Appalachians

Although not readily identifiable by race, gender, or surname, Appalachians are a distinct cultural group (Sullivan & Miller, 1990). Appalachians are indi-

viduals who were born, or whose ancestors were born, in the federally defined
Appalachian region of 397 counties and 5 independent cities in portions of the
following 13 states: Alabama, Georgia, Kentucky, Maryland, Mississippi, New
York, North Carolina, Ohio, Pennsylvania, South Carolina, Tennessee, Virginia, and West Virginia (McCoy & Watkins, 1980).

Appalachian migration to urban areas began before World War II and
peaked during the 1950s. Borman and Obermiller (1994) described several
stages in the process during which Appalachians became **urban Appalachians**. First, the newcomers were obviously migrants, with the Appalachian individual being viewed as transient and adults being perceived as undepend-
able because of absenteeism related to visits "back home." During the next
stage, Appalachians were not regarded as transients but were seen as a social
problem, a perception that was heightened by federal and state social **welfare**
programs. As social advocacy organizations developed in urban Appalachian
neighborhoods, a third stage of identity began to emerge: the movement to
establish an ethnic identity for urban Appalachians. In the current stage of
identity formation for urban Appalachians, an ecological point of view has
emerged, keeping in mind the existence of a distinctive, positive Appalachian
culture. Positive aspects of the Appalachian culture include strong family social and economic support networks and a sense of self-reliance (Obermiller &
Maloney, 1994). The term *urban Appalachian* itself was coined in the early
1970s by Appalachians living in midwestern cities to describe themselves after
realizing that, because of their permanence, the term *Appalachian migrant*
was no longer appropriate (Obermiller & Maloney, 1994).

Urban Appalachian youth remain on the economic margins of society
(Borman & Stegelin, 1994), avoiding more challenging opportunities outside
their neighborhoods because such jobs disrupt important social networks of
exchange among kin and peers. Without mentors, role models, and sponsors
outside the neighborhood, these young adults remain adrift, keeping afloat
through a series of odd jobs and exchange strategies.

Heath (1983) conducted an ethnographic study of two working-class Appalachian communities and described the mismatch of school and home play
and communication patterns. Heath found that indirect questions used at
school rather than direct commands generally used in the home were difficult
for Appalachian children to understand. Penn, Borman, and Hoeweler (1994)
also reported this mismatch among urban Appalachian adolescents and found
that these individuals had a need for a more person-oriented than work-
oriented communication style.

The impact of the cultural mismatch between school and home for urban
Appalachian students is exemplified by studies conducted in the city of Cincinnati, Ohio. Urban Appalachian neighborhood enclaves ranked higher than
either predominantly African American or other Caucasian areas both in the
high percentage of dropouts and in the percentage of the population between
16 and 25 years of age who were neither high school graduates nor currently
attending high school (Penn et al., 1994). Those students who remained in
school were achieving at significantly lower levels than their non-Appalachian
peers. In schools serving urban Appalachian children, the decline in scores on
the California Achievement Test was two or three times greater than the de-
clines for Cincinnati public schools as a whole. The Appalachian dialect and

the cultural emphasis on individualism are in conflict with standard English and the conformity anticipated in many schools.

Migrants

The children of migrant families are significantly at risk for educational problems and disabilities. In the United States, migrant children are the most underserved and inappropriately served group (Interstate Migrant Council, 1984). Migrants are individuals or groups who move frequently to find work. In the United States, there are approximately 800,000 migrant students. Of this number, only about 1% receive special education services as compared with about 10% of the students in the general student population (Perry, 1982).

Several factors in the lifestyles of migrant families expose their children to risk for educational problems and disabilities:

1. High mobility
2. Low socioeconomic status
3. Language and cultural differences
4. Poor general health and nutrition

According to Baca and Harris (1988), migrant children have several unique educational needs, such as native language development and instruction as well as instruction in English as a second language. There is a great need for self-concept enhancement, along with familiarization with European American culture without denigration of the native culture. The family also needs services, including service coordination, and involvement with school and community personnel.

Your Turn . . .

Relating one's own experiences to newly presented material reinforces learning. Throughout this book, the reader will occasionally be asked to give a personal response to the content presented in each chapter.

In this "Your Turn . . . ," reflect on your own learning about diversity. At what age did you become aware of cultural, ethnic, or linguistic diversity? How did this learning occur? How did it change your interactions with others?

LEARNING OBJECTIVE 2: To be able to describe issues related to diversity that individuals experience, including gender and disability

When using the term *diversity,* culture, ethnicity, and language usually come to mind. Gender and disability are also elements of diversity, however. In this section, issues related to gender and disability are described.

Gender

In the search for social justice, efforts are being made to eradicate discrimination between males and females, and, at the same time, gender differences are being rediscovered and examined in the social sciences (Gilligan, 1982). Male and female perspectives on relationships, for example, are being differentiated. Generally, women perceive others on their own terms and in context, whereas men base judgments on equality and reciprocity. Women are typically interdependent in relationships with others; men are autonomous, equal, and independent in relationships. Women tend to emphasize discussion and listening in order to understand others; men emphasize the need to maintain fairness and equality in dealing with others (Lyons, 1985).

In special education, even though boys significantly outnumber girls, research has rarely focused on gender issues. The more subjective the diagnosis (e.g., serious emotional disturbance, learning disabilities), the higher the representation of boys (American Association of University Women [AAUW], 1992). In *How Schools Shortchange Girls* (AAUW, 1992), the traditional explanation for the disproportionate number of boys in special education programs (that more boys are born with disabilities) is challenged by a thorough review of the literature. Medical reports on learning disabilities and attention-deficit/hyperactivity disorder indicate that they occur almost equally in boys and girls (Shaywitz, Shaywitz, Fletcher, & Escobar, 1990). Yet schools continue to identify many more boys than girls in these **disability** areas. In addition, girls who are identified as having learning disabilities have lower tested intelligence quotients than do boys referred to these classes (Vogel, 1990). The AAUW report suggested that girls who sit quietly are ignored, and boys who act out are placed in special education programs.

In extracurricular activities and sports, the participation of boys has been reported to be almost twice that of girls (National Federation of State High School Associations, 1990). The state of Michigan (Michigan Department of Education, Office of Equity in Education, 1990), in a statewide study, reported that students perceive clear gender-biased standards and expectations that favor males in physical education classes. Many girls wrote that they would play and enjoy sports more when asked, "How would your life be different if you were a boy?" Of the school districts surveyed, 70% did not provide girls with athletic opportunities comparable to those available to boys, though equal opportunities have been required by federal law since 1972, when Title IX of the Education Amendments (PL 92-318) was passed.

At the elementary school level, gifted females and males report similar interests. By secondary school, however, gifted females develop lower career aspirations than gifted males (Kerr, 1985). Subtle teacher behaviors have been reported that may socialize gifted girls to lower their expectations. For example, a study of science classes found that when teachers needed assistance in carrying out a demonstration, they selected boys to help 79% of the time (Tobin & Garnett, 1987). In addition, the "cultural underachievement" of women appears to be related to women's needs to balance professional interests and higher education while fulfilling traditional sex roles (Davis & Rimm, 1985).

People with Disabilities

In *No Pity: People with Disabilities Forging a New Civil Rights Movement,* Shapiro (1993) wrote of the changing paradigm or standard on the basis of which people with disabilities judge themselves and wish others to judge them. This standard has evolved from one of pity to one of respect and dignity. Shapiro described this evolution in a discussion of the "poster child": "No other symbol of disability is more beloved by Americans than the cute and courageous poster child—or more loathed by people with disabilities themselves" (1993, p. 12). He reported the evolution of the poster child, who in the 1940s was projected as someone who, if people sent in their money, would be cured. Because cures were few, children with disabilities were perceived as "damaged goods" who had to "try harder" to prove themselves worthy of charity and respect.

As a result of an attitude of pity toward people with disabilities, the "inspirational disabled person" emerged as someone who was presumed to be deserving of pity until proved capable by overcoming a disability through an extraordinary feat. A consequence of and central to the Civil Rights movement for people with disabilities is the concept that disability itself is not tragic or pitiable.

In the 1990s, people with disabilities began to challenge the professionals whose function it is to support and help them. Stefans, for example, discussed the actions that professionals take, which he described as "beyond professionalism" (1994, p. 19) in the effort to work with and serve people with disabilities effectively. He challenged professionals to adapt their training to existing realities for people with disabilities rather than to professionals' perception of that reality. Stefans urged professionals to seek consumers' input into their professional roles and functions and to attempt conscientiously to think of consumers as people first.

Another facet of disability has emerged through Biklen's (1993) work with people with autism. In discussing the use of facilitated communication, a supported communication strategy, he reported that one of the most consistent and frequently heard communications is "I am not retarded." He contended that these individuals are rejecting the perception that they are fundamentally different from other people, that their whole being can be defined as "disabled." Rather, he suggested, they generate voices filled with expectation and determination.

According to the U.S. Department of Education (1996), during the 1994–1995 school year, 5,439,626 children between birth and 21 years of age were served as people with disabilities. This number represents a 3.2% increase over the previous school year and represents approximately 7.5% of the resident population of children. The number and percentage of school-age children with disabilities has increased annually since the 1976–1977 school year. Four groups account for 92.3% of the learners with disabilities: specific learning disabilities (51.1%), communication disorders (20.8%), mental retardation (11.6%), and serious emotional disturbance (8.7%).

Using a social systems perspective as an organizational framework for an extensive discussion of information about people with disabilities, Shea and Bauer (1994) classified learners with disabilities into three broad groups:

1. Learners who vary from their peers in their interactions
2. Learners who vary from their peers in gaining access to the environment
3. Learners who vary from their peers in their learning styles and rates

The first group of learners subsumes the traditional categories of learners identified with behavior disorders and those from diverse ethnic, cultural, and linguistic groups. Learners with communication disorders, physical and other health impairments, visual impairments, or hearing impairments are included in the second group, that is, learners who vary from their peers in the ways in which they gain access to the environment. Learners who vary in learning styles and rates, the third group, include those traditionally classified as learners with mental retardation requiring intermittent or limited supports, learning disabilities, severe and multiple disabilities, and other mild disabilities.

From the social systems perspective that Shea and Bauer (1994) applied, the learner is seen as an inseparable part of the environment, both immediate and extended, in which the individual functions. Consequently, Shea and Bauer posited that it is impossible to understand disabilities without examining the contexts (family, classroom, school, community, and society) in which the individual is developing and ascertaining their impact on the individual.

Your Turn . . .

When did you first become aware of disability? What was the disability demonstrated by the individual with whom you interacted? What presumptions did you make about the individual?

LEARNING OBJECTIVE 3: To be able to discuss diversity within the caregiving environments that children and youth experience

In an effort to characterize the changing nature of the caregiving environment, the Children's Defense Fund (1994) offered some "moments in America for children":

- Every 30 seconds a baby is born into poverty.
- Every 34 seconds a baby is born to a mother who did not graduate from high school.
- Every 2 minutes a baby is born to a mother who had late or no prenatal care.
- Every 4 minutes a baby is born to a teenage mother who already has a child.

These "moments" challenge society to address the needs of an ever-increasing number of children living in poverty, children living in single-parent families, children of divorce, children living in stepfamilies, children living in families in which there is substance abuse, and children who are being maltreated.

Children in Poverty

Infants born to families living in poverty are at substantial risk for physical or learning disabilities. These children face a cycle of poverty and poor health throughout their lifetime. The White House Task Force on Infant Mortality (1989) stated that poor families have, by definition, limited resources for such basics as food, housing, transportation, and health care. In addition, poverty contributes to stress, a lack of social support, exposure to environmental toxins, low educational attainment, and difficulty in keeping families together. Poor families often survive through government support or "welfare." Governmental reforms in the 1990s are making uncertain the future of assistance to families living in poverty. Generally, "welfare" refers to TANF, which is part of the Welfare Reform Act of 1996 (PL 104-193). (Its predecessor, AFDC, began in 1935 as part of the Social Security Act [PL 74-271].) Only families with children qualify for TANF, which, though funded by both federal and state governments, is administered by the states. The Children's Defense Fund (1994) reported that the maximum cash grant for a mother and two children in the typical state is $367 per month, although each state sets its own funding level. The typical monthly grant, even combined with food stamps, is about 70% of the poverty level. Of all people receiving TANF, 70% leave the program within 2 years and 50% leave within 1 year. Only 15% of those families on TANF stay with the program for more than 5 years (Children's Defense Fund, 1994); however, a substantial number of individuals leaving the program return at a later date because of unemployment or the inability to find or afford child care services.

The impact of poverty on children's development has been referred to as *double jeopardy* because the factors of biological vulnerability secondary to prematurity, maternal depression, temperamental passivity, inadequate environmental stimulation, and insufficient social support available to the poor serve to potentiate each other (Parker, Greer, & Zuckerman, 1988). According to Gelfand, Jenson, and Drew (1988), three times as many (15%) European American infants of low socioeconomic status (SES) experience complications at birth as

European American infants of high SES. In addition, as a group, more than half of the nonwhite infants of low SES experience birth complications. Baumeister, Kupstas, and Klindworth (1990) suggested that, without specific prevention efforts, a "biologic underclass" of children will emerge whose problems are related to poverty, a lack of adequate and timely prenatal care, and prevalence of human immunodeficiency virus (HIV) and other ongoing illnesses.

Learners from Single-Parent Families, Families of Divorce, and Stepfamilies

Of the learners who are not living with two biological parents, children in never-married, single-parent homes are at greatest risk for school failure (Carlson, 1992). Children in single-parent homes are least likely to experience adverse effects if they fit the following profile:

1. They are female.
2. Their custodial parent is confident, mentally healthy, educated, and authoritative.
3. The family is economically secure and resides in a community with resources oriented to the well-being of children.
4. Relationships between the single custodial parent and other family system members, including the noncustodial parent, are cooperative and free of conflict.

The second-highest risk group are those learners with families that have experienced divorce (Carlson, 1992). The transition of a family from being a two-parent family to being a single-parent family is usually accompanied by reduction in income stability, lower income, and changes in residence and school. Divorce remains the single most common psychological stressor for children (Guidubaldi & Perry, 1985). Wallerstein and Blakeslee (1989) described several differences between the impact of divorce and other life crises such as death, illness, and unemployment. Divorce more often involves anger, which may be expressed verbally or physically, or in both of those ways. Rather than strive to ensure their children's safety and emotional security, parents in the process of seeking a divorce frequently give priority to their adult problems. This diminishes their capacity to parent. In addition, during the process of divorce, the usual social supports available to parents and children are less available because relatives and friends tend to withdraw from the conflict occurring within the family.

Children living in a home with a stepparent are least likely to experience adverse effects if

1. They are male
2. They are of younger school age or older adolescents
3. They reside in the stepfather's home
4. The stepparent does not attempt to become a parent too quickly
5. The remarried biological parent does not expect the stepparent–stepchild relationship to replicate a biological relationship (Carlson, 1992)

Substance Abuse

According to the National Institute on Drug Abuse (1981), substance abuse is the use of any chemical substance that causes physical, mental, emotional, or social harm to an individual or those close to him or her. Substance abuse in a

family has two primary effects on children. First, typical parent–child interactions do not occur because of the parents' preoccupation with obtaining and
using drugs. Second, as a result of the parents' preoccupation with activities
associated with their addiction, family life is disorganized. Children living
with parents who are abusing controlled substances live in unstable, often
dangerous environments and are cared for inconsistently by parents who frequently have psychological and physical problems.

Because of the potential serious effects of any maternal use of drugs during pregnancy, children whose mothers used alcohol or drugs of any kind during any time of the pregnancy are referred to as *prenatally exposed*. This
category includes far more children than those born addicted to a controlled
substance.

There are two groups of children associated with substance abuse in families who are of significance to educators. The first group is composed of children prenatally exposed to cocaine, usually in the form of alkaloidal cocaine
(i.e., "crack"). The second group is composed of children prenatally exposed to
alcohol. These two groups are not always mutually exclusive, and many children are referred to as having "polydrug" exposure, including cocaine, alcohol,
amphetamines, heroin, marijuana, and other drugs.

Children prenatally exposed to alcohol are classified into two groups: children with **fetal alcohol syndrome (FAS)** and children with possible **fetal
alcohol effects (FAE)** (Abel, 1984). In 1980, the Fetal Alcohol Study Group
of the Research Society on Alcoholism (Rossett & Weiner, 1984) presented min-
imal criteria for the diagnosis of FAS. The diagnosis is suggested when the
child has symptoms in each of the following categories:

- Prenatal and/or postnatal growth retardation and weight, length, and/or
  head circumference below the tenth percentile when corrected for gesta-
  tional age
- Central nervous system involvement, including neurological disorders
  such as seizure disorder and attention-deficit/hyperactivity disorder, developmental delay, or intellectual impairment
- Common facial characteristics with at least two of these three symptoms:
  microcephaly; microophthalmia and/or widely spaced eyes; poorly developed median groove between the upper lip and the nose, thin upper lip, or
  flattening of the upper jaw

Abel (1984) suggested that if only one or two of these symptoms are evident,
and if the mother is suspected of alcohol use during pregnancy, then a diagnosis of possible FAE may be made.

The emphasis in the popular media on maternal cocaine use has contributed to a perception that cocaine abuse is the sole contributor to poor infant health among substance-abusing women (Koren, 1989). Yet, according to
data from the 1990 Household Survey on Drug Abuse (Khalsa & Groefrer,
1991), there were 60 million women of childbearing age (ages 15–44 years) in
the United States who abused substances. Of these, an estimated 50.8% used
alcohol; 29% smoked cigarettes; and 8% used illicit drugs, including 6.5% who
used marijuana and 3.5% who used cocaine.

In view of the limitations involved in studying mothers who are engaging
in substance abuse and in view of the fact that few women use cocaine alone,

studies have reported that women who use cocaine throughout pregnancy are at increased risk for premature labor and delivery, miscarriage, poor maternal weight gain, hypertension, inadequate prenatal care, and having children who have growth retardation (Zaichkin & Houston, 1993). Most women with chemical dependency are polydrug users who have poor general health and nutrition, do not follow a health care plan, seek little or no prenatal care, and run a high risk of exposure to contaminants from street drugs and infection, including hepatitis and HIV (Adams, Eyler, & Behnke, 1990). Their infants often have decreased birth weight and length, are less awake and aware, express less interest and joy in learning, and have difficulty in establishing the relationship between events and their contingencies (Alessandri, Sullivan, Imaizumi, & Lewis, 1993). These families and children are seriously at risk for developmental disabilities.

Child Maltreatment

According to the American Humane Association (1987), there were approximately 2 million official reports of **child maltreatment** in the United States in 1985. The term *maltreatment* is used to describe both child abuse and child neglect. From a developmental perspective, child maltreatment is not a single or fixed incident but ongoing transactions or patterns of behavior wherein the individuals involved reciprocally influence each other to cause disturbances in the caregiving process (Cicchetti, Toth, & Hennessy, 1989). The Child Abuse Prevention and Treatment Act (PL 93-245) uses the terms *child abuse* and *child neglect* to refer to the physical or mental injury, sexual abuse, or neglect of a child younger than age 18 by a person responsible for the child's welfare under circumstances that indicate that the child's health or welfare is harmed or threatened.

In their review of the literature, Youngblade and Belsky (1989) concluded that child maltreatment is associated with dysfunctional parent–child relationships, with the children forming an insecure attachment to the maltreating parent. They further concluded that the effects of maltreatment are not limited to familial relationships. They concluded that there were repeated indications that maltreatment was associated with difficulty in forming relationships with peers.

Cicchetti and colleagues (1989) found that, as early as 30 months of age, children who had been maltreated used proportionally fewer words to describe their internal psychological states than did their peers who had not been maltreated. In older elementary school students, maltreatment is reflected in a negative self-image, which leaves students feeling less competent and less academically motivated than their peers.

Children who are maltreated exhibit more avoidance and aggressive behavior toward peers. As a group, they are more anxious, inattentive, and apathetic than other children and rely heavily on teachers for encouragement and approval. Maltreated children were disruptive and defiant in their confrontations with peers and teachers (Crittenden, 1989). Children who have been maltreated need to learn to 1) predict events in their environment; 2) achieve their goals in socially conventional ways; 3) communicate openly with others and use developmentally appropriate cognitive and language skills; 4) develop trust through carefully regulated, unambiguous, and consistent affective experiences; and 5) develop the self-confidence, self-motivation, and self-control necessary to enjoy and benefit from the intellectual stimulation of education programs (Crittenden, 1989).

LEARNING OBJECTIVE 4: To be able to discuss the emerging issues of empowerment and natural support

According to Spindler and Spindler (1994), school is a calculated intervention in the lives and learning of children. As an intervention, school mandates that certain topics be taught (regardless of whether they are learned) and that certain things be excluded. From a cultural perspective, the intervention of school is culturally constructed by the determinations of the dominant culture of any society. Children may fail in school because they do not perceive, understand, or master the instrumental relationships (those relationships that are "instrumental" in perceived success) upon which schoolwork is based (Spindler & Spindler, 1994). Children from various minority groups may develop low self-esteem and low estimates of self-efficacy in the school environment; however, these children may preserve an enduring self-identity that is comparatively intact and positive and is formed and sustained in nonschool contexts. Professionals must separate the child whom they see as being challenged by the mainstream culture of school from the child as he or she successfully navigates his or her own cultural interactions.

Another issue for students from diverse ethnic, cultural, and linguistic groups is a lack of congruence between what happens in and out of school. Resnick (1987) suggested that school learning is discontinuous in several important respects with daily life of learners from various cultural and ethnic groups. First, in schools, individual rather than shared cognition is valued. Students ultimately are judged by what they can do themselves. In work, personal life, and recreation, however, the individual's ability to function successfully depends on what others do and how several individuals' mental and physical performances mesh and contribute to the task.

Schools also vary from real life in that, in school, pure mental processing rather than tool manipulation is emphasized. As an institution, school values independent thought processes. In schools, abstract symbols rather than contextualized reasoning are manipulated; manipulation takes place outside of school. Finally, in schools, all children are required to be generalists; outside of school, children are required in many contexts to be specialists.

Spindler and Spindler (1994) suggested that when people experience cultural conflict and instrumental failure, they respond in predictable ways. They may reaffirm their culture and try to sustain a recognizable way of life in line with their culture's values and beliefs. They may withdraw, so torn by conflict that they cannot identify with either their traditional culture or the dominant culture. They may, as a consequence, vegetate or engage in substance abuse. They may construct a marginal existence, forming a personal culture that was productive initially but usually constituted several different segments. Alternatively, individuals may assimilate, sometimes trying to be more respectable than members of the dominant culture.

According to Bandura (1986), self-efficacy has an extremely powerful influence on an individual. If learners do not believe that they are capable of producing desired results efficiently, then every difficulty encountered confirms that belief. Consequently, goals, persistence, and the explanations of the outcomes of their efforts are all affected (Bandura, 1986). The position taken in this book is that educators, by accepting and celebrating children for who they are, can indeed help all children to believe that they are capable learners.

LEARNING OBJECTIVE 5: To be able to explain the premises on which this book is written

This book presumes that all classrooms are inclusive. A classroom may have

- Learners from diverse cultural, ethnic, or linguistic groups, including African American, Asian American, European American, Hispanic American, Appalachian, and Native American learners and all of the ethnic, religious, and cultural subgroups that these larger groups encompass
- Learners who vary in their ways of interacting, including males and females, learners with various challenging behaviors, and learners with identified behavior disorders
- Learners who vary in their learning styles and rates, including all of the various mode preferences (auditory, visual, and kinesthetic learners), learners who are academically gifted or challenged, learners identified as having learning disabilities, and learners identified with mental retardation
- Learners who vary in their ways of gaining access to the environment, including any of a wide range of physical, health, visual, hearing, or communicative issues

The issue of self-efficacy is true for teachers as well as for learners. If the teacher perceives him- or herself as able to meet the needs of the learners assigned to his or her classroom, then the teacher will find ways to meet those needs. The problem is not the child but the context in which the child is attempting to function.

Children construct their own knowledge as a result of their interaction with the social and physical environments. The role of the teacher in **constructivism** is one who is capable of and responsible for learning about children within his or her care. The teacher then uses this knowledge to construct practices that are developmentally appropriate for individual children in particular contexts (Mallory & New, 1994).

In this constructivist role, the teacher engages in what is becoming known as "critical pedagogy." In critical pedagogy, the teacher incorporates into the teaching and learning process students' experiences, background knowledge, and authentic tasks that are meaningful to the students and reflect students' interests. The teacher places emphasis on meaning rather than on form, and on creativity and divergent thinking rather than on correctness. The teacher interacts and dialogues with students rather than directing instruction and assesses students by contrasting the students' unassisted performance with their assisted performance in authentic tasks. In order to serve in a critical pedagogical classroom environment, teachers need to be well informed regarding community history, the history of the cultural group with whom they are working, and community resources, including individuals as well as community centers, that can provide additional information and support to themselves and their students (Goldstein, 1996).

The instruction methods and management strategies presented in this book provide teachers with practical knowledge and skills to be applied in teaching all of the children in their classrooms. Each chapter begins with learning objectives and key words and phrases. By modeling these teaching routines, the learning objectives and key words and phrases also will become a part of readers' professional practice. In addition, because active participation is more effective for many learners, each chapter in the book contains

- "Your Turn" boxes to be completed by the reader, which provide a stimulus to reflect on the content of the learning objective
- Self-evaluation activities, including multiple-choice questions at the end of each chapter
- Vocabulary exercises, to help readers make the language of the profession their own
- Application activities, to relate the content to practice and field experience

SUMMARY

This chapter addresses the following major concepts:

1. Every classroom is an inclusive classroom, with learners from diverse cultural, linguistic, and ethnic groups; learners who vary in their learning styles and rates; learners who vary in their interactions; and learners who vary in the ways in which they gain access to the environment.
2. The number of students from diverse cultural, linguistic, and ethnic groups in public schools is increasing, and an awareness of the characteristics of each culture and a recognition of the uniqueness of each individual are needed by teachers.
3. Attitudes toward people with identified disabilities are evolving from pity to respect.
4. The caregiving environment of children has changed greatly and may be affected by changes in the structure of the family, poverty, substance abuse, and maltreatment.

TEST YOUR KNOWLEDGE

Completion of the "Self-Evaluation," "Make the Language Your Own," and "Application Activities" sections will aid readers in understanding and retaining the information presented in this chapter. Answer keys for the "Self-Evaluation" and "Make the Language Your Own" sections are located in the Appendix at the end of the book.

Self-Evaluation

Select the most appropriate response to complete each of the following statements:

1. The concepts of minority and majority have been redefined because
   a. Legislation has increased equity among diverse cultures
   b. European Americans are the numerical minority in many education environments, such as many urban school districts
   c. Previous definitions have maintained stereotypes

2. One of the most important concepts regarding cultural, linguistic, and ethnic groups is that
   a. Characteristics among members of the group are consistent
   b. There is great heterogeneity within any group
   c. Members of cultural, linguistic, and ethnic groups are most appropriately educated by members of their groups

3. Much of the research about minority families
   a. Questions the ability of these families in childrearing
   b. Has perpetuated the notion of lower-class subculture
   c. Demonstrates an ability to gain access to resources

4. Women may demonstrate underachievement because of
   a. Unequal treatment by teachers
   b. Differences in their abilities
   c. Genetic reasons

5. The "poster child" perception of people with disabilities
   a. Is useful in getting resources to people with disabilities
   b. Perpetuates images of disability as tragic and pitiable
   c. Provides people with disabilities with successful models

6. Families living in poverty
   a. Generally remain dependent on TANF until their children leave the family
   b. Are multiply at risk because of limited resources and increased stressors
   c. Are provided adequate support through the "welfare" system

7. The children at greatest risk for school failure are
   a. Children of never-married single parents
   b. Children living with a stepparent
   c. Children in families that have experienced divorce

8. Among women with chemical dependency, the most common substance of choice is
   a. Cocaine
   b. Marijuana
   c. Alcohol

9. Children who have been maltreated have difficulty interacting with
   a. Their parents
   b. Their peers
   c. Peers as well as parents and other adults

10. Children from minority groups may
    a. Have an enduring, successful self-identity in the community
    b. Be consistently challenged by failure in school and the community
    c. Manage in a similar fashion across environments

Make the Language Your Own
Match the following terms with their definitions:

1. _____ European American
2. _____ Cultural pluralism
3. _____ Substance abuse
4. _____ African American
5. _____ Appalachian
6. _____ Welfare
7. _____ Culture
8. _____ Disability
9. _____ Ethnicity
10. _____ Asian American
11. _____ Fetal alcohol syndrome
12. _____ Child maltreatment
13. _____ Hispanic American
14. _____ Urban Appalachian
15. _____ Native American
16. _____ Fetal alcohol effects

a. Caucasian Americans of European ancestry
b. Membership in a group of people who share a unique social and cultural heritage that is transmitted through generations
c. Covert and overt beliefs, expectations, and values of people and institutions
d. Mutual appreciation and understanding of the various cultures in society
e. Americans of African ancestry
f. Americans of Asian ancestry
g. Americans of all races whose heritage is tied to the use of Spanish language and Latino culture
h. Americans with ancestry in one of the native populations of North America
i. Americans with ancestry in the federally defined Appalachian region of 397 counties and 5 independent cities in Alabama, Georgia, Kentucky, Maryland, Mississippi, New York, North Carolina, Ohio, Pennsylvania, South Carolina, Tennessee, Virginia, and West Virginia
j. Appalachians who are residents of urban areas outside the Appalachian region
k. Limitation that requires support
l. Common reference for TANF (formerly known as AFDC)
m. Use of any chemical substance that causes physical, mental, emotional, and social harm to an individual or to those close to the individual
n. Syndrome caused by prenatal alcohol consumption by the mother,

identified by prenatal and postnatal growth retardation, central
nervous system involvement, and
common facial characteristics

o. Prenatal and postnatal growth retardation and central nervous system involvement caused by prenatal
alcohol consumption

p. Child abuse and child neglect

Application Activities

1. Observe the students in a classroom for at least 30 minutes. Through a
seating chart such as the one that follows, indicate in the appropriate box
for each student the occurrences of the teacher calling on (CA), responding
to (RE), correcting (C), reprimanding (R), commenting to (CT), or praising
(P) the student indicated. Write the symbols in the box (e.g., the first box,
European American Male, may have (RE, RE, R, R, R) written in it by the
end of the observation period. Are any patterns generated by your data?
Who seems to be most often praised? reprimanded? commented to? ignored?

European American male	European American female	African American male	European American male
European American female	European American female	Hispanic male	Hispanic female
Asian American male	European American female	European American female	European American male
Asian American female	European American female	European American female	European American female
European American female	African American male	African American female	European American female

2. Observe a meeting in which men and women are attempting to come to a
consensus. What patterns of interaction do you observe? Who talks? Who
is silent? Who interrupts? Who apologizes?

REFERENCES

Abel, E.L. (1984). Prenatal effects of alcohol. *Drug and Alcohol Dependence, 13,* 1–10.

Adams, C., Eyler, F., & Behnke, M. (1990). Nursing intervention with mothers who are
substance abusers. *Journal of Perinatal and Neonatal Nursing, 3,* 43–52.

Alessandri, S.M., Sullivan, M.W., Imaizumi, S., & Lewis, M. (1993). Learning and
emotional responsivity in cocaine-exposed infants. *Developmental Psychology, 29,*
989–997.

Allen, L., & Majidi-Ahi, S. (1989). Black American children. In J. Gibbs & L. Huang (Eds.), *Children of color* (pp. 143–178). San Francisco: Jossey-Bass.

American Association of University Women (AAUW). (1992). *How schools shortchange girls.* Washington, DC: Author.

American Humane Association. (1987). *Highlights of official child neglect and abuse reporting.* Denver: Author.

Baca, L.M., & Harris, K.C. (1988). Teaching migrant exceptional children. *Teaching Exceptional Children, 20*(4), 32–35.

Bandura, A. (1986). *Social foundations of thought and action.* Upper Saddle River, NJ: Prentice-Hall.

Baumeister, A.A., Kupstas, F., & Klindworth, L.M. (1990). New morbidity: Implications for prevention of children's disabilities. *Exceptionality, 1,* 1–16.

Biklen, D. (1993). *Communication unbound: How facilitated communication is challenging traditional views of autism and ability/disability.* New York: Teachers College Press.

Borman, K., & Obermiller, P. (1994). Introduction. In K. Borman & P. Obermiller (Eds.), *From mountain to metropolis: Appalachian migrants in American cities* (pp. xvii–xxi). Westport, CT: Bergin & Garvey.

Borman, K., & Stegelin, D. (1994). Social change and urban Appalachian children: Youth at risk. In K. Borman & P. Obermiller (Eds.), *From mountain to metropolis: Appalachian migrants in American cities* (pp. 167–180). Westport, CT: Bergin & Garvey.

Brendtro, L.K., Brokenleg, M., & Bockern, S.V. (1990). *Reclaiming youth at risk: Our hope for the future.* Bloomington, IN: National Education Service.

Brod, R.L., & McQuiston, J.M. (1983). American Indian adult education and literacy: The first national survey. *Journal of American Indian Education, 1,* 1–16.

Buenning, M., Tollefson, N., & Rodriguez, F. (1992). Hispanic culture and the schools. In M.J. Fine & C. Carlson (Eds.), *The handbook of family–school intervention: A systems perspective* (pp. 86–101). Needham Heights, MA: Allyn & Bacon.

Carlson, C. (1992). Single parenting and stepparenting: Problems, issues, and interventions. In M.J. Fine & C. Carlson (Eds.), *The handbook of family–school intervention: A systems perspective* (pp. 188–214). Needham Heights, MA: Allyn & Bacon.

Child Abuse Prevention and Treatment Act of 1997, PL 93-245, 42 U.S.C. § 5161 *et seq.*

Children's Defense Fund. (1994). *Congressional workbook 1994.* Washington, DC: Author.

Cicchetti, D., Toth, S., & Hennessy, K. (1989). Research on the consequences of child maltreatment and its application to educational settings. *Topics in Early Childhood Special Education, 9*(2), 33–55.

Commins, N.L., & Miramontes, O.B. (1989). Perceived and actual linguistic competence: A descriptive study of four low-achieving Hispanic bilingual students. *American Educational Research Journal, 26,* 443–472.

Crittenden, P.M. (1989). Teaching maltreated children in the preschool. *Topics in Early Childhood Special Education, 9*(2), 16–32.

Dao, M. (1991). Designing assessment procedures for educationally at-risk southeast Asian-American students. *Journal of Learning Disabilities, 24,* 594–601, 629.

Davis, G.A., & Rimm, S.B. (1985). *Education of the gifted and talented.* Upper Saddle River, NJ: Prentice-Hall.

Delgado-Gaitan, C., & Trueba, H.T. (1985). Ethnographic study of participant structures in task completion: Reinterpretation of "handicaps" in Mexican children. *Learning Disabilities Quarterly, 8,* 67–75.

Education Amendments of 1972, PL 92-318, Title IX, 20 U.S.C. § 72235.

Fradd, S., Figueroa, R.A., & Correa, V.I. (1989). Meeting the multicultural needs of Hispanic students in special education. *Exceptional Children, 56,* 102–104.

Garcia-Preto, N. (1982). Puerto-Rican families. In M. Goldriek, J.K. Pierce, & J. Gordano (Eds.), *Ethnicity and family therapy* (pp. 75–101). New York: Guilford Press.

Gelfand, D.M., Jenson, W.R., & Drew, C.J. (1988). *Understanding child behavior disorders* (2nd ed.). Austin, TX: Holt, Rinehart & Winston.

Gilligan, C. (1982). *In a different voice: Psychological theory and women's development.* Cambridge, MA: Harvard University Press.

Goldstein, B.S.C. (1996). Critical pedagogy in a bilingual special education classroom. In M.S. Poplin & P.T. Cousin (Eds.), *Alternative views of learning disabilities: Issues for the 21st century* (pp. 145–167). Austin, TX: PRO-ED.

Grimm, L.L. (1992). The Native American child in school: An ecological perspective. In M.J. Fine & C. Carlson (Eds.), *The handbook of family–school intervention: A systems perspective* (pp. 102–118). Needham Heights, MA: Allyn & Bacon.

Grossman, H. (1992). Special education in diverse society: Improving services for minority and working class students. *Preventing School Failure, 36*(1), 19–27.

Guidubaldi, J., & Perry, J.D. (1985). Divorce and mental health sequelae for children: A two-year follow-up of a nationwide sample. *Journal of the American Academy of Child Psychiatry, 24,* 531–537.

Hanna, J. (1988). *Disruptive school behavior: Class, race, and culture.* New York: Holmes & Meyer.

Heath, S.B. (1983). *Ways with words.* New York: Cambridge University Press.

Ho, M.K. (1992). Asian-American students: Family influences. In M.J. Fine & C. Carlson (Eds.), *The handbook of family–school intervention: A systems perspective* (pp. 75–85). Needham Heights, MA: Allyn & Bacon.

Hyland, C.R. (1989). What we know about the fastest growing minority population: Hispanic Americans. *Educational Horizons, 67*(4), 124–130.

Inclan, J. (1985). Variations in the value orientations in mental health work with Puerto Ricans. *Psychotherapy, 33,* 324–334.

Interstate Migrant Council. (1984). *National policy workshop on special education needs of migrant handicapped students: Proceedings report.* Denver: Education Commission of the States.

Kerr, B.A. (1985). Smart girls, gifted women: Special guidance concerns. *Roeper Review, 8,* 30–33.

Khalsa, J.H., & Groefrer, J. (1991). Epidemiology and health consequences of drug abuse among pregnant women. *Seminars in Perinatology, 15*(4), 265–270.

Kochman, T. (1991). *Culturally based patterns of difference.* Paper presented at the University of Cincinnati, OH.

Koren, G. (1989, December 16). Bias against the null hypothesis: The reproductive hazards of cocaine. *Lancet,* 1440–1442.

Kugelmass, J. (1993). The challenge of cultural diversity. In A.M. Bauer (Ed.), *Children who challenge the system* (pp. 117–144). Greenwich, CT: Ablex Publishing Corp.

LaFramboise, T.D., & Low, K.G. (1989). American Indian children and adolescents. In J. Gibbs & L. Huang (Eds.), *Children of color* (pp. 114–147). San Francisco: Jossey-Bass.

Leap, W.L. (1981). American Indian language maintenance. *Annual Review of Anthropology, 10,* 271–280.

Lynch, E.M. (1993). Negotiating status and role: An ethnographic examination of verbal dueling among students with behavior disorders. In A.M. Bauer (Ed.), *Children who challenge the system* (pp. 29–44). Greenwich, CT: Ablex Publishing Corp.

Lyons, N. (1985). *Visions and competencies: Men and women as decision-makers and conflict managers.* Cambridge, MA: Harvard University Press.

Mallory, B.L., & New, R.S. (1994). Social constructivist theory and principles of inclusion: Challenges for early childhood special education. *Journal of Special Education, 28,* 322–337.

McAdoo, H.P. (1978). Minority families. In J.H. Stevens & M. Matthers (Eds.), *Mother–child, father–child relationships* (pp. 35–57). Washington, DC: National Association for the Education of Young Children.

McCoy, C.B., & Watkins, V.M. (1980). Drug use among urban ethnic youth. *Youth and Society, 11,* 83–106.

Michigan Department of Education, Office of Equity in Education. (1990). *The influence of gender role socialization on student perceptions.* Lansing: Author.

Mindel, C.H., & Habenstein, R.W. (Eds.). (1981). *Ethnic families in America: Patterns and variations* (2nd ed.). New York: Elsevier Science Publishers.

National Federation of State High School Associations. (1990). *1990–1991 handbook.* Kansas City, MO: Author.

National Institute on Drug Abuse. (1981). *Adolescent peer pressures: Theory, correlates, and program implications for drug and abuse prevention.* Washington, DC: U.S. Government Printing Office. (DHHS Publication No. ADM 81-1152)

Obermiller, P.J., & Maloney, M. (1994). Living city, feeling country: The current status and future prospects of urban Appalachians. In K. Borman & P. Obermiller (Eds.), *From mountain to metropolis: Appalachian migrants in American cities* (pp. 3–12). Westport, CT: Bergin & Garvey.

Parker, S., Greer, S., & Zuckerman, B. (1988). Double jeopardy: The impact of poverty on early childhood development. *Pediatric Clinics of North America, 35,* 1227–1240.

Penn, E.M., Borman, K.M., & Hoeweler, F. (1994). Echoes from the hill: Urban Appalachian youths and educational reform. In K. Borman & P. Obermiller (Eds.), *From mountain to metropolis: Appalachian migrants in American cities* (pp. 121–140). Westport, CT: Bergin & Garvey.

Pepper, F. (1976). Teaching the American Indian child in mainstream settings. In R.L. Jones (Ed.), *Mainstreaming and the minority child* (pp. 85–97). Reston, VA: Council for Exceptional Children.

Perry, J. (1982). The ECS interstate migrant education project. *Exceptional Children, 48,* 496–500.

Peters, M. (1981). Parenting in Black families with young children. In H. McAdoo (Ed.), *Black families* (pp. 21–35). Thousand Oaks, CA: Sage Publications.

Poplin, M.S., & Wright, P. (1983). The concept of cultural pluralism: Issues in special education. *Learning Disabilities Quarterly, 6,* 367–371.

Ramirez, O. (1990). Mexican American children and adolescents. In J.T. Gibbs & L.N. Huang (Eds.), *Children of color* (pp. 224–250). San Francisco: Jossey-Bass.

Resnick, L.B. (1987). Learning in school and out. *Educational Researcher, 16*(9), 13–20.

Roberts, E. (1994). Conversations with Ed. *The Mouth, 2,* 2.

Rossett, H., & Weiner, L. (1984). *Alcohol and the fetus.* New York: Oxford University Press.

Shapiro, J.P. (1993). *No pity: People with disabilities forging a new civil rights movement.* New York: Times Books.

Shaywitz, S., Shaywitz, B., Fletcher, B., & Escobar, M. (1990). Prevalence of reading disabilities in boys and girls: Results of the Connecticut longitudinal study. *JAMA: Journal of the American Medical Association, 264,* 998–1002.

Shea, T.M., & Bauer, A.M. (1994). *Learners with disabilities: A social systems perspective of special education.* Madison, WI: Brown & Benchmark.

Smith, E. (1981). Cultural and historical perspectives in counseling blacks. In D.W. Sue (Ed.), *Counseling the culturally different: Theory and practice* (pp. 175–191). New York: John Wiley & Sons.

Social Security Act of 1935, PL 74-271, 42 U.S.C. §§ 301 *et seq.*

Spindler, G., & Spindler, L. (1994). What is cultural therapy? In G. Spindler & L. Spindler (Eds.), *Pathways to cultural awareness: Cultural therapy with teachers and students* (pp. 1–35). Thousand Oaks, CA: Sage Publications.

Stefans, V. (1994). The six steps beyond professionalism. *The Mouth, 3,* 9.

Steward, R.J., & Logan, S.L. (1992). Understanding the black family and child in the school context. In M.J. Fine & C. Carlson (Eds.), *The handbook of family–school intervention: A systems perspective* (pp. 57–74). Needham Heights, MA: Allyn & Bacon.

Sullivan, M., & Miller, D. (1990). Cincinnati's Urban Appalachian Council and Appalachian identity. *Harvard Educational Review, 60*(1), 106–124.

Taylor, D., & Dorsey-Gaines, C. (1988). *Growing up literate: Learning from inner-city families.* Portsmouth, NH: Heinemann.

Tobin, K., & Garnett, P. (1987). Gender related differences in science activities. *Science Education, 71,* 91–103.

U.S. Department of Education. (1996). *Eighteenth annual report to Congress on the implementation of the Individuals with Disabilities Education Act.* Washington, DC: Author.

Valdivieso, R. (1990). *Demographic trends of the Mexican-American population: Implications for schools.* Charleston, WV: ERIC Clearinghouse on Rural Education and Small Schools. (ERIC No. ED 321961)

Vogel, S.A. (1990). Gender differences in intelligence, language, visual-motor abilities, and academic achievement in students with learning disabilities: A review of the literature. *Journal of Learning Disabilities, 23,* 44–52.

Wallerstein, J., & Blakeslee, S. (1989). *Second chances: Men, women, and children a decade after divorce.* New York: Ticknor & Fields.

Welfare Reform Act of 1996, PL 104-193, 42 U.S.C. §§ 607 *et seq.*

White House Task Force on Infant Mortality. (1989). *Infant mortality in the United States* (Draft report). Washington, DC: Author.

Yates, J.R. (1987). Current and emerging forces. *Counterpoint, 7*(4), 4–5.

Youngblade, L.M., & Belsky, J. (1989). Child maltreatment, infant–parent attachment security, and dysfunctional peer relationships in toddlerhood. *Topics in Early Childhood Special Education, 9*(2), 1–15.

Zaichkin, J., & Houston, R.F. (1993). The drug-exposed mother and infant: A regional center experience. *Neonatal Network, 11*(3), 41–48.

Legal Supports for Inclusion

All across our Nation mothers are giving birth to infants with disabilities. So I want to dedicate the Americans with Disabilities Act to these, the next generation of children and their parents. With the passage of ADA, we, as a society, make a pledge that every child with a disability will have the opportunity to maximize his or her potential to live proud, productive, and prosperous lives in the mainstream of our society. We love you all and welcome you into the world. We look forward to becoming your friends, your neighbors, and your co-workers. We say, whatever you decide as your goal, go for it. The doors are open and the barriers are coming down!

U.S. Senator Tom Harkin (D-Iowa) (1993, p. 3),
in a speech on the day the
Americans with Disabilities Act (ADA) of 1990
passed on the Senate floor

Senator Harkin's comments are a reminder that, in some cases, government
has intervened on behalf of individuals with disabilities. This chapter focuses
on this essential aspect of diversity in American society—that of legal protections for those who are perceived to vary from their peers. More specifically,
the chapter discusses the legal supports for inclusion of all learners in the general
classroom.

LEARNING OBJECTIVES

After completing this chapter, readers will be able to

1. Describe the development of legal supports for people with disabilities
   in the United States and Canada
2. Discuss the basic principles underlying special education law
3. Discuss school practices related to the rights of learners with disabilities and their parents
4. Discuss the effects of the legal aspects of inclusion on the general education teacher

---

KEY WORDS AND PHRASES

appeal—the process during which an appeals court reviews the records and judgments of a lower court to determine whether an error was made that might lead to a reversal or a change in the lower court's decision

class action—a civil suit or action brought on behalf of the plaintiffs who are named in the suit as well as on behalf of all other people similarly situated to vindicate their legally protected interests (Turnbull, 1993)

confidentiality—the protection of information from unauthorized disclosure

directory information—informa-tion that may include students' names, addresses, and telephone numbers; the nature of directory information is determined by each school district

due process of law—a right to have any law applied reasonably

and with sufficient safeguards by the federal and state govern-ments, such as through hearings and notice, to ensure that an indi-vidual is dealt with fairly

individualized education program (IEP)—a written commitment for the delivery of services to meet the student's educational needs

individualized family service plan (IFSP)—a plan of services and outcomes for the family of a child with a disability who is younger than age 3 years

least restrictive environment (LRE)—the environment in which learners with disabilities can suc-ceed that is most similar to the environment in which his or her peers are educated (Shea & Bauer, 1994)

mandated—required by law

transition services—services to fa-cilitate the individual's movement between education programs and other service programs; between school programs; or from school to work, to advanced training, or to postsecondary education

zero reject—the philosophy that no child, regardless of the severity of his or her disability, should be excluded from school on the basis of that disability

LEARNING OBJECTIVE 1: To be able to describe the development of legal supports for people with disabilities in the United States and Canada

The first federal laws of the United States designed to support individuals with disabilities were passed in 1798. At that time, the Fifth Congress **mandated** a Marine Hospital Service for seamen who were ill or had disabilities. By 1912, as a result of the expansion of the services provided and the population served, the Marine Hospital Service program had evolved into the U.S. Public Health Service (National Information Center for Children and Youth with Disabilities [NICHCY], 1991b). In 1912, Congress created the U.S. Children's Bureau to investigate and report on matters related to the lives and welfare of all American children (Kauffman, 1993).

Prior to World War II, there were few federal laws authorizing special benefits for people with disabilities, and the existing federal laws were written almost exclusively with regard to military service–related disabilities (NICHCY, 1991b). The development of legal supports for services, especially education services, for people with disabilities is summarized in Table 1.

Beginning in 1965 and continuing through the late 1990s, Congress enacted a series of laws that gradually increased federal support and requirements for special education services for individuals with disabilities. In 1965, the first federal support for education occurred in the Elementary and Secondary Education Act (ESEA) (PL 89-10). That same year, Congress enacted a federal grant program specifically for individuals with disabilities.

In 1966, the Elementary and Secondary Education Act (PL 89-750) established the Bureau for the Education of the Handicapped and the National Advisory Council on Disability. Three years later, the Elementary and Secondary Education Amendments of 1967 (PL 90-247) mandated discretionary programs for regional resource centers, services for children with dual sensory impairments, and research in special education.

In the early 1970s, two **class action** lawsuits paved the way for further legislation regarding the rights of children with disabilities (see Table 2). In the *Pennsylvania Association for Retarded Children (PARC) v. Pennsylvania* (1972) case, a consent decree by the commonwealth of Pennsylvania specified that children with mental retardation had to have access to a free public education and that the commonwealth had to identify and provide a free public education to individuals who previously had been excluded from education. The *Mills v. Board of Education* (1972) case specified that the District of Columbia must provide all children with disabilities a free public education, regardless of the severity or the nature of their disabilities. Both of these cases were based on the finding of the landmark *Brown v. Board of Education* (1954) case, which ended racially segregated schools. In the *Brown* decision, the court ruled that separate education of people of different races was not equal education.

Table 1.   U.S. laws involving services for people with disabilities

Legislation	Effect
Elementary and Secondary Education Act of 1965 (PL 89-10)	Provided first direct federal support for the education of children; aimed at strengthening and improving educational quality and opportunity in elementary and secondary schools
School Districts—Federal Aid (1965) (PL 89-313)	Authorized first federal grant program for children and youth with disabilities and grants to educate children with disabilities in state-operated or state-supported schools and institutions
Elementary and Secondary Education Act of 1966 (PL 89-750)	Established first federal grant program for the education of children with disabilities at the local school level; established the Bureau of the Education of the Handicapped and the National Advisory Council on Disability
Elementary and Secondary Education Amendments of 1967 (PL 90-247)	Established discretionary programs for regional resource centers, centers and services for children with dual sensory impairments, research in special education, and recruitment of special education personnel
Education of the Handicapped Act of 1970 (PL 91-230)	Consolidated programs for the education of children with disabilities
Education of the Handicapped Amendments of 1974 (PL 93-380)	Required states to establish a timetable for achieving full educational opportunity for children with disabilities; implemented procedural safeguards for the identification, evaluation, and placement of children with disabilities; and mandated integration into general classes when possible
Rehabilitation Act of 1973 (PL 93-112)	Section 504 of the Act ensured equal opportunities for children and youth with disabilities in schools receiving federal funds
Family Educational Rights and Privacy Act (FERPA) of 1974 (PL 93-380)	Parents and eligible students were granted the right to review and copy educational records, have records explained, and request that records be changed if they believe that information contained in them is inaccurate, misleading, or a violation of rights; records may not be destroyed if there is a request to inspect and review them
Education for All Handicapped Children Act of 1975 (PL 94-142)	Guaranteed free appropriate public education, ensured rights and due process, financially supported state efforts
Education of the Handicapped Act Amendments of 1983 (PL 98-199)	Expanded incentives for preschool special education programs, early intervention, and transition programs; formed the Office of Special Education Programs (OSEP) to replace the Bureau of the Education of the Handicapped
Carl D. Perkins Vocational Education Act (1984) (PL 98-524)	Required full range of vocational services and vocational education for students with disabilities
Handicapped Children's Protection Act of 1986 (PL 99-372)	Authorized the award of reasonable attorney fees to parents and guardians who prevail when there is a dispute with a school system regarding a child's right to a free appropriate public education
Children's Justice Act of 1986 (PL 99-401)	Funded respite care for children who have a disability or an ongoing illness
Education of the Handicapped Act Amendments of 1986 (PL 99-457)	Lowered eligibility age for special education services to 3 years; established the Handicapped Infants and Toddlers Program for children from birth to third birthday

(continued)

Table 1. *(continued)*

Legislation	Effect
Developmental Disabilities Assistance and Bill of Rights Act Amendments of 1987 (PL 100-146)	Authorized grants to support the planning, coordination, and delivery of specialized services to people with developmental disabilities
Technology-Related Assistance for Individuals with Disabilities Act of 1988 (PL 100-407)	Assisted states in developing comprehensive, consumer-responsive programs of technology-related assistance and extended the availability of assistive technology to individuals with disabilities and their families
Americans with Disabilities Act (ADA) of 1990 (PL 101-336)	Extended to individuals with disabilities all civil rights protection, including equal opportunity in employment, public accommodation, transportation, services, and telecommunications
Individuals with Disabilities Education Act (IDEA) of 1990 (PL 101-476)	Expanded discretionary programs; modified language; included transition services and assistive technology services as special education services; expanded to more fully include children with autism and traumatic brain injury
Individuals with Disabilities Education Act (IDEA) Amendments of 1997 (PL 105-17)	Mandated transition services be provided to children beginning at age 14; previously, IDEA had required that transition services be provided beginning at age 16

Source: National Information Center for Children and Youth with Disabilities (1991b, 1992).

In Canada, educational issues traditionally have been resolved through political change rather than judicial decisions. Indeed, there is a lack of federal involvement in Canadian education that makes it quite different from U.S. education (MacKay, 1986). The practices of school boards vary significantly even within Canada's individual provinces. The Canadian Charter of Rights and Freedoms, enacted in 1985, provides general assurances regarding education.

Your Turn . . .

Consider the ways in which inclusion in general education for learners with disabilities has evolved. Do you feel that such changes would have occurred without the involvement of the courts? Would American society have included individuals who vary from their peers without legislation? Why or why not?

Table 2. U.S. federal court cases involving services for people who vary from their peers

Case	Effect
Brown v. Board of Education (U.S. 1954)	Separate education was deemed not to be equal education.
Pennsylvania Association of Retarded Children (PARC) v. Pennsylvania (E.D. Pa. 1972)	All children with mental retardation must be provided an education; those previously excluded must be identified and provided an education.
Mills v. Board of Education (D.D.C. 1972)	All children with disabilities must be provided an education.

LEARNING OBJECTIVE 2: To be able to discuss the basic principles underlying special education law

The Education for All Handicapped Children Act of 1975 (PL 94-142) mandated services for students with disabilities and provided procedures related to the provision of those services. Amendments to that act, including the Individuals with Disabilities Education Act (IDEA) of 1990 (PL 101-476), the Individuals with Disabilities Education Act (IDEA) Amendments of 1991 (PL 102-119), and the Individuals with Disabilities Education Act (IDEA) Amendments of 1997 (PL 105-17), continue its legacy by guaranteeing the availability of special education programs to eligible children and youth with disabilities, ensuring that decisions made about providing special education are fair and appropriate, and providing federal financial assistance to state and local governments to educate children with special needs (NICHCY, 1992). Basically, in order to remain eligible for federal funds under the law, states must ensure that the educational rights and procedures described in the following sections are provided (NICHCY, 1991a).

Turnbull (1993) described six key principles underlying special education law. These principles state that every child has a right to

1. A free appropriate public education (FAPE)
2. A fair evaluation
3. An individualized and appropriate education
4. An education in the **least restrictive environment (LRE)**
5. Procedural **due process of law**
6. Parents' participation and shared decision making

These principles provide the structure for this chapter's discussion of special education mandates in the United States and Canada.

A Free Appropriate Public Education

The provision of free public education to children with disabilities has not been controversial. The issue of providing an *appropriate education* to these individuals, however, has been open to various interpretations. Congress did not clearly define the term *appropriate* when it mandated that all children with disabilities receive a FAPE (Osborne, 1988). As a consequence, lower courts ruled that PL 94-142 required a school to maximize the potential of each learner with disabilities commensurate with the opportunities provided to students who were not identified as having disabilities. The Supreme Court, however, in the *Rowley v. Hendrick Hudson School District* (1982) decision, ruled that a school district satisfied the mandate to provide a FAPE if it provided individualized instruction and services that brought about educational benefit and that the plans for such instruction and services were delineated in a procedurally correct **individualized education program (IEP)**. For students who received the majority of their instruction in the general classroom, instruction was required to be sufficient to allow the student to attain passing grades and be promoted annually. The specific ruling in *Rowley* was to deny an American Sign Language (ASL) interpreter for a high school student with a hearing impairment because the student was advancing from grade to grade without great difficulty. The *Rowley* decision implied that learners with disabilities need only achieve at a level commensurate with that of their peers rather than to their fullest potential.

The interpretation of the term *appropriate* also has become an issue in the education of preschool children with disabilities. In the view of the *Rowley* court, programs for preschool children are appropriate if they are reasonably calculated to enable the child to progress educationally (Edminster & Elkstrand, 1987). Some parents of preschool children, however, maintain that a full-day program is more beneficial for their children than a half-day program. Edminster and Elkstrand found that the amount of time that children actually engaged in learning in a full-day program was not significantly greater than it was in the half-day program because of the frequent breaks, lunchtime, and naps they experienced in the full-day program. Data (Edminster & Elkstrand, 1987) appear to demonstrate that the half-day program meets the requirements for a FAPE for many preschool children with disabilities.

Section 504 of the Rehabilitation Act of 1973 (PL 93-112) provides additional support for the right of every child to a FAPE. According to Section 504, people with disabilities, regardless of the nature or severity of their disabilities, must be provided a free public education. These requirements are designed to ensure that no child is excluded from school on the basis of disability. This concept is frequently referred to as the **zero reject philosophy**.

The Canadian Charter of Rights and Freedoms forbids discrimination against people with disabilities in employment, employment applications and advertisements, the provision of goods and services, and accommodations. In this way, the charter provides a broad, positive guarantee of an education for all children.

Fair Evaluation

The initial educational evaluation that PL 94-142 and its amendments requires must take into account all aspects of the child's development and must include information about the child's total environment. The law requires that the evaluation include the observations of professionals who have worked with the child; the child's medical history (when it is relevant to the child's educational experience at school); information provided by and observations of the family about their child's school experiences, abilities, needs, and behavior outside of school; and the child's feelings about school (NICHCY, 1991b).

PL 94-142 requires that diagnostic evaluation instruments be administered in the child's native language or mode of communication, be valid for the
purpose for which they are being administered, and be administered by qualified personnel. In addition, no single instrument may be used as the basis for
the decision with regard to the child's eligibility for special education services
(Shea & Bauer, 1994).

Learners can be referred for evaluation in several ways. The child's parents may request that the school evaluate their child. If the school refuses to
evaluate the child, written notice that explains the reasons for the refusal and
outlines due process rights must be provided to the parents. The school may
request the parents' permission to evaluate the child, or the child's teacher or
doctor may request an evaluation.

The Canadian Charter of Rights and Freedoms grants no specific directions regarding the evaluation of learners with disabilities. Section 7 of the
charter, however, guarantees the principles of fundamental justice, which
would support fair evaluation.

Individualized and Appropriate Education

PL 94-142 first presented the concept of an IEP. What PL 94-142 requires is a
guideline, not a contract, for individualized instruction. The school is responsible for providing the instruction services listed in the learner's IEP but not
for ensuring the learner's progress. The IEP serves as a written commitment
for delivery of services to meet a learner's educational needs.

Section 614(d)(1)(A) of the Individuals with Disabilities Education Act
(IDEA) Amendments of 1997 (PL 105-17) clarified the required contents of the
IEP. Under that section, the IEP is to include

- A description of the child's present level of educational performance, including, for school-age children, a description of how the child's disability
  affects his or her involvement and progress in the general education classroom (For preschool children, the description should describe, as appropriate, how the child's disability affects his or her participation in appropriate activities.)
- A statement of measurable annual goals, including benchmarks or short-
  term objectives, related to meeting the child's needs due to the disability
  and enabling the child to be involved and progress in the general curriculum, as well as other educational needs
- A statement of the special education and related services and supplementary aids and services to be provided to the child and a statement of the
  program modifications or supports for school personnel that will be provided for the child to progress toward annual goals; to be involved and
  progress in general education, including extracurricular and nonacademic
  activities; and to be educated with and participate with other children with
  or without disabilities in general education, including extracurricular and
  nonacademic activities
- An explanation of the extent to which the child will not participate with
  children without disabilities in general education
- A statement of any individual modifications in the administration of state-
  or districtwide assessments of student achievement that are needed in
  order for the child to participate in such assessment (If the IEP team de-

termines that the child will not participate in a particular state- or districtwide assessment, a statement of why that assessment is not appropriate for the child and how the child will be assessed must be included.)

- The projected date for the beginning of the services and modifications written in the IEP and the anticipated frequency, location, and duration of those services and modifications
- Beginning at age 14 and updated annually thereafter, a statement of the transition service needs of the child under the applicable components of the child's IEP that focuses on the child's courses of study (e.g., participation in advanced placement courses or a vocational education program)
- Beginning at age 16 (or younger if the IEP team determines it is appropriate), a statement of needed transition services for the child, including, when appropriate, a statement of the interagency responsibilities or any needed linkages
- A statement of how the child's progress toward annual goals will be measured and how often and how the child's parents will be informed regularly of their child's progress (In addition, the 1997 IDEA Amendments clarified the rights of children who attain majority while in school. Beginning at least 1 year before the child reaches the age of majority under state law, a statement must be included in the IEP that the child has been informed of the rights that will transfer to him or her on reaching the age of majority.)

The IEP team is composed of parents and professionals. According to Section 614(d)(1)(B) of the 1997 IDEA Amendments, the parents are key members of the team. In addition, if the child has been participating in general education, at least one general education teacher is included on the team in addition to at least one special education teacher or special education provider. Another member of the team is a representative of the local education agency (LEA) who is qualified to provide or supervise the provision of special education, is knowledgeable about the general education curriculum, and is knowledgeable about the availability of the resources of the LEA. An individual who can interpret the instructional implications of evaluation results also is included on the team. If the parent or the agency so requests, other individuals who have knowledge or special expertise regarding the child, including related-services personnel, can be included as appropriate. Finally, whenever appropriate, the child with a disability is a member of the IEP team.

There are several special factors that the IEP team must consider (1997 IDEA Amendments § 614[d][3]). When the child's behavior may have an impact on his or her learning or on the learning of others, strategies, including positive behavioral interventions and supports, must be described in the IEP. When the child has limited English proficiency, his or her language needs must be considered. For students with visual impairments, a statement regarding instruction in braille must be included. If the child has a hearing impairment, the communication needs of the child, with opportunities for direct communications with peers and professional personnel and direct instruction in the child's language and communication mode, must be addressed. Any assistive technology must be described clearly.

PL 94-142 required that a multidisciplinary team of individuals meet to share their evaluation results and determine whether the child is indeed eligible for special education services. This team usually includes both the general education teacher, who provides information about the child's current level of participation in the classroom, and the special education teacher, who provides information from systematic observation of the child. Parents, as active and contributing members of the team, provide information on the child's development, developmental level, and the ways in which they work with the child; the child's behavior in the home and the community; and their perceptions of the child's strengths and weaknesses. A psychologist collects and presents information regarding the child's cognitive development, learning styles, and coping skills. A social worker may present information regarding the child's social history. Others who may be members of the multidisciplinary team include the communication specialist, an audiologist, an occupational or physical therapist, a vision specialist, and medical personnel. The specific makeup of the team depends on the nature of the problem. For example, if concerns are raised about the child's hearing, an audiologist participates. The information gathered is used to determine the eligibility of the child for special education services.

The Education of the Handicapped Act Amendments of 1986 (PL 99-457) extended to children ages 3–5 years the right to have an IEP. State grants for children from birth through 2 years of age are provided in this law. The involvement of parents and families is ensured through the use of **individualized family service plans (IFSPs)**, which are developed by a multidisciplinary team and the child's parents. The IFSP includes

- A statement of the infant's or the toddler's developmental level
- A statement of the family's strengths and needs as related to the infant or toddler
- A statement of the anticipated outcomes for the infant or toddler and the infant's or toddler's family and the criteria, procedures, and time lines used to determine the degree to which progress is made and whether revisions of the anticipated outcomes are necessary
- A description of the specific early intervention services that are necessary to meet the unique needs of the infant or toddler and the infant's or toddler's family
- The projected dates of initiation of services and the anticipated duration of the services
- The name of the service coordinator who performs the service most relevant to the needs of the infant or toddler and the infant's or toddler's family; this individual is responsible for the implementation of the IFSP and the coordination with other agencies and other professionals
- A plan for the transition of the infant or toddler to preschool services

The IFSP is reviewed semiannually and evaluated annually. When the toddler enters preschool at 3 years of age, the IEP becomes the document used for service and placement descriptions. The IFSP is used rather than the IEP for young children because the family is the focus of services for infants and toddlers.

Included in the IEP mandate is the provision of related services for individuals with disabilities. IDEA defined *related services* as

Transportation, and such developmental, corrective, and other supportive services (including speech pathology and audiology, psychological services, physical and occupational therapy, recreation, including therapeutic recreation and social work services, and medical and counseling services, including rehabilitation counseling, except that such medical services shall be for diagnostic and evaluation proposes only) as may be required to assist a child with a disability to benefit from special education. (20 U.S.C. § 1401[17], cited in NICHCY, 1991b)

The related services described in PL 94-142 are summarized in Table 3.

In order to receive related services under the auspices of IDEA, children must be enrolled in special education. The IEP serves as a written commitment for delivery of services to meet a student's educational needs. If the parent is dissatisfied with related services, he or she may 1) request an independent evaluation at the school district's expense; 2) pay for an independent evaluation, in which case the school district must take the results of the independent evaluation into account; or 3) negotiate with the district to determine whether the child is eligible for related services under Section 504 of the Rehabilitation Act of 1973 and request a hearing. Under Section 504, the par-

Table 3.   Related services described in the Education for All Handicapped Children Act of 1975 (PL 94-142)

Service	Description
Transportation	Providing travel to and from school, between schools, and around school buildings
Speech-language pathology	Identifying, diagnosing, and appraising speech or language disorders
Audiology	Identifying students with a hearing loss; evaluating the loss; language, auditory, and speech-reading training; evaluating and implementing amplification
Psychological services	Administering tests, interpreting information about learning styles, consulting with staff
Physical therapy	Services provided by physical therapist
Occupational therapy	Activities to improve independent functioning and prevention of further loss of function
Recreation	Assessing leisure skills; conducting leisure education and recreation programs
Early identification	Generating plans to identify disabilities as early as possible
Medical services	Providing the services of a physician to determine medical disabilities that result in the need for special education and related services
School health services	Providing services of a school nurse or other qualified person
Counseling	Providing the services of social workers, psychologists, counselors, or other qualified personnel
Social work	Preparing social or developmental histories; counseling
Parent counseling and training	Helping parents understand the special needs of their child and providing them with information about child development

ents, if dissatisfied, can file a complaint with the U.S. Office of Civil Rights (NICHCY, 1991a).

Least Restrictive Environment

The implementation of the LRE has become one of the most controversial aspects of PL 94-142 (Biklen, 1992). Biklen suggested that if the law had merely required school districts to educate all children without regard to the location of children's classrooms, school districts could have simply established more programs, with many presumably being situated in separate locations. The LRE provision gave parents a basis on which to challenge segregation of learners with disabilities. According to PL 105-17,

> (5)   Least Restrictive Environment.—
>   (A)   In general.—To the maximum extent appropriate, children with disabilities, including children in public or private institutions or other care facilities, are educated with children who are not disabled, and special classes, separate schooling, or other removal of children with disabilities from the regular educational environment occurs only when the nature or severity of the disability of a child is such that education in regular classes with the use of supplementary aids and services cannot be achieved satisfactorily. (1997 IDEA Amendments § 612[a][5][A])

These regulations mandate that learners with disabilities be placed in the LRE in which they can function effectively.

The LRE mandate also applies in preschool programs. Edminster and Elkstrand (1987) suggested that PL 99-457 requires equal opportunities for preschool children with disabilities. Most states that provide preschool programs for children with disabilities, however, do not provide general education programs for preschool-age children who have not been diagnosed with a disability. The U.S. Department of Education, Office of Special Education Programs and Rehabilitative Services (OSERS), maintains that if there are programs available within a jurisdiction for preschoolers who have not been diagnosed with disabilities, then opportunities for inclusion are required. OSERS has determined that if programs for preschool children without disabilities are not provided within a jurisdiction, local education agencies (LEAs), if possible, must coordinate preschool special education programs with other existing public education programs such as Head Start and include children with disabilities in these programs. If, however, these service and program coordination efforts fail, school systems are not required to create preschool programs for children without identified disabilities or to enter into contracts with private facilities for the sole purpose of implementing inclusion.

The Individuals with Disabilities Education Act (IDEA) Amendments of 1997 (PL 105-17) increased the emphasis of IDEA on inclusion in early intervention programs. The 1997 IDEA amendments require that policies and procedures ensure that

> (A) to the maximum extent appropriate, early intervention services are provided in natural environments; and (B) the provision of early intervention services for any infant or toddler occurs in a setting other than a natural environment only when early intervention cannot be achieved satisfactorily for the infant or toddler in a natural environment. (1997 IDEA Amendments § 635[a][16])

A justification must be included in the IFSP of the extent, if any, to which services are not to be provided in a natural environment (NICHCY, 1997).

Taylor (1988) described several pitfalls in the LRE principle. First, it legitimizes and allows for placement of children in restrictive environments. In addition, on the surface, the principle assumes that intensive services cannot be provided in inclusive environments. Taylor also argued that professionals who emphasize the economic aspects of provision of services rather than the provision of services in the LRE continue to dominate decision making.

Yell (1995) described the impact of three court cases on the educators' approaches to providing services in the LRE. In *Daniel R.R. v. State Board of Education* (1989), the court noted that the school had not violated the LRE requirements of PL 94-142 in removing a boy with Down syndrome from general education classrooms to a special education classroom. Rather, the court noted that the school district had implemented a continuum of classroom environments and experimented with various placements. The court delineated the "Daniel test," which indicated that schools must ask themselves the following questions in determining the LRE for any given child with disabilities:

1. Can education in the general education classroom with the use of supplementary aids and services be achieved satisfactorily for the child?
2. If satisfactory education cannot be achieved in the general classroom and the school intends to remove the child from the general education classroom, has the school included the child in the general classroom to the maximum extent possible?

The Daniel test was applied in the case of *Oberti v. Board of Education* (1992), in which the child's parents opposed the school district's decision to place the child in a segregated special education classroom outside the district rather than in the general education classroom in the neighborhood school. The district court found that the school district had not provided appropriate aids and services to keep the student in the general education classroom and that the district had not considered less restrictive placements. The courts also ruled that the school district failed to provide adequate accommodations in *Greer v. Rome City School District* (1990), in which three crucial mistakes were found in the contested IEP:

1. By failing to consider a range of supplementary aids, school officials had not taken steps to accommodate the child in the general education classroom.
2. School officials had made no attempt to modify the kindergarten curriculum for the child.
3. School officials had developed the child's IEP before the IEP meeting and had made no realistic attempts to inform the child's parents of the range of options available.

Biklen (1992) reported that Section 15 of the Canadian Charter of Rights and Freedoms provides that "every individual is equal before and under the law" and has provided the basis for legal challenges to segregated special schools. Other provisions of the charter allow individual provinces to argue that certain provincial laws must operate outside the reach of the charter's general protection policy. The practices of Canadian school boards vary significantly, with some supporting inclusion and others supporting education in separate facilities. Great variability in education of children with disabilities exists even within individual Canadian provinces. In Ontario, for example, several publicly funded Catholic school districts include learners with severe disabilities in general education classes, but their counterpart public school boards in the same regions segregate learners with disabilities from learners in general education classrooms (Biklen, 1992).

Due Process

To receive federal funds under IDEA, education agencies must give assurances to the U.S. Department of Education, OSERS, Office of Special Education Programs, that it has adopted appropriate due process procedures. The LEA must give prior notices to parents, guardians, or surrogate parents whenever it proposes to initiate or to change, or refuses to initiate or to change, a child's identification, evaluation, or placement and the provision of a FAPE. The notice must be written in language understandable to the public and provided in the native language of the parent or in another mode of communication that the parent uses unless it is not feasible to do so (Turnbull, 1993).

The procedural safeguards provide that parents may request a hearing that is conducted by a hearing officer independent of the local school authorities at a time and place that are convenient for the parents. Parents have the right to present evidence and cross-examine witnesses, to **appeal**, to obtain a record of the hearing, and to receive a statement of the hearing officer's decisions and reasons for the decisions (Turnbull, 1993).

Section 7 of the Canadian Charter of Rights and Freedoms guarantees principles of fundamental justice and is considered the closest equivalent of the United States' due process clause. Although specific references to special education are not made, the Canadian Charter has been used to support due process.

Parent Participation

According to PL 94-142 and its amendments, parents must give consent for any evaluation, assessment, or placement of their child. In addition, parents must be notified of any changes in their child's placement and must be included in decision making regarding IEPs. PL 94-142 supports the right of parents to challenge and appeal any decision and initiate due process procedures. Parents' participation, however, is more than simply notification and consent; it includes **confidentiality** and parents' rights to information and advisory panels.

Confidentiality of Information and Parents' Rights to Information

There are several issues related to parents' rights to information about their children's school records. These rights, grounded in the Family Educational Rights and Privacy Act (FERPA) of 1974 (PL 93-380), are summarized in Table 4. Parents have the right to gain access to confidential information about their children without unnecessary delay and may request explanations and interpretations of the information contained in their children's school records. Students who are 18 years of age or older have access to their own school records; parents retain their right to inspect their children's school records if their children are claimed as dependents for income tax purposes. Other than parents, the only people who may have access to children's school records are school officials who have a legitimate educational interest in the records, officials of an-

Table 4.   Parents' rights under the Individuals with Disabilities Education Act (IDEA) of 1990 (PL 101-476)

---

1.   Parents must be notified that personally identifiable information is on file.
2.   Parents must be provided with a summary of the school's procedures for storing, releasing, or destroying information.
3.   Parents and their representatives have the right to personally inspect identifiable information in their child's records within 45 days of their request and may request an explanation, interpretation, or copies of information.
4.   Parents may request that records be amended and may formally or informally challenge the accuracy of the contents.
5.   Schools must obtain parents' consent before releasing identifiable information to anyone other than school officials.
6.   Schools must notify parents when personally identifiable information is no longer needed.
7.   When the student reaches 18 years of age, parents' rights are transferred to the student.

Source: Turnbull (1993).

other school system if the parent has notified the requesting school district, federal or state program auditors, representatives of accrediting organizations, organizations conducting studies, or any other individual or entity by court order. The school district must maintain a record of 1) each disclosure of information regarding a student's school records that contain any personal identification of the student and 2) requests for such disclosure (Hartshorne & Boomer, 1993).

Canada maintains few common-law and statutory protections regarding confidentiality of school records, with protections being mostly in the form of school board policies (MacKay, 1986). Teachers may disclose **directory information** about a student unless that information may be harmful (e.g., attendance at a segregated school for learners with disabilities, which would automatically identify the student as a person with disabilities). The school district must notify parents regarding what that particular district considers directory information. A teacher's personal notes disclosed to no one but a substitute teacher are not considered educational records. If the teacher shares the written information with anyone, however, that information is no longer personal but is an educational record (Hartshorne & Boomer, 1993).

Advisory Panels

IDEA requires state education agencies to create advisory panels of members appointed by the governor or by other officials. This panel is to be composed of individuals involved or concerned with the education of children with disabilities, including at least one representative of individuals with disabilities, teachers of children with disabilities, parents, state and local education officials, and administrators of programs for learners with disabilities. The panel is to advise the state education agency of the needs of learners with disabilities, comment on the state's plan to serve children with disabilities, and assist in developing and reporting data and evaluations required.

Other Legal Protections Under Section 504 of the Rehabilitation Act of 1973

Students do not need to be enrolled in special education to receive related services under Section 504 of the Rehabilitation Act of 1973 (PL 93-112). The legislation pertaining to related services for people with disabilities under Section 504 states that "education may consist of either regular or special education and must include any related aids or services necessary to provide a free, appropriate, public education designed to meet the individual students' needs" (cited in NICHCY, 1991b).

Americans with Disabilities Act of 1990

With the enactment of the Americans with Disabilities Act (ADA) of 1990 (PL 101-336), the goal of the right to full participation of individuals with disabilities in American society was recognized. Among the provisions of the ADA are a modification of the definition of *individuals with disabilities* and requirements in the areas of transportation, telecommunications, employment, and public accommodations for people with disabilities, as well as those with acquired immunodeficiency syndrome (AIDS) and human immunodeficiency virus (HIV). Learners who are not determined to be eligible for special education services under IDEA may be provided with accommodations through the ADA.

Your Turn . . .

In the United States, the six basic principles underlying special education that Turnbull (1993) outlined apply only to learners with disabilities. Learners who are not identified as having disabilities have no federal right to a FAPE. Select one of the principles. Reflect on your own education. How would your education have been different had that principle been applied to you in your educational experience?

LEARNING OBJECTIVE 3: To be able to discuss school practices related to the rights of learners with disabilities and their parents

School practices other than the ones described in the preceding sections have emerged that are related to the rights of learners with disabilities and their parents. Two practices that have been addressed in the courts are graduation and disclosure of information about students.

Graduation

With regard to graduation, the courts have limited their reviews of cases pertaining to learners with identified disabilities and students in special education programs to procedural concerns. Kortering, Julnes, and Edgar (1990) generated several guidelines for school districts related to their detailed review of court actions. First, the local school district has the discretion to restrict the award of standard diplomas. Kortering, Julnes, and Edgar contended that procedures that may result in awarding nonstandard diplomas to learners with identified disabilities and students in special education programs are intended to ensure that the standard diploma retains its value in the community and to improve the quality of education through maintaining higher standards. These procedures, however, should be based on standards that are fair and have been articulated to the student and his or her parents. All students with identified disabilities or in special education programs must be given the opportunity to satisfy the standards of a standard diploma when standards exist or through the provision of reasonable accommodations. The goals and objectives stated on the learner's IEP have been used to provide a proper means for evaluating whether the learner will graduate.

Disclosure of Information About Students

Although there are protections for parents and students regarding the disclosure of information, there are two circumstances in which teachers must disclose information. One case is that of suspected incidents of child abuse and neglect. Reporting suspected abuse or neglect is mandatory in most states and provinces, with criminal penalties being imposed in some cases for teachers' failure to report abuse or neglect. The second instance in which teachers are required to disclose information is in cases in which information communicated by the student may bear upon the student's commission of a felony. Privacy is ensured under FERPA.

 LEARNING OBJECTIVE 4: To be able to discuss the effects of the legal aspects of inclusion on the general education teacher

The legal aspects of inclusion have had a significant impact on the role of the general education teacher. The principle that all people are to be provided with a FAPE forces the teacher to become more reflective; to carefully select instruction goals, objectives, activities, and evaluation practices; and to ensure that the education provided to students is indeed appropriate. Fair evaluation has led teachers to explore creative and innovative ways of measuring learners' progress, including portfolios and curriculum-based assessment.

The use of IEPs has spread in some districts to all learners, recognizing that all children have individual strengths and needs. Meeting individualized education goals and objectives in inclusive classrooms has made supports and related services available to teachers at unprecedented levels. The principle of providing a FAPE in the LRE has given impetus to the whole inclusion movement. In addition, it has changed the ways in which children come to school and participate in curricular and co-curricular activities. Finally, the partnership of educators and related-services professionals with parents and the recognition of parents as sharing in decision making with professionals have had a positive impact on general education. Chapter 3 further studies the impact of the principles of inclusion of learners with disabilities in the general classroom on the school, the classroom, and the teacher.

SUMMARY

This chapter addresses the following major concepts:

1. The emergence of federal support for inclusive education for learners with disabilities has been an evolutionary process.

2. There are six basic principles in special education legislation and case law. These principles are committed to
   a. A FAPE
   b. Unbiased evaluation
   c. An appropriate IEP
   d. Education in the LRE
   e. Procedural due process
   f. Parents' participation and shared decision making

3. In the United States, Section 504 of the Rehabilitation Act of 1973 and the ADA provide protections for people with disabilities. The Canadian Charter of Rights and Freedoms provides support of procedural due process, nondiscriminatory treatment, and allegiance to the principles of fundamental justice.

TEST YOUR KNOWLEDGE

Completion of the "Self-Evaluation," "Make the Language Your Own," and "Application Activities" sections will aid readers in understanding and retaining the information presented in this chapter. Answer keys for the "Self-Evaluation" and "Make the Language Your Own" sections are located in the Appendix at the end of the book.

Self-Evaluation

Select the most appropriate responses to complete the following statements:

1. U.S. federal laws prior to 1900 regarding people with disabilities
   a. Provided for the needs of children
   b. Protected children with disabilities from abuse
   c. Provided services for people with disabilities that were related to their military service

2. Initial federal support for education
   a. Began with providing incentive funding for serving learners with disabilities
   b. Addressed concerns regarding elementary and secondary education
   c. Mandated the zero reject principle

3. With regard to the mandate for FAPE, controversy has surrounded the issue of
   a. Defining an *appropriate education*
   b. Funding of free education
   c. Public education versus private education of people with disabilities

4. A learner with a disability
   a. May receive accommodations only if the learner is determined to be eligible for the accommodations through a fair evaluation
   b. May receive accommodations only under the provisions of Section 504 of the Rehabilitation Act of 1973
   c. May receive accommodations and related services under the provisions of Section 504 of the Rehabilitation Act of 1973 and the ADA

5. Related services
   a. Must be provided if needed for the learner to profit from special education
   b. Are provided on an as-available basis
   c. Are not provided in inclusive education environments

6. The principle of the LRE
   a. Mandates inclusion for all learners
   b. May in itself be restrictive in that it legitimizes restrictive placements
   c. Emphasizes the provision of services in an economically efficient manner

7. In the design and provision of special education services, parents are
   a. Equal participants in decision making
   b. Consultants
   c. Informed of the decisions after the fact

8. Federal privacy law requires that
   a. No identifying information be released to anyone but the learner's parents
   b. Directory information, as defined by the district, may be released
   c. Information regarding abuse and neglect must be reported anonymously

9. Learners with identified disabilities
   a. Are ineligible for diplomas
   b. Receive diplomas because requirements are waived with their identification as learners with disabilities
   c. Must be given the opportunity to satisfy the requirements of the standard diploma through provision of reasonable accommodations

10. Teachers must disclose information when
    a. There is suspected child abuse or neglect
    b. Outside agencies are providing services to the child
    c. The teacher's personal notes about the child are shared with someone in addition to a substitute teacher

Make the Language Your Own
Match the following terms with their definitions:

1. _____ "Zero reject" philosophy or policy
2. _____ Appeal
3. _____ Mandated
4. _____ Directory Information

a. Required by law
b. The process during which an appeals court reviews the records and judgment of a lower court to determine whether an error was made that might lead to the re-

5. _____ IEP

6. _____ Transition services

7. _____ Class action

8. _____ IFSP

9. _____ Confidentiality

10. _____ Due process

11. _____ LRE

    versal of or a change of the lower court's decision

c. Information that may include learners' names, addresses, and telephone numbers

d. A civil suit brought on behalf of the plaintiffs as well as all other people similarly situated

e. A written commitment for the delivery of services to meet the student's educational needs

f. The protection of information from unauthorized disclosure

g. A right to have any law applied both reasonably and with sufficient safeguards

h. A plan of services and outcomes for the family of a child with a disability who is younger than 3 years of age

i. Learners with disabilities are to be educated with their peers to the maximum extent appropriate

j. Services to facilitate the individual's movement between programs

k. No child, regardless of severity of disability, is excluded from school on the basis of disability

Application Activities

1. Interview a teacher who works in an inclusive classroom environment. What are the related services provided to his or her students? Where are these services provided? What is the teacher's participation in providing these related services?

2. Obtain the information that a school district provides for parents regarding special education identification and services. How is the eligibility determination process described? How is the role of the parents described?

3. Interview parents who have participated in an IEP meeting. What was their perception of their role? What influence did they have in the decisions made?

REFERENCES

Americans with Disabilities Act (ADA) of 1990, PL 101-336, 42 U.S.C. §§ 12101 *et seq.*

Biklen, D. (1992). *Schooling without labels.* Philadelphia: Temple University Press.

Brown v. Board of Education, 347 U.S. 483 (1954).

Canadian Charter of Rights and Freedoms, Constitution Act C.11 (1985).

Carl D. Perkins Vocational Education Act, PL 98-524, 98 Stat. 2435, 20 U.S.C. §§ 2301 *et seq.* (1984).

Children's Justice Act of 1986, PL 99-401, 100 Stat. 903.

Daniel R.R. v. State Board of Education, 874 F.2d 1036 (5th Cir. 1989).

Developmental Disabilities Assistance and Bill of Rights Act Amendments of 1987, PL 100-146, 42 U.S.C. §§ 6000 et seq.

Edminster, P., & Elkstrand, R.E. (1987). Preschool programming: Legal and educational issues. *Exceptional Children, 54,* 130–136.

Education for All Handicapped Children Act of 1975, PL 94-142, 20 U.S.C. §§ 1400 et seq.

Education of the Handicapped Act Amendments of 1983, PL 98-199, 97 Stat. 1357.

Education of the Handicapped Act Amendments of 1986, PL 99-457, 20 U.S.C. §§ 1400 et seq.

Education of the Handicapped Act of 1970, PL 91-230, 20 U.S.C. §§ 1400 et seq.

Education of the Handicapped Amendments of 1974, PL 93-380, 88 Stat. 576.

Elementary and Secondary Education Act of 1965, PL 89-10, 20 U.S.C. §§ 6301 et seq.

Elementary and Secondary Education Act of 1966, PL 89-750, 20 U.S.C. §§ 6301 et seq.

Elementary and Secondary Education Amendments of 1967, PL 90-247, 20 U.S.C. §§ 877b et seq.

Family Educational Rights and Privacy Act (FERPA) of 1974, PL 93-380, 20 U.S.C. §§ 1221 et seq.

Greer v. Rome City School District, 762 F. Supp. 936 (N.D. Ga. 1990).

Handicapped Children's Protection Act of 1986, PL 99-372, 100 Stat. 796.

Harkin, T. (1993). Passage of the ADA. *Mouth, 1,* 3.

Hartshorne, T.S., & Boomer, L.W. (1993). Privacy of school records: What every special education teacher should know. *Teaching Exceptional Children, 25*(4), 32–35.

Individuals with Disabilities Education Act (IDEA) Amendments of 1991, PL 102-119, 20 U.S.C. §§ 1400 et seq.

Individuals with Disabilities Education Act (IDEA) Amendments of 1997, PL 105-17, 20 U.S.C. §§ 1400 et seq.

Individuals with Disabilities Education Act (IDEA) of 1990, PL 101-476, 20 U.S.C. §§ 1400 et seq.

Kauffman, J.M. (1993). *Characteristics of emotional and behavioral disorders of children and youth* (5th ed.). New York: Macmillan/Merrill.

Kortering, L., Julnes, R., & Edgar, E. (1990). An instructive review of the laws pertaining to the graduation of special education students. *Remedial and Special Education, 11*(4), 7–13.

MacKay, A.W. (1986, March). The Charter of Rights and special education: Blessing or curse? In Canadian Department of Education (Ed.), *Proceedings of the Canadian Symposium on Special Education Issues* (pp. 20–43). Ottawa, Ontario: Author.

Mills v. Board of Education, 348 F. Supp. 866 (D.D.C. 1972).

National Information Center for Children and Youth with Disabilities (NICHCY). (1991a). Related services for school-aged children with disabilities. *NICHCY News Digest, 1*(2), 1–23.

National Information Center for Children and Youth with Disabilities (NICHCY). (1991b). The education of children and youth with special needs: What do the laws say? *NICHCY News Digest, 1*(1), 1–15.

National Information Center for Children and Youth with Disabilities (NICHCY). (1992). *Questions often asked about special education services.* Washington, DC: Author.

National Information Center for Children and Youth with Disabilities (NICHCY). (1997). *PL 105-17 Part C: Impact on infants and toddlers with disabilities.* Washington, DC: Author.

Oberti v. Board of Education, 789 F. Supp. 1322 (D.N.J. 1992).

Osborne, A. (1988). The Supreme Court's interpretation of the Education for All Handicapped Children Act. *Remedial and Special Education, 9*(3), 21–25.

Pennsylvania Association for Retarded Children (PARC) v. Pennsylvania, 343 F. Supp. 279 (E.D. Pa. 1972).

Rehabilitation Act of 1973, PL 93-112, 29 U.S.C. §§ 701 et seq.

Rowley v. Hendrick Hudson School District, 458 U.S. 176 (1982).

School Districts—Federal Aid, PL 89-313, 79 Stat. 1158 (1965).

Shea, T.M., & Bauer, A.M. (1994). *Learners with disabilities: A social systems perspective of special education.* Madison, WI: Brown & Benchmark.

Taylor, S. (1988). Caught in the continuum: A critical analysis of the principle of the least restrictive environment. *Journal of The Association for Persons with Severe Handicaps, 13,* 41–53.

Technology-Related Assistance for Individuals with Disabilities Act of 1988, PL 100-407, 29 U.S.C. §§ 2201 *et seq.*

Turnbull, H.R., III. (1993). *Free appropriate public education: The law and children with disabilities* (4th ed.). Denver: Love Publishing Co.

Yell, M.L. (1995). The least restrictive environment mandate and the courts: Judicial activism or judicial restraint? *Exceptional Children, 61*(6), 578–581.

Qualities of Inclusive Schools and Classrooms

On Aaron's birthday, our family went to a nearby restaurant for dinner. The moment we entered the lobby, a young woman joyfully greeted Aaron. "Oh Aaron, it's so good to see you. I can't wait to tell Amanda I saw you—how are you doing?" At first, he wouldn't give her eye contact, then, as she kept twisting her body to force him to look at her, he finally gave her the biggest grin. She was so rewarded by his smile and the twinkle in his eyes, she gave him a big hug. When I asked the young woman how she knew Aaron, she introduced herself as Laura. She explained she had graduated from Lakota High School last year, and she often looked through her memory album, in which there were many pictures of Aaron. They had done all their workouts together in weight training class and

"Aaron was just looking so muscular and strong—was he having a good year?" We chatted for several minutes, and the only verbal word that Aaron said was "bye" when Laura went back to work at her station. Later she brought a group over to sing "Happy Birthday to You" as Aaron spelled out he wanted "iced tea" on his facilitated communication board. We told her Aaron was in general academic classes for the first time, and her eyes teared up. "How exciting! Aaron, you have made my day!" she exclaimed emotionally.

Mary Ulrich, Aaron's mother,
describing how inclusion has changed their lives;
Aaron, identified as having autism, attended an inclusive classroom

 This chapter discusses the qualities of inclusive schools and classrooms. To begin this discussion, an inclusive school must first be defined. An *inclusive school* is one in which all students—typical students, students at risk, students with disabilities, and students from diverse cultural backgrounds—are included in general education classes and are provided with 1) appropriate education experiences that are challenging yet geared to their capabilities and needs and 2) any support or assistance that they or their teachers require (Stainback & Stainback, 1991).

What are inclusive schools? They are environments in which there are in force various assumptions regarding the learning community, teachers, structures, parent participation, ethics, and the nature of the problem when coping with learners who vary from their peers. This chapter explores each of these issues and discusses professional practice within an inclusive learning community.

LEARNING OBJECTIVES

After completing this chapter, readers will be able to

1. Describe basic assumptions regarding inclusive learning communities
2. Describe basic assumptions regarding teachers in inclusive learning communities
3. Describe some of the structures that are common in inclusive learning communities
4. Recognize the role of parents in inclusive learning communities
5. Describe ethical practices with regard to all learners
6. Discuss the differences between the problem-solving and behavior problem perspectives on learners

KEY WORDS AND PHRASES

behavior problem model—a perception that behavior problems exist within the child and are addressed by changing the child rather than the environment or behavior of those around the child

criterion of the least dangerous assumption—criterion that, in the absence of conclusive data, education decisions ought to be based on assumptions that, if incorrect, are likely to have the least deleterious effect on the individual's ability to function independently as an adult

inclusive school—a school in which all students are included in classes and are provided with 1) appropriate education experiences that are challenging yet are geared to students' capabilities and needs and 2) any support or assistance that they or their teachers require

natural proportions—circumstance in which the students assigned to a classroom reflect the composition of the community at large

principle of dignity and worth of the individual—principle stating that people with disabilities should be treated as human beings

principle of fairness—principle stating that problem solving regarding learners with disabilities should begin with a consideration of the needs of learners with disabilities

principle of normalization—principle stating that people with disabilities should be provided with education and life experiences that are as close as possible to those of their peers

problem-solving model—a perception that the source of the problem is a situation and that the appropriate intervention involves changing the situation to support the learner

LEARNING OBJECTIVE 1: To be able to describe the basic assumptions regarding inclusive learning communities

Inclusive learning communities assume significantly different learning outcomes than those generally accepted by the existing education community. The purpose of schooling in inclusive learning communities is to enable all students to participate actively in their communities so that others care enough about what happens to them to look for a way to include them as part of those communities (Ferguson, Meyer, Jeanchild, Juniper, & Zingo, 1992). This explicit value base suggests that all members of the school and the community are connected and belong and that learners not only collaborate with each other in the learning process but also are empowered to make substantive decisions about classroom processes (Salisbury, Palombaro, & Hollowood, 1993). As Schwartz suggested, the goals of inclusion "include more than behaviors that can be measured on standardized assessment; inclusion is about belonging and participating in a community of one's peers. It is about being supported to succeed in an accepting, yet challenging environment" (1996, p. 204).

The value base assumed by **inclusive schools** suggests some specific goals (Stainback & Stainback, 1990a). These goals include

1. Meeting the unique educational, curricular, and instructional needs of all students within general education classes
2. Helping all students to feel welcome and secure through the development of friendships and peer supports
3. Challenging every student to go as fast and as far as possible toward fulfilling his or her unique potential
4. Developing and maintaining a positive classroom atmosphere conducive to learning for all students
5. Arranging physical and organizational variables to accommodate the unique needs of each student
6. Providing every student with any support services that he or she might need, such as physical, occupational, or speech-language therapy; instruction in braille, American Sign Language, or English as a second language; orientation and mobility training; and assistive technology supports such as augmentative or alternative communication devices

Caring is inherent in inclusion. Buber (1965) used the term *inclusion* to refer to the relational process by which one who cares assumes a dual perspective and can see things from both his or her own point of view and the point of view of the cared-for person. The most frequent etiology mentioned in the life histories of children who are at risk for developmental delays and children with behavior problems is the lack of adequate caring (Morse, 1994). Yet, among highly effective and gifted teachers, Morse found empathy and caring to be their most common characteristic.

The inclusive learning community is a caring school. Sapon-Shevin (1990a) suggested some basic assumptions of schools as caring places. The school assumes a philosophy of caring and honors and celebrates diversity. Cooperation is emphasized over competition, with each individual—administrator, support personnel, teacher, student, and parent or caregiver—empowered as a full participant in the community. Sapon-Shevin suggested that all labels be removed from students, teachers, and facilities.

Noddings (1984) also discussed a caring school. She suggested that when teachers care, ideally they should be able to present reasons for their actions or inactions that would persuade a reasonable, disinterested observer that appropriate action had been taken on behalf of the cared-for person. She contended that students, as the people cared for, have the greatest effect on the student–teacher relationship. If the student perceives the teacher's caring and responds, he or she is giving the teacher what is most needed by the teacher to continue to care.

A primary goal and challenge of an inclusive school is fostering peer support and friendships. With the great diversity among learners, however, how can peer support and friendships be developed and maintained? Stainback and Stainback (1990a) suggested that schools should increase the proximity of learners to one another by helping students become involved in co-curricular activities; by arranging for peer tutoring, buddy systems, and cooperative learning; by seating isolated students next to sensitive, outgoing, and accepting students; and through contrived activities such as pairing students and having them participate together in a free-time activity. Support and friendship development should be encouraged through making students more aware of each other's needs, cuing students to work together, and reinforcing students when they are exhibiting positive friendship and support behavior. Peer support and friendship skills, such as taking the perspective of others and sharing and providing support should be taught. An understanding and respect for learners' diversity should be fostered. Finally, teachers themselves should serve as positive supports for each other and for students and should provide models of friendships.

 LEARNING OBJECTIVE 2: To be able to describe the basic assumptions regarding teachers in inclusive learning communities

The assumptions regarding inclusive learning communities discussed in the previous section force one to make assumptions about the responsibilities of teachers. In inclusive learning communities, teachers are responsible for

- Educating all of the students assigned to them
- Making and monitoring instruction decisions
- Providing instruction according to the typical curriculum while adapting the particulars when children's progress is discrepant from that which is anticipated
- Managing instruction for diverse populations
- Seeking, using, and coordinating support for students who require more intense services than those provided to their peers (Jenkins, Pious, & Jewell, 1990)

Teachers have not always been prepared in their training for the responsibilities generated by inclusive learning. Giangreco, Dennis, Cloninger, Edelman, and Schattman (1993) described teachers' transformational experiences as they became inclusive teachers. These were gradual transformations and involved teachers who were willing to interact with students who varied from their peers, learn the skills needed to teach all students, and change their attitudes toward learners who vary from their peers. These teachers took several approaches, including treating students with disabilities like any other member of the class and including them in the same activities though their learning objectives may be different; engaging students in cooperative learning and group problem solving; and using active and participatory strategies, such as manipulatives, games, projects, labs, or field studies.

Inclusive learning communities change the role of the teacher in many ways. Lipsky and Gartner (1991) suggested that teachers become broad enablers of student's learning, working collegially with other professionals across disciplines, without the artificial distinction between special and general educators. Teachers engage in a variety of interactions with students, and each child is known as an individual. In addition, teachers have a broader involvement with other adults, including out-of-school learning resource professionals and parents. Teachers who view their efforts to include individuals with disabilities as personal and professional challenges have been reported to have more favorable attitudes toward inclusion, whereas the amount of external school support teachers receive has been found to have little bearing on how they perceived inclusion (Schechtman, Reiter, & Schanin, 1993).

In a study of inclusive preschool environments, a wide range of roles emerged for teachers (Fleming, Wolery, Weinzierl, Venn, & Schroeder, 1991). In both Head Start and other preschool programs, teachers were primarily instructors (e.g., teaching content, directing group activities) and monitors (e.g., checking on students' progress, suggesting alternatives, encouraging persistence). Teachers also assumed the role of co-player, participating in the child's activity, or of observer, purposefully watching the children. Teachers were materials managers, behavior managers, and caregivers as well as entertainers who strove to keep children's attention. Fleming and colleagues suggested that, rather than adapting activities to learners' needs, teachers in inclusive preschool environments should adapt their roles in response to learners' needs.

LEARNING OBJECTIVE 3: To be able to describe some of the structures common in inclusive learning communities

Successful inclusion necessitates more than providing one or two supports. Often an array of structures including buddies, friendships, peer tutors, professional peer collaborators, team teachers, teacher and student assistance teams, consultation, and time for planning and working together are required (Stainback & Stainback, 1990b). For example, McEvoy, Shores, Wehby, Johnson, and Fox (1990) suggested direct work on the attitudes of peers, organizing classroom environments to enhance interaction, and specific prompts for interactions and teacher praise that is contingent on interaction. Villa and Thousand (1990) contended that consensus for inclusion must be developed through in-service and professional development activities, development of a mission statement, and incentives for successful inclusion efforts.

Inclusive learning communities encourage teaming to the extent that, in one study, staff and administrators made reference to the team as *family* (Salisbury et al., 1993). Ysseldyke, Thurlow, Wotruba, and Nania (1990) found that in inclusive classrooms, there was usually a teacher or assistant who functioned in the same manner as instructional support in environments without learners with disabilities. Grouping was heterogeneous, which was also common in these environments. The most frequent methods of instruction were direct instruction followed by cooperative groups, discovery learning, independent work, and multimethod instruction. Two of the most common adaptations teachers reported were holding the student accountable for his or her performance and quality of work and altering instruction so that the student experienced success.

Meeting the needs of diverse learners is a challenge; no single type of support can provide the range of assistance needed by teachers and students. To provide these supports, Stainback and Stainback (1990a) suggested support networks. These support networks assume that everyone is capable and has strengths, gifts, and talents. Everyone is involved in helping and supporting one another, both formally and informally. An underlying assumption in using support networks is that natural, supportive relationships such as those among peers, friends, and colleagues are as important as professional support. In view of the uniqueness of each individual, supports cannot be based on a predefined list of options.

Staffing in Inclusive Communities

Forming inclusive communities forces changes in school structures (Stainback & Stainback, 1990a). Student–teacher ratios must be lowered, perhaps through methods such as team teaching. A wide range of resources and expertise must be available for teachers, as must time for teachers to meet and problem solve. Stainback and Stainback suggested including on the teaching team a support facilitator who collaborates with teachers and students to determine, through joint problem solving, the supports that they would like to have and their needs in the classrooms. The support facilitator must have a working knowledge of the resources available in the school and must be able to assess and match the needs of students and teachers to applicable support options and resources.

Natural Proportions

One concept that affects the structure of inclusive learning communities is that of **natural proportions** (Stainback & Stainback, 1991). This concept suggests that students should not be clustered by ability, disability, gender, culture, or any other characteristic. Rather, the students assigned to a classroom should reflect the characteristics of the community at large.

Early Childhood Education

New structures are also apparent in inclusive early childhood education environments. Bruder (1993) suggested that there are several structures needed for effective service delivery within early childhood programs. For example, a consistent and ongoing system for family involvement must be developed. Services for families should be based on the premise that the family is the enduring and central force in the life of the child. A system for team planning and program implementation in which members share roles and cross their professional service boundaries systematically is also necessary. Effective service delivery requires a system of collaboration and communication with other agencies that provide services. Well-constructed individualized education programs (IEPs) or individualized family service plans (IFSPs) with functional goals that are embedded in daily activities and routines are needed. In addition, the delivery of education and related services capitalizes on the child's interests, preferences, and initiations rather than on the service provider's choice. Effective programs also have a consistent, ongoing system for training and staff development and a comprehensive system for evaluating program effectiveness.

Cooperative Classrooms

In inclusive learning communities, classrooms are not competitive places in which students attempt to prove themselves but are cooperative environments in which students support and nurture each other's learning (Sapon-Shevin, 1990b). Students and teachers work together in these classrooms to accomplish goals, accommodate each other's differences, and find ways to encourage and nourish a high level of achievement and positive interaction. Competitive symbols, such as posting grades or star sheets and displaying the best papers, would be eliminated. The inclusive classroom community is built on sharing and having everybody participate in common activities. Students are encouraged to use one another as resources. Desks are clustered, and, before asking the teacher, students must consult with other students or look in the classroom Yellow Pages listing individual students and their talents and skills. Students are encouraged to take note of each other's accomplishments. Students' working together, whether through tutoring or through other cooperative modes, provides unique opportunities for improving the education of all students (Gartner & Lipsky, 1990).

LEARNING OBJECTIVE 4: To be able to recognize the role of parents in inclusive learning communities

In inclusive learning communities, parents are meaningful members of the education team, meeting with professionals on a regular basis, sharing responsibility, and developing a meaningful relationship with these professionals (Schattman & Benay, 1992). The Minnesota Governor's Planning Council on Developmental Disabilities (1992) described shifting patterns in parents' participation in inclusive communities. They stated that these shifting patterns are caused by

- The system setting the agenda for individuals and families to individuals and families setting and pursuing their own agendas
- Information provided to families so that they will know what the experts think is best and act appropriately to a focus on assisting families in developing skills and information so that they can pursue what they think is best
- A focus on changing families to a focus on families changing the system
- A focus on families as informed followers to a focus on families as leaders
- A focus on self-improvement to a focus on self-determination, self-creation, advocacy, and systemic improvement

   The Minnesota council encourages families to develop a Personal Futures Plan (Mount & Zwernik, 1988). In the planning process, the individual with disabilities and the individual's friends and family define what life would be like for the individual's family in the future. A team of family and friends who are close to the individual join efforts to address the individual's future. The focus is on the strengths, gifts, and capacities that the individual and the individual's family and friends have to contribute to the individual's future. In addition, the focus is on the individual's dreams for the future with regard to relationships, community, choice, and competence.

LEARNING OBJECTIVE 5: To be able to describe ethical practices with regard to all learners

In working with people with disabilities, ethical practice—or "doing the right thing"—involves choosing and acting on the course of action that will bring the greatest benefit to those individuals who are affected by the decision (Gardner,

1992). In addition, there is the challenge to do the right thing for the right reason. To act on behalf of others, knowing the possible risks and consequences, Gardner suggested, exemplifies courage and perpetuates a ripple of hope.

Your Turn . . .

Gardner (1992), in suggesting that professionals must "do the right thing" regardless of risk, offered the following strategy for evaluating decisions:

1. Describe the decision needed.
2. Describe your course of action.
3. Check all of the reasons that apply:

____ The rules say so.	____ It is compatible with my values.
____ It is cost effective.	____ It is administratively sound.
____ It is politically correct.	____ It is expected and predictable.
____ It will get me noticed.	____ It is the traditional response.
____ It will get me published.	____ I believe it is right.
____ My conscience says it is correct.	____ It is fashionable.
	____ It is what others tell me to do.
____ It will benefit others.	____ Other:
____ Others will agree with it.	

Consider a recent decision you made that had an impact on the lives of others. Reflect on this evaluation. How did you feel? What reasons seemed most appropriate? Which reasons seemed least important?

An assumption regarding individuals with disabilities that has a significant impact on ethical interventions has emerged. O'Brien and O'Brien (1993) commented that people with disabilities should be considered choice makers who are capable of contributing to and forming rewarding relationships. In view of this assumption, an individual's abilities and needs can best be understood in the context of trusting relationships in which others join in responding to opportunities, problems, and risks. To improve the quality of interventions with individuals with disabilities, teachers and related-services professionals must invest in relationships and learning.

In describing obligations to people with disabilities in supported living environments, O'Brien (1993) provided guidelines that are pertinent to the education of all learners. O'Brien suggested that, in order to help the individual with disabilities, the helper must earn the individual's trust and recognition as an ally by

- Treating the individual with respect
- Learning about the individual's interests and preferences
- Learning with the individual about the type, amount, and style of assistance needed for success
- Working with the individual and the individual's family and friends to establish the life that the individual desires and the assistance needed in order to achieve that life
- Being flexible and creative with all of the resources available to respond to the individual's needs
- Minimizing intrusion
- Sticking with the individual in difficult times
- Learning from mistakes
- Following through on commitments

These considerations support what Donellan (1984) described as the **criterion of the least dangerous assumption.** This criterion suggests that, in the absence of conclusive data, educational decisions ought to be based on assumptions that, if incorrect, would have the least dangerous effect on the likelihood that learners would be able to function independently as adults. In making decisions, educators must ask themselves, "Which of my actions will have the least dangerous effect on the likelihood that the goal will be attained?"

In 1969, Allen proposed three principles for members of the helping professions to apply in actions toward consumers, both children and adults:

1. Normalization
2. Fairness
3. Respect for the dignity and worth of the individual

The principles are recommended here as a foundation for intervention decisions.

Normalization

The **principle of normalization** states that individuals with disabilities should attain a daily existence as close to that of other individuals as possible (Allen, 1969; Nirje, 1967). When applying this principle, the professional must use the child's real environment as well as the ideal environment as points of reference. The principle demands that professionals understand the similarities and differences among various groups and subgroups in the community. The professional must base decisions on knowledge of the individual child's growth and development, needs, interests, strengths, and disabilities. Many children who are diagnosed with mental retardation, emotional disturbance, and other disabilities are classified as such simply because of their cultural diversity. African Americans; Hispanic Americans; Native Americans; Asian Americans; people of low socioeconomic status; and children who are physically different, slow learners, poor readers, or socially inept receive such diagnoses at higher rates than children from the dominant American culture (Grossman, 1992).

Fairness

The **principle of fairness** states,

> Fundamental fairness—due process of law—requires that in decision-making affecting one's life, liberty, or vital interests, the elements of due process will be observed, including the right to notice, to a fair hearing, to representations by counsel, to present evidence, and to appeal an adverse decision. (Allen, 1969, p. 2)

At times, interventions are arbitrarily applied on the whim of a professional without concrete evidence that the child is, in fact, exhibiting the presenting problem. Unfairness is evidenced when a professional refuses to apply an intervention that is obviously needed if the child is to function in school. If the principle of fairness is to be implemented, all professionals must make decisions from the point of view of the child's welfare and ask the question, What does this child need?

Respect for the Dignity and Worth of the Individual

The **principle of respect for the dignity and worth of the individual** is "one's right to be treated as a human being, and not as an animal or statistic" (Allen, 1969, p. 2). This principle requires that, in their actions toward children, professionals must demonstrate respect for children as human beings. The following are examples of interventions that demonstrate a lack of respect for the dignity and worth of the individual: physical punishment (e.g., spanking, slapping, paddling), psychological punishment (e.g., sarcasm, embarrassment, name calling), deprivation (e.g., deprivation from typical opportunities for success), segregation (e.g., arbitrary special class placement), isolation (e.g., inconsistent long-term use of time-outs and restraints), medication (e.g., capricious use of symptom control medication for the benefit of the parents or the teacher), and inhumane punishments (e.g., restraints, electric shocks). All of these interventions have been applied and remain in use in American society. They are applied by those professionals who justify the use of any means to attain their desired ends. To effectively teach all learners, it is absolutely necessary that all professionals and parents develop and apply an ethical system that incorporates the principles of normalization, fairness, and respect for the dignity and worth of the individual.

LEARNING OBJECTIVE 6: To be able to discuss the differences between the problem-solving and behavior problem perspectives on learners

As professionals, teachers share ownership of problems when management and instruction are less than successful (Bauer & Sapona, 1991). In the traditional **behavior problem** or **student problem model**, however, assessment of problems usually occurs outside the classroom context and focuses on the learner. The focus in inclusive environments is on addressing problem situations rather than on behavior problems. This emphasis forces the analysis of actual environments, roles, skills, and interests of both learner and teacher (Barnett & Carey, 1992). The problem-solving emphasis stresses existing teacher competencies rather than demanding new skills and thus may enhance the self-efficacy of teachers (Barnett, Ehrhardt, Stollar, & Bauer, 1994).

In both the **problem-solving model** and the student problem model, the reason for teacher and parent concerns originates in a difference between the learner's performance and others' expectations for the learner's performance (Iowa Department of Education, 1990). The assessment and nature of intervention differ significantly between the two models, however. The traditional student problem model focuses on the presence of student characteristics that account for the student's performance problems. These characteristics of the student should therefore be identified and removed so that the student will no longer have the problem. The student's problems can be identified by studying the student's characteristics and abilities in a quantitative way and making comparisons with a group of students who are developing typically. Interventions are then provided to eliminate the student's problem characteristics. If the problem is not resolved, then the inability to change these characteristics is assumed to be a function of the system doing the best it can by matching students with programs and providing services within that framework.

The problem-solving model provides a significant contrast to the behavior problem model. The problem, rather than being seen as related to student characteristics, is seen as being based on what people expect the student to do to be successful in the classroom environment and what people expect the student's performance to be. By intervening in the situation and using teaching strategies to increase the match between performance and expectations, success is achieved. The behavior problem and problem-solving models are contrasted in Table 1.

SUMMARY

This chapter addresses the following major concepts:

1. Inclusive learning environments are based on assumptions regarding the purpose of schooling and values regarding meeting the needs of all students and developing and maintaining a caring environment.
2. Inclusive learning environments assume that teachers are responsible for the education of all of the students assigned to them and that supports will be provided to them to fulfill this responsibility.
3. An array of support structures is often necessary for successful inclusion.
4. The use of teams and networks provide support to teachers, learners, and families.
5. Successful inclusion may require teachers to assume new roles, such as that of inclusion facilitator.
6. In inclusive learning communities, parents are essential members of the education team.
7. Ethical treatment of all learners assumes that professionals support normalization, are fair, and respect the dignity of each learner.

8. In inclusive learning communities, the emphasis is on problem situations rather than on behavior problems.

TEST YOUR KNOWLEDGE

Completion of the "Self-Evaluation," "Make the Language Your Own," and "Application Activities" sections will aid readers in understanding and retaining the information presented in this chapter. Answer keys for the "Self-Evaluation" and "Make the Language Your Own" sections are located in the Appendix at the end of the book.

Table 1. Comparing the student problem approach and the problem-solving approach

Issue	Student problem	Problem solving
Reason for concern	The student's performance differs from expectations.	The student's performance differs from expectations.
Problem definition	The problem is the presence of student characteristics that may contribute to or account for performance problems.	The problem is based on what people expect the student to do to be successful in that environment and on the student's performance.
Assumptions regarding assessment	Identify and remove the student's characteristics, and then the student will no longer have the problem.	Success is supported by using educational solutions to increase the match between performance and expectations.
Purpose of assessment	Explain the student's problems by studying the student's characteristics and abilities; data are similar across students in terms of, for example, IQ score, achievement, and birth history.	Clarifies factors affecting the student's performance; questions are identified that cannot be answered by using existing data; data collection is unique for each student
Role of team members	The roles and functions of professionals are highly predictable across cases.	The functions performed by specialists are unique to each case.
Analysis of assessment data	Quantitative analysis with comparisons with a norm-referenced group	Qualitative analysis of the student's performance within an environment in which the problem exists; any comparison is with peers in same environment
Intervention focus	Interventions for students with given characteristics are provided in programs for students with similar labels.	Interventions are designed to serve as corrective actions.
Goal setting and monitoring	Goals are set and measures of progress are often standardized.	Goals are set and monitored frequently by taking direct measures of behaviors of concern.
Student outcome focus	Change in student characteristics so services may be discontinued	Reduction of problem behavior
Client satisfaction	Assumed to be a function of the system doing the best it can by matching students with programs and providing services within that framework	Client satisfaction is based on demonstrated successful outcomes as observed in student's performance.

Source: Iowa Department of Education (1990).

Self-Evaluation

Select the most appropriate response to complete each of the following statements:

1. In inclusive learning communities,
   a. Supports are provided as the teacher perceives needs
   b. Learners are empowered to make substantive decisions about the classroom process
   c. Learners are provided supports as their parents identify their needs

2. In preschool environments, teachers may
   a. Only adapt the curriculum to meet the needs of learners
   b. Adapt their roles in response to learners' needs
   c. Only adapt the classroom's structure in response to learners' needs

3. Support networks
   a. Provide compensatory teacher activities to meet learners' needs
   b. Assume that everyone is involved in helping and supporting one another, both formally and informally
   c. Provide a mandated effort to support learners with disabilities

4. In inclusive learning communities,
   a. Student–teacher ratios are lowered
   b. Classroom size is increased to enhance the potential for diversity in the classroom
   c. Student–teacher ratios are increased as related services are provided

5. In cooperative classrooms,
   a. Grades, star sheets, and other recognition of quality work are emphasized
   b. Students work together to mutually encourage achievement
   c. Teachers assign peer tutors to include students in the learning process

6. Parents' roles
   a. Are similar in cooperative and competitive learning environments
   b. Are essential only for support and information sharing
   c. Have shifted significantly with the emergence of inclusive learning communities

7. The quality of interventions with learners increases as teachers and related-services professionals
   a. Gain more information regarding the deficits of disabilities
   b. Simply adhere to legal requirements
   c. Invest in relationships with learners

8. The principle of respect for the dignity and worth of the individual assumes that
   a. Professionals be allowed to use their judgment in selecting and implementing interventions
   b. Some interventions in and of themselves demonstrate a lack of respect and dignity
   c. Parents have the right to prohibit the use of some interventions

Make the Language Your Own

Match the following terms with their definitions:

1. _____ Normalization

2. _____ Inclusive school

3. _____ Problem-solving model

4. _____ Behavior problem

5. _____ Dignity and respect

6. _____ Fairness

7. _____ Natural proportions

8. _____ Least dangerous assumption

a. Decisions are based on assumptions that, if incorrect, would have the least deleterious effect on the individual.

b. All students are included in classes and are provided with appropriate, challenging educational experiences and the support or the assistance that they or their teachers require.

c. Students assigned to a classroom reflect the composition of the community at large.

d. People with disabilities are treated as human beings.

e. Problem solving begins with a consideration of the learner's needs.

f. Providing the individual with an existence that is as close to that of his or her peers as possible.

g. Problems exist within the child and are addressed by changing the child.

h. The source of the learner's problem is a situation, and intervention involves changing the situation to support the learner.

Application Activities

1. Observe a teacher in an inclusive classroom for at least 2 hours. Describe the roles that the teacher assumes. Does the teacher appear to adapt activities or roles to include or accommodate learners with disabilities?

2. Interview the parent of a learner in an inclusive learning community. What role does the parent assume? Does the parent perceive that his or her role has changed during the past several school years?

3. Interview the principal of an inclusive school. What structural changes have occurred as the school has moved toward inclusion?

REFERENCES

Allen, R.C. (1969). *Legal rights of the disabled and disadvantaged* (GPO 1969-0-360-797). Washington, DC: U.S. Department of Health, Education and Welfare, National Citizens Conference on Rehabilitation of the Disabled and Disadvantaged.

Barnett, D.W., & Carey, K.T. (1992). *Designing interventions for preschool learning and behavior problems*. San Francisco: Jossey-Bass.

Barnett, D.W., Ehrhardt, K.E., Stollar, S.A., & Bauer, A.M. (1994). PASSKey: A model for naturalistic assessment and intervention design. *Topics in Early Childhood Special Education, 14,* 350–374.

Bauer, A.M., & Sapona, R.H. (1991). *Managing classrooms to facilitate learning.* Upper Saddle River, NJ: Prentice-Hall.

Bruder, M.B. (1993). The provision of early intervention and early childhood special education within community early childhood programs: Characteristics of effective service delivery. *Topics in Early Childhood Special Education, 13*(1), 19–37.

Buber, M. (1965). *Between man and man* (R.G. Smith, trans.). New York: Macmillan.

Donellan, A.M. (1984). The criterion of the least dangerous assumption. *Behavioral Disorders, 9,* 141–149.

Ferguson, D.L., Meyer, G., Jeanchild, L., Juniper, L., & Zingo, J. (1992). Figuring out what to do with the grownups: How teachers make inclusion "work" for students with disabilities. *Journal of The Association for Persons with Severe Handicaps, 17,* 218–226.

Fleming, L.A., Wolery, M., Weinzierl, C., Venn, M.L., & Schroeder, C. (1991). Model for assessing and adapting teachers' roles in mainstreamed preschool settings. *Topics in Early Childhood Special Education, 11*(1), 85–98.

Gardner, J.B. (1992). Doing the right thing. *Cutting Edge, 8*(3), 1–2.

Gartner, A., & Lipsky, D.K. (1990). Students as instructional agents. In W. Stainback & S. Stainback (Eds.), *Support networks for inclusive schooling: Interdependent integrated education* (pp. 81–98). Baltimore: Paul H. Brookes Publishing Co.

Giangreco, M.F., Dennis, R., Cloninger, C.V., Edelman, S., & Schattman, R. (1993). I've counted Jon: Transformational experiences of teachers educating students with disabilities. *Exceptional Children, 59,* 359–372.

Grossman, H. (1992). Special education in a diverse society: Improving services for minority and working class students. *Preventing School Failure, 36,* 19–27.

Iowa Department of Education. (1990). *Trial sites draft: 2/12/90.* Des Moines: Iowa Department of Education.

Jenkins, J.R., Pious, C.G., & Jewell, M. (1990). Special education and the regular education initiative: Basic assumptions. *Exceptional Children, 56,* 479–491.

Lipsky, D.K., & Gartner, A. (1991). Achieving full inclusion: Placing the student at the center of educational reform. In W. Stainback & S. Stainback (Eds.), *Controversial issues confronting special education: Divergent perspectives* (pp. 3–12). Needham Heights, MA: Allyn & Bacon.

McEvoy, M.A., Shores, R.E., Wehby, J.H., Johnson, S.M., & Fox, J.J. (1990). Special education teacher's implementation procedures to promote social integration among children in integrated settings. *Education and Training in Mental Retardation, 25,* 267–276.

Minnesota Governor's Planning Council on Developmental Disabilities. (1992). *Shifting patterns.* St. Paul: Author.

Morse, W.C. (1994). The role of caring in teaching with behavior problems. *Contemporary Education, 65,* 3.

Mount, B., & Zwernik, K. (1988). *It's never too early, it's never too late: A booklet about Personal Futures Planning* (Pub. No. 421-88-109). St. Paul, MN: Governor's Planning Council on Developmental Disabilities.

Nirje, B. (1967). The normalization principle and its human management implications. In R. Kugel & W. Wolfensberger (Eds.), *Changing patterns of residential services for the mentally retarded* (pp. 42–65). Washington, DC: President's Committee on Mental Retardation.

Noddings, N. (1984). *Caring: A feminine approach to ethics and moral education.* Berkeley, CA: University of California Press.

O'Brien, J. (1993). *Supported living: What's the difference?* Syracuse, NY: Center on Human Policy.

O'Brien, J., & O'Brien, C.L. (1993). *Assistance with integrity: The search for accountability and the lives of people with developmental disabilities.* Lithonia, GA: Responsive Systems Associates.

Salisbury, C.L., Palombaro, M.M., & Hollowood, W.M. (1993). On the nature and change of an inclusive elementary school. *Journal of The Association for Persons with Severe Handicaps, 18,* 75–84.

Sapon-Shevin, M. (1990a). Initial steps for developing a caring school. In W. Stainback & S. Stainback (Eds.), *Support networks for inclusive schools: Interdependent integrated education* (pp. 241–248). Baltimore: Paul H. Brookes Publishing Co.

Sapon-Shevin, M. (1990b). Student support through cooperative learning. In W. Stainback & S. Stainback (Eds.), *Support networks for inclusive schooling: Interdependent integrated education* (pp. 65–79). Baltimore: Paul H. Brookes Publishing Co.

Schattman, R., & Benay, J. (1992). Inclusive practices reform special education. *Administrator, 49*(2), 8–12.

Schechtman, Z., Reiter, S., & Schanin, M. (1993). Intrinsic motivation of teachers and the challenge of mainstreaming: An empirical investigation. *Special Services in the Schools, 7*(1) 107–121.

Schwartz, I.S. (1996). Expanding the zone: Thoughts about social validity and training. *Journal of Early Intervention, 20*(3), 204–205.

Stainback, S., & Stainback, W. (1990a). Facilitating support networks. In W. Stainback & S. Stainback (Eds.), *Support networks for inclusive schooling: Interdependent integrated education* (pp. 25–36). Baltimore: Paul H. Brookes Publishing Co.

Stainback, S., & Stainback, W. (1990b). Inclusive schooling. In W. Stainback & S. Stainback, (Eds.), *Support networks for inclusive schooling: Interdependent integrated education* (pp. 3–23). Baltimore: Paul H. Brookes Publishing Co.

Stainback, S., & Stainback, W. (1991). Schools as inclusive communities. In W. Stainback & S. Stainback (Eds.), *Controversial issues confronting special education: Divergent perspectives* (pp. 29–43). Needham Heights, MA: Allyn & Bacon.

Villa, R.A., & Thousand, J.S. (1990). Administrative supports to promote inclusive schooling. In W. Stainback & S. Stainback (Eds.), *Support networks for inclusive schooling: Interdependent integrated education* (pp. 201–218). Baltimore: Paul H. Brookes Publishing Co.

Ysseldyke, J.E., Thurlow, M.L., Wotruba, J.W., & Nania, P. (1990). Instructional arrangements: Perceptions from general education. *Teaching Exceptional Children, 22*(4), 4–8.

Inclusive Services

The teacher's special work calls upon him to take more serious note of diversities than resemblances. The philosopher in his study, the psychologist or logician, may lay down the general laws of the growth of mind or the conditions of valid inferences, but the teacher has to keep his wits alert to modify his treatment from time to time so that it may suit Tom, Dick, and Harry at different times, in different places, and with different subject matter.

P.A. Barnett (1902, p. 2)

In 1902, in his book *Common Sense in Education and Teaching: An Introduction to Practice,* Barnett wrote, "The endeavor to lay down rigid rules of procedure is a serious error in education. . . . For the teacher the important fact is diversity" (p. 1). Later in the same book, he wrote,

> We have come next to recognize not only that children generally must be treated as persons in process of development rather than as persons developed, but also that children differ among themselves, mentally and physically, and in antecedents and habitual development. (p. 3)

Recognizing the diversity among students in a classroom, then, is not new. Meeting their needs through adaptation has been perceived as common sense for nearly a century. This chapter explores the emerging characteristics of individualized programming. In addition, the chapter discusses when the need for individualization, supports, and accommodation is pervasive enough to warrant a learner's referral for special education services. The evaluation, classification, and placement process regarding special education services is also discussed.

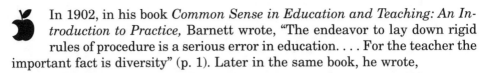

LEARNING OBJECTIVES

After completing this chapter, readers will be able to

1. Describe the nature of individualized programming in inclusive classrooms
2. Participate in the evaluation, classification, and placement processes
3. Describe the recursive cycle of assessment, design, implementation, and reassessment

KEY WORDS AND PHRASES

assessment—the process of collecting data to specify and verify problems and make decisions regarding learners and programs

classification—the determination of eligibility for special services

differentiated instruction—an instruction system in which the teacher employs varied approaches to content, process, and product in anticipation of learners' varying degrees of readiness and divergent interests and learning needs

individualized education program (IEP)—the plan for a student's special education program

individualized family service plan (IFSP)—an annual plan of services and outcomes for the family of a child with disabilities who is younger than 3 years of age

interventions—specific supports designed to meet the specific needs of children

micronorms—the standards for a single situation or environment, such as a classroom

multifactored evaluation—a process engaging a team of individuals from various disciplines in studying a student and his or her developmental contexts to determine the nature, cause, and circumstances of a problem, if, in fact, there is a problem

referral—a request for assistance from a parent or from a professional

screening—the collection of preliminary information to determine whether more comprehensive study is needed

LEARNING OBJECTIVE 1: To be able to describe the nature of individualized programming in inclusive classrooms

The individualization required in inclusive services at the turn of the 21st century is not the individualized instruction of the 1970s. During the 1970s, individualized instruction meant providing each of the 30-plus students in a classroom with a different set of assignments that were matched precisely to each student's entry level and working on each student's individual skills. Teachers found such planning exhausting, and students did not develop a sense of community. The individualized programming required by inclusive service programs at the turn of the 21st century is more appropriately called **differentiated instruction** than *individualized instruction*.

Tomlinson (1995) offered an excellent description of the flow of instruction in classrooms in which there is differentiated instruction: a repeated rhythm of whole-class preparation, review, and sharing followed by individual or small-group exploration, sense making, extension, and production representing a recursive pattern of teaching and learning. More specifically, Tomlinson described a repeated rhythm or flow of instruction in which

- The teacher and the whole class begin to work on a topic or concept.
- The students use varied materials, depending on their readiness and strengths, to explore the topic or concept further.
- The teacher and the whole class come together to share what they have learned and to pose further questions.
- The students work on tasks that the teacher suggests, which are designed to help them make sense of key ideas at varied levels of complexity and at varied rates.
- The teacher and the whole class again come together to review key ideas and extend their study by sharing.
- In small, student-selected groups, students work together to solve teacher-generated problems related to their study.
- The teacher instructs students in the skills that the students will need later to make a presentation about the teacher-generated problems.
- Students self-select interest areas through which they will apply and extend their learning.
- The teacher and the class share individual study plans and establish the ways in which their projects will be evaluated.

According to Tomlinson, "The teacher plans and carries out varied approaches to content, process, and product in anticipation of responding to student differences in readiness, interest, and learning needs" (1995, p. 10). How does this recursive pattern fit into individualizing instruction in inclusive classrooms? The following case studies clarify how the needs of individuals with disabilities may be met in the general education classroom and how the

individualized education program (IEP), the written plan for each student with a disability, supports the student.

David

Mrs. Tom's first graders are beginning to work on combining three sets in addition, addressing problems such as 2 + 4 + 1. Mrs. Tom meets with the entire group, showing examples by using objects, moving next to pictures, and then to the chalkboard with written examples. The students then begin their assignment. The teacher continues to work with a small group, including David, a student with disabilities whose IEP indicates a need to develop one-to-one correspondence in counting. As the other students work individually, in pairs, or in small groups, completing tasks related to three-number addition, Mrs. Tom brings a tub of "teddy bear counters" to the table where David and three students who do not have identified disabilities are meeting with Mrs. Tom. Mrs. Tom encourages each student to take a handful of teddy bears and place these on the table in front of them. With the students, Mrs. Tom works through the first problem. Rather than combine sets with David, the teacher encourages David to count each bear while touching it. As the other three students use the manipulatives, count out the total number, and write the numerals on their sheets, Mrs. Tom provides David with the number of bears that represents the sum of the problem, which she again encourages David to count, touching each teddy bear as it is counted. Tomorrow David will work with a partner, again counting each manipulative and touching it, working on his one-to-one counting while his partner works on combining sets.

Michael

Mr. Story, a fifth-grade teacher, and his class are beginning a unit on biographies. Michael, a student in the class with identified disabilities, has an IEP goal of increasing his reading comprehension. Each student has a packet regarding biographies that he or she must complete. The assignment in the packets varies from student to student. To complete the project, the information gathered by each individual student is combined with the information gathered by other members of a small group. Michael's packet, which varies from that of his peers, includes a biography that is shorter and at a reading level that is lower than that of his peers. Rather than being assigned a written report, Michael's packet requires him to complete a story board on the individual's life, thus accommodating his difficulties in written language while providing practice in comprehension and sequencing.

Mrs. Tom and Mr. Story found goals for David and Michael that then became the basis for their instruction on David's and Michael's IEPs. David's objective of increasing his counting with a one-to-one relationship became a basis of his mathematics instruction. It was reinforced throughout various activities conducted individually, with a partner, in a small group, or in the large group. Michael was given a successful way to complete his portion of the project on biographies while addressing a skill (reading comprehension) in which he needed practice. The IEP, then, provides the basis for planning instruction.

The IEP-planning process requires that the individuals responsible for the student's education engage in two activities: 1) a meeting during which parents and school personnel jointly determine the student's education program, and 2) writing the IEP document itself, which becomes a written record of the meeting.

The National Information Center for Children and Youth with Handicaps (NICHCY) (1990) described several purposes and functions of the IEP:

- The IEP is a communication vehicle, enabling parents and school personnel to jointly determine, as equal partners, students' needs, the services that will be provided to meet those needs, and the anticipated outcomes.
- The IEP provides an opportunity for resolving differences between learners' parents and the school.
- An IEP puts in writing a commitment of resources necessary to enable learners to receive needed special education and related services.
- An IEP is a management tool that ensures that students are provided the special education and related services that learners need.
- The IEP is a monitoring document used by authorized personnel from various government levels to determine whether learners are actually receiving the free, appropriate public education (FAPE) on which the parents and the school have agreed.
- An IEP serves as an evaluation device to determine the extent of learners' progress toward projected outcomes.

The IEP is the document by which students receive special education services. David's IEP is presented in Figure 1. The next section describes how students become eligible to receive special education services and how the IEP is developed.

Your Turn . . .

Consider the case of David. In his first-grade classroom, groups of students are completing projects around their social studies unit on families. What meaningful contributions could David make to the unit? How could these contributions be related to his IEP?

Riverside School District

Student's name: David Jones   **Birth date:** 6/21/92

School: Riley Primary School   **Date of conference:** 9/15/99

Date of initial placement in program: 7/15/95

Summary of present levels of performance
Strengths: Enthusiastic, attempts all tasks, gross motor skills are similar to those of peers, initiates play on playground, prints first name, prints numerals 1–20, rote counts to 100, remains at task for 20 minutes, begins to identify some words
Weaknesses: Legibility of printing, fine motor skills, responding with appropriate volume in classrooms (usually either does not respond or shrugs), one-to-one correspondence in counting, sight-word vocabulary, speech is difficult to understand when the context is not apparent

Annual goals	Amount of time in general education	Additional considerations	Committee members present
1. David will increase his verbal language in the classroom 2. David will increase his concepts of quantity and numeration 3. David will increase his sight-word vocabulary to 50 words 4. David will increase the legibility of his printing	100%	1. Will not participate in state proficiency testing 2. Will not receive extended school year services	Sue Tracker, Chair Sarah Jones, Parent Sy Jones, Parent Terry Tyson, Teacher

Committee recommendations for specific procedures/techniques:	Objective evaluation criteria for annual goal statements:
Recommended for occupational therapy evaluation David's daily parent–teacher journal	Permanent products will be maintained in portfolio Anecdotal records

Short-term objectives	Specific educational and/or support services	Person responsible	Amount of time	Beginning date	Review date
• David will initiate at least one comment to a peer.	Communication specialist	Teacher	100%	9/15/99	9/14/00
• David will initiate at least one comment per work session in small-group time.	Consult with teachers			12/1/99	9/14/00

Figure 1. David's individualized education program.   *(continued)*

Figure 1. *(continued)*

• With cues from teacher, David will initiate a comment at least twice daily in whole class.				3/15/00	9/14/00
• David will count out 10 objects independently.					
• David will count out 20 objects independently.	Teacher	Teacher	100%	9/15/99	1/31/00
• David will participate in peer tutoring using sight-word cards.				2/1/00	9/14/00
• David will participate in reading group with peers.	Teacher, special education consultant	Teacher	100%	9/15/99	9/14/00
• David will write his first and last name legibly.					
• David will copy from paper on desk with 80% accuracy.	Teacher	Teacher	100%	9/15/99	9/14/00

LEARNING OBJECTIVE 2: To be able to participate in the evaluation, classification, and placement processes

The previously introduced case studies of David and Michael are next elaborated to clarify the ways in which a learner may become eligible for special education services.

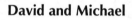

David and Michael

When David was born, he was identified as having Down syndrome. Immediately after this diagnosis, David began receiving early intervention services. His family was provided with a service coordinator who, working with them, developed an **individualized family service plan (IFSP).** An IFSP is an annual plan of services and outcomes for the family of a child with a disability who is younger than 3 years of age. When David approached his third birthday, his family and the service coordinator visited several preschool programs and developed a transition plan to facilitate his movement into an inclusive preschool. After a **multifactored evaluation,** David continued at the preschool until he was 5 years old. At that time, during reevaluation, representatives from the school district that David would attend the following year came to David's IEP meeting to discuss David's needs and the transition from preschool to kindergarten. As a consequence, David's IEP included support services in kindergarten and related services (communication therapy and occupational therapy). When David was assigned to Mrs. Tom's first-grade classroom, he had an IEP with goals and objectives developed by the kindergarten teacher, the special education teacher who supported David's inclusion in kindergarten, the communication specialist, and the occupational therapist.

Michael, unlike David, was not referred for special education services by his parents. He attended general education classes without special education services during the first and second grades. Both teachers were concerned about Michael's reading problems, yet they felt that they could meet his needs adequately. During the third grade, however, Michael began to fall further and further behind his peers. His teacher met with the parents and, with their permission, initiated a series of instruction strategies to improve Michael's performance in reading. The teacher documented these efforts. Unfortunately, little progress was made, and Michael became frustrated and began to act out in the classroom. The teacher, after consulting with Michael's parents, referred Michael for a multifactored evaluation. His parents, after giving written consent for the evaluation, were provided with notification of who would evaluate their son and which types of tests and other **assessment** techniques would be used in the evaluation. The parents were asked to complete a social and family history form. After the evaluation was completed, Michael's parents met with the evaluation team members, who summarized and interpreted evaluation results and identified Michael as having a mild disability. Following this eligibility meeting, an IEP meeting was held at a mutually agreed on time and place. The parents and team members jointly developed Michael's IEP, including a description of Michael's strengths, needs, annual goals, and short-term objectives, and appropriate special education and related services. It was determined that Michael required accommodation related to his reading activities in the classroom. A special education teacher began weekly consultation and problem-solving meetings with his teacher. During reading class, the special education teacher, serving as co-teacher, instructed Michael and two other students in the class who, according to their IEPs, had similar needs.

The cases of David and Michael provide examples of some of the variations that may occur during the eligibility and evaluation phases of special education. David was identified at a young age, his parents referred him for services, and he began to receive services in an early intervention program. Annual reviews resulted in the continuation of these services through his placement in the third grade. Unlike David, Michael was identified as having a disability while attending school and was referred for evaluation by his teacher. His first IEP was not written until he was in the third grade. It documented the need for accommodations and the provision of services in Michael's general education classroom. In both cases, the students came to the attention of individuals around them as varying from their peers. Help was sought, David and Michael were evaluated, and it was determined that David and Michael needed special education services. In formal terms, these processes are known as **referral** and **screening**, multifactored evaluation, and **classification** and placement through the IEP meeting.

Referral and Screening

Salvia and Ysseldyke (1991) described referral as a request for assistance from a parent or professional. Upon referral, the representative from the school district reviews the available information, studies attempts that have been made to address the referral issue, and determines whether to refer the child or youth for multifactored evaluation. Screening, the other way in which students come to the attention of the school district by referrals, is the collection of preliminary information to determine whether more comprehensive study is needed. Screening involves collecting adequate data to make a knowledgeable decision about the need for further evaluation (Salvia & Ysseldyke, 1991).

In inclusive classrooms, accommodation and supports are the rule rather than the exception. How does one determine, then, that the accommodation and supports being provided are so extensive that a referral for special education services is appropriate? Barnett and Bell (1997) suggested looking at the **micronorms** of the classroom. *Micronorms* are the standards for a single situation or environment—in the cases of David and Michael, a classroom. To develop micronorms, Barnett and Bell suggested observing three peers who are functioning adequately in the classroom. Their behavior then forms a basis for comparison with the student of concern. For example, the three peers may need reminders to return to their work twice a day. If the student of concern requires a reminder only twice a day, then he or she may not vary to the extent that referral is necessary. If, however, the student needs 8–10 such reminders and often needs to be led back to his or her seat, the variation from the micronorm may be extensive enough to warrant referral.

Multifactored Evaluation

If it is agreed that an evaluation is appropriate, the parents' written consent to evaluate is requested. Parents are notified of who will complete the evaluation and the procedures, including tests and other techniques, to be used to evaluate the student. Next, information from both the parents and the student's teachers is gathered.

The evaluation must look at the whole child and include information about the student's total environment. It may include observations by the professionals who have worked with the student as well as the student's medical history, when relevant to the student's performance at school, and information and observations from the family about the student's experiences, abilities, needs, and behavior outside school. The evaluation must use multiple means of measurement, must be in the student's native language, and must be culturally appropriate (NICHCY, 1992).

Culturally appropriate evaluation should include consideration of the student's cultural background and its possible relationship to the reason for referral. In addition, previous evaluation records should be reviewed for indications of cultural bias. McIntyre (1995) recommended gathering assessment information on individuals from the student's cultural background and conducting a functional analysis of the behavior to understand the motivations behind the student's actions. Instruments should be used that minimize cultural bias. In addition, McIntyre suggested that the expected standards of behavior for the student should take into account the student's cultural characteristics and that, whenever possible, at least one person with the same cultural background as the student's be on teams involved in referral and placement decisions.

The Individuals with Disabilities Education Act (IDEA) Amendments of 1997 (PL 105-17) incorporated additional safeguards for parents (Turnbull, Rainbolt, & Buchele-Ash, 1997). Parents as well as qualified professionals must be active members of the evaluation team. In addition, parents must receive a copy of the evaluation report and documentation of their child's eligibility for special education. The parent may also submit and require the evaluation team to consider evaluations and information that they themselves contribute to the evaluation process.

When the evaluation is complete, the team meets to review the information. At that point, the student's profile is compared with the definition of various disabilities provided in the state or provincial guidelines for eligibility for special education services. If the student's profile meets the criteria, the team will determine a time and place for the IEP meeting. If the student's profile does not meet the criteria and thus the student is not eligible for services, the team may determine appropriate modifications or **interventions** that may be conducted in the classroom without special education services. In addition, the team may consider whether the student is eligible for services under Section 504 of the Rehabilitation Act of 1973 (PL 93-112). Finally, the team notifies parents of their right to an independent evaluation if they disagree with the evaluation results.

Classification and Placement Through the Individualized Education Program Meeting

At the IEP meeting, the parents and other members of the educational team write

- A description of the student's level of educational performance (Under the 1997 amendments to IDEA, this statement of the level of educational performance must include how the student's disability affects his or her involvement and performance in the general education curriculum or, for a preschool-age child, age-appropriate activities.) (Turnbull et al., 1997)
- Annual goals that are directly related to the student's level of performance and that the student can reasonably be expected to accomplish within a 12-month period in the special education program
- Short-term instruction objectives that are measurable, intermediate steps between the student's present levels of educational performance and the annual goals established for the student; these short-term objectives are a logical breakdown of the major components of the student's annual goals and, under the 1997 IDEA amendments, must be related to the student's needs that result from his or disability to enable him or her to be involved and to progress in the general education curriculum (Turnbull et al., 1997).
- A description of the specific special education and related services to be provided to the student and the extent to which the student participates in general education programs
- Projected dates for initiation of services and anticipated duration of services
- The criteria by which it will be determined (at least annually) whether the short-term instruction objectives for the student are being achieved (NICHCY, 1990)

The team should discuss several additional issues during the IEP meeting. The student's participation in various proficiency tests, if required by the student's state or province, should be discussed, as should the issue of whether the student should receive extended school year services. If those services are needed, they should be included in the IEP. Discussed and planned during the IEP meeting are the student's transition from early childhood special education to school-age services; the transitions among school-age services; and the transition from school-age services to work, postsecondary education, and community living. Under the 1997 amendments to IDEA, when the child is 14 years old, an individualized transition plan (ITP) must be written. The ITP is based on the student's needs, preferences, and interests. Behavior support plans should be discussed if the student's behavior significantly interferes with his or her opportunity to learn, and physical education programs that address the student's individual needs should be discussed. Finally, the team should discuss needs specific to the student's disability, such as braille instruction for a student with visual impairments or the provision of an interpreter and American Sign Language (ASL) instruction for a student with hearing impairments (State of Ohio, 1997).

If the IEP planning process proceeds as intended by design, then its goals and objectives drive the identification of needed services and accommodations. When developing and writing goals and objectives, emphasis should be placed on those keystone behaviors that, if established, will facilitate further learning. For example, for a young child, diligence at a task for 15 minutes is a keystone behavior; once the student is able to work at a task for at least 15 minutes, his or her ability to complete a wide range of academic tasks is enhanced. Other keystone behaviors include communication (e.g., expressing needs, initiating conversation, taking turns).

One of the key ways to determine the content of the IEP is to look at the student's subsequent educational and life environment—the next step, so to speak—and likely long-term educational and life environments. The goals and objectives on the IEP should be related to one or both of these environments. Once a skill is determined to be necessary, the team should consider whether the student will ultimately complete the skill-building activity independently or whether accommodations are necessary. For example, a student may be unable to learn the formula necessary to complete long-division problems independently but may be able to understand the concepts of division and when to use division to solve problems and how to complete problems by using a calculator. Is it necessary, then, for the student to learn the formula?

Section 504 of PL 93-112 does not require a student to be enrolled in special education in order to receive related services. Rather, Section 504 indicates that in elementary and secondary education, an individual is determined to have a disability if he or she is 1) of an age at which people without disabilities are provided services, 2) of an age at which it is mandatory under state law to provide services to people with disabilities, or 3) a person to whom a state is required to provide a FAPE.

 LEARNING OBJECTIVE 3: To be able to describe the recursive cycle of assessment, design, implementation, and reassessment

This book proposes a problem-solving model for the provision of services to students with disabilities. Problem solving is a systematic process that includes the assessment of children and their environments, the identification of children's needs, the development and implementation of supports to meet those needs, and the monitoring and evaluation of outcomes (Salvia & Ysseldyke, 1991). A problem-solving model assumes that assessment, design, implementation, and reassessment occur in a recursive cycle throughout the student's educational career. This recursive cycle is depicted in Figure 2.

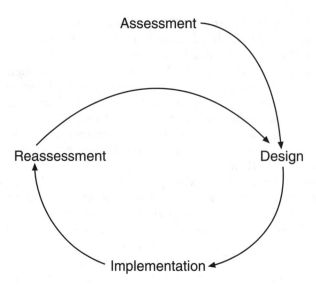

Figure 2.   The assessment, design, implementation, and reassessment process.

Assessment is the process of collecting data for the purpose of specify-ing and verifying problems and making decisions about students (Salvia & Ysseldyke, 1991). It is not testing, which Salvia and Ysseldyke described as "exposing a person to a particular set of questions in order to obtain a score" (1991, p. 3).

The purpose of assessment is to design interventions. Interventions are specific supports implemented to meet the specific needs of a student. Inter-ventions can include activities to increase children's competence and skills. They can also include environmental or instructional modifications designed to facilitate the acquisition of such skills (Canter et al., 1994).

Assessment may serve several purposes. Referral, screening, and classifi-cation, all of which are purposes of assessment, are discussed elsewhere in this chapter. In the classroom, the teacher is likely to use assessment for two other purposes: 1) instruction planning, which includes the development of specific goals, objectives, and intervention strategies; and 2) monitoring progress, which evaluates the extent to which students are or are not meeting specific in-tervention goals and objectives. In any case, assessment remains the way in which teachers make informed decisions about intervention plans and their outcomes for students (Salvia & Ysseldyke, 1991).

Assessment is incorporated into collaborative problem solving through

1. Problem identification and definition
2. Problem analysis, in which comprehensive information is collected sys-tematically to generate and explore hypotheses about the child's charac-teristics, environmental factors, and interactions between the child and the environment
3. Plan design
4. Progress monitoring and outcome evaluation; assessment continues over time as supports, services, and interventions are evaluated for effective-ness

Canter and colleagues (1994) suggested that there are several essential characteristics of assessment within a problem-solving model. Students' natural environments should be included as the environment of the assessment process; in fact, studying the students' natural environments may be key to effective intervention design. In addition, multiple procedures and methods of assessment must be applied. If the goal is to make well-informed decisions about needed supports, services, and interventions by integrating multiple methods, then the team must have access to the broad range of information necessary to define problems, design strategies, implement plans, and monitor outcomes. In any assessment, the individual's culture, race, ethnicity, native language, and gender should be considered and respected.

SUMMARY

This chapter addresses the following major concepts:

1. Individualized instruction in inclusive classrooms is most likely to take the form of differentiated instruction, with a repeated pattern of whole-class, small-group, and individual work.
2. IEPs are composed of two parts:
   a. A meeting during which parents and school personnel jointly determine the student's education program
   b. The writing of the IEP document itself
3. The IEP is the document that presents and describes the special education and related services to be provided to a student with disabilities.
4. Students may be referred for an evaluation by parents or professionals, or they may be identified through screening.
5. An evaluation must describe the whole child and include information about the child's total environment.
6. Students who are not classified as needing special education services may receive services through Section 504 or other non–special education service interventions in the general education classroom.
7. In developing the IEP, individualized goals and objectives drive identification and provision of services and accommodations for the student.
8. Problem solving is a systematic process that includes the assessment of the child and his or her environment, identification of his or her needs, planning and implementation of supports and accommodations designed to meet the child's identified needs, and the monitoring and evaluation of outcomes of intervention.
9. Assessment, design, implementation, and reassessment represent a recursive cycle in classrooms.

TEST YOUR KNOWLEDGE

Completion of the "Self-Evaluation," "Make the Language Your Own," and "Application Activity" sections will aid readers in understanding and retaining the information presented in this chapter. Answer keys for the "Self-Evaluation" and "Make the Language Your Own" sections are located in the Appendix at the end of the book.

Self-Evaluation

Select the most appropriate response to complete each of the following statements:

1. Differentiated instruction involves
    a. Decreasing homework assignments to students' abilities
    b. A recursive pattern of teaching and learning
    c. Individually assigning independent work

2. In inclusive classrooms, accommodations are
    a. Designed only for learners identified as having disabilities
    b. The rule rather than the exception
    c. Implemented without documentation

3. Micronorms are
    a. Developed to apply standardized test results to learners with disabilities
    b. The standards for a single situation or environment
    c. Set by the school

4. Before evaluations can be conducted,
    a. Parents must provide their written consent
    b. Interventions must have failed
    c. Students must be identified as having disabilities

5. The evaluation
    a. Studies the specific environment in which the child is challenged
    b. Studies the whole student and the student's total environment
    c. Involves parents, teachers, and related-services personnel

6. If a student's profile does not meet the criteria for eligibility for special education services,
    a. The student must remain in the same education program
    b. The student can be reevaluated by using different tools
    c. Modifications or interventions may be developed that do not involve special education services

7. Participation in proficiency tests should
    a. Not be addressed in the IEP
    b. Not be an issue for learners with disabilities
    c. Be monitored, and appropriate accommodations should be provided

8. A key way to determine the content of the IEP is to
    a. Determine which subjects are the most challenging
    b. Interview parents regarding their concerns
    c. Look at the student's subsequent educational and life environments

9. A student may receive related services
    a. Only if enrolled in special education
    b. Through an IEP or through Section 504
    c. At a parent's or a teacher's request

10. The purpose of assessment is to
    a. Identify the student's weaknesses for remediation
    b. Design interventions
    c. Identify strengths for compensation programs

Make the Language Your Own

Match the following terms with their definitions:

1. _____ Assessment

2. _____ Differential instruction

3. _____ Classification

4. _____ Individualized education program (IEP)

5. _____ Individualized family service plan (IFSP)

6. _____ Intervention

7. _____ Micronorms

8. _____ Multifactored evaluation

9. _____ Referral

10. _____ Screening

a. The process of engaging a team of individuals from various disciplines in studying a student and his or her developmental contexts to determine the nature, cause, and circumstances of a problem if there is, in fact, a problem

b. An instruction system in which the teacher employs varied approaches to content, process, and product in anticipation of varied student readiness, interests, and learning needs

c. A request for assistance made by a parent or a professional

d. The process of collecting data to specify and verify problems and make decisions regarding students and programs

e. Specific supports designed to meet the specific needs of children

f. The standards for a single situation or environment (i.e., a classroom)

g. The collection of preliminary information to determine whether more comprehensive study is needed

h. The plan for a student's special education program

i. The determination of eligibility for special education services

j. An annual plan of services and outcomes for a family of a child with a disability who is younger than 3 years of age

Application Activity

1. Observe an inclusive classroom for 20 minutes. List the subtle accommodations that the teacher employs to engage all students in the activities and lessons.

REFERENCES

Barnett, D.W., & Bell, S.H. (1997). *Peer micronorms in the assessment of young children.* Unpublished manuscript, University of Cincinnati, OH.

Barnett, P.A. (1902). *Common sense in education and teaching: An introduction to practice* (4th ed.). New York: Longmans, Green & Co.

Canter, A.S., Crockett, D.P., Dawson, M.M., Graden, J., Harrison, P.L., Kovaleski, J.F., & Reschly, D.J. (1994). *Assessment and eligibility in special education: An examination of policy and practice with proposals for change.* Alexandria, VA: U.S. Department of Education, Office of Special Education Programs.

Individuals with Disabilities Education Act (IDEA) Amendments of 1997, PL 105-17, 20 U.S.C. §§ 1400 *et seq.*

McIntyre, I. (1995). Focus on cultural sensitivity. *Council for Children with Behavioral Disorders Newsletter, 9*(3), 7–8.

National Information Center for Children and Youth with Handicaps (NICHCY). (1990). *Individualized education programs.* Washington, DC: Author.

National Information Center for Children and Youth with Handicaps (NICHCY). (1992). *Questions often asked about special education services.* Washington, DC: Author.

Rehabilitation Act of 1973, PL 93-112, 29 U.S.C. §§ 701 *et seq.*

Salvia, J., & Ysseldyke, J.E. (1991). *Assessment in special and remedial education* (5th ed.). Boston: Houghton Mifflin.

State of Ohio. (1997). *Whose IDEA is this? A resource guide for parents.* Columbus, OH: Author.

Tomlinson, C.A. (1995). *How to differentiate instruction in mixed-ability classrooms.* Washington, DC: Association for Supervision and Curriculum Development.

Turnbull, H.R., Rainbolt, K., & Buchele-Ash, A. (1997). *What does IDEA '97 say about evaluations, eligibility, IEP's and placements?* Lawrence: University of Kansas, Beach Center.

Collaboration

Working as a Member
of an Instruction Team

When we first started our student assistance teams, I was doubtful. I had always had principals who wanted you to handle things by yourself; to keep things under control. Now, here was this principal, setting up this team, and telling us we should have other teachers come in and observe when we're having trouble. As far as I was concerned, the least likely time I'd invite someone in to observe was when I was having trouble. But slowly, the culture of the school changed. It became known that good teachers ask for help, mediocre teachers just go ahead and limp along. I'm a good teacher—I ask for help.

*A fifth-grade teacher
in an inclusive elementary school*

In inclusive educational environments, collaboration is essential to the effective service of learners who vary from their peers. The first section of this chapter is devoted to the discussion of the instruction team. The role and functions of the team members are reviewed. Teams may include the general education teacher, the special education teacher, parents, aides, and the principal. Related-services personnel such as the social worker, nurse, counselor, and school psychologist may be included on the **instruction** team as needed. The purpose of the instruction team is to provide effective services to the student. In the second section of the chapter, various models for cooperative teaching or co-teaching teams composed of general and special educators are presented and discussed. The uses and advantages of the teacher assistance team, its composition, and its functions are discussed in the fourth section of the chapter. Strategies that encourage successful collaboration are discussed.

LEARNING OBJECTIVES

After completing this chapter, readers will be able to

1. Describe the nature of instruction teams in inclusive learning environments
2. Identify potential instruction team members in inclusive learning environments
3. Describe a structure for the cooperative teaching of general and special educators
4. Describe the use of teacher assistance teams
5. Identify strategies to encourage successful collaboration

KEY WORDS AND PHRASES

collaborative consultation—a partnership involving sharing and commitment between team members to facilitate effective services

collaborative teaching (co-teaching)—a strategy in which the general education teacher and the special education teacher work together and jointly teach students in an inclusive environment

instruction team—an organizational and instructional arrangement of two or more members of the school and the greater community who distribute among themselves planning, instruction, and evaluation responsibilities for the same students on a regular basis for an extended period of time (Thousand & Villa, 1990)

itinerant service model—services delivered by education and related-services personnel who travel from school to school

natural proportion—condition in which the number of students with disabilities in a classroom reflects the number of individuals with disabilities generally found in the community

role release—sharing by a team member of expertise and helping other team members to provide service in that unique area of expertise

teacher assistance team—teacher-centered instruction alternative support systems (Hayek, 1987)

LEARNING OBJECTIVE 1: To be able to describe the nature of instruction teams in inclusive learning environments

An instruction team is "an organizational and instructional arrangement of two or more members of the school and greater community who distribute among themselves planning, instructional, and evaluation responsibilities for the same students on a regular basis for an extended period of time" (Thousand & Villa, 1990, p. 151). The instruction team increases the potential for differentiating instruction and thus for increasing students' success.

In instruction teams, responsibilities for planning, instructing, evaluating, and supporting a common group of students are distributed among the team members (Thousand & Villa, 1990). The roles of instruction team members demand a clear delineation of responsibility and accountability. Thousand and Villa suggested that the team functions with a "positive sink or swim together" (1990, p. 151) sense of interrelatedness. Members of instruction teams provide support to each other so that all students can actively participate in classroom learning activities. The team may provide teaching support (i.e., support in the planning and the delivery of instruction), prosthetic support (e.g., being positioned well, having a backup strategy for assisting each other), and interpretive support (i.e., providing explanations regarding individual styles and strengths) (Ferguson, Meyer, Jeanchild, Juniper, & Zingo, 1992). Teams wrap around the student, with individual team members providing each other with the support needed for success throughout the school day. Teachers working with the support of other team members generally demonstrate strong self-efficacy; they know that they can make a difference in the child's life.

LEARNING OBJECTIVE 2: To be able to identify potential instruction team members in inclusive learning environments

On an effective education team, members feel that they belong, have support, and have power. Vandercook and York (1990) suggested that on an effective team, the need for belonging is satisfied by the sense of caring among the members for each other and for their students. The need for power is satisfied by giving each member the opportunity to be heard and affirmed.

The Student

The student, whether actually present or whose presence is implied, is a constant reminder to team members that their ability and willingness to work together creatively and collaboratively has an impact on someone else's—the student's—quality of life (Vandercook & York, 1990). In addition, all of the students in the classroom provide evidence that each student's needs are valued and accepted.

The General Education Teacher

As a member of the instruction team, the general education teacher has a unique vantage point to view each student individually and the students as a group; the teacher views the individual student as a member of the classroom group. From this vantage point, general education teachers can contribute information about the classroom curriculum, instruction strategies, management strategies, and routines and rules. In addition, the teacher is an ongoing model of appropriate interaction and communication for the student of concern to imitate (Vandercook & York, 1990).

The relationships between general educators and special educators are crucial to effective collaboration for learners who vary from their peers in inclusive learning environments (Stanovich, 1996). As the individual with the major responsibility for instruction, the general educator is an essential partner in the education process of students with disabilities, from the development of the individualized education program (IEP) through the annual review of the IEP. Stanovich maintained that teaming should occur throughout the processes of assessment, selection of goals and objectives, delivery of instruction and management strategies, and evaluation and monitoring of goals and objectives.

According to Reeve and Hallahan (1994), the general education teacher is knowledgeable with regard to curriculum and curricular sequencing and skilled in large-group management. The general education teacher is responsible for

- Educating the students assigned to the classroom
- Making and monitoring instructional decisions for all the students, providing instruction that follows a developmental curriculum, and adapting that curriculum to students' progress
- Managing instruction for diverse populations
- Seeking, using, and coordinating assistance for students (Jenkins, Pious, & Jewell, 1990)

The Special Education Teacher

As a member of the instruction team, the special education teacher contributes to the development of the IEPs of students with disabilities, accommodations, and **collaborative teaching** or **co-teaching** arrangements. Models for co-teaching are discussed later in the chapter. The special educator is skilled in task analysis, curriculum modification, and planning and implementing behavior management strategies (Reeve & Hallahan, 1994).

Parents

Parents of children with disabilities have legal rights and responsibilities as partners with professionals in their children's education. Parents need frequent and meaningful goal-directed interactions with teachers if they are to be viewed as true partners in their child's education (Stanovich, 1996). Parents also can collaborate among themselves, formally and informally, for the benefit of themselves, their children, and other parents.

Aides

The collaboration of aides is essential to effective general education classroom programming for learners who vary from their peers. Stanovich (1996) suggested that working as team members is sometimes challenging for aides because of the difference in status between the teacher and the instructional assistant (i.e., the professional and the aide). Aides should be invited to team meetings, and the team should make an effort to develop mutual respect among all team members and make a commitment to shared goals.

Principals

Principals play an essential role in collaboration by supporting the team activities of faculty and staff. Principals can advocate for programs, visibly participate on the team, and support team efforts (Gerber, 1991). Stanovich suggested that team members keep the principal involved by

- Keeping the principal informed of team activities
- Including the principal in group meetings, when appropriate
- Making the principal aware of scheduling, caseloads, equipment, supply, and other logistics needed to support the team model
- Encouraging the principal to participate or at least to visit and see the team in action

Hines and Johnston (1997) suggested that principals adhere to several major requirements in support of inclusion in their schools. First, they should provide support for general education teachers. This support can include special instruction materials or technologies that facilitate the differentiation of instruction in the general education classroom. Staff development opportunities that emphasize inclusive practices should be made available. Second, Hines and Johnston suggested that teachers' efforts to facilitate and implement inclusion be supported by the principal by making sure that class sizes are not increased when co-teachers are added and that **natural proportions** of students with disabilities are not violated in the composition of the inclusive classroom. Third, they contended that team member participation be voluntary in co-teaching situations and that the team members be compatible with regard to teaching styles and philosophies.

Lindsey suggested that principals influence inclusive practices in their schools by

- Developing a vision
- Advocating for all students being part of the school community
- Redesigning service configurations and delivery of instruction
- Building comprehensive support systems
- Developing and supporting curriculum modifications
- Facilitating transitions
- Building a professional development agenda (1997, p. 8)

Related-Services Personnel

The **itinerant service model**, in which related-services personnel go from school to school, greatly reduces the opportunity for working as a member of an instruction team (Jordan, 1994). Frequent, open communication is essential when related-services personnel are shared among schools. Open communication and team participation by itinerant educational and related-services personnel can be facilitated by carefully scheduling team meetings and instructional activities. Team membership varies with the abilities and skills of the students as well as with those of the personnel serving the students.

LEARNING OBJECTIVE 3: To be able to describe a structure for the cooperative teaching of general and special educators

Cooperative teaching, sometimes called *co-teaching,* has emerged as a model with great potential in inclusive classroom environments. In cooperative teaching, general and special educators work collaboratively to jointly teach students in inclusive environments. In this model, general and special education teachers are simultaneously present in general education classrooms, maintaining shared responsibilities for instruction. In this environment, what the teachers do is based on performance assessments of the skills and strengths of individual teachers, not on artificially determined categories of students with disabilities (Bauwens, Hourcade, & Friend, 1989).

The emphasis in cooperative teaching is on having each teacher do what he or she does best. Bauwens and colleagues (1989) suggested, as an example, that the majority of general educators are knowledgeable in the curriculum, the scope and sequence of curriculum, and the traditional content areas. General educators are also skilled in large-group management. Special educators have expertise in targeting areas within a curriculum, analyzing and adapting instruction materials and strategies, developing IEPs, and handling small-group and individual behavior management interventions.

Bauwens and colleagues (1989) identified several variations of cooperative teaching. The first is complementary instruction, which perhaps works best at the secondary level. In complementary instruction, the general education teacher maintains primary responsibility for teaching the specific content area, and the special educator assumes responsibility for students' mastery of the academic survival skills necessary for effective performance in the class. For example, the general educator may provide instruction through lectures, discussions, field trips, and in-class activities. The special educator may provide units of instruction on paying attention, taking notes, and finding the main idea in a lesson. The special educator is teaching survival skills to the students who need such instruction, whereas the general educator is engaged in enrichment activities with students without disabilities.

Another model that Bauwens and colleagues (1989) described is team teaching. In team teaching, the general and special educators jointly plan and teach academic subject content to all students. Teachers rotate responsibilities, assuming primary responsibility for specific types of instruction or portions of the curriculum. For example, the special educator might introduce new vocabulary words to the whole class by using direct instruction. The general educator might then complete the lesson.

Another model of co-teaching suggested by Bauwens and colleagues (1989) is supportive learning activities. During supportive learning activities, the general education teacher maintains responsibilities for delivering the essential content of the curriculum to the class, whereas the special education teacher assumes responsibility for developing and implementing related supplementary activities designed to enrich the specific content presented by the general educator. Both teachers are present in the instruction environment and cooperatively monitor learning activities.

As a result of the observations they conducted in 70 classrooms, Vaughn, Schumm, and Arguelles (1997) identified five practices that teachers implement in co-teaching:

1. Teaching on purpose
2. Two teachers teaching the same content to two heterogeneous groups
3. One teacher reteaching previously presented content and the other teaching alternative information to two groups
4. Multiple-groups model
5. Two teachers teaching one group the same content

Vaughn and colleagues called these practices the ABCDEs of co-teaching. In the first model, there is one lead teacher. The other teacher engages in teaching on purpose. *Teaching on purpose* is giving 1-minute, 2-minute, or 5-minute lessons to individual students, to pairs of students, or even to small groups of students. It involves checking, following up on, and extending the lead teacher's instruction. The second model involves two heterogeneous groups with two teachers instructing the same content. The third model involves two groups to which one teacher reteaches previously presented content and the other teacher teaches alternative information. The fourth arrangement is the multiple-groups model, which according to Vaughn and colleagues, is much like using learning centers or cooperative learning groups. The teachers engage in one or more of the following roles: monitoring progress, instructing minilessons, or instructing one group of learners while the other teacher is monitoring. The fifth model involves one group with two teachers teaching the same content.

Communication is essential to cooperative teaching. Salend and colleagues (1997) maintained that teachers need to devise strategies for communicating their needs and feelings and for understanding the perspectives and experiences of their teaching partners. They found that a dialogue journal was a useful tool in which teachers recorded, communicated, and reflected on their concerns, hopes, perspectives, and experiences.

The practice of co-teaching involves planning, providing, and evaluating instruction. White and White (1992) contended that joint decision making is an important element in selecting the ways in which instruction is evaluated. They suggested completion of assignments, earning daily points, turning in homework, completing projects, and participating in group activities as evaluative activities. Planning time is needed to allow teachers to review students' daily and weekly performance.

Lesson presentation, White and White (1992) stated, is the responsibility of both teachers involved in co-teaching. They argued that one teacher should not be viewed as the real teacher and the second as the helper. They provided several examples of the ways in which co-teaching can occur:

1. The general education teacher presents new information, and the special education teacher writes notes on the chalkboard to support the presentation. At the end of the presentation, the special education teacher reviews the main points of the lesson from the chalkboard.
2. The special education teacher organizes students into cooperative groups; both teachers move about the room and answer questions and provide assistance and feedback.

3. Before a test, both teachers plan and develop questions for a study session using a game show format. One teacher serves as the moderator, and the other serves as the scorekeeper.
4. Both teachers support students in developing organizational skills through the use of individual notebooks.

Classroom management is an essential, shared responsibility in co-teaching. Each teacher is responsible for modeling appropriate behavior, intervening when necessary if students exhibit inappropriate behavior, and problem solving and planning ways in which to maintain an orderly classroom (White & White, 1992). Wiedmeyer and Lehman (1991) suggested that in co-teaching situations, both teachers are responsible for monitoring students. Ways in which teachers may monitor students are presented in Table 1.

Co-teaching is not easy. Bauwens and colleagues (1989) suggested that the major problems in co-teaching are time (planning time is essential), cooperation (teachers must be able to work together), and workload (teachers need to understand that the workload will become easier as teachers use their strengths and as others supplement their weaknesses). Another challenge in co-teaching that teachers have reported is learning to work together (Fager, Andrews, Shepherd, & Quinn, 1993). Most teacher education programs tend to emphasize working independently. Learning to work cooperatively with others takes time. Phillips, Sapona, and Lubic (1995) reported that not only must logistical and territorial issues be resolved but concerns about being observed constantly by another professional also must be confronted.

Walther-Thomas (1997) found that the most persistent barriers to implementing cooperative teaching were problems in scheduled planning time, student scheduling, caseload concerns, and staff development opportunities. Finding time during the school day for co-teachers to plan together was a serious problem. In many elementary schools, planning periods were broken into small segments of time, which made in-depth planning difficult. In terms of student scheduling, though it may seem easy, assigning students in order to maintain heterogeneous classroom groups required thoughtful consideration. Closely related to scheduling problems were concerns about the special educator's caseloads. Special educators may float among several classrooms, making the number of students with disabilities with whom they work very large. A difficult professional development situation was noted by participating teachers who, though identified as the experts in their districts, reported serious gaps in their skills.

Table 1.   Monitoring students in co-teaching

- Checking for eye contact and attending behaviors
- Checking for correct notetaking (writing down of assignments, taking notes from board and during lecture)
- Working one-to-one with students
- Visually checking for understanding prior to reteaching
- Providing supplementary notetaking
- Checking for efficient use of class time

Adapted from Wiedmeyer and Lehman (1991).

Although cooperative teaching may be difficult at times, it has been reported to make teaching enjoyable, stimulating, and encouraging as teachers attempt new teaching methods (Giangreco, Baumgart, & Doyle, 1995). As teachers work together, they develop relationships with colleagues outside their classroom, which improves both teachers' morale and students' performance (York, Vandercook, Macdonald, Heise-Neff, & Caughey, 1992). In a case study of two cooperative teachers, Salend and colleagues reported that though teachers initially were concerned about ownership, teaching spaces, roles, philosophical differences, and use of language, the team evolved into one that shared responsibility and accountability and engaged in cooperative decision making. The teachers learned to blend their skills and areas of expertise, take risks, respect and trust each other's professionalism, and experiment with new teaching methods.

Co-teaching is an alternative that provides classroom teachers with help in developing, delivering, and evaluating effective instruction programs. It provides special educators with information and experience about classroom environment demands, teachers' expectations, and how students actually perform in the classroom. This information helps special educators provide more appropriate recommendations for others' instruction and for the instructing they do themselves. Co-teaching encourages ongoing support, collaborative problem solving, and professional development for all involved.

Your Turn . . .

Reflect on the challenges presented regarding co-teaching. How would you address the need for planning time? develop ways to gain administrative support? keep the numbers of individuals with whom special educators interact reasonable? improve the teaching skills of everyone involved?

LEARNING OBJECTIVE 4: To be able to describe the use of teacher assistance teams

Even in co-teaching environments, teachers sometimes need assistance in their efforts to respond to the unique needs of each student. **Teacher assistance teams** are designed to provide such support. Teacher assistance teams are "teacher-centered instructional alternative support systems" (Hayek, 1987). During team meetings, members generate ideas, methods, techniques, and activities to facilitate the teacher's efforts to provide effective instruction and management interventions. The goal of the team meeting is to develop ways in which the teacher or the teaching team can better meet students' needs.

Teacher assistance teams are usually ad hoc groups assembled at the request of the teacher or teachers working with a student. The request is often made on a referral form such as the one presented in Figure 1. In teacher assistance teams, the teacher or teachers involved may request peer observation, materials, assistance in problem solving, references, or other supports. Essential to the team's effectiveness is the willingness to help the teacher or teachers develop the skills needed to support the student or students or with other

---

Team Plan and Commitments

Teacher(s): Mrs. Keener and Ms. Chavez

Issue, student need, or concern: 5 of our 24 students are having difficulty with succeeding on the multiple-choice tests that come with the text.

Strategies suggested by team:

• Let students practice writing multiple-choice questions from the material that will be tested.

• Provide more practice in vocabulary, using flash cards and practicing in pairs. Most of the questions seem to be about vocabulary.

• Review students' notebooks to make sure that they have listed key words and meanings.

• "Talk through" the items that most of the students missed in class.

Time line:

Mrs. Keener and Ms. Chavez will try Item 3 first; if the students do have the key words listed, they will proceed with Items 1 and 2. Starting with the next test (November 7), they will do Item 4 with the class.

Commitment:

Mrs. Keener and Ms. Chavez will each write in their journals their perceptions of these efforts.

Next meeting:

November 13 (Students will have had another test by that date.)

Figure 1. Teacher assistance team referral form.

issues of concern. In addition, the team provides the teachers with a vehicle for the discussion of their earlier attempts at supporting the student or addressing the issue and developing new ways to respond to the student's needs.

A successful teacher assistance team meeting concludes with a plan designed to assist the teacher and, as a consequence, the student. The plan provides specific strategies and materials for the teacher to implement and a time when the teacher will report back to the team. For example, assume that Mrs. Keener and Ms. Chavez are co-teaching in a fifth-grade classroom. Several students, including some without identified disabilities, are having difficulty with multiple-choice social studies tests. The principal and the teachers feel strongly that they should use these tests as one measure of the students' learning because of the emphasis of such tests in the junior high school that the students will be attending the following year. Earlier attempts at working with the students to study more effectively for multiple-choice tests were not successful. During the teacher assistance team meeting, the team members develop the strategies and plan presented in Figure 2.

Teacher(s): _____

Issue, student need, or concern: _____
_____
_____

Efforts to address issue, student need, or concern: _____
_____
_____

Results of these efforts: _____
_____
_____

Suggested members of teacher assistance team: _____
_____
_____

Other comments or concerns: _____
_____
_____

Figure 2.   Sample teacher assistance team plan.

There are several advantages to using teacher assistance teams. First, the emphasis is not on the student and his or her problem. Rather, the emphasis is on building the teacher's capacity to meet the needs of the student. Teachers are provided with an opportunity to practice articulating their efforts to assist the student and problem-solve with their peers. In addition, teachers increase their skills as a result of information received from their peers. For teacher assistance teams to be effective, it is essential that it be considered good professional practice within the culture of the school for teachers to ask for help to improve their skills.

 LEARNING OBJECTIVE 5: To be able to identify strategies to encourage successful collaboration

Collaboration is more than just being a member of a team. Collaboration implies a partnership, a sharing, and a commitment among team members. Cook and Friend (1995) and Friend and Cook (1996) suggested that collaboration

- Is voluntary
- Requires parity among participants
- Is grounded in mutual goals
- Is dependent on participants' shared responsibility for participation and decision making
- Requires sharing of resources
- Requires sharing of accountability for outcomes

Collaboration usually occurs when teachers are consulting about a specific issue or concern. The term **collaborative consultation** is sometimes used to describe this activity. In collaborative consultation, interaction is reciprocal and involves all professionals involved in the issue or concern under discussion. The goal of this collaboration is to develop further the independent problem-solving skills of the individuals involved. Everyone in a school should be involved in collaborative consultation at one time or another during a school year. The language used during consultation should be as free of professional jargon as possible (Pugach & Johnson, 1988).

An additional essential aspect of collaboration in inclusive classrooms is **role release**. Lyon and Lyon (1980) described role release as sharing between two or more members of a team on three levels:

1. All members of the team share general information regarding their individual expertise, duties, and responsibilities.
2. Each team member teaches other team members to make specific teaching decisions within their own areas of expertise.
3. Team members share the skills specific to their areas of expertise.

Rather than owning a specific area, in role release, a professional shares his or her expertise and helps other collaboration team members provide direct services related to their unique areas of expertise. For example, rather than referring students to the occupational therapist for one-to-one work related to handwriting, the occupational therapist works with the teacher, provides a variety of materials and information, and allows the teacher to determine when the students need a soft-grip or hard-grip writing instrument, unlined or lined paper, or fat or thin pencils.

Pugach and Johnson (1995) suggested that active listening skills can facilitate effective communication in collaboration. These skills include

- Offering support—that is, communicating to a colleague that you are there to listen and help him or her work through a concern
- Using general nonthreatening openings, asking questions such as "Would you like to talk?" or "How are things going?" rather than asking "What are you angry about?"
- Reflecting, or restating, the key information from the sender in order to gain greater clarity in the message
- Stating the implied, or verbalizing what you understand to be the underlying message being sent
- Requesting clarification, or seeking a greater understanding of the information being sent
- Remaining silent, or avoiding the need to speak because no one else is speaking or communicating more information
- Placing events in context, that is, placing events into their proper order to help identify issues that are unrelated to the issue under examination
- Summarizing—that is, providing both individuals with an opportunity to review key points and to agree on what was said or to disagree and revise the content and making public the action that everyone is to take

In addition to these skills, Pugach and Johnson suggested that there are several barriers that may influence the communication necessary for effective collaboration. The most common error is giving advice, the impact of which can negate the professionalism of a collaborative relationship. In addition, giving false reassurances is not helpful and can be a deterrent to further collaboration. Misdirected questions also can be a problem and may prevent a colleague from developing a clear line of thought in the discussion. Participants' inattention and wandering interactions also are a problem and should be brought into focus by a request for clarification. Interruptions or changing the subject can also disrupt the flow of the conversation and hinder problem solving. Resorting to clichés can diminish the feelings of participants in the interaction. Using clichés can also minimize the feelings of the individuals involved, which may inhibit further collaboration. Moving too quickly to solve a problem can also be damaging to a collaborative relationship. If there were quick fixes, colleagues in collaboration would have applied them already.

SUMMARY

This chapter addresses the following major concepts:

1. Instruction teams are responsible for planning, instructing, evaluating, and supporting a group of students.
2. Instruction teams may include, as appropriate, the student, the general education teacher, the special education teacher, parents, aides, the principal, and related-services personnel.

3. Cooperative teaching (co-teaching) has emerged as a model for use in in-
    clusive learning environments. In this model, general educators and spe-
    cial educators are simultaneously present in the general education class-
    room and share responsibilities for instruction and management.
4. Teacher assistance team activities may include peer observation, use of
    materials, and assistance in problem solving.
5. Role release is an essential aspect of collaboration.

TEST YOUR KNOWLEDGE

Completion of the "Self-Evaluation," "Make the Language Your Own," and "Application Activities" sections will aid readers in understanding and retaining
the information presented in this chapter. Answer keys for the "Self-Evaluation"
and "Make the Language Your Own" sections are located in the Appendix at the
end of the book.

Self-Evaluation

Select the most appropriate response to complete each of the following statements:

1. The roles of instruction team members
    a. Can develop as the team works
    b. Demand a clear delineation of responsibility and accountability
    c. Are interchangeable

2. In instruction teams, the need for control or power
    a. Is ignored for the good of the team
    b. Is satisfied by giving each member the opportunity to be heard
    c. Is managed through democratic processes

3. Aides
    a. Are not officially members of the team because of challenges to
        liability
    b. Are challenged by the difference in status between the teacher and
        the instruction assistant (professional and aide)
    c. Should not be engaged in team activities but should support indi-
        vidual children

4. In co-teaching, general educators
    a. Jointly teach students with special educators
    b. Receive consultation from special educators
    c. And special educators plan cooperative learning strategies in the
        classroom

5. In co-teaching classrooms,
    a. It is clear to the students who is the "real" teacher
    b. Instruction is the responsibility of both teachers
    c. General educators take the lead and are supported by special
        educators

6. Co-teaching
   a. Is easy to implement
   b. Allows teachers to work independently
   c. Requires time for teachers to learn to work together

7. Teacher assistance teams
   a. Remove students with disabilities from the classroom for brief periods of time
   b. Provide support to teachers with regard to the unique needs of each student
   c. Provide instruction aides for teachers in inclusive classrooms

8. Successful teacher assistance team meetings conclude with
   a. A shared commitment to help the student involved
   b. A commitment to communicate
   c. A plan with specific strategies and materials

9. Collaboration should be
   a. Mandatory
   b. Voluntary
   c. Mandated

10. In role release, professionals share
    a. Their expertise
    b. Credentials
    c. Participation with parents

Make the Language Your Own
Match the following terms with their definitions:

1. _____ Instruction team

2. _____ Co-teaching

3. _____ Role release

4. _____ Natural proportions

5. _____ Collaborative consultation

6. _____ Itinerant service model

7. _____ Teacher assistance team

a. General education and special education teachers working collaboratively to jointly teach students in an inclusive environment

b. A partnership, a sharing, and a commitment among team members to facilitate effective services

c. An organizational and instructional arrangement of two or more members of the school community and the greater community who distribute among themselves planning, instruction, and evaluation responsibilities for the same students on a regular basis for an extended period of time (Thousand & Villa, 1990)

d. Services delivery by education and related-services personnel who travel from school to school

e. The condition in which the number of students with disabilities in

a classroom reflects the number
of individuals with disabilities
found in the greater community

f.   Sharing of expertise among team
members and helping other team
members to provide services

g.   Teacher-centered instructional alternative support systems (Hayek,
1987)

Application Activities

1.   Interview a general education teacher and a principal who work in a
school in which teacher assistance teams are used. Discuss with each of
these individuals the purpose of the teams, how the teams functions, and
the effectiveness of the teams. If possible, discuss the teacher assistance
team with other professionals and aides in the school.

2.   For one school day, observe and then discuss with the general education
teacher and the special education teacher involved their functioning as
members of the instruction team. Discuss the teaching models that they
employ, the roles that they assume, the reactions of the students to their
co-teaching activities, and the effectiveness of their efforts.

REFERENCES

Bauwens, J., Hourcade, J.J., & Friend, M. (1989). Cooperative teaching: A model for
general and special education integration. *Remedial and Special Education, 10*(2),
17–22.

Cook, L., & Friend, M. (1995). Co-teaching: Guidelines for creating effective practices.
Focus on Exceptional Children, 28(3), 1–16.

Fager, P., Andrews, T., Shepherd, M.J., & Quinn, E. (1993). Teamed to teach: Integrating teacher training through cooperative teaching experiences at an urban professional development school. *Teacher Education and Special Education, 16*(1), 51–59.

Ferguson, D.L., Meyer, G., Jeanchild, L., Juniper, L., & Zingo, J. (1992). Figuring out
what to do with the grownups: How teachers make inclusion "work" for students
with disabilities. *Journal of The Association for Persons with Severe Handicaps, 17*,
218–226.

Friend, M., & Cook, L. (1996). *Interactions: Collaboration skills for school professionals*
(2nd ed.). White Plains, NY: Addison Wesley Longman.

Gerber, S. (1991). Supporting the collaborative process. *Preventing School Failure,
35*(4), 48–52.

Giangreco, M.F., Baumgart, D.M.J., & Doyle, M.B. (1995). How inclusion can facilitate
teaching and learning. *Interaction in School and Clinic, 30*, 273–278.

Hayek, R.A. (1987). The teacher assistance team: A prereferral support system. *Focus
on Exceptional Children, 20*(1), 1–7.

Hines, R.A., & Johnston, J.H. (1997). *Promoting achievement in inclusive classrooms:
The principal's role.* Washington, DC: National Association of Secondary School Principals.

Jenkins, J.R., Pious, C.G., & Jewell, M. (1990). Special education and the Regular
Education Initiative: Basic assumptions. *Exceptional Children, 55*, 147–158.

Jordan, A. (1994). *Skills in collaborative classroom consultation.* London: Routledge.

Lindsey, C. (1997). The principal's role in inclusion. *Missouri Innovations in Special
Education, 24*(4), 8–9.

Lyon, S., & Lyon, G. (1980). Team functioning and staff development: A role release approach to providing integrated educational services to severely handicapped students. *Journal of The Association for Persons with Severe Handicaps, 5*, 250–263.

Phillips, L., Sapona, R.H., & Lubic, B.L. (1995). Developing partnerships in inclusive education: One school's approach. *Intervention in School and Clinic, 30*(5), 262–278.

Pugach, M., & Johnson, L.J. (1988). Rethinking the relationship between consultation and collaborative problem-solving. *Focus on Exceptional Children, 21*(4), 1–8.

Pugach, M., & Johnson, L.J. (1995). *Collaborative practitioners, collaborative schools.* Denver: Love Publishing Co.

Reeve, P.T., & Hallahan, D.P. (1994). Practical questions about collaboration between general and special educators. *Focus on Exceptional Children, 26*(7), 1–12.

Salend, S.J., Johansen, M., Mumper, J., Chase, A.S., Pike, K.M., & Dorney, J.A. (1997). Cooperative teaching: The voices of two teachers. *Remedial and Special Education, 18*(1), 3–11.

Stanovich, P.J. (1996). Collaboration: The key to successful instruction in today's inclusive schools. *Intervention in School and Clinic, 32*(1), 39–42.

Thousand, J.S., & Villa, R.A. (1990). Sharing expertise and responsibilities through teaching teams. In W. Stainback & S. Stainback (Eds.), *Support networks for inclusive schooling: Interdependent integrated education* (pp. 151–166). Baltimore: Paul H. Brookes Publishing Co.

Vandercook, T., & York, J. (1990). A team approach to program development and support. In W. Stainback & S. Stainback (Eds.), *Support networks for inclusive schooling: Interdependent integrated education* (pp. 95–122). Baltimore: Paul H. Brookes Publishing Co.

Vaughn, S., Schumm, J.S., & Arguelles, M.E. (1997). The ABCDEs of co-teaching. *Teaching Exceptional Children, 30*(2), 4–10.

Walther-Thomas, C.S. (1997). Co-teaching experiences: The benefits and problems that teachers and principals report over time. *Journal of Learning Disabilities, 30*(4), 395–407.

White, A.E., & White, L.L. (1992). A collaborative model for students with mild disabilities in middle schools. *Focus on Exceptional Children, 24*(9), 1–12.

Wiedmeyer, D., & Lehman, J. (1991). The "house plan" approach to collaborative teaching and consultation. *Teaching Exceptional Children, 23*(3), 6–10.

York, J., Vandercook, T., Macdonald, C., Heise-Neff, C., & Caughey, E. (1992). Feedback about integrating middle school students with severe disabilities in general education classes. *Exceptional Children, 58*, 244–259.

6

Parent and Family Involvement

Our teenage son has autism. One day my husband was in line with him at McDonald's. The kid working the counter said, "Hi, Aaron," and to my husband said, "Did you know Aaron has a girlfriend?" It seems that every day in the weight training class, Aaron rides a stationary bike, with Lauren beside him. The day before, Lauren wasn't there, and when another student tried to use the bike, Aaron had a tantrum. His teenage classmate figured out that Aaron was "saving" the bike for his girlfriend. Why didn't the teacher or aide tell us about this? Don't they understand how important these little bits of normalcy are to us? Instead, all we hear is that Aaron had a tantrum in the weight room.

Mary Ulrich, parent of a young adult with autism

In this chapter, attention is given to several topics that are essential to parent and family involvement with educators and other professionals on behalf of learners who vary from their peers and who are being served in inclusive environments. The first section of the chapter discusses several challenges that confront all parents and families raising children with or without disabilities. Among those challenges are the need for both parents to work, family and sexuality education, after-school and evening activities for children, life skills and parenting instruction, and the cost of education. Some families are confronted with the concerns of divorce, foster care, substance abuse, and poverty. Several questionable presumptions regarding the parents and families of learners who vary from their peers are discussed. These presumptions have a significant impact on services for learners who vary from their peers and for the parents and families of these learners. The chapter next discusses the rights and responsibilities of parents of learners who vary from their peers. This is a discussion of the rights of parents under the Individuals with Disabilities Education Act (IDEA) of 1990 (PL 101-476) and other federal legislation. Written communication, conferences, support groups, helping with homework, serving as volunteers in classrooms and in schools, and participating in educational decision-making activities are suggested as ways to increase parents' participation in their children's education. Parents also can facilitate school outreach and multicultural education programs.

LEARNING OBJECTIVES

After completing this chapter, readers will be able to

1. Identify challenges that confront all families
2. Discuss presumptions regarding parents of learners who vary from their peers
3. Describe the rights and responsibilities of parents of learners who vary from their peers
4. Identify ways to increase the participation of all parents

KEY WORDS AND PHRASES

acculturation—the extent to which members of one culture adapt to a new culture

bicultural competence—an ability to function in both the home culture and the school culture

conferences—focused conversations regarding a student's participation in the school environment

empowerment—a group of processes and activities that involve people in determining their own future and possibly the future of their community

family—a social system composed of two or more interdependent members who engage in reciprocal interactions over time

foster care—a planned, temporary placement of a child in out-of-home service for the purpose of strengthening the natural family

normalization—the belief that families with learners who vary from their peers should function in as typical a manner as they desire and as is possible

LEARNING OBJECTIVE 1: To be able to identify challenges that confront all families

It has never been easy to be a parent. In America's complex society, however, families are becoming progressively less well equipped to support their children's education. More than ever, college costs are seen as a government responsibility; after-school and summer school activities have decreased parents' responsibility for their children; parental authority over college and high school–age students has relaxed; and socialization activities, such as **family** and sexuality education, after-school activities, life-skills instruction, and even parenting instruction, are increasingly being turned over to the schools (Coleman, 1987).

The Children's Defense Fund (1996) stated that there are several enormous challenges that families face:

- The number of children reported to have been abused or neglected has nearly doubled since the late 1980s.
- The number of children in **foster care** has increased by about two thirds over the 1-day count recorded in the late 1980s.
- An estimated 1 million children run away each year, and another 300,000 are homeless.
- Families with children are not better off financially than they were in the late 1970s. In addition, there is a widening gap between families at the highest and lowest income levels.

One issue that commonly affects families and children is divorce. Guidubaldi and Perry (1985) described divorce as the most pervasive, severe psychological stressor for children. In families in which the parents divorce, family structures no longer match family members' emotional needs (Wallerstein & Blakeslee, 1989). For example, rather than serving as a place where a child can rest, the home often becomes a place of significant stress.

Because of the many challenges that families confront, children are more likely to be placed in foster care than ever before in U.S. history. Foster care placement, intended as a planned, temporary service implemented to strengthen families, is changing. Children in foster care have been found to experience more frequent health care problems, developmental delays, and educational problems than do their peers (Schorr, 1988; Silver, Amster, & Haecker, 1999).

Parents may be engaged in substance abuse. When a parent is involved in substance abuse, the interactions that usually occur between parents and young children may not occur because of the parents' preoccupation with obtaining and using drugs. In addition, the primary concern of parents engaged in substance abuse is acquiring their drug of choice rather than caring for their children.

Poverty is another challenge to families. Young children living in poverty are confronted with the double jeopardy of biological problems and the insufficient social support available to those who are poor. Parker, Greer, and Zuckerman (1988) suggested that working with families in poverty should involve both strengthening relationships and providing social supports for children. They suggested that even in families under stress, the presence of a good relationship with one parent reduces the risk for children.

Your Turn . . .

Reflect on your childhood and those of your parents or guardians. What were the societal issues that confronted your grandparents in raising your parents? What societal issues confronted your parents during your childhood? What issues confront or will confront you as a parent?

LEARNING OBJECTIVE 2: To be able to discuss presumptions regarding parents of learners who vary from their peers

It is difficult to discuss parents without discussing families. Families are not just collections of people; families are social systems. Because families are social systems, their interactions within and outside their homes cannot be described by linear, cause-and-effect relationships (Johnston & Zemitzsch, 1988).

How are families like social systems? First, families are structured wholes composed of interdependent elements. As in all social systems, interactions in the family are reciprocal and represent a continuous give-and-take rather than a cause-and-effect pattern. Families also try to maintain stability or homeostasis; however, families also are constantly changing. Although changes occur constantly in families, families make an effort to stay with old patterns and resist change, as is common in all social systems (Minuchin, 1974).

The most common presumption regarding parents of learners who vary from their peers is that, when adjusting to the birth or the diagnosis of a child with disabilities, these parents progress through a series of psychological stages similar to those that individuals grieving a death experience: shock, denial, bargaining, anger, depression, and acceptance (Kroth & Otteni, 1985). Families are viewed as grieving the loss of their perfect child (Hinderliter, 1988). After an extensive review of the literature, however, Blacher (1984) concluded that these stages are a result of professionals' judgments rather than an analysis of objective data. In another review, Allen and Affleck (1985) reported that they found no support for any stagelike progression of parents' reactions.

Seligman and Darling (1989) argued that the strength of families of learners who vary from their peers is demonstrated by the fact that, given many obstacles and challenges, most are able to achieve a nearly typical lifestyle. They suggested that **normalization** is the most common adaptation found among families of children with disabilities in American society, though it remains difficult for some families. In order to cope, these families develop other adaptations. Crusadership—one alternative adaptation—is a result of parents' attempts to bring about social change. These parents engage in campaigns to increase public awareness, testify before congressional committees, or wage legal battles with the school system. They are advocates who try to change the opportunity structure for their own and other people's children. Some "crusadership" families may eventually achieve normalization as they withdraw from involvement in advocacy groups.

Seligman and Darling (1989) referred to another adaptation pattern as *altruism*. Rather than withdraw from advocacy groups, some families who have achieved normalization remain active for the sake of others, representing successful role models for the parents of younger children. A fourth pattern, *resignation,* includes families who, despite their inability to achieve normalization, never become involved in crusadership activity. Rather, these families become resigned to their problematic existence and, lacking access to supportive resources, become isolated.

One presumption about parents is that they resent their children's receiving special education services. Green and Shinn (1995), however, found that parents reported liking what special educators do (or what the parents think special educators do) for their children. Parental satisfaction, however, was not always related to their children's academic performance. Rather than improved achievement outcomes as a basis of their satisfaction, parents stressed individual attention to their children, caring teachers, and their children's increased self-esteem as the basis for their satisfaction.

Another difficulty that parents of children who vary from their peers confront is the presumption of professionals that they should be active advocates for their children. Mlawler (1993) suggested that parents and professionals have created an advocacy expectation that runs counter to the philosophy of normalization, the belief that families should function in as typical a manner as they desire and as is possible. Professionals rather than parents have the obligation to serve as advocates. Moreover, to truly empower parents, programs must be developed that are capable of engaging in advocacy along with and on behalf of parents. These programs should be available regardless of income, well publicized, and easily accessible. Mlawler suggested that, rather than use parents as advocates, there should be a corps of independent, uncompromised special educators available to serve as experts on behalf of students.

Professionals often presume that parents' stress is related to the severity of their child's disability. In fact, parents' stress is primarily a function of their personalities and psychological makeup and may not be a consequence of the nature of their child's disability (Bradshaw, 1978; Koch, 1982). Stress, however, may be related to the amount of time that parents devote to caregiving, concern over present and future needs, and uncertainty about the child's progress (Frey, Greenberg, & Fewell, 1989).

LEARNING OBJECTIVE 3: To be able to describe the rights and responsibilities of parents of learners who vary from their peers

One primary aspect of IDEA and its amendments is the direct involvement of parents in decision making. IDEA details how decision making in the school context is to proceed, but situations exist in which school personnel and families may find it difficult to reach agreement. The reasons for this circumstance may include the following:

- Parents are not sure that they are qualified to play an active role in decision making regarding their child.
- Parents and teachers lack the communication skills needed to cooperate effectively.
- Some school systems approach decision making regarding placement and planning informally, thus making the parents feel as if decisions are being made without their input.
- Parents and school professionals have a full partnership yet disagree on specific decisions.
- Their previous experiences make it difficult for professionals and parents to collaborate.
- School professionals may not view parents as equal partners in the school environment (Gerry, 1987).

IDEA includes many procedural safeguards for families. These safeguards are presented in Table 1. Parents have the right to initiate a due process hearing for many reasons. The request for a due process hearing must be completed in writing and may be initiated if the school district proposes to initiate a change in the identification, evaluation, or placement of the student or a provision in the student's individualized education program (IEP). Parents may also initiate a due process hearing if they request, and the school district fails to initiate or change, 1) the identification, evaluation, or placement of the student or 2) the student's IEP. Finally, parents may request a due process hearing when they request, and the school district refuses or fails to amend, the child's education records.

Table 1. Safeguards provided in the Individuals with Disabilities Education Act (IDEA) of 1990 (PL 101-476)

1. Written notice to parents before the school initiates, changes, or refuses to initiate or change the identification or placement of a student
2. Direct participation in the development of and annual review of the individualized education program (IEP)
3. Written, informed parental consent before initiating a formal evaluation and assessment and before initial placement
4. Parents' inspection and review of any education records that the school maintains regarding their child; access must be granted without unnecessary delay and before any meeting regarding the IEP or before hearings, evaluations, or placement
5. The right to request information on where independent educational evaluations may be obtained; a parent has the right to an independent educational evaluation at public expense if the parent disagrees with an evaluation obtained by the local school district; school districts, however, may initiate due process hearings to show that the original evaluation was appropriate

LEARNING OBJECTIVE 4: To be able to identify ways to increase the participation of all parents

Dauber and Epstein (1993) found that in determining whether parents will become involved in their child's education, how schools encourage parents' participation is more important than families' characteristics, such as parents' levels of education, families' sizes, families' socioeconomic status, or children's grade levels. As children grow older and progress through the school system, parents have less positive contact with the school. Puma, Jones, Rock, and Fernandez (1993) reported that during the first grade, slightly more than 50% of the interactions between families and schools are positive and that only 20% are negative. By the seventh grade, the proportion of positive interactions drops to 36%. Classroom volunteerism levels drop from 33% of first-grade parents to 8% of seventh-grade parents.

Teachers often talk about the importance of parent–school communication. This communication is often one-sided, however, based on information gleaned from notes, newsletters, and annual parent–teacher **conferences**. If parents are to be true partners in the education of their children, then communication must flow both ways. The National Parent Teacher Association (1997) identified six components of effective parent involvement:

- Regular, meaningful, two-way communication should exist between home and school.
- Parenting skills should be promoted and supported.
- There should be active parent participation in student learning.
- Parents should be welcomed as volunteer partners in schools.
- Parents should be full partners in school decisions that affect children and families.
- Outreach to the community for resources to strengthen schools should be engaged in.

The preceding components are used to structure the discussion of parent participation that follows.

Regular, Meaningful, Two-Way Communication

Open communication is essential in inclusive classrooms. Some parents may have concerns about the inclusive learning community and about whether their children's needs will be met. Clear communication of the classroom goals in a welcome letter may increase parents' comfort. Enclosing in the welcome letter a listing of whom to call for what information or services can give parents a sense of security. An example of a welcome letter is provided in Figure 1.

In addition to the welcome letter, a follow-up letter can be sent to invite parents to participate with school personnel in their children's education. Examples of such a letter and an attached questionnaire are provided in Figures 2 and 3. A common form of communication between teacher and parents is a note. Effective notes are clear, concise, and positive and are written in the parents' primary language. Rutherford and Edgar (1979) suggested that notes and letters serve four purposes:

Dear *[Insert parents' or guardians' names]*,

Welcome to Room 304! We are so pleased to have you and your child join us this year. We look at Room 304 as a place where everyone will have the opportunity to be successful and to learn to the best of his or her ability.

There are 23 students in our classroom. This year, in addition to emphasizing the basic skills of reading, writing, and mathematics, we have identified the theme of "Our School, Our Community" for our work this year. Social studies, science, health, art, and music activities will all involve exploring our school environment and our community environment. We'll be calling on you, as members of this community, to join us in any way you are able. We'll be asking if you'd like to send in photographs, notes, and newsletter articles or whether you'd like to join us in our classroom.

Let me tell you a little about our teaching team. Because my name is a bit long (Mary Elizabeth Trizinski), the students call me Ms. T. This is my fifth year teaching the third grade at Ellendar Elementary School. In addition to having my early childhood (kindergarten through third grade) teaching license, I am licensed to teach learners with learning disabilities. I have three children, one of whom is now in college and will be joining us every now and then as a volunteer!

John Huedefeld is my co-teacher. Mr. Huedefeld has a teaching license in learning disabilities and behavior disorders. He has taught at Ellendar for 3 years in the fourth- to fifth-grade support area. We are thrilled that he will be in the classroom with us all day, every day this year.

In the near future, Mr. Huedefeld and I will be meeting with each of you to discuss your child's education program and to gather information regarding your goals for your child this year. If your child has an individualized education program (IEP), we will use this conference to review the IEP with you and determine whether any amendments are needed or whether a new IEP is necessary. We will discuss expectations for your child this year and ways in which you can help your child at home and at school.

We are looking forward to a very rewarding and productive school year. If you have any questions or concerns, please call. And speaking of calling, we have attached a brief list of "whom to call for what."

Best wishes for a wonderful new school year,

Mary Elizabeth Trizinski
John Huedefeld

Whom to Call for What

Bus problems	Louise Farber	555-2938
Making sure my child gets his or her medication	Catherine Dennis	555-3958
Hearing/vision testing	Catherine Dennis	555-3958
Parent Teacher Association	Joelle Francke	555-0857
Lunch program	Dolly Pratte	555-3957
After-school care	Tasha Graymeier	555-6830
Classroom questions	Mary Elizabeth Trizinski	555-3955
	John Huedefeld	555-3955
School concerns	Jeri Jerold	555-3959
Questions about my child's IEP	John Huedefeld	555-3955
Communication specialist	Martha Vendome	555-3955

Figure 1. Welcome letter.

Dear *[Insert parents' or guardians' names]*,

Again, welcome to Room 304. With this letter, we would like to invite you to participate with us! We have several opportunities available for your participation. Please feel free to take advantage of as many of these opportunities as you are comfortable with. There are activities that can be done at home, in the classroom, or in the school. Our Parent Involvement Program is your program; please feel free to add any other suggestions or activities in which you would like to be engaged.

Please complete the attached form and return to school with your child by October 1. As always, if you have any questions at all, please call.

Thanks for your help!

Mary Elizabeth Trizinski
John Huedefeld

Figure 2.   Follow-up to welcome letter.

1. To praise the child's general academic performance or behavior
2. To informally and positively address specific academic and behavior problems
3. To informally evaluate the child's performance
4. To provide a structured performance evaluation, similar to a report card

Shea and Bauer (1991) suggested that the following guidelines be adhered to in all written communication with parents:

1. Be brief. (Both parents and teachers are busy.)
2. Be positive. (Parents know that their children are challenged and challenging and do not need to receive negative reminders of these facts.)
3. Be honest. (Do not say that a child is doing fine if he or she is not. Write noncommittal comments and request a person-to-person or telephone conference.)
4. Be responsive. (If the parent asks for help, respond immediately.)
5. Be informal. (All participants working on behalf of a child are equals.)
6. Be consistent. (If notes are the communication system of choice, use them consistently.)
7. Avoid jargon. (Parents may not understand special education jargon.)
8. Be careful. (Do not project personal feelings or the frustrations of a bad day onto a child or a parent.)

It is essential to be cautious in writing notes and letters to parents. Marion (1979) provided the following guidelines for writing to parents from diverse cultural, linguistic, or ethnic groups, which are applicable to written communication to all parents:

1. Determine the parents' education level before sending written communications to them. By adjusting the language of the message accordingly, teachers increase the likelihood that the parents will understand it and perceive it as positive. To find information about parents' background, ask another teacher who is familiar with the family or review the fam-

Name: _____   **Date:** _____

Child's name: _____

Oral communication

I would like a monthly phone call from the teachers.   Yes   No
I would like a monthly conference with the teachers.   Yes   No
I would like a conference once a quarter with the teachers.   Yes   No
Other:

Written communication

I would like to receive weekly notes on my child's progress.   Yes   No
I would like to receive a biweekly newsletter.   Yes   No
I would like to send a dialogue notebook back and forth with my child.   Yes   No
Other:

Volunteer opportunities

I would like to help with the phone chain.   Yes   No
I would like to help on the playground.   Yes   No
I would like to help during art or music.   Yes   No
I would like to chaperon field trips.   Yes   No
I would like to send treats for parties.   Yes   No
I would like to help during parties.   Yes   No
I would like to help prepare educational materials.   Yes   No
I would like to help tutor.
                                                                             Yes   No
I would like to read with children.   Yes   No
I would like to teach an art project or a craft project.   Yes   No
I would like to share my job/occupation/career with the children.   Yes   No
Other:

Education

I would like information on literacy and reading.   Yes   No
I would like information on learning math.   Yes   No
I would like information on learning disabilities or behavioral disorders.   Yes   No
I would like information on parenting.   Yes   No
Other:

Home

I would like information on homework.   Yes   No
I would like a home/school check-off sheet.   Yes   No
I would like to work with my child at home.   Yes   No
Other:

THANK YOU FOR YOUR HELP!!

Figure 3. Parent participation questionnaire.

ily's background in the learner's cumulative record. Use clear, direct prose, avoiding indirect language. For example, rather than writing, "Luis appears to be challenged by the amount of work required in fourth grade," write, "Luis is not completing as much work as the other students in his class." Remember that not all parents can read and write standard English.

2.   Affix Mr., Ms., or Mrs. (whichever is appropriate) to all written communications to parents.

3. Guard against writing with a condescending or superior tone. Avoid phrases such as "If only you would . . . ," "If you had considered . . . ," or "Please try to remember . . . ," which connote that the parent has somehow failed to do his or her duty. Statements such as "At school, we do not tolerate cursing" may appear to a parent who is reading it that the teacher believes that the parent condones such behavior.

4. If requesting that the parent visit for a conference, offer a clear reason for the request. Parents resent losing time and wages from work or home tasks for unclear reasons.

Parent conferences are a common communication tool that teachers use. When using parent conferences for communication, teachers should remember that some parents may have had experiences in which they not only were faced with a litany of complaints about their child during a conference but also were offered little or no constructive criticism or assistance. Parents may have been summoned to school when a teacher was frustrated and did not know what to do, and as a result the teacher blamed the parent for the child's in-school problem (DiCocco, 1986).

Shea and Bauer (1991) suggested that in order to set a positive, proactive tone for parent conferences, teachers should provide parents with an explanation of the purpose of the conference and a written agenda (see Figure 4). In many situations, the conference is a show-and-tell session in which the teacher presents and discusses the student's work and the instruction materials used in the education program. Parents may be provided with an opportunity to manipulate the materials.

Dear Parents,

Each quarter, we meet with each child's parents in order to describe their child's participation in educational activities in Room 304. These conferences are a way for us to have a conversation about your child's progress, review the educational materials we are using, and answer any questions that either teachers or parents may have about better supporting the child. Thirty minutes are set aside for each conference, with most lasting between 20 and 30 minutes.

During the conference, we would like to follow this agenda:

1. Your goals for your child
2. Our educational goals for your child
3. How your child is progressing toward those goals
4. Materials being used with your child
5. Ways that we could work together to support your child

We hope you will take advantage of this opportunity to discuss your child's progress. We have set aside 3 days for these meetings, with times available in the morning, afternoon, or evening. If none of these times is convenient for you, we can schedule individual conferences at a later date. We will be sending home a request for you to express your meeting time preferences early next week.

Again, if you have any questions, please call.

Mary Elizabeth Trizinski
John Huedefeld

Figure 4. Parent conference letter.

As in all communications with parents, teachers should begin with a positive statement. Teachers guide the actual conference, systematically following the agenda and encouraging and responding to the parents. After making sure that the parents are comfortable at the beginning of the session, teachers should clarify the time available for discussion. Parents and teachers may want to take notes during the conference, but the teacher should make sure that all participants are comfortable with note taking and should not take notes if doing so appears to be intrusive. Immediately after the conference, the teacher should write a conference summary, attach any reports, and make a copy for parents and the student's file. Conferences can be an effective tool for enhancing communication between parents and teachers. As in all involvement activities, parents are equal partners in the discussion.

Parenting Skills Should Be Promoted and Supported

All families need support at some time. Miller and Hudson (1994) described the use of support groups for families. They suggested that the families themselves should be used to form a committee to establish such a group. Miller and Hudson suggested that meetings should have an informal tone and emphasize parents' comfort. As parents arrive, they may be invited to sign a guest book and help themselves to refreshments. Meetings may begin with introductions, followed by the structured content of the meeting. Following the conclusion of the structured content of the session, parents' questions may be addressed, and their general comments may be tied in to the topic encouraged. Next, the group may break into smaller groups for brainstorming regarding the application of the content. The meeting concludes with each member completing an evaluation sheet. A sample meeting agenda is presented in Figure 5.

Active Parent Participation in Students' Learning

Parents should be active participants in their children's learning. Their participation may range from providing a quiet spot for homework to implementing a behavior management plan. Although parents can participate in their children's learning, teachers should remember that parents have many roles and responsibilities. Some activities in which parents can actively participate include

- Supervising homework
- Reviewing material learned in school
- Reading with their children
- Participating in book sharing with their children
- Completing learning projects at home
- Implementing specific IEP objectives
- Implementing behavior change plans

Parents as Volunteers

Parents are able to make a significant contribution to schools. Shea and Bauer (1991) suggested that there are several keys to successful parent volunteer programs. First, volunteers should participate in an in-service program in which school and classroom procedures are introduced, roles and responsibilities are clarified, and ways to request assistance are delineated. Next, the volunteers' abilities, interests, and special skills should be matched with the volunteer activities available or with activities that could be made available.

Guest book sign-in and refreshments	5 minutes
Welcome from group facilitator	5 minutes
Introduction of participants	10 minutes
Guest speaker/film/videotape	25 minutes
Group questions	10 minutes
Small-group discussion	30 minutes
Closing remarks from group facilitator	2 minutes
Evaluation forms distributed and collected	3 minutes

Figure 5.   Sample parent support meeting agenda.

In addition to supporting the education program, parents can support other parents by serving as parent partners. Parent partners may be assigned to parents who are new to the school in order to provide an informal source of information regarding the culture and practices in the school. For example, parents may feel more comfortable asking another parent about how birthdays are celebrated in the classroom, whether the students carry lunchboxes or brown bags to school, or what rainy day recess policies are.

Parents as Partners in Decision Making

A recurrent theme in the professional and popular literature on the participation of parents and families in education is **empowerment**. *Empowerment* usually refers to a group of processes and activities that involve people in determining their own future and possibly the future of their community (Thompson et al., 1997). For parents, empowerment occurs when individuals are confident that they have the information and problem-solving abilities necessary to deal with challenging situations (Balcazar, Seekins, Fawcett, & Hopkins, 1990). Empowerment in education requires professionals and parents to restructure their traditional relationships. Professionals empower parents by sharing information with them and welcoming them as partners in decision making. Parents are equal partners and decision makers; professionals do not always know what is best for parents and children.

Parents have long been asked to support their children's education at home in safe, routine ways such as by making sure children are well fed and well rested and have completed their homework. Parents have also been encouraged to participate in their children's education as described above. Engaging parents in shared decision making, however, remains a challenge for many teachers. On the whole, parents have essentially served as consent givers, with the decision-making power resting primarily with the professionals (Harry, 1992).

Harry (1992) argued that parents must be offered and must assume new roles if they are to have greater power in the educational partnership. The first step, she argued, is to truly engage parents in the assessment. Parents should be team members in the assessment of their children. Parents should be encouraged to present reports during team meetings. These reports, along with the reports of professional team members, should become a part of the meeting record and be taken into account in decision making. Harry also argued that parents should be policy makers, serving on school-based advisory committees. She also suggested that parents serve as advocates and as peer supports for other parents. By engaging parents in these roles, they are more likely to develop a sense of competence and share their learning with other parents.

Comer (1988) described a school–home program that has been successful in engaging poor families in school governance. In that program, parents are encouraged to participate as part of a governance and management team that plans academic programs and improvements in school involvement. In addition, parents receive education related to how children learn. Workshops, dinners, and other events are planned that bring parents and school staff together.

One way in which parents can be actively engaged is through parent advisory councils. When issues emerge, teachers are then able to turn to parents for help. Parents can serve on advisory committees related to curriculum, extracurricular activities, dress code, school facilities, school transportation, fund raising, textbook and instruction materials review, and program evaluation.

Outreach for Resources

Parents can be actively involved in connecting schools to other community and business resources. Business partners in education can be a source not only of volunteers but also of materials and funding for special projects. Parents working with local community centers can bring after-school and before-school care to the school building. Parents working with public health and mental health services can help make these and other services available at the school. Parents can lobby effectively to make immunization and vision and hearing screenings available at the school.

CULTURAL ISSUES

Essential to working collaboratively with parents and families is recognizing the role of culture. The majority of educators are female European Americans. As discussed previously, the student population of U.S. schools is becoming more and more diverse.

Salend and Taylor (1993) described several issues that must be considered when working with families from a variety of cultural, ethnic, and linguistic groups. **Acculturation,** for example, is the extent to which members of one culture adapt to a new culture. In terms of acculturation, children tend to adapt more rapidly than their parents. Children, then, may assume roles such as shopping, managing money, or interacting with social institutions rather than with the parents. In addition, the cultural, ethnic, or linguistic group's prior history with regard to discrimination must be considered. For example, the families of Japanese Americans who were interned during World War II may be less likely to maintain their Japanese customs than Japanese Americans who lived in Hawaii, who were not interned. Families may not attend meetings if they have experienced discrimination or disrespect at any meetings or in individual interactions. The structure of the family also must be considered; in many cultures, the roles of the fathers, extended-family members, or elders may have a significant influence on who attends conferences and meetings, which family member should be addressed first, how family members should be addressed, or even seating arrangements.

The behavioral and developmental expectations of families vary according to their culture of origin. Children from culturally diverse families must develop **bicultural competence**, or an ability to function in both their home culture and their school culture. In some African American families, for example, it is important to be independent and assertive, whereas Asian American families may urge their children to defer to authority. Concern over whether children are reaching developmental milestones varies from culture to culture. Mexican American and Native American families, who encourage their children's emotional development and familial attachment more than achievement and competitiveness, tend to downplay efforts to help children reach milestones. Appropriate behavior, however, is expected of adults in these cultures. The degree of discipline that parents employ varies among families. Teachers must interact with parents in a nonjudgmental manner to identify and adapt interventions that while helping the child will not alienate the family. Family members' beliefs about the etiology of disability may also affect interactions with professionals. Problems may be perceived as extrinsic to the child or as the child's being out of harmony.

Salend and Taylor (1993) described linguistic patterns that must be considered when working with families from various cultural, ethnic, and linguistic groups. In communication patterns, personal space, eye contact, waiting time, voice quality, word choice, facial expressions, and touching all vary among ethnic, cultural, and linguistic groups. Meeting structures may need to be adjusted to respond to families' communication patterns. For example, people from some cultures may need little time to express themselves or chat; people from other cultures may prefer that the professional appear authoritative, competent, and reserved. Language differences may be compounded because educational jargon may not have counterparts in the parents' native language. In addition, Salend and Taylor suggested that socioeconomic factors must be considered in communicating with families from diverse cultural backgrounds. Families from minority cultural, ethnic, or linguistic groups are more likely to live in poverty than are members of the dominant culture. They may work long hours, experience many time conflicts and transportation problems, and have child care needs that make attending meetings difficult for them. In some families, parent training should be offered to extended-family members as well as to the immediate family. This training should be related to the family's needs. An ongoing goal should be empowering these families to address their children's needs in education and social service environments.

Thorp (1997) contended that teachers should examine their classroom environment and curriculum practices as these relate to students' cultural backgrounds. Teachers should create classroom and school environments in which all families feel welcome. All aspects of the environment should be evaluated to determine whether various cultures are represented in a stereotypic manner. All books, pictures, and resources should reflect cultural diversity. The "tourist approach" to cultures, restricting the celebration of community diversity to a designated cultural awareness week or heritage month, should be avoided. Rather, teachers should consider how families can be validated and supported in their roles of transmitting cultural learning and supporting children's cognitive development. Families can support the literacy of their children through their own stories, written or oral. Opportunities should be provided for families to link with each other and share sources of information.

Collaborating with parents should emphasize individualized programming. Shea and Bauer (1991) described a recursive system of family involvement in which the steps in the model are revisited as family collaboration develops over time. The phases include engaging in introductory activities and assessment of parent and family needs, selecting goals and objectives, planning and implementing activities, and evaluating activities. In the recursive system model, family collaboration is an ongoing process that continues until the student leaves the school or program.

Your Turn . . .

Reflect on yourself as a teacher. In which activities will you engage to increase the participation of parents and families? What are some of the challenges that will confront you as a teacher as you engage in these activities in an inclusive learning community?

SUMMARY

This chapter addresses the following major concepts:

1. With the increasing complexity of American society, families need more help in supporting their children's education.
2. Families are social systems that, while striving to maintain the status quo, are constantly undergoing change.
3. Most families of learners with disabilities are able to achieve a nearly typical lifestyle.
4. Parents have a legal right to direct involvement in educational decision making.
5. Communication with parents should be regular and meaningful and should provide a full exchange of information.
6. Recognizing the role of culture is essential in working with parents and families.

TEST YOUR KNOWLEDGE

Completion of the "Self-Evaluation," "Make the Language Your Own," and "Application Activities" sections will aid readers in understanding and retaining the information presented in this chapter. Answer keys for the "Self-Evaluation" and "Make the Language Your Own" sections are located in the Appendix at the end of the book.

Self-Evaluation

Select the most appropriate response to complete each of the following statements:

1. Because of the increased complexity of American society,
   a. Parents' responsibility for children has decreased
   b. Parents' parental authority has increased
   c. Socialization activities within the family have increased

2. Among families under stress,
   a. Child abuse is most common
   b. The presence of a good relationship with one parent reduces risk
   c. Foster care often provides stability for children

3. Like all social systems, families
   a. Strive to change
   b. Strive to remain the same
   c. Follow cause-and-effect patterns

4. When adjusting to the birth or diagnosis of a child with a disability, families
   a. Usually achieve a nearly typical lifestyle
   b. Progress through a predictable set of stages
   c. Become consumed by grief

5. The most common adaptation of families with members with disabilities is
   a. Crusadership
   b. Normalization
   c. Resignation

6. Parents usually
   a. Are satisfied when their children receive individual attention and care
   b. Resent special education services
   c. Want improved academic performance as a product of special services

7. Parents' stress related to their children's disabilities is related to
   a. The severity of the child's disability
   b. The parents' personality and coping skills
   c. Special education placement

8. As a result of IDEA, the role of parents is that of
   a. Consultant
   b. Expert adviser
   c. Decision maker

9. Parents' involvement is related to
   a. The severity of their children's disabilities
   b. How schools encourage participation
   c. Parents' levels of education
10. By junior high school, most family–school interactions are
   a. Negative
   b. Positive
   c. Nonexistent

Make the Language Your Own

Match the following terms with their definitions:

1. _____ Conferences

2. _____ Acculturation

3. _____ Foster care

4. _____ Normalization

5. _____ Family

6. _____ Bicultural competence

7. _____ Empowerment

a. A social system composed of two or more interdependent members who engage in reciprocal interactions over time

b. An ability to function in both the home culture and the school culture

c. The extent to which members of one culture adapt to a new culture

d. A group of processes and activities that involve people in determining their own futures

e. Focused conversations regarding a student's participation in the school environment

f. A planned, temporary placement of a child in out-of-home service for the purpose of strengthening the natural family

g. The belief that families with learners who vary from their peers should function in as typical a manner as they desire and as is possible

Application Activities

1. Interview the parent of a child with a disability regarding the family's adaptation to the child's disability.
2. Discuss with a teacher the way in which he or she prepares for parent–teacher conferences. What are his or her goals for these conferences? What materials does he or she provide to parents?

REFERENCES

Allen, D.A., & Affleck, G. (1985). Are we stereotyping parents?: A postscript to Blacher. *Mental Retardation, 23,* 200–202.

Balcazar, F., Seekins, T., Fawcett, S., & Hopkins, B. (1990). Empowering people with physical disabilities through advocacy skills training. *American Journal of Community Psychology, 18,* 281–296.

Blacher, J. (1984). Sequential stages of parental adjustment to the birth of a child with handicaps: Fact or artifact. *Mental Retardation, 22*(2), 55–68.

Bradshaw, J. (1978). Tracing the causes of stress in families with handicapped children. *British Journal of Social Work, 8,* 181–192.

Children's Defense Fund. (1996). *The state of America's children yearbook.* Washington, DC: Author.

Coleman, J. (1987). Families and schools. *Educational Researcher, 165*(6), 32–38.

Comer, J.P. (1988). Educating poor minority children. *Scientific American, 259*(5), 42–48.

Dauber, S.L., & Epstein, J.L. (1993). Parents' attitudes and practices of involvement in inner-city elementary and middle schools. In N. Chavkin (Ed.), *Families and schools in a pluralistic society* (pp. 53–72). Albany: State University of New York Press.

DiCocco, B.E. (1986) A guide to family/school interventions for the family therapist. *Contemporary Family Therapy, 8,* 50–61.

Frey, K.S., Greenberg, M.T., & Fewell, R.R. (1989). Stress and coping among parents of handicapped children. A multidimensional approach. *American Journal of Mental Retardation, 94,* 240–249.

Gerry, M. (1987). How parents and educators make decisions together and how disputes arise. *News Digest, 7,* 1–7.

Green, S.K., & Shinn, M.R. (1995). Parent attitudes about special education and reintegration: What is the role of student outcomes? *Exceptional Children, 61*(3), 269–281.

Guidubaldi, J., & Perry, J.D. (1985). Divorce and mental health sequelae for children: A two-year follow-up of a nationwide sample. *Journal of the American Academy of Child Psychiatry, 24,* 531–537.

Harry, B. (1992). Restructuring the participation of African-American parents in special education. *Exceptional Children, 59,* 123–131.

Hinderliter, K. (1988). Death of a dream. *Exceptional Parent, 18*(1), 48–49.

Individuals with Disabilities Education Act (IDEA) of 1990, PL 101-476, 20 U.S.C. § 1400 *et seq.*

Johnston, J.C., & Zemitzsch, A. (1988). Family power: An intervention beyond the classroom. *Behavioral Disorders, 14*(1), 69–79.

Koch, A. (1982, November). *Conceptualizing family stress: A systemic revision of Hill's ABCX model.* Paper presented at the annual meeting of the National Council on Family Relations, Washington, DC.

Kroth, R.L., & Otteni, H. (1985). *Communicating with parents of exceptional children: Improving parent–teacher relationships* (2nd ed.). Denver: Love Publishing Co.

Marion, R. (1979). Minority parent involvement in the IEP process: A systematic model approach. *Focus on Exceptional Children, 10*(8), 1–15.

Miller, S.P., & Hudson, P. (1994). Using structured parent groups to provide parental support. *Intervention in School and Clinic, 29*(3), 151–155.

Minuchin, S. (1974). *Families and family therapy.* Cambridge, MA: Harvard University Press.

Mlawler, M.A. (1993). Who should fight? Parents and the advocacy expectation. *Journal of Disability Policy Studies, 4*(1), 105–116.

National Parent Teacher Association. (1997). *Teacher's guide to parent and family involvement.* Chicago: Author.

Parker, S., Greer, S., & Zuckerman, B. (1988). Double jeopardy: The impact of poverty on early child development. *Pediatric Clinics of North America, 35,* 1227–1240.

Puma, M.J., Jones, C.C., Rock, D., & Fernandez, R. (1993, May). *Prospects: The Congressionally mandated study of growth and opportunity* (Interim rep.). Bethesda, MD: ABT Associates.

Rutherford, R.B., Jr., & Edgar, E. (1979). *Teachers and parents: A guide to interaction and cooperation* (Abr. ed.). Needham Heights, MA: Allyn & Bacon.

Salend, S.J., & Taylor, L. (1993). Working with families: A cross-cultural perspective. *Remedial and Special Education, 14*(5), 25–32.

Schorr, E.L. (1988). Foster care. *Pediatric Clinics of North America, 35*(6), 1241–1252.

Seligman, M., & Darling, L.B. (1989). *Ordinary families, special children.* New York: Guilford Press.

Shea, T.M., & Bauer, A.M. (1991). *Parents and teachers of children with exceptionali-
ties: A handbook for collaboration* (2nd ed.). Needham Heights, MA: Allyn & Bacon.

Silver, J.A., Amster, B.J., & Haecker, T. (1999). *Young children and foster care: A guide
for professionals.* Baltimore: Paul H. Brookes Publishing Co.

Thompson, L., Lobbs, C., Elling, R., Herman, S., Jurkiewicz, T., & Hulleza, C. (1997).
Pathways to family empowerment: Effects of family-centered delivery of early intervention service. *Exceptional Children, 64,* 99–113.

Thorp, E.K. (1997). Increasing opportunities for partnership with culturally and lin-
guistically diverse families. *Intervention in School and Clinic, 32*(5), 261–269.

Wallerstein, J., & Blakeslee, S. (1989). *Second chances: Men, women, and children a
decade after divorce.* New York: Ticknor & Fields.

Assessment and Evaluation

I know it may not be the sort of thing a "good" parent may say, but I dread coming to school to review how my child is doing. Marco is a good boy; he tries, he is wonderful with younger kids, he almost seems to feel what they need. He's been babysitting since he was 11, and he's the most responsible child you'd want. But when I come to school, I get this shopping list—he can't do this, he can't do that. Tell me what he can do—tell me where to go from here. Tell me how you're going to help him. I know what he can't do. I live with him.

Latricia, parent of a 15-year-old student
receiving special education services

This chapter discusses in detail assessment and evaluation, two topics that are essential to the provision of effective and efficient services for learners with disabilities in inclusive school environments. The chapter begins with a thorough discussion of the role of assessment and evaluation in inclusive school environments. Strategies applied in ecological assessment are reviewed in the second section of the chapter. Next, the use of portfolios and "A Day's Worth of Work" as techniques for assessing student progress are explained. The applications and advantages of curriculum-based assessment, rubrics, and similar strategies to evaluate students' content area learning are reviewed in some detail. Functional assessment is discussed as a useful technique to ascertain students' readiness to live and work in the community. The final section of the chapter reviews the controversial topics of testing and assigning grades to learners with disabilities in inclusive classrooms. Each of the assessment and evaluation strategies discussed in the chapter is supported with an example.

LEARNING OBJECTIVES

After completing this chapter, readers will be able to

1. Discuss the role of assessment and evaluation in inclusive classrooms
2. Describe ecological assessments and strategies
3. Use portfolios and "A Day's Worth of Work" to assess students' progress
4. Use curriculum-based assessment, rubrics, and other strategies to measure content area learning in inclusive environments
5. Use functional assessment strategies in the classroom
6. Recognize issues related to testing and assigning report card grades in inclusive classrooms

KEY WORDS AND PHRASES

assessment—the process by which needed changes in the learner's behaviors or environments are identified

curriculum-based assessment—the evaluation of instructional needs through ongoing measurement of students' performance within the local school curriculum

ecological assessment—assessment that addresses the impact of the environment on students' behavior and performance

functional assessment—the assessment of outcomes related to

living and working as part of the community

grade—an arbitrary symbol reflecting a value judgment concerning the relative quality of a student's achievement

observation—systematically collecting data about behavior in specific environments by watching and recording events

portfolio—a systematically organized collection of evidence for monitoring children's growth and development

rating scales—checklists and standardized rating forms

review of records—the process of reviewing previous grades, assessment findings, attendance records, and other information

rubric—a scaled set of criteria

LEARNING OBJECTIVE 1: To be able to discuss the role of assessment and evaluation in inclusive classrooms

This book describes **assessment** in terms of what is often referred to as *assessment for intervention*. The primary purpose of assessment for intervention is to identify changes that are needed in the learner's behavior or environments and decide how to accomplish the goals of the needed changes (Barnett et al., 1997). Assessment for intervention, however, has been seriously neglected. Dunlap and Childs (1996), in their review of 13 years of intervention research, reported that interventions were rarely individualized or based on assessment data. In fact, they found that interventions often were designed independent of any assessment information about students.

According to the National Center for Fair and Open Testing (1989), more than 1 million standardized tests were administered annually to public school students in the 1980s. Although standardized tests are useful for planning and intervention purposes, teachers should keep in mind the following assumptions underlying appropriate assessment:

- Differences among learners derive their meanings from the situations in which they occur.
- Tests are samples of behavior; decisions cannot be based on test results alone.
- The purpose of assessment is to improve instruction or the planning of the intervention.
- Assessment must be conducted by well-prepared, knowledgeable professionals.
- No assessment strategy is free from errors (Witt, Elliott, Kramer, & Gresham, 1994).

Canter and colleagues (1994) described several methods of assessment. Tests and **rating scales** include any standardized instrument used for obtaining a sample of behavior that typically results in a score. Tests and rating scales may be standardized, norm-referenced, or standardized methods for collecting **curriculum-based assessments** or for conducting **portfolio** assessments or performance-based assessments. Rating scales may include checklists and standardized rating forms to be completed by parents, teachers, or the students themselves.

Another method of assessment that Canter and colleagues described was a **review of records.** A *review of records* refers to any method of reviewing existing student data sources or permanent products for pertinent information about present concerns. Review of records includes review of previous **grades,** previous assessment findings, attendance records, records of intervention outcomes, responses to services received, and examination of classroom and homework assignments. **Observation**, a third method of assessment, is carried out by systematically collecting data about behaviors in specific situations or environments by watching and recording events. Interviewing, another method, refers to using informants to collect perspectives concerning students' behaviors, situations, and environments.

A comprehensive assessment system has several characteristics. Comprehensive assessment uses multiple data sources in multiple domains and multiple environments across time. Canter and colleagues urged that any assessment plan link assessment to students' needs and to interventions. Assessment should serve as a means of monitoring progress toward outcomes and encouraging greater participation and collaboration among parents and professionals during the assessment process. Assessment should be a data-driven process in which a wide range of traditional and innovative techniques are systematically selected to address comprehensively the particular needs of the individual (Canter et al., 1994). Assessment is most effective when it includes a systematic search for those supports, services, and interventions that allow learners to make meaningful progress in their present and future environments.

Answering the "how" of assessment requires first determining "what," or the purpose of assessment. Redding (1992) described the "big outcomes" or goals of education, all of which should be considered in inclusive school environments. These "big outcomes" include encouraging students to become self-directed learners who are collaborative workers, complex thinkers, quality producers, and community contributors. In addition, teachers should engage in self-assessment to determine whether their personal activities are addressing these future-oriented outcomes. Redding's (1992) outcomes and their component skills are provided in Table 1.

In the 1990s, assessment has begun to shift from traditional, norm-referenced, standardized testing to performance assessment. Performance assessment allows students to demonstrate their knowledge in thoughtful ways in a number of contexts. Various forms of performance assessment include 1) authentic assessment, in which students apply their knowledge to challenging, real-life situations; and 2) portfolio assessment (Darling-Hammond, Ancess, & Falk, 1995). Performance assessment can have a positive impact in inclusive classrooms. Authentic assessments expose students to real-life experiences, allowing them to rehearse a variety of real-life situations. Performance assessment increases the ways in which students can demonstrate their knowledge (Fuchs, 1994). Such assessment may increase a sense of accomplishment and independence among learners (Darling-Hammond et al., 1995). The portfolio as an assessment technique is discussed in a subsequent section of this chapter.

LEARNING OBJECTIVE 2: To be able to describe ecological assessments and strategies

The systems perspective presented in this book recognizes that learning does not take place in a vacuum. Rather, a student's behavior in the classroom

Table 1. The "big outcomes" of education in inclusive school environments

Students should become

1. Self-directed learners who can
   - Set personal priorities and attainable goals
   - Monitor and evaluate progress
   - Generate opinions
   - Assume personal responsibility
   - Create a positive vision for themselves and their future

2. Collaborative workers who can
   - Monitor personal behavior as group members
   - Assess and manage group functioning
   - Demonstrate interactive communication
   - Demonstrate consideration for diversity

3. Complex thinkers who can
   - Use a wide variety of strategies for managing issues
   - Select strategies appropriate to the resolution of issues
   - Accurately and thoroughly apply strategies
   - Access and use relevant knowledge

4. Quality producers who can create products that
   - Achieve their purposes
   - Are appropriate for the intended audience
   - Employ resources and technology

5. Community contributors who
   - Demonstrate knowledge about their communities
   - Take action
   - Reflect on the role of community contributor

Source: Redding (1992).

takes place in a complex developmental context in which many variables interact to support the student's behavior. In order to determine the impact that factors in the instructional environment have on students' performance, **ecological assessment** techniques are applied (Graden, Casey, & Christensen, 1986). Welch (1994) suggested that ecological assessment is collaborative in nature because it requires ongoing communication between the individuals who work and live with the child. He suggested informal classroom environment inventories that can be designed individually to address the "who, what, where, when, and why" of activities in the classroom.

For example, assume that Luisa, a fourth grader, is having difficulty during social studies. In order to gather more information on the problem, her teacher devised the worksheet shown in Figure 1. Using this worksheet, Luisa's teacher was able to identify some of the complex issues that contributed to Luisa's difficulties in that subject area. By using the worksheet, Luisa's support teacher was able to identify several issues or concerns and areas for potential intervention. The teacher, who had taught older students previously, may have expectations for her present students that are slightly beyond Luisa's ability to perform. By discussing Luisa's maturity level and development, the teacher may have a better understanding of how to adapt to her needs. The teacher relies heavily on the text, manual, work-

Problem: Luisa's behavior and learning in social studies

Who?   Teacher is new to fourth grade and usually teaches sixth grade.
                        Luisa has experienced difficulty in adapting to departmentalization.
                        Luisa does not have an identified "study buddy," because her teacher
                          believes having Luisa have a partner is disruptive.

What?   Materials include textbook and accompanying student workbook, atlas, and
                          student folders.
                        Student workbook requires a great deal of inference; students must draw
                          conclusions; workbook pages are assigned as independent work or for
                          homework.
                        Teacher uses tests that come with the text, which are in multiple-choice,
                          fill-in-the-blank, and short-essay test formats.

Where?   Teacher has positioned Luisa front and center and has reported that Luisa's
                          attention is better since she has moved her to this position; teacher uses a
                          signal system with Luisa so that Luisa knows when her turn to read is
                          coming up.

When?   Social studies immediately follows lunch; Luisa may be having a difficult time
                          cuing back in to work.

Why?   Luisa is not completing workbook sheets (is 8–10 pages behind), has not
                          turned in an outline for her long-term project, and is not doing well on unit
                          tests.

Figure 1.   Sample ecobehavioral checklist for Luisa.

book, and tests in the social studies series. Again, adaptations may not only help Luisa but also support the learning of her peers. Although the time when the class occurs cannot be changed, recognizing that Luisa may have difficulty in shifting gears may help the teacher understand her difficulties in attending. The teacher has devised a way to keep Luisa engaged and on the right page, even though the teacher does not want Luisa to use a partner during her class.

The ecobehavioral interview is another common ecological assessment strategy. Barnett, Carey, and Hall (1993) described two important functions of the ecobehavioral interview. First, the interview can be used to develop detailed descriptions of behaviors across environments, clarifying the concerns of teachers and helping them to develop the intervention plans. Teachers use interviews to gather information on events such as entering school, class activities, transitions, and lunchtime. Second, the ecobehavioral interview can be used to analyze specific situations in depth, helping to identify key people, environments, times, and circumstances related to the issue of concern.

Wahler and Cormier (1970) conducted early work in the development of the ecobehavioral interview. The interview was designed to determine the specific behavior of concern and the contexts in which the behavior occurs. Prior to the interview itself, the teacher or the parents are provided with a behavior checklist to complete. This information is brought to the interview for discussion. During the interview, the consultant determines the social contingencies that are maintaining the behavior problems, the people providing those contingencies, and how they are provided. A sample school behavior checklist is presented in Figure 2.

In the case of Luisa, an ecobehavioral interview could show that across several environments, Luisa is demonstrating similar problems. When she arrives at school, Luisa experiences difficulty in finding the materials in her book bag that she needs for the morning and in being ready for morning work with her peers. In social studies, she is having difficulty in finding the appropriate page and staying with the group. At lunchtime, she frequently forgets an item in the lunch line, and, after she makes several return trips for a spoon, a napkin, and a straw, for example, she has little time to eat. She frequently forgets to bring her physical education uniform to school. By assessing Luisa's behavior across several school environments, a keystone behavior, that of organization, emerges as Luisa's primary problem. Looking at Luisa's entire day helps her teachers develop a plan for intervention with Luisa that can be applied across several subject areas and activities.

 LEARNING OBJECTIVE 3: To be able to use portfolios and "A Day's Worth of Work" to assess students' progress

The purpose of a portfolio is to showcase learning (Keefe, 1994). Portfolios are a collection of evidence that is systematically collected and organized in some way and used by both teacher and student to monitor the student's growth and development (Vavus, 1990). The purpose of the portfolio is to document students' progress over an extended period of time, usually the academic year (Hamm & Adams, 1991).

Wesson and King (1996) described several advantages of portfolios. Portfolios are formative and allow the teacher and the student to monitor the student's progress over the course of the school year. They provide a way for students to assess and reflect on their growth. Through portfolios, students assume ownership of their learning and are encouraged to become more invested in their learning. Finally, portfolios emphasize the breadth and scope of learning, which is a more sensitive approach to student growth than a list of a limited set of learned skills.

A portfolio is not simply a collection of a student's work; rather, a portfolio is organized around a focus or guidelines. Portfolios, which typically belong to students, are kept in the classroom and are shared with parents, peers, and teachers (Goerss, 1993). Goerss, in her work with teachers who were using portfolios, identified several themes surrounding the development and use of portfolios. Teachers emphasized the importance of a clear purpose and identifiable objectives in the portfolio. They indicated that, at times, they had difficulty in relinquishing control over students' choices and grading every paper. One of the greatest challenges that the teachers described was the time that they needed for review of the portfolios submitted at the end of a marking period.

Portfolios may include a wide range of materials. Sample items may include an audiotape or videotape of the student reading, presenting, or inter-

School Behavior Checklist

This checklist allows teachers to describe a student's behavior in various environments. On the left-hand side of the checklist, list specific activities or environments. On the righthand side of the checklist, write a description of the student's behavior during that activity or in the environment.

Bus or transportation behavior

Arriving at school

Morning work

Transitions between periods,
    lessons, and activities

Recess

Lunch

"Specials" (art, music,
    physical education)

Moving in the hall

Rest room

Large-group instruction

Small-group work

Independent work

Figure 2. Sample school behavior checklist.

acting with other students; a checklist of skills that the student has learned; the student's reading journal for the subject that lists his or her outside reading and opinions; copies of stories, including drafts; pictures of projects; notes that the teacher has made in conference with the student; or the student's learning log. The most common portfolios, and perhaps the most comfortable for beginning teachers, are those related to language arts.

To initiate the portfolio assessment process, the teacher writes a note, such as the following sample, to the students, reminding them of the impending portfolio due date:

Dear students,

We are approaching the end of this grading period, and it is time for you to evaluate your work. In a letter to your portfolio reviewers (two students and me, your teacher), answer these questions:

- What is in your portfolio?
- What does your portfolio show about you as a reader and writer?
- Which item in the portfolio do you think represents your best work?
- What challenges are you facing as a reader and writer?
- What are your plans for meeting these challenges?
- What are your goals for next quarter?

In addition to their letter to the reviewers, students are often provided with self-evaluation materials. An example of these materials is provided in Figure 3.

Another helpful technique for organizing the portfolio is providing a caption for each of the portfolio items (Swicegood, 1994). The caption describes the item and its significance to the portfolio. For example, a writing sample could be captioned, "Student was able to identify the sentence fragment after reading the writing sample out loud." A caption for a spelling test could include a statement such as, "After erasing the first three words and rewriting them several times, the student missed the fourth and fifth words. These words were provided after the other students completed the test." The caption can provide a necessary context for each item in a portfolio.

Remember that a portfolio is more than a simple collection of work. Swicegood (1994) offered a variety of examples of portfolios, each with a specific purpose:

- Goal-based portfolios provide a concrete display of a learner's best work and a concrete view of the learner's development.
- Activity-based portfolios display the range of learning experiences or activities in which the student has engaged.
- Reflective portfolios provide a way for the student and the teacher to reflect on learning goals, including attitudes, knowledge, and strategies.
- Dialogue portfolios encourage discussion and collaboration among educators and between the teacher and the student.

Some of Swicegood's suggestions for developing a portfolio are presented in Table 2. Swicegood also suggested that the individualized education pro-

Personal Assessment of Portfolio

Student's name: _____

Your portfolio consists of all writing assignments (including drafts) that you have completed this quarter, your reading log, and all language arts assignments and projects. This form will help you monitor your portfolio and determine your strengths and weaknesses in language arts.

I. Respond to each statement:

My portfolio contains all of the required items. If no, why not?	Yes	No
My portfolio shows that I have improved. If no, why not?	Yes	No
My portfolio demonstrates that I can write accurate directions. If no, why not?	Yes	No
My portfolio shows that I reflect on my reading. If no, why not?	Yes	No
My portfolio demonstrates that I can write effectively. If no, why not?	Yes	No
My portfolio demonstrates that I can think and write creatively. If no, why not?	Yes	No

II. In assessing my overall portfolio, I find it to be [*circle one*]

Very satisfactory   Satisfactory   Somewhat satisfactory   Unsatisfactory

My goals and strategies for next quarter are:

Goals	Strategies
1.	1.
2.	2.
3.	3.

Student's comments:

Reviewer A comments:

Reviewer B comments:

Reviewer C comments:

Figure 3.   Sample portfolio self-evaluation form.

Table 2.   Possible items for student portfolios

1. Indicators of behavioral and adaptive functioning, including
    • Anecdotal records
    • Behavior checklists
    • Interviews about interests, motivation, and attributions
    • Videotapes of student behaviors
2. Indicators of academic and literacy growth, including
    • Criterion-referenced tests
    • Curriculum-based assessments
    • Teacher-created tests
    • Analysis of oral reading
    • Writing samples
    • Photographs of student projects
3. Indicators of strategies and self-management, including
    • Checklists of skills or strategies
    • Student self-evaluations
    • Interviews with the student about his or her performance
    • Student "think aloud"
4. Indicators of language and culture, including
    • Cultural interviews with the student and the student's parents
    • Primary language sample
    • Observations
    • Simulations and role-plays

Source: Swicegood (1994).

gram (IEP) be linked to a student's portfolio. Portfolio components, including work products that show progress toward the IEP objectives, can be evaluated by reviewing the portfolio. Periodic conferences regarding the portfolio can then assist the student in becoming more accountable for progress toward his or her objectives.

In summary, portfolios can function both as a student's résumé and as a way to demonstrate growth (Nolet, 1992). Portfolios

- Include samples of students' work collected over time
- Employ data generated in several ways under a variety of conditions, all of which pertain to performance in a specific skill or content area
- Include tasks that are regularly performed in natural contexts
- Include at least two types of data: raw data (i.e., work samples) and summarizing data (i.e., teacher's and student's comments)
- Involve at least some degree of student participation (Nolet, 1992)

Another application of the portfolio concept is "A Day's Worth of Work." For this portfolio, a teacher simply collects all of the materials, projects, papers, and activities that a student has produced during 1 day. Through this collection, a teacher is able to describe better the student's task engagement and completion and participation in class. In addition, "A Day's Worth of Work" is helpful when sharing information with parents regarding a student's performance in a classroom.

Your Turn . . .

Select one content area for a specific grade level. Review a curriculum for this content area. Looking at one unit or objective, what are some of the items that could be included in a student's portfolio to demonstrate that the student has accomplished the objective?

LEARNING OBJECTIVE 4: To be able to use curriculum-based assessment, rubrics, and other strategies to measure content area learning in inclusive environments

One of the challenges confronting teachers in inclusive learning communities is that of content area assessment. Weekly quizzes, multiple-choice tests, and teachers' questions may not provide an accurate measure of a student's content area learning. Several strategies, including curriculum-based assessment and rubrics, have emerged as promising ways to assess content area learning.

Curriculum-Based Assessment

Curriculum-based assessment is the evaluation of instructional needs through ongoing measurement of student performance in the local school curriculum (Fuchs, Fuchs, & Hamlett, 1989). Curriculum-based assessment subsumes a variety of practices.

Curriculum-based assessments are developed directly from a school district's curriculum (Paulsen, 1997). For example, Paulsen developed a series of curriculum-based measures from the reading series used by the school district. The measures included

- *Reading fluency,* which is evaluated by having students read a passage aloud and determining the number of words read per minute
- *Reading comprehension,* which involves students' filling in the blanks in sentences from stories so that the sentences make sense
- *Word recognition,* which involves asking students to read from flash cards

Curriculum-based assessment can be thought of as testing what is taught.

Rubrics

A **rubric** is a scaled set of criteria that clearly communicates to both the student and the teacher the range of acceptable and unacceptable performance in a particular skill or activity. Each criterion includes a description of the level of performance and an assigned value (Herman, Aschbacher, & Winters, 1992). Rubrics can be applied to the learning process as well as to content and can be presented prior to the beginning of a unit or activity to clarify the teacher's expectations.

Pate, Homestead, and McGinnis (1993) maintained that rubrics should provide sufficient detail so that there are few questions regarding the student's performance. In developing a rubric, they suggested the guidelines presented in Table 3. A sample rubric is presented in Figure 4.

In the example presented in Figure 4, the teacher has developed with the students a rubric for book sharing in the fourth-grade classroom. The teacher began developing the rubric by providing the students with an outline of the areas of book sharing that she believed were important, that is, basic information; information about genre; characters, setting, and plot; eye contact and posture; and organization and time. The teacher asked the students to describe the performance needed in each of these areas to earn a grade of "Excellent" or "A." The teacher then asked the students to describe the performance necessary in each area to earn a grade of "Unacceptable." With the students, the teacher then developed the two intermediate steps of performance between "Excellent" and "Unacceptable." The weight to be assigned to each of the levels of performance was then determined by the teacher and the students.

Your Turn . . .

Identify an activity, assignment, or project that you have observed being used with students. What are the areas of performance important to this activity, assignment, or project? What would be the top level of performance? How would unsatisfactory performance be measured? Using this information, develop a rubric for the activity, assignment, or project.

Table 3.   Guidelines for developing a rubric

---

1.   List the most important parts of a learning activity. Use this list to develop rubric
     sections, including process, content, mechanics, presentation, source variety, and
     neatness.
2.   List in each of the sections the behavior that earns an excellent or "A" perfor-
     mance, then list in each of the sections the behavior that would be unsatisfactory.
     Generate intermediate levels of performance.
3.   Assign weights to the rubric sections if appropriate. Assign the greatest amount of
     weight to each of the rubric sections.

Other Strategies

There are other strategies that can be applied on a daily basis to assess students' performance in content areas. Espin and Foegen (1996) explored the validity of three such strategies: vocabulary, comprehension, and maze. In vocabulary, students were quizzed regarding the vocabulary that was unique to
the unit or subunit being studied. Comprehension measures involved asking
students questions after they had read a section without instruction. In addition to daily testing, comprehension measures required a 1-week posttest. The
third strategy was called *maze*. In maze, after the first sentence in the passage, every seventh word was deleted and replaced with a multiple-choice
item. If the student understood the content, he or she would be able to answer
with the correct item. After employing these strategies, Espin and Foegen
found that all were valid predictors of student performance on comprehension
questions, daily tests, and posttests. Vocabulary, however, added significantly
to the prediction of content area success and was the strongest predictor of student performance. They suggested that vocabulary may be a good way to measure content area learning.

**LEARNING OBJECTIVE 5: To be able to use functional assessment
strategies in the classroom**

Functional assessment is grounded in functional outcomes of education—
those outcomes related to living and working as part of the community. Clark
(1994) suggested a series of questions for reflection to determine whether information or skills are functional:

- Is the content appropriate for meeting the student's personal, social, daily
  living, or vocational needs?
- Does the content focus on knowledge and information needed for the student to live independently?
- Is the content part of a scope and sequence toward the student's future
  needs?
- Do the student's parents think the content is important for the student's
  current and future needs?
- Does the student think the content is important for his or her current and
  future needs?
- Is the content appropriate for the student's chronological age and current
  performance?
- What will happen if the student does not learn the concepts and skills?

Category	Criterion 1	Criterion 2	Criterion 3	Criterion 4	Score x Weight = Total
Basic information	Does not name author or title	Names either title or author but not both	Names title and author	Names title, author, other books by same author	__ x 3 =
Information about genre	Does not name genre	Names genre but no reasons	Names genre and one reason	Names genre and two or more reasons	__ x 3 =
Characters, setting, and plot	Names some characters but does not describe setting or plot	Names characters; unclear about plot	Names characters, mentions setting, and briefly describes plot	Describes characters, lays out story line clearly, and indicates why setting is important to story	__ x 5 =
Eye contact and posture	Rarely; slouches, fidgets	Not often; sometimes slouches	Stands straight and makes frequent eye contact		__ x 2 =
Organization and time	Audience could not follow; less than 5 minutes	Interesting but not logical; 5–7 minutes	Interesting and logical; 7–9 minutes	Interesting, logical, and entertaining; 10+ minutes	__ x 5 =
					TOTAL =

Figure 4.   Sample rubric.

Functional assessment is also applicable in the inclusive classroom. The skills and information that a student needs to function independently may be taught and maintained in an inclusive environment by using the general education curriculum as the means rather than the ends of instruction. Field, LeRoy, and Rivera (1994) developed a matrix to depict the "how" and "where" of the functional goals and objectives of a student's IEP. For example, the functional skill "turn taking" can be practiced during several daily activities, including playing a game, answering a question in response to the teacher, and waiting in line for a drink.

Making Action Plans (MAPS) (Pearpoint, Forest, & O'Brien, 1996) is one strategy for identifying functional goals for the student. By asking the following questions, MAPS focuses the discussion of the education team providing support for the student on the student and the student's family, friends, and significant others:

- What is the student's history?
- What is your dream for the student?
- What is your nightmare for the student?
- Who is the student?
- What are the student's strengths, gifts, and abilities?
- What are the student's needs?

Visits to classrooms, schools, and vocational environments that the student may attend in the future can be helpful in determining what will be functionally appropriate for the student.

 LEARNING OBJECTIVE 6: To be able to recognize issues related to testing and assigning report card grades in inclusive classrooms

As more U.S. states and Canadian provinces require proficiency testing, questions regarding the participation of students with disabilities in these tests have emerged. Each student's IEP should contain a statement indicating whether the student will participate in the state and district testing programs, which areas are appropriate for testing, modifications in testing procedure required, and a justification for the decision related to participation. The Wisconsin Department of Public Instruction (1996) developed a series of questions for teachers and administrators to use when determining whether proficiency testing is appropriate for a student:

- Are the goals for the student similar to those covered by the proficiency test?
- Will the student be presented with material similar to the material on the test?
- Is the student's reading level similar to that of students in the general education program?
- Can the student read the test materials?
- Is the student motivated to do well on the test?
- Is the student motivated to participate in the test with his or her unidentified peers?
- Will modifications enhance his or her ability to take the test?

The student should participate in proficiency testing to the extent that the responses to these questions are positive. Some parts of the testing program may be appropriate for the student, and some parts may not, however.

Although raised for proficiency-testing programs, the suggestions that the Wisconsin Department of Public Instruction made would be appropriate for a variety of testing sessions in which students with disabilities participate along with their unidentified peers. These suggestions are summarized in Table 4.

Although these modifications may support learners with disabilities, attending to format issues and the presentations of test items and directions can be of assistance to all learners. Salend (1995) suggested that teachers can minimize format problems by making sure that tests

- Include only necessary information
- Are clearly and darkly printed on plain paper
- Are typed or written in a type font with which the student is familiar

- Have items that are properly spaced and sequenced
- Do not require students to transfer answers to a separate sheet
- Present questions in a predictable sequence that support transition
- Provide adequate space for response

Cues can be embedded in the format of the test to help learners with disabilities comprehend and comply with directions. For example, the word *Circle* in the direction *Circle the correct response* is itself circled. A model for each item can be presented in a box to identify a new type of item that is being presented. Stop signs can be used to indicate the end of a section.

Multiple-choice questions, often used in the middle and upper grades, can be constructed to increase students' understanding by making

1. Item stems and choices grammatically correct and free of double negatives
2. Response choices shorter than item stem
3. Item stems relate to only one major point and contain only the information needed to answer the question
4. Only one correct response
5. Presenting choices in a vertical format

Matching items also can be formatted to enhance students' performance. Wood (1988) contended that there should be no more than 10 item pairs in lists of matching questions. The list of matching questions should contain an equal number of choices in both columns. Both columns of the matching list should be on the same page.

Report Card Grades

Assigning grades is a persistent challenge in inclusive classrooms. Rojewski, Pollard, and Meers (1990) defined grades as arbitrary symbols reflecting a stu-

Table 4. Modifications for testing situations

Time	• Use shorter testing sessions.
	• Provide more breaks or rest periods.
	• Administer the test during the time the student is most likely to do well.
	• Allow additional time to complete the test.
Environment	• Administer tests in small groups or individually.
	• Allow the student to complete the test in a study carrel.
	• Allow the student to work in the place in the room where he or she is most comfortable.
	• Allow someone other than the teacher to administer the test.
Format	• Enlarge print.
	• Use braille or recorded questions.
	• Provide additional practice tests or examples.
	• Assist the student in tracking items by pointing to the items or placing the student's finger on the items.
	• Use a paper mask so that the student sees only one item at a time.
	• Use American Sign Language instructions or directions.
	• Use the technology that the student uses for other tests and schoolwork.
Recording	• Have someone record the student's responses.
	• Use a computer board, communication board, tape recorder, or computer to record the student's responses.

Source: Wisconsin Department of Public Instruction (1996).

dent's quality of work. They are a value judgment concerning the relative quality of a student's achievement. Rojewski and colleagues described the following grading practices:

- Traditional grading (i.e., A, B, C, D)
- Pass or fail (i.e., student has or has not met predetermined standards)
- Checklists (i.e., listings of skills)
- Contract grading (i.e., an agreement for a predetermined grade by student and teacher)
- Narratives (i.e., a written description)
- Blanket grades (i.e., all students receive the same grade)

In a national survey of classroom practices (Bursuck et al., 1996), teachers reported that letter and number grades were more helpful for students without disabilities and pass-or-fail grades and checklists were more helpful for students with disabilities. Many teachers modified the criteria on which grades for students with disabilities were based, including effort, improvement on IEP objectives, and adjusting grades according to ability. Across all grade levels, homework, tests, and quizzes accounted for most of the students' grades.

Rojewski and colleagues found six practices and techniques successful for grading learners with disabilities. First, there should be individualization and modification of instruction techniques and evaluation based on the students' abilities. Second, teaching and evaluation methods should be flexible. Third, special educators and other support staff should collaborate on behalf of the student. Fourth, prestated objectives, competencies, and standards should be used. Fifth, multiple evaluation methods should be employed. Finally, positive aspects of performance should be emphasized with students and parents.

Teachers must protect the confidentiality of their students' grades. Students should not be required to read aloud their grade for the teacher (Friedman, 1996). Students should not be forced to share personal assessment information with their peers by posting papers with grades or by listing grades in any way.

SUMMARY

This chapter addresses the following major concepts:

1. The primary purpose of assessment for intervention is to identify changes needed in the learner's behavior or environments and determine how to accomplish the goals of those changes.
2. Ecobehavioral assessment is used to describe the impact of the instruction environment on students' performance and behavior.
3. Portfolios may be used by both the teacher and the student to monitor the student's growth and development.
4. Curriculum-based assessment, developed directly from the school district's curriculum, is designed to measure what is taught.
5. Rubrics are used in communicating to both student and teacher detailed information regarding the student's performance.
6. Functional assessment emphasizes the functional outcomes of education—those outcomes related to living and working as part of the community.
7. Modifications for testing and grade assignment can benefit all learners in the inclusive classroom.

TEST YOUR KNOWLEDGE

Completion of the "Self-Evaluation," "Make the Language Your Own," and "Application Activities" sections will aid readers in understanding and retaining the information presented in this chapter. Answer keys for the "Self-Evaluation" and "Make the Language Your Own" sections are located in the Appendix at the end of the book.

Self-Evaluation

Select the most appropriate response to complete each of the following statements:

1. The reason for assessing students is to
   a. Document the need for additional supports
   b. Identify changes needed in the environment and how to accomplish those changes
   c. Document lack of progress

2. Comprehensive assessment
   a. Identifies a strong tool and uses it across all areas
   b. Uses multiple data sources in multiple environments
   c. Includes parents and students in the process

3. Authentic assessment
   a. Has traditionally been used in special education environments
   b. Allows students to demonstrate their knowledge in a number of contexts
   c. Is most helpful when it is norm-referenced

4. Ecological assessment requires
   a. Careful observation and review of records
   b. Collaboration with individuals who work and live with the child
   c. Use of curriculum-based assessment

5. Ecobehavioral interviews determine
   a. The parent's and child's perceptions of the issue
   b. The specific behavior of concern and the contexts in which it occurs
   c. Environmental stimuli maintaining behaviors

6. Portfolios typically
   a. Are collections of work
   b. Are organized around a focus or guidelines
   c. Contain a record of performance on one item over time

7. Curriculum-based assessment is developed
   a. In response to national standards in content areas
   b. From the school district's curriculum
   c. From practical application of curriculum content

8. An example of a functional task is
   a. Writing a letter of complaint
   b. Writing a descriptive paragraph
   c. Writing a narrative

9.   Proficiency testing
     a.   Is inappropriate for individuals with disabilities
     b.   Should be addressed on each student's IEP
     c.   Is incompatible with curriculum-based assessment

10. Report card letter grades
     a.   Are an example of curriculum-based assessment
     b.   Are arbitrary symbols assigned to a value judgment
     c.   Are grounded in functional assessment

Make the Language Your Own
Match the following terms with their definitions:

1. _____ Assessment
2. _____ Curriculum-based assessment
3. _____ Ecological assessment
4. _____ Functional assessment
5. _____ Grade
6. _____ Observation
7. _____ Portfolio
8. _____ Rating scales
9. _____ Review of records
10. _____ Rubrics

a.   Systematically collecting data about behavior in specific environments by watching and recording events
b.   The process by which changes that are needed in the learner's behaviors or environments are identified
c.   Checklists and standardized rating forms
d.   An arbitrary symbol reflecting a value judgment concerning the relative quality of a student's achievement
e.   Evaluation of instructional needs through ongoing measurement of student performance within the local school curriculum
f.   The process of reviewing previous grades, assessment findings, attendance records, and other information
g.   A scaled set of criteria
h.   A systematically collected and organized collection of evidence for monitoring growth and development
i.   The assessment of outcomes related to living and working as part of the community
j.   Assessment that addresses the impact of the environment on the student's behavior and performance

Application Activities
1.   For the course for which you are using this book and in a discussion with your fellow students and instructor, plan and develop a portfolio. This portfolio will be used to evaluate your performance in the course.

2. Interview two general education and two special education teachers and discuss with them assessment and grading of learners with disabilities in their classes. Develop an interview protocol containing the topics discussed in this chapter to guide your discussion.

REFERENCES

Barnett, D.W., Bauer, A.M., Barnhouse, L., Ehrhardt, K.E., Lentz, F.E., Macmann, G., & Stollar, S. (1997). Ecological foundations of early intervention: Planned activities and strategic sampling. *Journal of Special Education, 30*(4), 471–490.

Barnett, D.W., Carey, K.T., & Hall, J.D. (1993). Naturalistic intervention design for young children: Foundations, rationales, and strategies. *Topics in Early Childhood Special Education, 13*(4), 430–444.

Bursuck, W., Polloway, E.A., Plante, L., Epstein, M.H., Jayanthi, M., & McConeghy, J. (1996). Report card grading and adaptations: A national survey of classroom practices. *Exceptional Children, 63*(4), 301–318.

Canter, A.S., Crockett, D.P., Dawson, M.M., Graden, J., Harrison, P.L., Kovaleski, J.F., & Reschly, D.J. (1994). *Assessment and eligibility in special education: An examination of policy and practice with proposals for change.* Alexandria, VA: U.S. Department of Education, Office of Special Education and Rehabilitative Services, Office of Special Education Programs.

Clark, G.M. (1994). Is a functional curriculum approach compatible with an inclusive education model? *Teaching Exceptional Children, 26*(2), 36–39.

Darling-Hammond, L., Ancess, J., & Falk, B. (1995). *Authentic assessment in action: Studies of schools and students at work.* New York: Teachers College Press.

Dunlap, G., & Childs, K.E. (1996). Intervention research in emotional and behavioral disorders: An analysis of studies from 1980–1983. *Behavioral Disorders, 21*(2), 125–136.

Espin, C.A., & Foegen, A. (1996). Validity of general outcome measures for predicting secondary students' performance on content area tasks. *Exceptional Children, 62*(6), 497–514.

Field, S., LeRoy, B., & Rivera, S. (1994). Meeting functional curriculum needs in middle school general education classrooms. *Teaching Exceptional Children, 26*(2), 40–43.

Friedman, S.J. (1996). Who needs to know that Andy got a D? *Clearing House, 70*(1), 10–12.

Fuchs, L.S. (1994). *Connecting performance assessment to instruction.* (ERIC Document Reproduction Service No. ED 375565)

Fuchs, L.S., Fuchs, D., & Hamlett, C.L. (1989). Effects of instrumental use of curriculum-based measurement to enhance instructional programs. *Remedial and Special Education, 10*(2), 43–52.

Goerss, K.V. (1993). Portfolio assessment: A work in process. *Middle School Journal, 25*(2), 20–24.

Graden, J.L., Casey, A., & Christensen, S.L. (1986). Implementing a prereferral intervention system: Part 1. The model. *Exceptional Children, 51,* 377–384.

Hamm, M., & Adams, D. (1991). Portfolio: It's not just for artists anymore. *Science Teacher, 58*(2), 18–21.

Herman, J.L., Aschbacher, P.R., & Winters, L. (1992). *A practical guide to alternative assessment.* Alexandria, VA: Association for Supervision and Curriculum Development.

Keefe, C.H. (1994). Portfolios: Mirrors of learning. *Teaching Exceptional Children, 27,* 66–67.

National Center for Fair and Open Testing. (1989). *Fallout from the testing operation.* Cambridge, MA: Author.

Nolet, V. (1992). Classroom-based measurement and portfolio assessment. *Diagnostique, 18*(1), 5–10.

Pate, P.E., Homestead, E., & McGinnis, K. (1993). Designing rubrics for authentic assessment. *Middle School Journal, 25*(2), 25–27.

Paulsen, K.J. (1997). Curriculum-based measurement: Translating research into school-based practice. *Intervention in School and Clinic, 32*(3), 162–167.

Pearpoint, J., Forest, M., & O'Brien, J. (1996). MAPs, Circles of Friends, and PATH: Powerful tools to help build caring communities. In S. Stainback & W. Stainback (Eds.), *Inclusion: A guide for educators* (pp. 67–86). Baltimore: Paul H. Brookes Publishing Co.

Redding, N. (1992). Assessing the big outcomes. *Educational Leadership, 52,* 49–53.

Rojewski, J.W., Pollard, R.R., & Meers, G.D. (1990). Grading mainstreamed special needs students: Determining practices and attitudes of secondary vocational educators using a qualitative approach. *Remedial and Special Education, 12*(1), 7–28.

Salend, S. (1995). Modifying tests for diverse learners. *Intervention in School and Clinic, 31*(2), 84–90.

Swicegood, P. (1994). Portfolio-based assessment practices. *Intervention in School and Clinic, 30*(1), 6–15.

Vavus, L. (1990). Put portfolios to the test. *Instructor, 100*(1), 48–53.

Wahler, R.G., & Cormier, W.H. (1970). The ecological interview: A first step in outpatient child behavior therapy. *Journal of Behavioral Therapy and Experimental Psychology, 1,* 279–289.

Welch, M. (1994). Ecological assessment: A collaborative approach to planning instructional interventions. *Intervention in School and Clinic, 29*(3), 160–164.

Wesson, C.L., & King, R.P. (1996). Portfolio assessment and special education students. In E.L. Meyen, G.A. Vergason, & R.J. Whelan (Eds.), *Strategies for teaching exceptional children in inclusive settings* (pp. 293–302). Denver: Love Publishing Co.

Wisconsin Department of Public Instruction. (1996). *The testing of students with disabilities (exceptional educational needs students), handicapped students under Section 504, and limited-English-speaking students: DPI Guidelines for nondiscriminatory testing.* Madison: Author.

Witt, J.C., Elliott, S.N., Kramer, J.J., & Gresham, F.M. (1994). *Assessment of children.* Madison, WI: Wm. C. Brown Communications.

Wood, J. (1988). *Adapting instruction for the mildly handicapped student: A national perspective.* Paper presented at the annual meeting of the Council for Exceptional Children, Washington, DC.

8

Structures of Inclusive Schools and Classrooms

Aaron goes to our neighborhood high school with his brother. The captain of the varsity basketball team is trying to teach him to shoot hoops. A female friend, Chris, spots for him during his daily workouts on the weightlifting equipment. Aaron got "in trouble" in reading class because he and a general education student were playfully trading strange noises. For Aaron and our family, the difference in this new school has been that it is a friendlier, more accommodating environment with some dedicated staff who said they didn't know all the answers but were willing to try.

Mary Ulrich, describing changes in her son's life brought about by inclusion; Aaron is a young adult with autism

In this chapter, methods and strategies for organizing and managing inclusive schools and classrooms are discussed. The initial section is devoted to ways to organize and manage inclusive schools. Several models are presented for readers' consideration, adaptation, and adoption, including the new attitude (Means & Knapp, 1991) toward teaching and learning that builds on learners' strengths rather than on the remediation of weaknesses and on cultural sensitivity. Also discussed are 1) inquiring schools (Calfee, 1991), in which the entire learning community assumes a problem-solving stance and teachers apply modeling, coaching, scaffolding, articulation, reflection, and exploration; and 2) the cognitive apprenticeship (Collins, Hawkins, & Carver, 1991), which involves teaching the processes that experts use to handle complex tasks and learning through guided experiences in cognitive skills and processes rather than physical ones.

Cooperative classrooms, block scheduling, and parallel block scheduling are also discussed in the first section. The second section of the chapter discusses structures that are effective in inclusive classrooms. These structures include cues, engagement, and feedback. The third section of the chapter is a discussion of participation structures and ways to increase access for all students. The coexistence of the teacher's academic agenda and the students' social agenda during lessons is discussed. Participation structures such as taking turns, following the rules for speaking, knowing when to attend to the teacher and when to attend to classmates, and leading and following a discussion are presented. Signaling or cuing systems between teachers and students that allow both sides to continue functioning effectively and without disruption are discussed. The fourth section of the chapter discusses ways to manage the environment in inclusive classrooms to facilitate instruction and behavior management. Among the many variables or antecedents to instruction that teachers must consider in developing the classroom environment are the utilization of space, materials, and equipment; procedures for individual, small-group, and whole-group activities; rules; and transitions. The final section of the chapter discusses natural classroom supports for learners. Natural supports are the least-contrived and least-intrusive supports available in the environment in which performance is being exhibited.

LEARNING OBJECTIVES

After completing this chapter, readers will be able to

1. Describe ways to organize and manage an inclusive school
2. Describe structures that are effective in inclusive classrooms
3. Identify participation structures and ways to increase access for all students
4. Discuss ways to manage the environment of inclusive classrooms
5. Identify natural classroom supports for students

KEY WORDS AND PHRASES

block scheduling—scheduling time and space for periods longer than the traditional 45- to 50-minute class, thereby allowing for the integration of curriculum areas

cognitive apprenticeship—teaching the processes that experts use to handle complex tasks and learning through guided experiences in cognitive skills and processes rather than physical ones (Collins et al., 1991)

cooperative classrooms—classrooms in which students support and nurture each other's learning

inquiring schools—schools in which the entire learning community assumes a problem-solving stance and engages in modeling, coaching, scaffolding, articulation, reflection, and exploration (Calfee, 1991)

natural supports—the least-contrived and least-intrusive supports available in the environment in which performance is being exhibited

new attitude—a model for teaching and learning that builds on the strengths rather than remediating the weaknesses of learners and on cultural sensitivity (Means & Knapp, 1991)

parallel blocking schedule—a complex blocking schedule in which students are grouped in classrooms so that no single classroom has more than one third to one half of its students in the lower-ability group; teachers apply direct, large-group, and support and enrichment instruction

participation structure—the patterns of conversational turns or the allocation of interaction rights and obligations that occur in the classroom (Bauer & Sapona, 1991)

rules—statements of explicit limits

signaling or cuing system—the process of using symbols to communicate essential messages between individuals

transition—the movement from one activity to another

 LEARNING OBJECTIVE 1: To be able to describe ways to organize and manage an inclusive school

Many ways to organize and manage inclusive schools are evolving as inclusive communities become more common. Each of these ways describes a vision, a rethinking, or a reshaping of the traditional ways in which schools operate. Rather than prescribe a single vision as a model, readers are urged to review various models described in this chapter and identify those parts of each that would contribute to their efforts to meet the needs of particular students, parents, schools, and communities.

In 1991, Means and Knapp recommended adopting **the new attitude** toward teaching. In the new attitude, the intellectual accomplishments that all learners bring to school are to be valued. The emphasis in teaching is on building on learners' strengths rather than on remediating their impairments. Everyone working with students must learn about individual students' cultures and thus avoid mistaking cultural differences for impairments (Kalyanpur & Harry, 1999).

In addition to teachers' adopting a new attitude, the curriculum offered to the students must be reshaped. Means and Knapp (1991) suggested focusing the curriculum on complex, meaningful problems. Instruction in the basic skills is to be embedded in the context of more global tasks and issues. During teaching and learning, connections are made constantly with students' out-of-school experiences and cultures. New instruction strategies are applied that model powerful thinking strategies, encourage multiple approaches and solutions, provide scaffolding to enable students to accomplish complex tasks, and make dialogue the central medium for teaching and learning. Teachers are charged with the responsibility of seeking authentic problems as the context for their teaching and students' practicing skills. Teachers must become knowledgeable about their students' cultural backgrounds and draw on the strengths of those cultures.

Calfee (1991) referred to inclusive schools as **inquiring schools.** In this vision, the emphasis is on a few clearly articulated goals about the educational purpose of the school and the techniques used to achieve those goals. There are a small number of distinctive and overarching goals, all of which center around a common theme. The entire learning community assumes a problem-solving stance; the group takes charge of the problems rather than attributing its success to luck and its failure to lack of ability.

In inquiring schools, several instruction structures emerge. In modeling, the teacher performs a task so that students can observe. In coaching, the teacher observes and facilitates while the student performs the task. Teachers provide scaffolding, in which ongoing supports help the student successfully perform a task. Articulation is used as the teacher encourages students to verbalize their knowledge and thinking. In reflection, the teacher enables students to compare their performance with that of students around them. Finally, through exploration, the teacher invites students to pose and solve their own problems.

According to Calfee (1991), meaningful tasks of increasing difficulty are presented to the students. In addition, practice is provided in a variety of situations that emphasize broad applications. The **transition** is from global to local skills, with the focus on conceptualizing the whole task before executing its parts. Collins and colleagues (1991) suggested a **cognitive apprenticeship** as an approach to inclusion. This apprenticeship aims primarily at teaching the processes that experts use to handle complex tasks and learning through guided experiences in cognitive skills and processes rather than physical ones. In the cognitive apprenticeship, content differentiates various kinds of knowledge. Strategic knowledge underlies the students' ability to make use of concepts, facts, and procedures as necessary to solve problems and accomplish tasks. Domain knowledge comprises the concepts, facts, and procedures explicitly identified with particular subject matter that are generally presented in textbooks, class lectures, and demonstrations. Three forms of strategies are also at work in cognitive apprenticeships. Heuristic strategies are generally effective techniques and approaches used to accomplish tasks that might be regarded as tricks of the trade. Control strategies are used to control the process of carrying out a task. Learning strategies are strategies for learning any other type of content.

Several goals emerge in managing inclusive schools. Stainback and Stainback (1990) suggested that the goal of the school must be to meet the unique educational objectives and curricular and instructional needs of all students. This goal in itself has several implications for inclusive schools. Ways in which all children can be recognized for achievement must be developed. Competitive structures such as honor rolls cannot be used if the cause for celebration would be for every student to reach his or her potential. In the inclusive classroom environment, teachers teach all of the students to whom they are assigned and are responsible for everyone's learning. If a student is not reaching his or her unique educational objectives, the teacher and the educational team must develop alternative ways to meet those objectives. The assumptions are that all students can learn and that everyone belongs. The emphasis is on challenging every student to progress as far as possible toward fulfilling his or her potential rather than comparing students with each other. The structure of an inclusive school must create a sense of community while emphasizing the individual.

An inclusive school must make all students feel welcome and secure through friendships and peer supports (Stainback & Stainback, 1990). A positive classroom atmosphere that is conducive to learning for all students must be developed and maintained. Physical and organizational characteristics of the classroom must accommodate the unique needs of each student. The emphasis is on access; if an activity is planned, then everyone must be able to participate in that activity in some way. Sapon-Shevin (1990) described **cooperative classrooms**, in which students support and nurture each other's learning:

- Competitive symbols such as star charts, posted grades, and best papers are eliminated.
- Inclusive language, such as referring to "students" rather than "boys and girls," is used so that all students are encouraged to see the role that they have in helping other students to succeed.
- A sense of community is consciously developed through emphasizing activities in which everyone participates.
- Students act as resources for each other, desks are clustered, students are urged to consult with each other before they ask the teacher a question, and classrooms develop their own Yellow Pages listing individual students and their talents and skills.
- Students are encouraged to notice each other's accomplishments.
- Children's literature is used to explore real issues and concerns of the students.

Lipsky and Gartner (1992) argued that, to be inclusive, schools must shift from emphasizing the means of learning to emphasizing the outcomes of learning. In inclusive schools, they contended, respect for the actual and potential contributions to learning must be in place for all students. Students must be actively engaged in all aspects of the learning process, including determining what to learn, how to learn it, and how to measure growth in learning. Inclusive schools must believe that they are preparing students for a lifetime and that all learning is important. An additional emphasis in inclusive schools and classrooms is on "doing it right from the start"; that is, if a child fails, then the school has failed to meet the child's needs. Education planning must identify the instruction strategies and adaptations necessary for the child to do the work of learning.

Scheduling in Inclusive Schools

Restructuring a school as an inclusive community may require restructuring all of the school's resources, including staff, space, and time. The utilization and redistribution of staff are discussed in Chapter 5. Restructuring space and time is necessary to support efforts such as cooperative teaching.

Block scheduling is one means of rescheduling time and space. In block scheduling, the traditional 45- to 50-minute bells or periods are changed to longer periods that allow for the integration of curriculum areas. In elementary schools, integration of curricula may involve teachers' assigning the morning to two blocks: one for mathematics and one for language arts. The afternoon may be a single block involving an extended period of time for science or social studies in cooperative groups. In middle schools and secondary schools, block scheduling may be accomplished by collapsing individual bells or periods into longer periods and assigning classes to occur on A days or B days. Students have three classes every other day and one class and lunch daily. Sample elementary and secondary school schedules using block scheduling are depicted in Figure 1.

Snell, Lowman, and Canady (1996) described a more complex form of block scheduling, which they called the **parallel blocking schedule.** In parallel block scheduling, students are grouped in classrooms so that no single classroom has more than one third to one half of its students in the lower-ability group. Teachers form direct instruction groups for mathematics and reading, using children's interest areas and talents as the basis for instruction. Larger groups are scheduled for language arts, social studies, and science so that hands-on activities and cooperative learning can be used. To support the teacher's direct instruction, an extension center is developed. In the extension center, students engage in enrichment and support activities including journal writing, group reading, library use, computer support, English as a Second Language lessons, counseling, speech-language therapy, occupational or physical therapy, and individual educational interventions. All students visit the extension center; consequently, there is no stigma related to attendance. A variety of professionals and aides staff the extension center, including classroom teachers, special educators, speech-language pathologists, occupational and physical therapists, and tutors. An advantage of parallel block scheduling is that all students participate in the same environments and similar activities, and everyone receives individual help.

 LEARNING OBJECTIVE 2: To be able to describe structures that are effective in inclusive classrooms

Several classroom structures have been linked to highly effective inclusive classrooms. Goldstein (1996) reported that in these classrooms, students' experiences and background knowledge, authentic tasks that are meaningful to the student, and the student's interests are all incorporated into the teaching and learning processes. The emphasis in inclusive classrooms is on the meaning of learning experiences rather than on the form of those experiences. In addition, rather than correctness, emphasis is placed on creativity and divergent thinking. Interactions between teacher and student are grounded in dialogue.

Elementary School Schedule

Ms. Shadowarrior, Grade 3

8:30–8:50	Opening class meeting
8:50–10:15	Language arts block: Integrated reading, writing, English, spelling
10:15–10:30	Recess/break
10:30–12:15	Math block: Integrated mathematics and problem solving
12:15–1:00	Lunch/recess
1:00–1:30	Mondays: Sustained silent reading Tuesdays and Thursdays: Physical education Wednesdays: Art Fridays: Music
1:30–2:50	Content area block organized around thematic units; emphases alternate between science and social studies
2:50	Dismissal/buses

Secondary School Schedule

Christopher Joseph, Grade 10

7:55–8:11	Homeroom	
8:14–9:54	A days: Band	B days: Latin II
9:57–11:45	A days: Civics	B days: Computer Science
10:50–11:15	A and B days: Lunch	
11:25–12:57	A and B days: Biology and Biology Lab	
1:00–2:40	A days: Algebra II	B days: English II

Figure 1.   Sample elementary and secondary school block schedules.

Assessment and evaluation in these classrooms compare the students' unassisted performance with their assisted performance on authentic tasks.

Walberg (1990) described specific strategies that support effective inclusive classrooms. He grouped these strategies into three categories:

1. *Cues,* which show students what is to be learned and how to learn it
2. *Engagement,* in which students are encouraged to persistently and actively participate in learning until the appropriate responses are firmly entrenched in their repertoires
3. *Feedback,* which includes detecting difficulties rapidly; remedying them; and providing clear, appropriate reinforcement that also **signals** what to do next

Among **cues**, Walberg (1990) suggested the use of advanced organizers, or overviews that connect new learning to old learning. In addition, through the use of adjunct questions, students are alerted to questions that should be answered. Through goal setting, teachers suggest specific objectives, guidelines, methods, or standards. Walberg also suggested carefully sequencing material and using pretests to determine what the students need to learn.

In terms of engagement, Walberg (1990) argued that high expectations transmit high standards of learning. Frequent tests and questioning also have been related to more productive learning. With regard to feedback, homework may serve to reinforce students' learning. Classroom structures for students with intense needs or severe disabilities are often difficult for teachers in inclusive classroom environments. Woolery and Schuster (1997) grouped instruction strategies into the categories of ecological structuring, self-management, using the inclusive environment, and response-prompting procedures. Examples of strategies within each of these categories are presented in Table 1.

LEARNING OBJECTIVE 3: To be able to identify participation structures and ways to increase access for all students

All classrooms are complex academic and social environments. Throughout the school day, the teacher's academic task agendas are operating concurrently with the students' social participation agendas. Bremme and Evertson (1977) suggested that classrooms are as much social occasions as they are learning environments. Erickson (1982) referred to the complex interactions of students and teachers as *doing a lesson together.* Academic task structures, the teacher's agenda, are those constraints on the lesson that are related to the nature of the academic task itself. For example, if the academic task is related to writing sentences, then teachers and students must follow certain steps that are dictated by the task itself. The social participation agendas relate more specifically to the social context and interactions involved in teaching and learning.

Table 1.   Group instruction strategies

Classroom structure	Instruction strategy
Ecological structuring	Develop an appropriate schedule
	Use materials to structure activities
	Manage the number and proximity of peers
	Manage the number and proximity of adults
	Modify materials and activities
	Structure roles during free time
Self-management	Employ self-observation and recording
	Employ self-monitoring
	Use subtle cues
Using the inclusive environment	Use peers as competent interactive and communicative partners
	Use peers as models
Response prompting	Gradually increase delay between behavior and response
	Gradually reduce supports

Participation structures are the patterns of conversational turns or the allocation of interaction rights and obligations that occur in the classroom (Bauer & Sapona, 1991). Participation structures place communicative and behavioral demands on the students. In any classroom, participation structures include taking turns, following the **rules** about when to speak and when not to speak, knowing when to attend to the teacher and when to attend to classmates, and leading and following discussions. Students who do not engage as their peers do in the classroom's participation structures may be described as exhibiting behavior problems or demonstrating inappropriate behaviors (Erickson, 1982).

In group activities, instruction should be differentiated for individual students. Giangreco, Cloninger, and Iverson (1998) suggested that in group activities, the teacher may be able to use the same curriculum with no differentiation. In addition, the teacher has the option of using a multilevel curriculum in which all students work on the same content but may work at different levels to the extent that even the concepts being taught may be different. Finally, teachers may employ an overlapping curriculum in which students participate in the same activity but in which individual students may be working on varied content and concepts altogether.

Student–Teacher Signaling Systems

In inclusive classroom environments in which teachers may be working with individuals or groups, a signaling system between teachers and students should be in place. A signaling system allows a teacher to continue working with a student(s) while recognizing requests for help. The signaling system allows the class to continue to work with fewer distractions and allows the student in need of help to relax, knowing that the teacher will respond as soon as possible. In any signaling system, the student uses his or her signal for help and then switches to another task or backup work while awaiting assistance. The teacher must have backup tasks ready and available for the student. These backup tasks may be on the student's desk, on a nearby shelf, or in the student's cubbie. In addition, teachers should be on the lookout for signals and reinforce their use as quickly as possible.

A signal system may be referred to as a cuing system or as the process of using symbols to communicate essential messages between individuals. Cues not only reduce interruptions in ongoing classroom activities but also actually facilitate structure and provide routine (Legare, 1984; Olson, 1989). Cuing is a proactive, preventive behavior management intervention (Slade & Callaghan, 1988).

There are various cues or signals that can be used in the classroom. Such cues are most effective if developed collaboratively by students and teachers at the beginning of the school year. The following are among the many cues that may be implemented:

- Students place a sign or a flag in a holder on their desks when assistance is needed.
- Students write their names on the chalkboard when help is needed.
- Students take a numbered ticket (as at the supermarket delicatessen counter) when help is needed.

- Students use a cardboard symbol (e.g., "R" for restroom, "P" for pencil, "W" for water) instead of frequently asking questions.
- Teachers use a traffic signal to control noise levels (red meaning too loud, yellow meaning caution, and green meaning OK).
- Teachers turn the lights on or off to signal the beginning and end of activities.

Finally, teachers may use body language, hand signals, smiles, frowns, and schedules as cues (Rosenkoetter & Fowler, 1986). The design and application of cues and signals are limited only by the imagination of the teachers and students involved. Of course, cues should not be used in lieu of appropriate verbal communication.

Your Turn . . .

Develop a teacher–student signal system for a classroom. How will the students communicate that they need help? How will you communicate that you recognize their request? Where will backup tasks and activities be available? How will you instruct the students in the use of the signaling system?

LEARNING OBJECTIVE 4: To be able to discuss ways to manage the environment of inclusive classrooms

The effective classroom is planned and organized to facilitate instruction and behavior management (Montague, Bergerson, & Lago-Delello, 1997). The teacher must take into consideration a broad range of factors to enhance the probability that learning will occur. Among those factors are space utilization and storage, including procedures for the use of classroom and nonclassroom space, facilities, materials, and equipment. The teacher must develop procedures for individual, small-group, and whole-group activities; beginning and ending a school day or period; transitions; housekeeping; interruptions; visitors; fire drills; and various other activities. The teacher must consider classroom rules for behavior.

Murdick and Petch-Hogan (1996) discussed alternative intervention strategies for application with educational and behavior problems in inclusive classes prior to evaluating students for special education services. They suggested strategies designed to increase the probability that students with disabilities will remain in the general education classroom. Their suggestions focused on manipulating the antecedents of behavior and learning, such as the physical environment; the daily schedule; the instructional delivery system, including pre-instruction, during-instruction, and postinstruction variables; the management plan; and classroom rules. They also recommended that teachers analyze the methods (verbal and nonverbal) used to communicate with students.

The more thoroughly a classroom facility and program are planned, the greater the probability of success for both students and teacher. Although the majority of behavior management research focuses on the effects of manipulating the consequences of behavior, Wheldall (1991) reported some positive results from research that focuses on the effects of manipulating the antecedents of behavior. Munk and Repp (1994) reviewed the research literature on instructional variables that may decrease behavior problems in the classroom. The focus of their review was on positive or nonaversive strategies for reducing and preventing problem behaviors. Their review centered on the antecedents of instruction. Among the variables that they suggested may decrease problem behaviors were the student's choice of task, variation in tasks, instructional pace, interspersal of high-probability tasks, partial task versus whole-task training, decreasing task difficulty, and multielement packages.

The remainder of this section is devoted to an overview of the antecedents of effective instruction and classroom management. The suggestions presented are general in nature and must be modified to respond to the needs of a particular classroom environment.

Space, Materials, and Equipment

Teachers begin the school year by planning for the use of the space, materials, and equipment assigned to them and their students. They must give consideration to the space assigned to them and their students exclusively, as well as that shared with others, such as hallways, the lunchroom, the playground, the library, and the music room (Evertson et al., 1981).

Walls, Ceilings, and Bulletin Boards

Walls, ceilings, and bulletin boards are valuable spaces that can be used to display a variety of materials such as schedules, rules, seasonal and topical items, calendars, study assignments, "housekeeping" assignments, charts, maps, and so forth. It is prudent not to overdecorate; space should be reserved for students' work and items of current interest. Students can profit from helping to plan displays for bulletin boards. Materials displayed on walls, ceilings, and bulletin boards should be changed periodically so that the students will not become desensitized to its content.

Floor Space

The use of floor space will vary with the size of the room, the number of students and their characteristics, and the activities to be conducted in the room. The room must be arranged to ensure that the teacher can observe all areas in which students work and to ensure that the students are able to see the teacher and the work materials that the teacher is using for instruction. Students' desks and tables should be arranged away from high-traffic areas. If tables are used instead of desks, then space for storage of student materials must be planned. Space must be planned for individual, small-group, and whole-group activities. If learning centers (reading, mathematics, science, and others) are used, then space must be planned to include these areas. Centers that generate a high degree of activity and noise should not be located near centers that require a high degree of concentration. All needed materials and equipment should be located in the appropriate center.

The teacher must plan where common items such as plants, pet cages, fish tanks, bookcases, and storage cabinets will be located in the classroom. The teacher's desk, files, and other equipment must be located where they are easily accessible yet do not interfere with activities. Every effort should be made to maintain traffic lanes in the classroom to prevent confusion as students move about the room. If the classroom is serving learners who use wheelchairs or other adaptive equipment or students with visual impairments, free and stable traffic lanes must be maintained and space organized to ensure accessibility for these individuals.

Storage Space

There are various kinds of supplies, materials, and equipment used in the classroom: everyday supplies and materials, infrequently used supplies and materials, student supplies and materials, teacher supplies and materials, and the personal items of students and the teacher. The teacher must plan for their storage and use. Large, adaptive equipment poses a particular challenge and cannot be left in the hall, owing to fire regulations.

Everyday supplies and materials such as pencils, paper, and chalk should be stored in an easily accessible location. The teacher may wish to locate these items where they are available to the students. Students' instruction materials, such as texts, workbooks, dictionaries, and study guides, may be stored in students' desks, in bookcases, or in filing trays and cabinets. Infrequently used items such as seasonal and topical materials should be stored in the backs of cupboards. Equipment such as overhead projectors, record players, compact disc players, and movie projectors should be stored in a safe place when not in use but should be accessible. Each student should have a private place to store personal items such as clothing, gym shoes, lunchboxes, and prized possessions. The teacher must have a private space for his or her briefcase and other personal items as well as personal instruction materials and equipment. The personal and private spaces of all students and teachers must not be violated.

A challenge for teachers in inclusive classrooms is acquiring and maintaining materials that are appropriate for the wide range of instructional needs in the classroom. This challenge is even more evident in classrooms in which students with intense needs or severe disabilities are included. Woolery and Schuster (1997) suggested that materials can be used in several ways. First, materials can be used as target stimuli, acting as cues for specific behaviors. With all students, and particularly with students with intense needs or severe disabilities, materials that can provide multiple and realistic examples of how materials are used in the natural environment are recommended. For example, using real money is more realistic in counting change than using play money. When realistic examples cannot be used, simulations may be appropriate as long as strategies to generalize children's learning to real materials are planned.

A second use of materials described by Woolery and Schuster (1997) was that of setting the stage for children's behavior. For example, a teacher in the primary grades may provide only four chairs at each learning center, cuing students by the number of chairs that only four students may work at that center at one time. Materials may also be linked to peer interaction, and other materials may be linked to individual play (Rettig, Kallam, & McCarthy-Salm, 1993). Materials may also be strategically used to increase communication. Kaiser (1987) suggested that if the teacher's aim is to increase the communicative behavior of students, the teacher should

- Use materials that are interesting
- Place desired materials in view but out of reach
- Use materials for which students will need to request assistance
- Give students incomplete amounts of materials so that they need to interact communicatively to complete the activity
- "Sabotage" the material or activity so that the student needs to request help (i.e., give a student a blank instead of a printed piece of paper)

Woolery and Schuster (1997) also suggested that materials can be used to support adaptive behavior. Students may be taught to use materials specifically as resources for performing adaptive behavior. For example, language books can be used so that students may approach their peers or teachers to converse. Students who have difficulty in remaining seated can be placed in a cluster of students with their backs to the wall, making their leaving the group more difficult.

Another use of materials that Woolery and Schuster (1997) described was that of reinforcing and rewarding certain behaviors. Students with more intense needs or severe disabilities may not respond to the same rewards as their peers. Early research on working with students who engaged in self-injurious behavior showed that sensory stimuli may hold powerful reinforcing properties (Rincover, Newsome, Lovaas, & Koegel, 1977). Students who body rock may be reinforced for periods of stillness at their desk or table by being allowed to go to the rocking chair. Students who like to dangle strings before their eyes may be reinforced by sitting in front of a wind chime or may even be given a string to dangle.

Procedures

The teacher is responsible for developing a variety of classroom and nonclassroom procedures designed to ensure that students will learn and behave effectively and efficiently. The teacher must be sure that these procedures are compatible with general school policy.

Students' Use of Classroom Space and Facilities

Procedures should be established to facilitate the care of students' desks and storage areas. Procedures are established for the number of students permitted in various areas of the room at one time, including the sink, pencil sharpener, and other shared facilities, as well as for requests to use the drinking fountain and the rest room. Procedures for the use and care of common and personal instruction materials and with regard to students' and teachers' personal space and possessions must be developed and established. Procedures must be developed for students' leaving the classroom and the movement of individual students and groups of students throughout the school building.

Students' Use of Nonclassroom Space and Facilities

Procedures should be developed for the use of nonclassroom space and facilities such as rest rooms, drinking fountains, offices, the library, the media room, the resource room, and other areas. Playground activity procedures must be developed. These procedures should facilitate fair play and safety and enjoyment. Special procedures are frequently needed for the lunchroom because of the large number of students in the facility at one time and the limited amount of time available to eat.

Whole-Group, Small-Group, and Individual Activities

The teacher must establish procedures for a variety of individual, small-group, and whole-group activities. Procedures are developed for the conduct of discussions, answering questions during class, talking among students, out-of-seat behavior, and so forth. Students should be instructed about the cues and prompts that the teacher will use to obtain students' attention. Procedures are developed for making assignments to work groups, assigning homework, distributing supplies and materials, turning in work, returning assignments, and completing missed assignments. Students should know what they are expected to do when they have completed a task and have unscheduled time available.

Small-Group Activities Require Procedures

Students must know the cues that the teacher will use to begin and end small-group activities, what materials to bring, and behavioral expectations. Students who are not in a particular small group must know what is expected of them during other students' small-group activities. Students who are working independently must know how to obtain their work, where they are to work, what work to do, how to signal for assistance, and what to do when their work is completed.

Teachers are prudent to establish standard procedures for beginning and ending the school day or period. It is important to begin and end the day on a positive note. Students should know what behaviors are appropriate and inappropriate during this time. Students should know the procedures for reporting after an absence, tardiness, and early dismissal.

Procedures are developed for the selection and duties of classroom helpers. All students should participate in these activities. Finally, procedures should be established for students' conduct during classroom interruptions and delays and for fire, tornado, and earthquake drills and other infrequent and unplanned occurrences.

Rules

Rules of behavior are needed in all classrooms. According to Joyce and colleagues (1989), a rule specifies the relationship between two events. A rule may take the form of an instruction, a direction, or a principle. Students follow rules to obtain natural reinforcers (e.g., getting the correct answer, self-satisfaction) or artificial reinforcers (e.g., grades, points, free time). Teachers use various rules to organize classroom instruction and conduct. Rules usually are designed to apply to those activities and occurrences that are not governed by the classroom and nonclassroom procedures discussed previously.

Rules should be few in number. They should be brief and understandable to the students and positively stated. They should communicate expectations rather than prohibitions. It may be necessary, however, to state rules that prohibit specific behaviors. Rules are best developed through the collaborative efforts of students and the teacher (Murdick & Petch-Hogan, 1996; Thorson, 1996). When students are involved in developing the rules, they will think of the rules as "our rules" rather than as "the teacher's rules." When rules are set collaboratively, they may be changed only through discussion and consensus (Cheney, 1989). Rules should be posted in a highly visible location in the classroom and reviewed with the students frequently (Blankenship, 1986). During the initial weeks of the school year, the rules should be reviewed and discussed daily.

The teacher must give students repeated examples of the behaviors that a student demonstrates when following the rules. The function of a rule is to encourage appropriate behavior and prevent inappropriate behavior. Teachers are responsible for enforcing classroom rules with fairness and consistency (Rieth & Evertson, 1988). Four or five rules are more than adequate to govern classroom behavior. They should be general—but not so general as to be meaningless. Rules must be sufficiently objective to be exemplified by the teacher. The following are examples of general rules:

- Be polite and helpful.
- Keep personal space and materials in order.
- Take care of the classroom and school property.

Some teachers have certain highly specific rules. The following are examples of specific rules:

- Raise your hand before speaking.
- Leave your seat only with permission.
- Only one person is allowed in the rest room at a time.

Joyce and colleagues (1989) reminded teachers that students whose behavior is rule governed (i.e., under the control of reinforcers) may become insensitive to environmental conditions that make rule following inappropriate. To prevent the development of environmental insensitivity due to rule following, they suggested that students should be

1. Exposed to contingencies that are incompatible with specific rules
2. Provided various tasks for meeting the objective of the rule
3. Exposed to natural contingencies for appropriate classroom behavior
4. Overtly aided to make transitions from rule-governed behaviors that were in effect in previous environments

Transitions

Transitions are the movement from one activity to another. According to Rosenkoetter and Fowler (1986), transitions are complex activities that frequently result in classroom disruptions. Transitions should be carefully planned to minimize the loss of instruction time. Effective transitions teach students self-management skills.

In a study of 22 classes (15 general education and 7 special education) for young children (ages 4 and 5 years), Rosenkoetter and Fowler found that, on average, 18% of the school day was devoted to transitions. Special education and general education classes differed with regard to the management of transitions. General education teachers used more cues or signals than special education teachers did. Special education teachers used children's names as cues; general education teachers used group names. Individual cues in the general class were rare; when special education teachers used group cues, they followed them with individual cues. Special education teachers employed one- or two-step directions; general education teachers employed three- or four-step directions. Special education teachers often used proximity control. In the special education class, children frequently were not held responsible for their materials and were not taught group movement.

Rosenkoetter and Fowler discussed the implications of these differences for the inclusion of children in general education classes. They suggested several guidelines for special education teachers wishing to facilitate transition behaviors:

- Visit the general class to determine transition rules.
- Plan for transitions, and use shaping to assist students in learning appropriate behavior.
- Evaluate existing transition behaviors to determine whether students need more or less assistance.
- Move from individual to group cues or signals.
- Use a variety of cues or signals.
- Teach lining-up and moving-in-line behaviors.
- Teach students how to ask for assistance.

Teachers may use the following activities to facilitate transitions:

- Model appropriate transition behaviors.
- Signal or cue the beginning and the end of activities.
- Remediate transition difficulties such as slowness and disruptiveness.
- Observe students' performance during transitions, and, if students are experiencing difficulties, repeat the rules and practice until the behaviors are firmly established.
- Reinforce quick and quiet transitions (Shea & Bauer, 1987).

Effective transitions are essential to maximize engaged instruction time in the classroom.

LEARNING OBJECTIVE 5: To be able to identify natural classroom supports for students

The best supports for all learners are those that are most natural to the environment and the activity in which they are engaged (i.e., with the least contrived and the least intrusive supports). There are several strategies that can encourage social interaction among learners with disabilities and their classmates. In a preschool, Hanline (1993) found that an ongoing curriculum structure that enhances interactions, such as cooperative learning and curricula with social goals, are natural ways to support inclusion. In addition, interactions can be encouraged by placing and positioning learners with disabilities in ways that encourage participation (i.e., in the same areas as other children, as leaders in games and other activities). Social interactions can be encouraged. Hanline provided the example of a teacher saying to a peer without disabilities who is playing with clay, "Can Sarah have some of those pies you're making?" In this manner, the teacher includes a learner with disabilities in the activity. By modeling appropriate interactions, the teacher can facilitate the appropriate interactions of the students.

The most likely **natural supports** for learners with disabilities in inclusive classrooms are their peers. Stainback and Stainback (1990) suggested several strategies to foster these natural supports. They suggested increasing the proximity of students by having everyone engaged in extracurricular activities. Strategies such as peer tutoring, buddy systems, and cooperative learning, which are described in subsequent chapters, are also helpful. To stimulate these natural supports, Stainback and Stainback suggested contrived activities, such as pairing students and having them participate together in a free-time activity.

Stainback and Stainback also suggested increasing students' awareness of each other's needs. A welcoming committee of class members may be formed when a new student enters the group. In addition, a peer support committee of class members may focus on ways to be sure that all class members are accepted and supported within the group. Stainback and Stainback recognized, however, that teachers may need to teach peer support skills, such as helping students to develop a positive interaction style, learn to take the perspective of the other person, share and provide support, resolve conflicts, and develop friendship skills. Teachers should emphasize understanding and respect for individual differences and be models of positive support and friendship.

Salisbury, Gallucci, Palombaro, and Peck (1995) analyzed transcripts of interviews with teachers who were successful in inclusive classrooms to determine the strategies that they used to support their students. The themes that emerged from their analysis suggested active facilitation of social interaction among members of the class. The teachers used grouping, including cooperative learning groups. They arranged the classroom physically to support group work rather than individual work. The teachers emphasized collaborative problem solving, working with the students and capitalizing on discussions of interpersonal issues that would have yielded less understanding of social interaction if the teacher had solved them. The teachers employed peer tutoring and created jobs in their classrooms to promote children's learning and personal development. The teachers structured time to provide opportunities for interactions, thus allowing the students to make connections on their own.

SUMMARY

This chapter addresses the following major concepts:

1. The ways in which inclusive schools are structured present a reshaping of the traditional ways in which schools operate.

2. The emphasis in inclusive classrooms is on the meaning of learning experiences rather than on the form of those experiences.
3. Throughout the school day, the teacher's academic task agendas are operating concurrently with the students' social participation goals.
4. Teachers must develop procedures for individual, small-, and whole-group activities as well as for beginning and ending the school day or class periods, transitions, housekeeping, and other activities.
5. Rules are necessary in all classrooms.
6. Transitions are complex and can result in the loss of instruction time.
7. The best supports are those that are most natural to the environment.

TEST YOUR KNOWLEDGE

Completion of the "Self-Evaluation," "Make the Language Your Own," and "Application Activities" sections will aid readers in understanding and retaining the information presented in this chapter. Answer keys for the "Self-Evaluation" and "Make the Language Your Own" sections are located in the Appendix at the end of the book.

Self-Evaluation

Select the most appropriate response to complete each of the following statements:

1. In inquiring schools, the emphasis is on
    a. Broad-based goals that improve the student's quality of life
    b. Achievement
    c. A few clearly articulated goals

2. Cognitive apprenticeships are aimed at
    a. Mentoring
    b. Teaching the processes experts use through guided experiences
    c. Direct instruction in cognitive skills

3. In cooperative classrooms,
    a. Symbols such as star charts and posted grades are used to create a positive atmosphere
    b. Inclusive language is used
    c. Only the "best" work is displayed as a model

4. Inclusive schools shift from
    a. Emphasizing means to emphasizing results
    b. Inequality to complete equality
    c. Exclusion to partial participation

5. Block scheduling
    a. Shortens periods to increase the number of activities conducted
    b. Increases the options for pulling students into special help sessions
    c. Is grounded in blocks of objectives for each student

6. During lessons, teachers and students
    a. May have separate agendas
    b. Follow the same agenda
    c. Agree verbally on instruction goals and objectives

7. Students who do not engage as their peers do in classroom participation structures
   a. Usually have unidentified disabilities
   b. May be described as experiencing behavior problems
   c. May need separate instruction

8. The more thoroughly a classroom facility is planned,
   a. The more likely it is that students with disabilities will experience difficulties
   b. The more likely it is that students will challenge the teacher
   c. The greater the probability of success

9. Rules should
   a. State the punishments for inappropriate behavior
   b. Describe the inappropriate behavior
   c. Communicate expectations rather than prohibitions

10. Transitions
    a. Provide relief for students
    b. Are more readily managed in inclusive classrooms
    c. Frequently result in disruptions

Make the Language Your Own

Match the following terms with their definitions:

1. _____ Block scheduling
2. _____ Cognitive apprenticeship
3. _____ Cooperative classroom
4. _____ Inquiring schools
5. _____ Natural supports
6. _____ Parallel blocking schedule
7. _____ Participation structure
8. _____ Rules
9. _____ Signal or cuing system
10. _____ The new attitude
11. _____ Transition

a. The patterns of conversational turns or the allocation of interaction rights and obligations that occur in the classroom (Bauer & Sapona, 1991)

b. Classrooms in which students support and nurture each other's learning

c. Teaching the processes that experts use to handle complex tasks and learning through guided experiences in cognitive skills and processes rather than physical ones (Collins et al., 1991)

d. Schools in which the entire learning community assumes a problem-solving stance and engages in modeling, coaching, scaffolding, articulation, reflection, and exploration (Calfee, 1991)

e. A complex blocking schedule in which students are grouped in classrooms so that no single classroom has more than one third to one half of its students in the lower-ability group.

    f.   The specification of the relation-
ship between two events, which
may take the form of instruction,
direction, or principle (Joyce et al.,
1989)

    g. Scheduling time and space for pe-
riods longer than the traditional
45–50 minutes, which allows for
the integration of curriculum
areas

    h. The process of using symbols to
communicate essential messages
between individuals

    i.   The least-contrived and the least-
intrusive supports available in
the environment in which performance is being exhibited

    j.   An approach to teaching and learn-
ing that builds on the strengths
rather than remediates the weaknesses of learners, and employs
cultural sensitivity (Means &
Knapp, 1991)

    k. The movement from one activity
to another

Application Activities
1. Observe a classroom. What are the rules in the classroom? Are the rules
   posted? Are the rules evident in the ways in which the students interact?
2. Visit a classroom when the students are not present. Describe the general
   layout of the classroom. Identify the ways in which materials are stored
   and the ways in which students would be able to move about in the classroom.

REFERENCES

Bauer, A.M., & Sapona, R.H. (1991). *Managing classrooms to facilitate learning.* Upper
    Saddle River, NJ: Prentice-Hall.
Blankenship, C.S. (1986). Managing pupil behavior during instruction. *Teaching Ex-
    ceptional Children, 19,* 52–53.
Bremme, D.W., & Evertson, F. (1977). Relationship among verbal and nonverbal class-
    room behaviors. *Theory into Practice, 16,* 153–161.
Calfee, R. (1991). What schools can do to improve literacy instruction. In B. Means, C.
    Chelemer, & M.S. Knapp (Eds.), *Teaching advanced skills to at-risk students: Views
    from research and practice* (pp. 176–203). San Francisco: Jossey-Bass.
Cheney, C.O. (1989, August). First time in the classroom? Start off strong! *Exceptional
    Times,* 4.
Collins, A., Hawkins, J., & Carver, S.M. (1991). A cognitive apprenticeship for disad-
    vantaged students. In B. Means, C. Chelemer, & M.S. Knapp (Eds.), *Teaching ad-
    vanced skills to at-risk students: Views from research and practice* (pp. 216–243). San
    Francisco: Jossey-Bass.
Erickson, F. (1982). Classroom discourse as improvisation: Relationships between aca-
    demic task structure and social participation structure in lessons. In L.C. Wilkinson
    (Ed.), *Communicating in classrooms* (pp. 153–181). San Diego: Academic Press.

Evertson, C.M., Emmer, E.T., Clements, B.S., Sandford, J.P., Worsham, M.E., & Williams, E.L. (1981). *Organizing and managing the elementary school classroom.* Austin: University of Texas, Research and Development Center for Teacher Education.

Giangreco, M.R., Cloninger, C.J., & Iverson, V.S. (1998). *Choosing outcomes and accommodations for children (COACH): A guide to educational planning for students with disabilities* (2nd ed.). Baltimore: Paul H. Brookes Publishing Co.

Goldstein, B.S.C. (1996). Critical pedagogy in a bilingual special education classroom. In M.S. Poplin & P.T. Cousin (Eds.), *Alternative views of learning disabilities: Issues for the 21st century* (pp. 147–176). Austin, TX: PRO-ED.

Hanline, M.F. (1993). Inclusion of preschoolers with profound disabilities: An analysis of children's interactions. *Journal of The Association for Persons with Severe Handicaps, 28,* 28–35.

Joyce, B.G., Joyce, J. H., & Chase, P.N. (1989). Considerations for the use of rules in academic settings. *Education and Treatment of Children, 12,* 82–92.

Kaiser, A.P. (1987). *Teaching functional language skills.* Distinguished lecture series, University of Kentucky, Lexington.

Kalyanpur, M., & Harry, B. (1999). *Cultural underpinnings of special education: Building a posture of reciprocity in parent–professional relationships.* Baltimore: Paul H. Brookes Publishing Co.

Legare, A.F. (1984). Using symbols to enhance classroom structure. *Teaching Exceptional Children, 17,* 69–70.

Lipsky, D.K., & Gartner, A. (1992). Achieving full inclusion: Placing the student at the center of educational reform. In W. Stainback & S. Stainback (Eds.). *Controversial issues confronting special education: Divergent perspectives* (pp. 3–12). Needham Heights, MA: Allyn & Bacon.

Means, B., & Knapp, M.S. (1991). Introduction: Rethinking teaching for disadvantaged students. In B. Means, C. Chelemer, & M.S. Knapp (Eds.), *Teaching advanced skills to at-risk students: Views from research and practice* (pp. 1–26). San Francisco: Jossey-Bass.

Montague, M., Bergerson, J., & Lago-Delello, E. (1997). Using prevention strategies in general education. *Focus on Exceptional Children, 29*(8), 1–12.

Munk, D.D., & Repp, A.C. (1994). The relationship between instructional variables and problem behaviors: A review. *Exceptional Children, 60*(5), 390–401.

Murdick, N.L., & Petch-Hogan, B. (1996). Inclusive classroom management: Using preintervention strategies. *Intervention in School and Clinic, 31*(3), 172–176.

Olson, J. (1989). Managing life in the classroom: Dealing with the nitty gritty. *Academic Therapy, 24,* 545–553.

Rettig, M., Kallam, M., & McCarthy-Salm, K. (1993). The effect of social and isolate toys on social interactions of preschool-age children. *Education and Training in Mental Retardation, 28,* 252–256.

Rieth, H., & Evertson, C. (1988). Variables related to the effective instruction of difficult-to-teach children. *Focus on Exceptional Children, 20,* 1–8.

Rincover, A., Newsome, C.D., Lovaas, O.I., & Koegel, R.L. (1977). Some motivational properties of sensory stimulation in psychotic children. *Journal of Experimental Child Psychology, 24,* 312–323.

Rosenkoetter, S.E., & Fowler, S.A. (1986). Teaching mainstreamed children to manage daily transitions. *Teaching Exceptional Children, 19,* 20–23.

Salisbury, C.L., Gallucci, C., Palombaro, M.M., & Peck, C.A. (1995). Strategies that promote social relations among elementary students with and without severe disabilities in inclusive schools. *Exceptional Children, 62*(2), 125–137.

Sapon-Shevin, M. (1990). Student support through cooperative learning. In W. Stainback & S. Stainback (Eds.), *Support networks for inclusive schooling: Interdependent integrated education* (pp. 65–79). Baltimore: Paul H. Brookes Publishing Co.

Shea, T.M., & Bauer, A.M. (1987). *Teaching children and youth with behavior disorders* (2nd ed.). Upper Saddle River, NJ: Prentice-Hall.

Slade, D., & Callaghan, T. (1988). Preventing management problems. *Academic Therapy, 23,* 229–235.

Snell, M., Lowman, D.K., & Canady, R.L. (1996). Parallel block scheduling: Accommodating students' diverse needs in elementary schools. *Journal of Early Intervention, 20*(3), 265–278.

Stainback, S., & Stainback, W. (1990). Facilitating support networks. In W. Stainback & S. Stainback (Eds.), *Support networks for inclusive schooling: Interdependent integrated education* (pp. 25–36). Baltimore: Paul H. Brookes Publishing Co.

Thorson, S. (1996). The missing link: Students discuss school discipline. *Focus on Exceptional Children, 29* (3), 1–12.

Walberg, H.J. (1990). Productive teaching and instruction: Assessing the knowledge base. *Phi Delta Kappan,* 470–478.

Wheldall, K. (1991). Managing troublesome classroom behavior in regular schools: A positive teaching perspective. *International Journal of Disability, Development, and Education, 38*(2), 99–116.

Woolery, M., & Schuster, J.W. (1997). Instructional methods with students who have significant disabilities. *Journal of Special Education, 31*(1), 61–79.

Structuring Programs
for All Learners

Perhaps one of the most important findings [of this study] was that secondary teachers stated that they were willing to make changes in their instructional approaches when students with disabilities were mainstreamed in their classes, although the changes they were willing to make must be ones that were considered to be reasonable.

Linda Ellett (1993, p. 64), describing the results of a study of instruction practices in inclusive secondary classrooms

In this chapter, two factors that are essential to the effective instruction of all learners in inclusive classrooms are discussed. These factors are the nature of the variations among learners and the characteristics of effective teaching and learning environments. The variations among learners that are discussed include variations in learning styles and rates, interactions and behaviors, and ways of gaining access to the environment. The characteristics of effective teaching and learning environments that are reviewed are rules and routines and their roles in classroom management, the use of scripts in classroom management, and natural classroom supports.

LEARNING OBJECTIVES

After completing this chapter, readers will be able to

1. Describe the nature of variations among learners
2. Describe challenges presented by learners who vary from other students in their learning styles and rates
3. Describe challenges presented by learners who vary from other students in their interactions and behaviors
4. Describe challenges presented by learners who vary from their peers in the ways in which they gain access to the environment
5. Discuss characteristics of effective teaching and learning environments
6. Identify the roles of rules and routines in classroom management
7. Describe the role of explicitness and the use of scripts in classroom management
8. Identify natural classroom supports for learners

KEY WORDS AND PHRASES

explicitness—clear, specific, unambiguous cues for students

natural classroom supports—the least-contrived and least-intrusive means of enhancing students' opportunities for success in the classroom

routines—shared, cooperative scripts for completing common procedures in the classroom

rules—statements of explicit limits

scripts—a series of experience-based expectations about the way in which events occur that are developed and practiced to support students

 LEARNING OBJECTIVE 1: To be able to describe the nature of variations among learners

There is great variation among all learners—those with identified disabilities and those without identified disabilities. In inclusive learning communities, the individual learner's specific diagnostic classification (e.g., learning disabilities, mental retardation) generally is not relevant to the planning and implementation of an effective education program. During program planning and implementation, attention should be focused on how the learner learns and the manner in which the learner's disability affects the learning process. Programs should be based on the individual learner's strengths, challenges, and talents.

Learners vary from each other in three ways. First, learners vary in the ways and rates at which they learn. Those who require significant support in learning because of variations in the ways and rates at which they learn have traditionally been labeled *students with learning disabilities, students with mental retardation,* or *students who are gifted, creative, or talented.* Second, learners who differ in ways in which they interact with teachers and peers have traditionally been labeled as *students with emotional or behavioral disorders.* Other learners who vary in the ways in which they interact with teachers and peers may be experiencing a mismatch between the structures and expectations of the school or classroom environment and the interaction patterns that they usually practice because of variations in their ethnicity, culture, language, or gender and those of the teacher and other students in the classroom.

Third, learners vary in the ways in which they gain access to the environment and to information in the environment. Learners with visual disabilities are challenged in gaining access to visual information, and learners with hearing disabilities are challenged in gaining access to auditory information. Such students traditionally have been referred to as *blind* and *deaf,* respectively. Some learners have difficulty in communicating and, as a consequence, have difficulty in obtaining information through the use of spoken or written language. These learners have traditionally been labeled as *students with communication disorders.* Other learners may vary with regard to physical mobility or health, making their experiences in the environment different from those of their peers. These students have traditionally been referred to as *students with physical disabilities or health impairments.* Although each learner is unique, there are some general considerations concerning learners who vary in similar ways. These challenges are discussed in the following sections.

LEARNING OBJECTIVE 2: To be able to describe challenges presented by learners who vary from other students in their learning styles and rates

Learners who vary in their learning styles and rates are commonly identified as a result of a mismatch between the expectations and demands of the classroom and school and the ways in which and the speed with which these learners learn. The traditional classroom, with its work orientation, teacher-set standards, and evaluation of individual performance (Marshall, 1988) emphasizes the differences rather than the similarities between learners who vary from their peers in terms of their learning styles and rates. Inclusive classrooms support all learners and view such variations as natural rather than as problematic.

Learners with Learning Disabilities

The basis of identification of learning disabilities is a discrepancy between ability and academic functioning. Early definitions of *learning disabilities* excluded social skills as a factor. Current definitions, however, do include social skills as a significant factor in this disability. The National Joint Commission on Learning Disabilities (1987) contended in their definition that learning disabilities comprise a heterogeneous group of disorders that are manifested by significant challenges in learning and using speaking, reading, writing, reasoning, or mathematics. The commission contended that problems in self-regulation and social skills are commonly associated with learning disabilities, but they do not by themselves constitute a learning disability (Hammill, 1990).

Bryan (1991) summarized the social problems of learners with learning disabilities as related to three challenges. First, students with learning disabilities seem to have problems in acquiring positive notions about themselves and their self-efficacy. In addition, because of problems related to their interaction styles and social skills, learners identified as having learning disabilities may generate negative attitudes and judgments in others. As they attempt to interact, these learners are challenged in understanding and responding to complex, ambiguous social situations.

Learners with Mental Retardation

Perhaps the most frequently recognized characteristics of learners with mental retardation are related to their cognitive skills. Processing information may be less automatic for learners with mental retardation requiring intermittent or limited supports. In addition, problems may emerge in integrating or generalizing information (Ashman, 1983).

McLean and Snyder-McLean (1988) discussed four critical features of mental retardation. First, mental retardation is developmental in nature and is apparent throughout the developmental period (birth through age 18 years). Second, mental retardation is characterized by problems in general intellectual functioning. Third, mental retardation affects the learner's ability to function across environments. Fourth, mental retardation is identified only when challenges in adaptive behaviors, including independent self-care, language, self-direction, and socialization, are presented.

An alternative way of looking at mental retardation is through the response required by the people identified as having mental retardation. Gold (1980) suggested that mental retardation refers to a level of functioning that requires significant intervention, based on the power needed for the individual to learn. Gold's definition places the limitations imposed by mental retardation in the cultural and social contexts within which the individual functions.

Learners Who Are Gifted, Creative, or Talented

If one considers the distribution of tested intelligence on the typical or bell-shaped curve, the number of learners who are gifted, creative, or talented is limited, by definition, to 3%–5% of the general population. This definition imposes an artificial restriction on the number of learners who can be served as gifted, creative, or talented and leads to charges of elitism (Van Tassel-Baska, Patton, & Prillaman, 1989). Through efforts to widen the definition of gifted, creative, or talented students, more learners can be served through open learning and flexible study opportunities (Marjoram, 1986).

Learners who are gifted, creative, or talented present unique developmental challenges (Hilyer, 1988). Among these challenges are

- Confronting society's contradictory treatment of learners who are gifted, creative, or talented
- Labeling learners as gifted
- More rapid development
- Heightened sensitivity or oversensitivity
- Discrepancy between intellectual and social skills
- Unrealistic goals or expectations
- Perfectionism
- Stress, anxiety, and depression
- Difficulty in coping with failure and success

Your Turn . . .

Consider a simple household task that you completed before you left for class. What challenges would be presented to you in completing this task if you learned at a slower rate than your peers? if you processed information differently? if you processed information more rapidly?

LEARNING OBJECTIVE 3: To be able to describe challenges presented by learners who vary from other students in their interactions and behaviors

As noted in Chapter 1, American society is becoming increasingly diverse. Learners who vary in their interactions and behaviors often present challenges to the school system. These same learners, however, may be competent in other social systems such as family, playground, church, and community. The variations in their interactions may be due to cultural, ethnic, or linguistic diversity; gender; or emotional or behavior disorders.

Cultural, Ethnic, or Linguistic Diversity

In school, learners are socialized to act in specific ways. A conflict occurs when the values and expectations of the school contradict those that the learner has been taught in other social environments or when the same behavior has different meanings for the child and those in authority. Competence at school emerges not as the property of the learner but as the property of situations

presented in the school environment (Mehan, Hertweck, & Meihls, 1986). Inclusive learning communities strive to celebrate diversity.

Gender

Gilligan (1982) commented that, in efforts to eradicate discrimination between
the genders and achieve social justice for women, the differences between the
genders are being rediscovered and examined. Lyons (1985) contrasted male
and female interaction patterns. Whereas women tend to perceive others in
their own terms and in context, men see others in terms of equality and reciprocity. Whereas women are typically interdependent in their relationships
with others, men are autonomous, equal, and independent. Women make social attachments through their responses in social interactions and are concerned with the responsiveness and isolation of others. Men make social attachments through roles, obligations, and duties and are concerned with
equality and fairness in relationships. Women tend to emphasize discussion
and listening in order to understand others; men emphasize the need to maintain fairness and equality in dealing with others.

Learners with Emotional Disabilities or Behavior Disorders

Although an extremely diverse group, learners identified as having emotional
disabilities or behavior disorders present significant challenges to the school
system and the professionals serving them. Rhodes (1967) stated that behavior
disorders are as much a function of where and with whom a child interacts as
the child's behavior itself. Algozzine (1980) reaffirmed this position when he
suggested that the level and the type of behavior that the learner exhibits is not
"disturbed," but the particular set of characteristics that make him or her an individual may evoke different reactions from others within the environment.

   More than half of the referrals for learners for evaluation for emotional or
behavior disorders occur when the learner is in the third through the sixth
grades. Almost three fourths of the learners referred are boys (Hutton, 1985).
Most frequently these learners are identified for special help because of

- Poor peer relationships
- Frustration
- Low achievement
- Withdrawn behavior
- Disruptive behavior
- Fighting
- Refusal to work
- Short attention span

Poor interaction with peers is the most common problem among both boys and
girls.

   The Task Force on Definition of the National Mental Health and Special
Education Coalition (Council for Children with Behavior Disorders, 1990) presented a draft definition for *emotional or behavior disorders* that includes the
following points:

- *Emotional or behavior disorder* refers to a condition in which behavioral or
  emotional responses of a student are so different from those generally accepted as appropriate for the child's age, ethnicity, and culture that they

result in significant problems in self-care, social relationships, educational progress, classroom behavior, or work adjustment.

- Emotional or behavior disorders are more than a transient, expected response to stressors in the environment and resist interventions such as feedback to the student, consultation with parents or families, and modifications of the education environment.
- Multiple sources of data must be used to determine emotional or behavior disorders, and the problem must be present in at least two different environments.

Your Turn . . .

Observe a conversation between a man and a woman, a boy and a girl, or two individuals from different cultural, ethnic, or linguistic groups. What differences in interaction styles emerged in this conversation?

LEARNING OBJECTIVE 4: To be able to describe challenges presented by learners who vary from their peers in the ways in which they gain access to the environment

Spoken language is the medium for most teaching and the way in which most learners demonstrate what they have learned (Cazden, 1986). For learners whose communication, physical, and sensory systems are intact, the communicative process that occurs in teaching is automatic. For learners whose communication, physical, and sensory systems vary from those of their peers, however, the teaching–learning process in classrooms is often a challenge. Learners whose communication, physical, and sensory systems vary from those of their peers are confronted with the challenge of gaining access to the vast amount of information and interaction that occurs in the environment. Those with communication disorders may have difficulty in either the comprehension or the expression of language.

Learners with orthopedic disabilities or other health problems are challenged in gaining access to the physical environment and are limited in experiences that are common to others in interactions with objects, places and positions, or mobility. Learners with visual impairments are challenged in their acquisition of concepts that others learn vicariously through observation. Learners with hearing impairments are challenged in their acquisition of verbal language.

Learners with Communication Disorders

Learners with communication disorders are the second-largest group of individuals who receive special education services. (The largest group is individuals with learning disabilities.) In addition to those learners who receive services primarily because of their identification as students with communication disorders, about one fourth of the learners with other disabilities receive speech and language services as a related service.

There are two general categories of communication disorders: speech disorders and language disorders. Speech disorders are problems with the production of oral or spoken language. Disfluency, voice disorders, and articulation disorders are speech disorders. Language disorders are problems in the comprehension and/or use of the signs or symbols of language applied to express or receive ideas in a spoken, written, or other symbol system. These problems may include receptive (receiving and interpreting), expressive (developing and sending), or mixed (both sending and receiving) language disorders.

Learners with Physical Disabilities or Health Impairments

There are many physical and other health impairments. Perhaps the most recognizable of these are orthopedic disabilities, which affect an individual's participation in daily activities. In addition, ongoing illnesses and other health impairments, such as seizure disorders, human immunodeficiency virus and acquired immunodeficiency syndrome, are conditions with which the teacher needs to be familiar because of these conditions' impact on the functioning of individuals who have them.

With regard to learners with physical disabilities or health impairments, safety is of great importance. To ensure learners' safety, teachers must have pertinent information related to the nature of the physical disability or health impairment, medical procedures, and medications. The Utah State Department of Education (1992) developed a series of forms to be used in gathering safety information, which are presented in Figures 1–4.

A student information form (Figure 1) presents information regarding a student's ongoing health problem. The information provided on this form alerts the teacher to any treatment, medication, or accommodations required by the student. A physician's orders for health care procedures form (Figure 2) is typically required for students who need treatment either daily or on an as-needed basis. For example, the potential treatment may be as infrequent as an injection for a child with a serious allergy to bee stings or as frequent as scheduled snacks for a student with diabetes. Figure 3 is a form that is used to make teachers and school personnel aware of emergency plans for students. These emergency plans may describe what to do if a child with diabetes is having a reaction or a student has a seizure. The Medication/Treatment Administration Record (Figure 4) provides school personnel with information regarding the times, dosages, manner of administration, and potential side effects of medica-

Student's name: _____   Date of birth: _____

Name of person completing form: _____   Date: _____

Does the student . . .	Yes	No	Supports/Plan of action
Have a medical diagnosis of a chronic health problem? Condition:			
Receive treatment during or outside the school day? Treatment:			
Have frequent absences related to the condition?			
Have frequent hospitalizations?			
Receive ongoing medication for physical or behavior disorders? Medication:			
Need scheduling adjustment (e.g., rest following a seizure, limitation in physical activity, longer time between activities)?			
Need environmental adjustments (e.g., special seating, refrigeration of medication, temperature control)?			
Require safety considerations (e.g., lifting, transportation, emergency plan, positioning equipment, feeding equipment)?			

Figure 1. Sample student information form.

tion or treatment. In addition, the form provides an administration log to ensure that the medication is given at the correct time by the appropriate individual.

Learners with Visual Impairments

Learners with visual impairments are those whose sight is limited in some manner to the extent that special services are required. Many people with visual impairments have a degree of sight that is useful for some purposes (Finkelstein, 1989). Teachers should remember that vision is only one source of information for learners. Two large groups emerge among learners with visual impairments: those who are blind and require alternatives to print and visual materials and those who are partially sighted and may use print and

Student: _____

Condition for which procedure is required	
Description of standardized procedures	
Precautions and possible adverse reactions and interventions	
Time schedules and suggested environment procedures	
Procedure is to be continued as described above until [*insert a date*]	
Dietary recommendations	
Activity limitations	

Physician: _____

Physician's signature: _____

Contact person: _____

Figure 2.   Sample physician's orders for health care procedures form. (Orders must be updated at least annually.)

visual materials with the support of large-print reading materials, optical aids, technological aids, and education in the use of residual vision.

Learners with Hearing Impairments

Learners with hearing impairments may be deaf or hard of hearing. *Deafness* is defined as a hearing impairment that precludes successful processing of linguistic information through hearing, with or without amplification. Individuals who are hard of hearing have hearing ability that is adequate for successful processing of linguistic information through hearing with amplification (Report of the Ad Hoc Committee to Define Deaf and Hard of Hearing, 1975).

More than half of the school day of learners who are developing typically is devoted to listening, making it extremely difficult for the learner with hearing impairment to understand all of the information being presented auditorily. Although there is great controversy regarding the education of learners with hearing impairments, the Council on the Education of the Deaf (1976) formally stated that no single method of instruction or communication can best meet the needs of all students with hearing impairments.

Your Turn . . .

During 10 minutes of class time, assume that you vary from your peers in the ways in which you gain access to the environment and information in the environment. What challenges would be presented if you

- Had a hearing impairment?
- Had a visual impairment?
- Had difficulty with receptive language?
- Had difficulty with expressive language?
- Were unable to move your hands?
- Were unable to sit for extended periods of time?

LEARNING OBJECTIVE 5: To be able to discuss characteristics of effective teaching and learning environments

Effective teaching and learning environments include a fairly clear set of characteristics. These include

1. High expectations for students' learning
2. Clear and focused instruction
3. Close monitoring of students' learning
4. Reteaching using alternative strategies when children do not learn
5. Using incentives and rewards to promote learning
6. Efficient use of classroom **routines**
7. Enforced high standards for classroom behavior
8. Excellent personal interactions with students (Bain, 1989)

In Bain's (1989) study, effective teachers with excellent organizational skills had available to them almost 1 additional hour of teaching time per week for mathematics and reading than did less-well-organized teachers.

In addition to teacher-oriented indicators, three key elements may support prosocial behavior in inclusive environments (Cheney, 1989). These are organization; anticipation and redirection of student behavior; and positive, en-

Student: _____   Date: _____

Preferred hospital: _____

Physician: _____   Physician's telephone: _____

Contact person: _____

Student-specific emergencies

If you see the following . . .	Do the following . . .

If an emergency occurs:

1. Call 911 if it appears to be life threatening

2. Stay with the student or designate another adult to do so

3. Call, or ask someone to call, the principal and/or the child's parent

Figure 3.   Sample emergency plan form.

couraging interactions that serve to prevent disruptions in teaching and learning. Organization includes physical arrangement of the classroom, a consistent schedule of activities, procedures for classroom routines, and **rules**. Anticipation and redirection occur through lesson planning and delivery, specific teacher behaviors, and knowledge of individual students' behavior patterns. Positive, encouraging interactions are provided through students' success in classroom activities, encouraging rather than praising, and supporting rather than criticizing when errors in students' interactions occur (Cheney, 1989).

Multiple Concurrent Agenda of Classrooms

The interactions among the teacher, the learner, and the learning environment are complex and multiply determined. In any classroom, multiple, concurrent agendas are operating. One example of concurrent agendas involves two levels of student engagement. Nystand and Gamoran (1989) suggested that students are engaged in both procedural engagement (concerning classroom rules and regulations) and substantive engagement (sustained commitment to the content and issues of academic study) concurrently. Disengagement at either level adversely affects achievement. The teacher may increase

Student: _____   School: _____

Date of birth: _____   Grade: _____

Physician: _____   Date: _____

Employees designated and trained to
administer medication/treatment: _____

Medication/Treatment

Medication/treatment	Time(s)	Dosage	How given	Possible effects on learning and physical functioning

Medication/Treatment Administration Log

Date	Time	Signature	Date	Time	Signature

Figure 4.   Sample medication/treatment administration record.

substantive engagement by asking authentic or open-ended questions, incorporating students' previous answers into subsequent questions, and using students' responses in the subsequent discussion. One clear indicator of substantive engagement is the reciprocal interaction and negotiation between students and the teacher.

The social and academic agendas of classrooms also exist concurrently. Brown, Bauer, and Kretschmer (1995) reported that among children in a developmental kindergarten, the teacher perceived children's behaviors associated with connecting socially to be disruptive and often interrupted or redirected these behaviors. As the teacher attempted to proceed with her academic agenda, however, the students' social interactions became more covert. The students employed looks, gestures, and nods to connect socially. Teachers may be more successful in accomplishing their academic agenda if they balance the need for successful lesson completion with their students' needs to connect with each other socially.

Hidden agendas often are evident in education environments. Mills and Simpson (1986) suggested that hidden agendas are a consequence of personal values, culture-bound factors of communication, and the institutional approaches and practices of teachers. When there is a cultural mismatch between the teacher and the learner, a hidden agenda may preclude the learner's substantive engagement in the material being presented. Rather than attend to the task at hand, the learner must attend to adapting his or her cultural interaction style to that of the teacher.

LEARNING OBJECTIVE 6: To be able to identify the roles of rules and routines in classroom management

Inclusive classrooms are orderly places. Two essential aspects of creating and maintaining this order are rules and routines.

Rules

Rules are statements of explicit limits on behavior. Castle and Rogers (1994) suggested that teachers and learners collaboratively create classroom rules. During the collaborative process, learners not only engage in the meaningful experience of learning about and creating rules but also establish a positive sense of classroom community. As students suggest rules for discussion, reflection and inductive reasoning are used to problem-solve the content of the rule and its rationale, as well as the most accurate way to state the rule, and to meaningfully connect with the needs of the students. Through student-generated rules, greater respect for rules and a sense of community are encouraged.

Presentation of rules is also an essential part of effective management. Brooks (1985) indicated that, when reviewing each rule with the class, the teacher should

1. State the rule
2. Provide the reason behind the rule
3. Provide an example of appropriate behavior within the limits of the rule
4. Describe the consequences of breaking the rule

Routines

Routines are shared, cooperative **scripts** for completing common procedures in the classroom. Baron (1992) suggested that *classroom management* actually refers to the routines that a teacher uses to maintain a smoothly running classroom. Routines are invaluable in helping students make sense of the classroom and move through activities and the segments of the day (Schulz & Florio, 1979).

Routines allow teachers to model for students in a unique way. Routines provide clues to teachers' information-processing methods and ways of solving problems for their students. Experienced teachers, through the use of routines, are able to predict classroom conditions and execute their lessons in a single step rather than through a series of sequential directions (Bromme, 1982).

In addition to helping the day go smoothly, routines can be used to support the development of literacy skills among young children. Taylor and Gay (1988) described the efforts of an inner-city elementary school teacher to create a functionally literate environment in her classroom by linking written language to the classroom routines. By using written routines and increasing the learner's opportunities to write and receive written communication, the teacher created a print-rich environment.

LEARNING OBJECTIVE 7: To be able to describe the role of explicitness and the use of scripts in classroom management

A primary goal of all teachers is to increase academic learning time. Academic learning time includes allocated time (the actual time the learner has to work), engagement time (the proportion of allocated time during which the student is paying attention to the set tasks), and success rate (the amount of time during which the learner experiences varying levels of success on the set tasks) (Hardy, 1990).

Explicitness increases academic learning time. *Explicitness* means providing clear, specific, unambiguous cues for students. In an ethnographic study of the commonalities in teachers' and learners' perceptions of effective classroom learning, Cooper and McIntyre (1993) found that teachers and learners agreed that the teacher's making explicit the agenda for the lesson was valuable as an aid for learning and understanding. Other variables that teachers and learners reported that were related to explicitness and clarity in instruction are summarized in Table 1.

Scripts

Scripts are a series of experience-based expectations about the way in which events occur that are developed and practiced to support students. Scripts assist students in organizing the sequence of school activities as well as in interpreting and participating in common classroom events (Ranney, 1992). For example, a preschooler whose teacher refers to students as *bus riders* or *carpoolers* may act confused when a parent says he or she is going to "pick up [the preschooler]," asking, "Am I a bus rider or a carpooler?"

Scripts can be developed for students and teachers as a way of providing supports in the environment. In this situation, a script is essentially a person-

Table 1. Ways of increasing clarity and explicitness reported by both teachers and learners

Both teachers and learners reported that the following strategies were valuable to learning and understanding:

- Recapping previous lessons and highlighting continuity between lessons
- Teacher's storytelling to provide examples
- Oral explanation by the teacher, often combined with discussion/question-and-answer sessions and use of blackboard
- Blackboard notes and diagrams
- Pictures and other visual stimuli
- Use of models based on student work or generated by teacher
- Structure for written work generated and presented by teacher
- Printed text or worksheets
- Use of stimuli that relate to pupils' popular culture

Source: Cooper and McIntyre (1993).

alized and detailed guideline for providing instructions and/or managing behaviors (Barnett, Ehrhardt, Stollar, & Bauer, 1993). As such, students can be taught the sequence of events necessary to succeed in the classroom. For example, the "entering the classroom in the morning" script for a fourth grader may be as follows:

1. Enter the classroom.
2. Hang up your coat.
3. Take any notes out of your book bag.
4. Hang up your book bag.
5. Put your notes on the teacher's desk.
6. Go to your desk.
7. Check to see if your pencils need sharpening.
8. Sharpen your pencils if necessary.
9. Return to your seat; check the blackboard for morning work.
10. Begin your morning work.

If a student appears to be wandering around the classroom in the morning, he or she may need to be taught the script and may need prompts, such as a check sheet or a list of steps in the script to follow. Rather than reprimanding the student who is not coming to class and starting to work, providing a script is a proactive measure to ensure that the student knows what must be done. In this way, scripts can be developed and practiced to support students.

 LEARNING OBJECTIVE 8: To be able to identify natural classroom supports for learners

The most effective supports for any learner are those that are the most **natural classroom supports** (i.e., least contrived, least intrusive). Supports that occur naturally in the environment are more likely to help maintain behaviors that are generalizable to other environments (Barnett & Bauer, 1992). Natural supports are effective; inexpensive; controlled within the classroom; flexible; sustainable by using resources within the classroom; simple; and compatible with the needs, values, and customs of the teacher, the student, and the classroom (Fawcett, Mathews, & Fletcher, 1980).

Natural supports are developed based on an analysis of situations, through collaborative problem solving, and with consideration of the naturalistic basis for the support (Barnett & Bauer, 1992). There are, however, several strategies that can encourage social interactions among learners with disabilities and their classmates without disabilities.

In preschool, Hanline (1993) found that an ongoing curriculum structure that enhances interactions, such as cooperative learning and curricula that have social goals, is a natural way to support inclusion. In addition, learners' interactions can be encouraged by placing and positioning learners with disabilities in areas or in ways that encourage participation (e.g., placing in the same areas as other children, choosing learners with disabilities to lead games with support).

In addition, social interactions can be encouraged. For example, to include a learner with disabilities in an activity, Hanline suggested a teacher's saying to a peer who is developing typically and who is playing with clay, "Can Sarah have some of those pies you're making?" Through modeling appropriate interactions, the teacher can further the appropriate interactions of his or her students. In some situations, the teacher may need to interpret the behavior of learners with disabilities as meaningful by, for example, making statements such as, "When Mary is waving her hands like that, she's excited."

Hanline encouraged teachers to answer the questions of learners without disabilities about the children with disabilities as those questions occur. For example, a student might ask, "Why does Joey hit when he wants stuff?" The teacher could reply, "Joey isn't using many words yet. His way of getting things he wants is to hit. When Joey hits, say, 'No hitting, Joey. Sign WANT.'"

In elementary and secondary school, a buddy system is an effective natural support. Students naturally turn to a peer for help when they require brief supports or need the answer to a question. These supports may range from permitting a student to ask a nearby classmate for clarification when needed to having an assigned helper or arranging formal peer tutoring.

Four sets of variables emerge in formal peer support situations (i.e., tutoring) (Project STRETCH, 1980). First, students should be matched carefully, with partners being of comparable size and age. Second, the teacher should be conscious of each student's needs, recognizing that, for some students, peer tutoring may be distracting rather than facilitating. Third, students should be prepared to support their peers, with clear goals set for their interaction and assistance in developing their listening skills. The logistics of formal peer support should be considered, recognizing issues of space, noise, and time.

SUMMARY

This chapter addresses the following major concepts:

1. The nature of the variations among learners include variations in learning styles and rates, interactions and behaviors, and the ways in which students gain access to the environment.

2. Learners who vary in their learning styles and rates have traditionally been classified as having learning disabilities or mental retardation or as being gifted, creative, or talented.
3. Learners who vary from their peers in their interactions and behaviors may do so because of cultural, ethnic, or linguistic diversity or because of their gender; learners who vary to such an extent that they require special services traditionally have been classified as having emotional disabilities or behavior disorders.
4. Learners may vary in the ways in which they gain access to the environment and to information in the environment because of visual impairments, hearing impairments, communication disorders, physical disabilities, or other health impairments.
5. There are identifiable characteristics of effective teaching and learning environments.
6. Explicit rules and routines are necessary for effective classroom management.
7. Scripts may provide an explicit support to learners in working with their peers and teachers.
8. The most effective classroom supports frequently are the most natural.

TEST YOUR KNOWLEDGE

Completion of the "Self-Evaluation," "Make the Language Your Own," and "Application Activities" sections will aid readers in understanding and retaining the information presented in this chapter. Answer keys for the "Self-Evaluation" and "Make the Language Your Own" sections are located in the Appendix at the end of the book.

Self-Evaluation

Select the most appropriate response to complete each of the following statements:

1. Programs for learners who appear to vary from their peers should be
    a. The same as those for their peers
    b. Based on the traditional label used to describe the learner
    c. Based on the learner's strengths, challenges, and talents

2. Learners from diverse cultural, ethnic, or linguistic groups
    a. May experience a mismatch between the structures and expectations of the classroom and their community interaction patterns
    b. Are identified as having emotional disabilities or behavior disorders
    c. Are unable to use the scripts required in the classroom

3. Learners with physical disabilities or other health impairments vary from their peers without disabilities in
    a. Their learning styles and rates
    b. How they gain access to the environment and information in the environment
    c. Interactions with their peers

4. The medium of the majority of teaching in the classroom is
    a. Written language
    b. Spoken language
    c. Scripts and routines

5. Teachers in effective learning environments
   a. Use a clear scope and sequence for learning
   b. Enforce high standards for classroom behavior
   c. Vary their expectations according to individual learners' abilities

6. In procedural engagement, learners
   a. Are committed to the content and issues of academic study
   b. Demonstrate an understanding of routines
   c. Are concerned with classroom rules and regulations

7. Hidden agendas are a consequence of
   a. The teacher's efforts to engage students in critical thinking
   b. A lack of explicitness
   c. Personal values, culture-bound factors of communication, and institutional approaches and practices of teachers

8. Rules
   a. Demonstrate low teacher expectations for learners' behavior
   b. Express limits on learners' behavior
   c. Eliminate the need for sequential directions

9. Explicitness
   a. Reduces the learner's need to think critically
   b. Increases the learner's ability to think critically
   c. Increases academic learning time

10. Natural supports
    a. Require additional classroom personnel
    b. Are the least contrived supports
    c. Are least engaging for students

Make the Language Your Own
Match the following terms with their definitions:

1. _____ Routines

2. _____ Rules

3. _____ Scripts

4. _____ Explicitness

5. _____ Natural classroom supports

a. Clear, specific, unambiguous cues for students
b. The least-contrived and least-intrusive means of enhancing students' opportunities for success in the classroom
c. Shared, cooperative scripts for completing common procedures in the classroom
d. Statements of explicit limits
e. A series of experience-based expectations about the way in which events occur that are developed and practiced to support students

Application Activities
1. In a preschool, elementary school, or secondary school classroom, observe the interactions among participants during one period for 2 weeks. Interview the teacher regarding his or her assumptions, perceptions, and ex-

pectations of the students in the classroom. Summarize how the teacher's assumptions about the students affect his or her interactions with them. Describe briefly the assumptions and expectations of the teacher regarding students

    a.   Who the teacher perceives as varying in learning rate from other students

    b.   Who the teacher perceives as varying in learning style from other students

    c.   From minority cultures

    d.   Of each gender

    e.   With a hearing impairment, visual impairment, or physical disability

    f.   Who the teacher perceives as varying from peers in socioeconomic status and/or in physical appearance

2.   In classroom observations, consider the following questions:

    a.   What challenges are present for a learner whose learning rate varies (either faster or slower) from that of his or her peers?

    b.   What challenges are present for a learner from a minority culture?

    c.   What challenges are present for a male learner? a female learner?

    d.   What challenges are present for a learner who varies in his or her learning style? is more successful as an auditory learner? as a visual learner? as someone who learns by doing? as someone who learns by observation rather than by participation?

    e.   What challenges are present for a learner with a hearing impairment? with a visual impairment? with a physical disability involving balance, coordination, or wheelchair use?

    f.   What challenges are present for a learner who varies from his or her peers in terms of socioeconomic status? in terms of physical appearance?

REFERENCES

Algozzine, B. (1980). The disturbing child: A matter of opinion. *Behavioral Disorders, 5*(2), 112–115.

Ashman, A.F. (1983). Exploring the cognition of retarded persons: A brief report. *International Journal of Rehabilitation Research, 6,* 355–356.

Bain, H. (1989, April). *A study of fifty effective teachers whose class average gain scores ranked in the top 15 percent of four school types in Project STAR.* Paper presented at the annual meeting of the American Educational Research Association, San Francisco.

Barnett, D.W., & Bauer, A.M. (1992). *Designing interventions for young children: A model of service delivery for Ohio* [Grant proposal]. Cincinnati: Ohio Department of Education, Division of Early Childhood.

Barnett, D.W., Ehrhardt, K.E., Stollar, S.A., & Bauer, A.M. (1993, December). *PASSKey: A model for naturalistic assessment and intervention design.* Paper presented at the National Association of School Psychologists annual convention, Washington, DC.

Baron, E.B. (1992). *Discipline strategies for teachers.* Bloomington, IN: Phi Delta Kappa.

Bromme, R. (1982, April). *How to analyze routines in teachers' thinking processes during lesson planning.* Paper presented at the annual meeting of the American Educational Research Association, New York City.

Brooks, D.M. (1985). The teacher's communicative competence: The first day of school. *Theory into Practice, 24,* 63–70.

Brown, M.S., Bauer, A.M., & Kretschmer, R.R. (1995). Dual agenda: Social participation and teachers' lessons. *Qualitative Studies in Education, 8,* 265–280.

Bryan, T. (1991). Social problems and learning disabilities. In B.L.Y. Wong (Ed.), *Learning about learning disabilities* (pp. 195–229). San Diego: Academic Press.

Castle, K., & Rogers, K. (1994). Rule-creating in a constructivist classroom community. *Childhood Education, 70*(2), 77–80.

Cazden, C. (1986). Classroom discourse. In M.C. Wittrock, *Handbook of research on teaching* (3rd ed., pp. 432–463). New York: Macmillan.

Cheney, C.O. (1989, April). *Preventive discipline through effective classroom management.* Paper presented at the annual convention of the Council for Exceptional Children, San Francisco.

Cooper, P., & McIntyre, D. (1993). Commonality in teachers' and pupils' perceptions of effective classroom learning. *British Journal of Educational Psychology, 63*, 381–399.

Council for Children with Behavior Disorders. (1990, August). Coalition finalizes definition. *Council for Children with Behavioral Disorders Newsletter, 1.*

Council on the Education of the Deaf. (1976). *Resolution on individualized educational programming for the hearing impaired.* Washington, DC: Author.

Ellett, L. (1993). Instructional practices in mainstreamed secondary classrooms. *Journal of Learning Disabilities, 26*(1), 57–64.

Fawcett, S.B., Mathews, R.M., & Fletcher, R.K. (1980). Some promising dimensions for behavioral community technology. *Journal of Applied Behavior Analysis, 13*, 505–518.

Finkelstein, D. (1989). *Blindness and disorders of the eye.* Baltimore: National Federation for the Blind.

Gilligan, C. (1982). *In a different voice: Psychological theory and women's development.* Cambridge, MA: Harvard University Press.

Gold, M.W. (1980). An alternative definition of mental retardation. In M.W. Gold (Ed.), *"Did I say that?": Articles and commentary on the Try Another Way system* (pp. 17–25). Champaign, IL: Research Press Co.

Hammill, D.D. (1990). On defining learning disabilities: An emerging consensus. *Journal of Learning Disabilities, 23*, 74–84.

Hanline, M.F. (1993). Inclusion of preschoolers with profound disabilities: An analysis of children's interactions. *Journal of The Association for Persons with Severe Handicaps, 18*, 28–35.

Hardy, C.A. (1990). Teacher communication and time on-task. *Research in Education, 49*, 30–38.

Hilyer, K. (1988). Problems of gifted children. *Journal of the Association for the Study of Perception, 21*, 10–26.

Hutton, J.B. (1985). What reasons are given by teachers who refer problem behavior students? *Psychology in the Schools, 22*, 79–82.

Lyons, N. (1985). *Visions and competencies: Men and women as decision makers and conflict managers.* Cambridge, MA: Harvard University Press.

Marjoram, T. (1986). Better late than never: Able youths and adults. *Gifted Education International, 4*(2), 89–96.

Marshall, H.H. (1988). Work or learning: Implications for classroom metaphors. *Educational Researcher, 17*(9), 9–16.

McLean, J.E., & Snyder-McLean, L. (1988). Application of pragmatics to severely mentally retarded children and youth. In R.L. Schiefelbusch & L.L. Lloyd (Eds.), *Language perspectives: Acquisition, retardation, and intervention* (2nd ed., pp. 255–289). Austin, TX: PRO-ED.

Mehan, H., Hertweck, A., & Meihls, J.L. (1986). *Handicapping the handicapped: Decision making in students' educational careers.* Stanford, CA: Stanford University Press.

Mills, J.R., & Simpson, N. (1986). *Cross-cultural conflict in higher education* (Research Rep. No. 4). Chicago: National Association for Developmental Education.

National Joint Commission on Learning Disabilities. (1987). Adults with learning disabilities: A call to action. *Journal of Learning Disabilities, 20*, 172–175.

Nystand, M., & Gamoran, A. (1989). *Instructional discourse and student engagement.* Madison, WI: National Center on Effective Secondary Schools.

Project STRETCH. (1980). *Peer tutoring.* Northbrook, IL: Hubbard.

Ranney, S. (1992). Learning a new script: An exploration of sociolinguistic competence. *Applied Linguistics, 13*, 25–47.

Report of the Ad Hoc Committee to Define Deaf and Hard of Hearing. (1975). *American Annals of the Deaf, 120,* 509–512.

Rhodes, W.C. (1967). The disturbing child: A problem of ecological management. *Exceptional Children, 33,* 449–455.

Schulz, J., & Florio, S. (1979). Stop and freeze: The negotiation of social and physical space in a kindergarten/first grade classroom. *Anthropology and Education Quarterly, 10,* 166–181.

Taylor, N.E., & Gay, A. (1988). The search for a two-headed cat. *Momentum, 19*(2), 10–12.

Utah State Department of Education. (1992). *Guidelines for serving students with special health care needs.* Salt Lake City: Author.

Van Tassel-Baska, J., Patton, J., & Prillaman, D. (1989). Disadvantaged gifted learners at risk for educational attention. *Focus on Exceptional Children, 22*(3), 1–15.

Principles of Learning

It was amazing. It was like I was listening to myself. My fourth graders were in their cooperative learning groups with Katie, who has spina bifida and some pretty serious learning problems. She has a hard time attending for long periods of time. One of the girls would, every 2 or 3 minutes, pat Katie on the hand and say, "Thanks for staying with us, Katie!" or "Great job, Katie," or "Thanks for sharing, Katie." It showed me two things—first, that we are serious models for our students. Second, that kids can implement behavioral programs without any explicit instruction!

        Ms. N., a fourth-grade teacher in an inclusive classroom

According to King-Sears (1997), proactive behavior management is a recommended practice in inclusive classrooms. Proactive behavior management is a positive approach to managing behavior that is applied consistently throughout the school. The rules of behavior are clear to all members of the school community. Communication with families is frequent and positive. Collegial teams support individual teachers and students. In addition, the school is a safe, secure environment that is attractive to all members of the community. The amount of disruption caused by any behavior management intervention must warrant its application. Yeaton and Sechrest (1981) suggested that the strongest intervention is the weakest one that works. Weigle (1997) suggested positive behavioral support as a schoolwide approach to proactive behavior management. The foci of intervention in positive behavioral support are long-term goals and changes in behavior that ultimately decrease challenging behaviors. The following are the basic principles of positive behavioral support:

- The broad emphasis of behavior change is on lifestyle concerns, such as happiness with friends, positive and productive social interactions, and personal independence rather than on modifying specific challenging behaviors.
- Long-term goals and outcomes occurring over a period of years rather than short-term behavioral objectives are emphasized.
- Behavior management programs are based on the function of the behavior rather than on its topography (i.e., observable and measurable features).
- Interventions are based on individual needs and individual effectiveness rather than on hierarchies of intervention strategies.
- Functionally equivalent skills are taught to replace challenging behaviors.
- Behavior change plans are positive, emphasizing reinforcement procedures.
- Emphasis is placed on preventing the occurrence of challenging behaviors rather than on providing consequences for those challenging behaviors.
- Interventions may have multiple components, such as adapting the curriculum, preventing the occurrence of the behavior, and providing social skills programming.

This chapter contains a detailed discussion of behavior management interventions. The chapter provides information regarding an emphasis on positive reinforcement procedures. The behavioral interventions described in the chapter form one of the many components of a behavior management plan for a student or a group of students. Interventions discussed in the chapter include positive reinforcement, extinction, negative reinforcement, shaping, prompting, modeling, and token economy. Contingency contracting and the Premack principle are discussed. The chapter concludes with a discussion of the roles of partial participation and fading procedures in inclusive classrooms.

LEARNING OBJECTIVES

After completing this chapter, readers will be able to

1. Describe basic principles of learning, including the use of positive reinforcement, extinction, negative reinforcement, shaping, prompting, modeling, and token economy
2. Implement contingency contracting and the Premack principle in the classroom
3. Recognize the use of partial participation and fading in inclusive classrooms

KEY WORDS AND PHRASES

aversives—noxious and sometimes painful consequences of behavior; undesirable results of behavior that the individual typically wishes to avoid

baseline data—quantitative data collected on the target behavior before a behavior change intervention is implemented

contingency contracting—the process of contracting so that the student can do something that he or she wants to do following completion of a task the teacher wants the student to do

contract—an agreement, written or verbal, between two or more parties, individuals, or groups that stipulates the responsibilities of the parties concerning a specific item or activity

extinction—the discontinuation or withholding of a reinforcer that previously reinforced a behavior

fading—the systematic, gradual reduction of prompts and supports

intervention data—quantitative data collected on the target behavior during intervention

modeling—the provision of an individual or group behavior to be imitated or not to be imitated by an individual

negative reinforcement—the strengthening of a behavior as a consequence of the removal of an already-operating aversive stimulus

partial participation—the engagement of an individual with disabilities in a skill to the best of his or her ability in an age-appropriate, meaningful, natural environment

positive reinforcement—presentation of a desirable reinforcer after a behavior has been exhibited; the process of reinforcing a target behavior in order to increase the probability that the behavior will recur

Premack principle—principle stating that a behavior that has a high rate of occurrence can be used to increase a behavior with a low rate of occurrence

principles of reinforcement—a set of rules to be applied in the behavior change process; the rules of learning

prompting—the process of providing verbal, visual, aural, or manual assistance to a student during the behavior change process to facilitate the completion of a task

punishment—the addition of an aversive stimulus or the subtraction of a pleasurable stimulus as a consequence of behavior

reinforcer—the consequence (which may be tangible or social, positive or negative) of a behavior

shaping—the systematic, immediate reinforcement of successive approximations of a target behavior until the behavior is established

target behavior—the specific behavior to be changed as a result of intervention

token economy—a system of exchange in which the student earns tokens as reinforcers and exchanges them for tangible and social reinforcers

LEARNING OBJECTIVE 1: To be able to describe basic principles of learning, including the use of positive reinforcement, extinction, negative reinforcement, shaping, prompting, modeling, and token economy

Throughout the school day, teachers apply behavioral interventions grounded in the principles of learning. Although the emphasis in schools on the strict application of behavior modification interventions is waning, the use of **principles of reinforcement** and strategies derived from them, such as **positive reinforcement, extinction, negative reinforcement, shaping, prompting, modeling**, and **token economy**, are applied frequently and considered to be good teaching practices. The learning principles may be applied informally throughout the day, or they may be applied to specific students through the use of a behavior intervention plan. According to Walker and Shea (1995), the following are the principles of reinforcement:

- Reinforcement is dependent on the exhibition of the **target behavior**.
- The target behavior is to be reinforced immediately after it is exhibited.
- During the initial stages of the behavior change process, the target behavior is reinforced each time it is exhibited.
- The target behavior is reinforced intermittently after it reaches a satisfactory level.
- Social **reinforcers** are always applied with tangible reinforcers if tangible reinforcers are used.
- Social reinforcers are preferred.

The components of a behavior intervention plan include

- Selecting a target behavior
- Collecting and recording **baseline data**
- Identifying reinforcers
- Implementing the intervention and documenting its effects
- Evaluating the effects of the intervention

The decisions involved in the design of a behavior intervention plan for a student are complex. Cooper, Heron, and Heward (1987) suggested that there are nine issues that should be considered regarding these decisions. In Table 1, these issues have been reformulated as questions to facilitate the decision-making process.

Once the decision has been made to intervene in a learner's behavior, the target behavior is defined. The target behavior is the specific behavior to be changed as a result of intervention. The definition of the target behavior takes the form of a behavioral objective. The objective includes a description of what the student is expected to do, using action verbs to denote the behavior. The level of performance expected, if the student is successful, is included in the objective. The following are examples of behavioral objectives that may be used in inclusive environments:

- Jacob will initiate a play interaction with his buddy in the block area during choice time.
- Mickey will remain with his cooperative learning group for 10 minutes.
- Martina will make one comment or response using her educational interpreter during social studies.
- Jameel will complete the study guide for social studies group with the support of a scribe.
- Renaldo will complete the morning routine of entering the classroom, hanging up his book bag, removing his home folder, and placing the folder in the basket without teacher or peer cues.

Once the behavior is defined and written as an objective, the learner's current level of the behavior is documented. This documentation of the level of a behavior is referred to as *baseline data,* which are defined as quantitative data collected on the target behavior before a behavior change intervention is implemented. Gathering baseline data employs some sort of counting and charting. Various means of counting and charting baseline behavior and subsequent **intervention data** are presented in Figures 1, 2, and 3.

Table 1. Issues related to decisions regarding behavior plans

- Is the challenging behavior a danger to the student or to others?
- Is the behavior so frequent that it requires intervention? Or, are there so many opportunities for a new or replacement behavior to occur that it requires intervention to instate it?
- Has the challenging behavior been occurring for a long time? Or, has the student long needed a new or replacement behavior?
- Will the new or replacement behavior produce a higher level of reinforcement for the individual than the challenging behaviors? (Behaviors that produce high levels of reinforcement usually take priority over behaviors that produce a low level of reinforcement.)
- What is the impact of the behavior on the individual's skill development and independence?
- Will the behavior reduce the negative attention the student receives?
- Will the behavior increase reinforcement for others in the student's environment?
- How much time and energy will be expended to change the behavior?
- What is the cost to change the behavior?

Adapted from Cooper, Heron, and Heward (1987).

Behavioral objective: Renaldo will complete the morning routine of entering the classroom, hanging up his book bag, removing his home folder, and placing the folder in the basket, without teacher or peer cues.

Step	Level of assistance required									
Dates:										
Hangs up book bag	3	3	3	3	3	3	3	3	3	3
	2	2	2	2	2	2	2	2	2	2
	1	1	1	1	1	1	1	1	1	1
	0	0	0	0	0	0	0	0	0	0
Removes home folder	3	3	3	3	3	3	3	3	3	3
	2	2	2	2	2	2	2	2	2	2
	1	1	1	1	1	1	1	1	1	1
	0	0	0	0	0	0	0	0	0	0
Places home folder in basket	3	3	3	3	3	3	3	3	3	3
	2	2	2	2	2	2	2	2	2	2
	1	1	1	1	1	1	1	1	1	1
	0	0	0	0	0	0	0	0	0	0

Circle the number below representing the level of assistance Renaldo required to complete the task:

3   Independently completed the task
2   Required a verbal cue from teacher or peer
1   Required a demonstration from teacher or peer
0   Required physical assistance from teacher or peer

Figure 1.   Documenting level of assistance data.

After gathering baseline data, reinforcers to be used during intervention are identified. A reinforcer is the consequence of the behavior; it may be tangible or social and may be positive or negative. A reinforcer is not desirable because a teacher believes it is; reinforcers reinforce only if they change the learner's behavior, that is, by being reinforcing to the student whose behavior is being changed. Asking the student is the simplest way to determine what the student would like to be used as reinforcers. Another excellent way to determine what a student may like as a reinforcer is to observe what the student does during free or unstructured time. Individuals tend to do whatever they enjoy doing during free and unstructured time. In addition, teachers may interview parents or former teachers to identify reinforcers.

After determining the reinforcer, the behavior program is implemented and data are collected. After a predetermined period of time (usually no less than 2 weeks), the intervention program is revisited and evaluated using the data collected during the intervention. The effectiveness of the intervention is evaluated by comparing the intervention data with the baseline data.

Objective: Mickey will stay with his cooperative learning group for 10 minutes. (Time ends when Mickey physically leaves the group.)

Circle the number of minutes for which Mickey remains with his group.

[Date]	[Date]	[Date]	[Date]	[Date]	[Date]	[Date]	[Date]	[Date]	[Date]	[Date]
10	10	10	10	10	10	10	10	10	10	10
9	9	9	9	9	9	9	9	9	9	9
8	8	8	8	8	8	8	8	8	8	8
7	7	7	7	7	7	7	7	7	7	7
6	6	6	6	6	6	6	6	6	6	6
5	5	5	5	5	5	5	5	5	5	5
4	4	4	4	4	4	4	4	4	4	4
3	3	3	3	3	3	3	3	3	3	3
2	2	2	2	2	2	2	2	2	2	2
1	1	1	1	1	1	1	1	1	1	1
0	0	0	0	0	0	0	0	0	0	0

Figure 2. Documenting duration data.

Interventions that a teacher may implement in the inclusive classroom to increase students' learning and to maintain or increase appropriate behavior include positive reinforcement, extinction, negative reinforcement, shaping, prompting, modeling, and token economy. These interventions are discussed in the subsections that follow.

Positive Reinforcement

The most common application of the principles of reinforcement is positive reinforcement. *Positive reinforcement* is also known as *positive attention, social reinforcement, approval,* and *rewarding.* Positive reinforcement is the presentation of a desirable reinforcer after the behavior has been exhibited or the process of reinforcing a target behavior in order to increase the probability that the behavior will recur. In positive reinforcement, the teacher presents a positive consequence after the target behavior has been exhibited. The advantages of positive reinforcement are that 1) it is responsive to the student's natural need for attention and approval and 2) it decreases the probability that the student will exhibit challenging behavior in an effort to obtain needed attention.

Two rules are essential for the effective application of positive reinforcement. First, when the student is initially exhibiting a new appropriate behavior, it must be positively reinforced each time it occurs. Second, once the target behavior is established at a satisfactory rate, the student should be reinforced intermittently. Intermittent reinforcement ensures that the behavior will re-

Objective: Mickey will stay with his cooperative learning group for 10 minutes. (Time ends when Mickey physically leaves the group.)

Circle the number of times Mickey leaves the group during the first 10 minutes of the session.

[Date]	[Date]	[Date]	[Date]	[Date]	[Date]	[Date]	[Date]	[Date]	[Date]	[Date]
10	10	10	10	10	10	10	10	10	10	10
9	9	9	9	9	9	9	9	9	9	9
8	8	8	8	8	8	8	8	8	8	8
7	7	7	7	7	7	7	7	7	7	7
6	6	6	6	6	6	6	6	6	6	6
5	5	5	5	5	5	5	5	5	5	5
4	4	4	4	4	4	4	4	4	4	4
3	3	3	3	3	3	3	3	3	3	3
2	2	2	2	2	2	2	2	2	2	2
1	1	1	1	1	1	1	1	1	1	1
0	0	0	0	0	0	0	0	0	0	0

Figure 3. Documenting frequency data.

main at a satisfactory rate of occurrence. A note of caution for teachers applying positive reinforcement interventions: Public reinforcement is unwelcome to some students under some circumstances. Some students may be embarrassed by being positively reinforced in the presence of peers, teachers, parents, and others.

Extinction

Just as adding a positive reinforcer increases the exhibition of a behavior, removing the reinforcer that is sustaining a behavior will decrease it. This planned or systematic ignoring is referred to as *extinction*. Extinction is the discontinuation or withholding of the reinforcer of a behavior that previously reinforced it. The application of extinction presents some difficulties. First, ignoring is sometimes used by teachers as an unplanned intervention in the hope that the behavior will simply go away. Unfortunately, what may occur is an inconsistent ignoring and reinforcement of the behavior, which, in effect, may increase or maintain the very behavior that the teacher wishes to decrease. Specifically, the teacher must be consistent and persistent in the application of extinction if the reinforcer is to be effective. A second difficulty is the extinction burst. If the teacher systematically applies extinction, the target behavior in all probability will increase before it decreases, or the reverse may occur, depending on the desired direction of the behavior change and the specific behavior. An extinction burst occurs because the student is frustrated in his or her efforts to get the usual response from the teacher or others to a tried-and-true behavior; as a consequence, he or she tends to dramatically increase or decrease the frequency of the exhibition of the target behavior. Simple, nondangerous behaviors such as whining and tattling can be ignored, but these behaviors must be ignored every time they occur if they are to decrease. Some behaviors simply cannot be ignored in the classroom, and, as a consequence, extinction is contraindicated as an intervention in those cases.

Whining is a behavior that may be handled through extinction. If the students groan when given a homework or written assignment, the teacher may simply ignore their groaning. An extinction burst may occur in the form of increased groans and excuses. If the students persist with excuses, the teacher should merely repeat the assignment and go on. If the teacher should happen to respond to the increased groans and excuses with a shortened assignment, then the groaning and whining behavior will be maintained at that higher level.

Negative Reinforcement

Negative reinforcement is the strengthening of a behavior as a consequence of the removal of an already operating **aversive** stimulus (Walker & Shea, 1995). In negative reinforcement, the teacher removes something that a student dislikes when the student performs a specific behavior (Axelrod, 1983). Negative reinforcement is often confused with **punishment,** which is the addition of an aversive stimulus or the removal of a desired stimulus as the consequence of behavior. An example of negative reinforcement is a group of students working diligently at their desks after the teacher stated that they would not be required to do homework assignments that evening if their classroom assignments were completed during the allotted time during the school day. This example assumes that the teacher has assigned homework to the students previously and that doing homework is aversive for the students.

Shaping

One of the difficulties with positive reinforcement is that the behavior must occur before it can be reinforced. With some complex behaviors, occurrence of the target behavior as desired is unlikely without additional help. Shaping is a way to gradually develop a behavior or increase its occurrence. In shaping, the successive approximations of the target behavior are reinforced until the behavior is established (Shea & Bauer, 1987). For example, if the goal is for the student to remain with his group for 10 minutes and, at present, the student remains with the group for an average of 2 minutes, the teacher who is shaping the behavior may begin by reinforcing the student for staying with the group for 2 minutes. When the student is consistently with the group for 2 minutes, the teacher increases the requirement for reinforcement to 3 minutes, then 4 minutes, then 6 minutes and so forth until the goal of 10 minutes is attained. If the teacher wants a student to follow the classroom's morning routine, the student is systematically reinforced for completing aspects of the routine and gradually the number of steps that must be completed before reinforcement is increased.

Prompting

Prompting is a behavior that supports students in completing a behavior successfully (Wolery, Ault, & Doyle, 1992). Specifically, prompting is the process of providing verbal, visual, aural, or manual assistance to a student during the behavior change process to facilitate the completion of a task. Prompts are not part of the actual, final stimulus that evokes the target behavior; rather, they are hints, cues, gestures, manual guides, or other environmental modifications applied to evoke the behavior during the learning process. Prompts are gradually withdrawn as the student assumes increasing responsibility for successful completion of the task. For example, if Luis consistently forgets his lunch in the classroom when going to the cafeteria, the teacher may begin by prompting him, "Luis, remember your lunch." After Luis has consistently remembered his lunch with that prompt, she may simply say, "Luis. . . ." After Luis successfully remembers his lunch for several days with this shortened cue, the teacher may try to eliminate the prompts completely.

Modeling

People naturally learn through observation and imitation. *Modeling* is a term used to describe learning by observation. Specifically, modeling is the provision of an individual or group behavior to be imitated or not to be imitated by the student. Modeling can have three effects:

1. *Observational learning:* The model performs a behavior that the student imitates in substantially identical form. For example, the teacher names an object and the student repeats it, or the teacher forms a sign and the student forms the same sign.
2. *Inhibitory and disinhibitory effect:* The student observes a peer who is punished or ignored for engaging in a specific behavior, and, as a consequence, the student does not exhibit the behavior. For example, a student observes a peer being punished for being late for class and not having the required materials and, as a consequence, subsequently makes every effort to be on time for class with the required materials.
3. *Eliciting or response facilitation effect:* The student observes a model using a previously learned but dormant behavior and, as a consequence, exhibits that behavior. For example, a student who has been in a different classroom in which the students did not raise their hands to participate begins raising his or her hand in the new classroom after observing his or her peers doing so. The assumption here is that the student has learned handraising behavior in previous environments but was not required to use it in the immediately preceding environment (Bandura, 1969; Clarizio & Yelon, 1967).

The following factors are important when a modeling intervention is applied. First, the student must be ready developmentally and cognitively to imitate a model. Second, the student must be reinforced for imitating the model. Some students are not intrinsically reinforced for performing behaviors that others consider acceptable. Third, the model must be good or acceptable to the student. Just because the teacher or the parent thinks a student is an acceptable model for another student does not mean that the selected model is one whom the student will imitate. Finally, a model can be too good or too bright and therefore beyond the student's ability or desire to model the behavior, and consequently the model's behavior is rejected.

Token Economy

The token economy is undoubtedly one of the most versatile and widely used of the behavior modification interventions. It is an exchange system that provides the individual or the group whose behavior is being changed with immediate feedback cues on the appropriateness of their behavior. These cues, or tokens, are at a later time exchanged for backup reinforcers. Backup reinforcers can be tangible or social or both if a tangible reinforcer is used. Tokens are usually valueless to the student initially. Their value becomes apparent to the student when the student learns that they can be exchanged (i.e., traded) for backup reinforcers (i.e., items, activities).

When developing a token economy, the teacher must first select a target behavior or behaviors. These behaviors must be discussed and clarified with the student or the group. After selecting a token, a menu of backup reinforcers is developed and posted in the classroom. Time must be provided for the exchange of tokens. As the school year progresses, the teacher must revise the reinforcer menu and backup reinforcers frequently to avoid satiation. With proper management, the token economy is effective because students compete only with themselves and the reinforcer menu provides a variety of desirable reinforcers. Again, each of the learning principles described can be applied informally throughout the day. These learning principles are defined and exemplified in Table 2.

Your Turn . . .

Reflect on your own experience as a learner. Do you recall examples of your teachers using the learning strategies described in this chapter? What are some examples of the ways in which they applied (or misapplied) these principles?

Table 2.   Learning principles employed in developing a token economy

Principle	Definition	Example
Positive reinforcement	The teacher presents a positive consequence after the behavior has been exhibited.	The teacher pats on the back a student who has completed a problem correctly.
Extinction	The teacher systematically ignores a behavior.	The teacher turns away from a student who is whining.
Negative reinforcement	The teacher terminates a negative experience when the desired behavior occurs.	The teacher permits a student to join the group when work is completed.
Shaping	The teacher reinforces the successive approximations of the target behavior.	The teacher gradually increases the amount of time the student must stay in group to receive a reward.
Prompting	The teacher provides behaviors that support students in successfully completing a behavior.	The teacher works individually with students doing long division, reciting the process to them as they complete the problems.
Modeling	The teacher provides an adult or group behavior to be imitated by the child.	The teacher says, "I like the way Group 1 is ready to go!" Other groups settle down.
Token economy	An exchange system in which the student earns tokens and exchanges them for backup reinforcers	The student attends to assignment for 10 minutes, and the teacher awards a point. Later in the day, the student exchanges points for free time in the reinforcement area.

LEARNING OBJECTIVE 2: To be able to implement contingency contracting and the Premack principle in the classroom

In an education environment, **contingency contracting** is the process of contracting so that the student gets to do what he or she wants to do following the completion of what the teacher wants the student to do (Walker & Shea, 1995). In contingency contracting, the teacher serves as the contract manager, prescribing procedures and explaining principles to be followed. The teacher works with the child to ensure that the task and the reinforcer are fair to both the student and the teacher.

A **contract** is an agreement between two or more parties, individuals, or groups that stipulates the responsibilities of the parties concerning a specific item or activity. There are two types of contracts that are used in classrooms: verbal and written. Verbal contracts are used throughout the day, when the teacher makes statements such as, "Yiping, when you complete two more problems, you may get a drink," or, "As soon as the groups are quiet, we can watch the videotape."

Written contracts are more elaborate and are usually individualized. Walker and Shea (1995) suggested that contacts should:

- Be negotiated and freely agreed on by both student and teacher
- Include the target achievement or production level

- Be delivered consistently in accordance with the terms of the contract
- Include the date for review and renegotiation

The following are several steps that are useful in developing a contract. The teacher should:

- Establish and maintain rapport with the student
- Explain the purpose of the meeting as a way to support the student's efforts
- Provide the student with a simple definition of a contract as well as examples of contracts
- Explain that, together, the student and the teacher will write a contract
- Discuss with the student the tasks to be included in the contract
- Discuss with the student the reinforcers to be included in the contract
- Negotiate with the student the amount of the task that needs to be completed for a specific amount of the reinforcer to be awarded
- Identify the criteria for achievement
- Elicit the student's verbal affirmation to the contract terms
- Congratulate the student for making the contract

The teacher and the student should

- Agree on the time allocated for the task
- Discuss evaluation procedures
- Negotiate delivery of the reinforcer
- Agree on a date for renegotiation of the contract
- Write the contract together
- Read the contract together
- Sign the contract together (Shea, Whiteside, Beetner, & Lindsey, 1974)

An example of a completed contract is provided in Figure 4.

Contract

Date: 1-23-99

This is an agreement between Mickey and Ms. Farmer. The contract begins on 1-24-99 and ends on 1-31-99. It will be reviewed on 1-31-99.

In this contract, Mickey will complete the four pages of his spelling workbook for Unit 21. Mickey will complete these four pages using cursive handwriting. Mickey will have not more than two mistakes on these four pages.

If Mickey fulfills this contract, he will serve as the "Gerbil Monitor" from February 2 through February 8. He will care for the gerbils at school and take them home on the weekend.

Student's signature: _____
                                     Mickey

Teacher's signature: _____
                                     Ms. Farmer

Figure 4. Sample contract.

Contingency contracting is based on the **Premack principle** (Premack, 1965), which states that a behavior that occurs frequently can be used to increase a behavior with a low rate of occurrence. This principle can be restated as, "If you do *X,* then you can do or get *Y*" (Walker & Shea, 1995, p. 139). Some examples follow:

"If you eat your spinach, then you can have some ice cream."
"If you clean your room, then you can go to the theater."
"If you wash the car, then you can go for a drive."

The Premack principle can be applied to the structuring of activities in the classroom. Teachers can alternate more desirable and less desirable activities during a single period or throughout the school day. In a single lesson, teachers can begin with a more desirable activity, follow with a less desirable activity, and end the period with a more desirable activity. It is generally recommended that the period begin and end with a desirable activity (i.e., on a positive note).

Throughout the school day, the teacher may apply a schedule based on the Premack principle. The daily schedule begins and ends with a desirable activity and more desirable and less desirable activities are alternated throughout the remainder of the day. A partial daily schedule based on the Premack principle is presented next. In the schedule, the smile (☺) denotes a more desirable activity, and the frown (☹) denotes a less desirable activity.

☺ 9:00 A.M.—Free time to play quietly with classroom toys, talk with friends, or read

☹ 9:10 A.M.—Return to seats for individual study during attendance, lunch count, and so forth

☺ 9:15 A.M.—Circle sharing time or pow-wow

☹ 9:35 A.M.—First reading group; others, individual study

☺ 9:55 A.M.—Transition time, drinks, rest room

☹ 10:00 A.M.—Second reading group; others, individual study

☺ 10:20 A.M.—Recess

LEARNING OBJECTIVE 3: To be able to recognize the use of partial participation and fading in inclusive classrooms

When applying behavioral interventions in inclusive learning communities, two additional strategies should be considered for implementation. These strategies are **partial participation** and **fading**. Both have implications for all students but have a significant impact on the functioning of students with severe disabilities or intense educational needs in inclusive classrooms.

Partial Participation

Partial participation is the engagement of an individual with disabilities in a skill to the best of his or her ability in an age-appropriate, meaningful, natural environment (Walker & Shoultz, 1996). Partial participation emerged from efforts to provide recreation activities for individuals with severe disabilities along with their peers without disabilities (Baumgart et al., 1982). Traditionally, individuals with disabilities have been excluded from sponsored activities such as scouting, sports, dances, and art classes unless a parent provided one-to-one support during the activity (Walker, 1990). Many agencies are exploring how to provide support for individuals with disabilities within their common programs rather than providing segregated activities (Walker & Shoultz, 1996).

Partial participation is based on several assumptions. First, the provision of supports to individuals with disabilities is based on a value or a belief in inclusion for all. Second, supports should promote social integration and friendships. Third, supports to individuals with disabilities in age-appropriate activities should be both individualized and flexible. At times, an adult or older peer is required to support the partial participation of an individual with disabilities (Walker & Edinger, 1988). There are several strategies that this support person may use to facilitate participation of the individual with disabilities that is as complete as possible:

- Get to know the students who do not have identified disabilities, engage them, and provide them with a connecting link with the student with disabilities. The support person should not be seen as someone who is there only to interact with the student with disabilities.
- Model interactions for the other participants, assist them in communicating with the person with disabilities, and respond appropriately to behavior that is not desirable during the activity.
- Do not place too many limits on behaviors that occur in the presence of the student with disabilities; back off (Savard, 1988) and let interactions emerge (i.e., let kids be kids).
- Be sensitive to the interactions of others involved in the activities. The support person should notice and promote opportunities for interaction, which may necessitate flexibility and even serendipity. Nonverbal interactions, including interactions that are as simple as sitting together, should be encouraged.
- Provide opportunities for students to have fun, get acquainted, develop friendships, and experience increased attachments to their peers.

Developing individualized and flexible supports is essential to effective partial participation. To effectively implement supports, it is important that the support person and the student with disabilities get to know each other and that time is allotted for the support person to determine which are the most helpful supports. In addition, the support person may at times need to teach skills to the student with disabilities. Sometimes skills and behaviors indirectly associated with an activity (e.g., learning to cheer for a team) are important. Sometimes adaptations are necessary to facilitate participation. Adaptations may be physical (e.g., a ramp for an individual to roll the bowling ball down the alley) or may shift the focus of the activity (e.g., the student with disabilities guards the base, makes a ruling on who is "out" and who is "it"). Again, the key to effective partial participation is that help should be offered only when it is needed. Too much visibility by the support person can create barriers (Schleien, Ray, & Green, 1997).

Your Turn . . .

Choose one activity that may occur in an inclusive classroom. What would some aspects of partial participation of this activity be? What sorts of supports would an individual with severe disabilities or intense educational needs require?

Fading

Supports can sometimes be reduced, or faded, as the student becomes more proficient or skilled at a behavior. Fading may include reducing the amount and quality of physical assistance, verbal assistance, or concrete supports that have been used to structure an activity (Walker & Shea, 1995).

The key to the inclusion of students with disabilities is the implementation of the accommodations needed for them to function effectively within their peer group. These accommodations may or may not be faded. If an individual is successfully participating in an activity with supports, those supports may not necessarily be reduced. The emphasis should be on providing the most natural accommodation and continuing to use that accommodation with the student as long as necessary. For example, an individual who has difficulty with writing may continue to use a computer throughout his or her life rather than move from computer usage to cursive handwriting. An individual who uses a calculator may continue to use one rather than spend additional time remediating mathematics skills. A student who successfully completes a routine by using a reminder list may continue to carry the reminder list throughout the school year.

It may be possible, however, to fade some of the accommodations that the individual with disabilities initially used to function in the inclusive environment. For example, suppose an individual initially needed a buddy when learning to run the bases during a baseball game. As the individual became more proficient at the game, the buddy would fade his or her support. Alternatively, suppose a student needed assistance from a support person when learning to approach and conduct a brief conversation with a peer or an adult. Initially, the support person would monitor and facilitate the conversation; but as the student learned effective conversation skills, the support that the adult provided would be faded.

In inclusive environments, successful participation is the goal rather than fixing the disability. Dedicating large amounts of time to drills, fading efforts, or learning inconsequential skills is neither efficient nor effective. Rather, identifying accommodations that allow for participation that is as complete as possible and then maintaining those accommodations may be the most helpful support for the student.

SUMMARY

Although the strict application of behavior modification interventions is decreasing, the use of principles of reinforcement and strategies derived from them, such as positive reinforcement, extinction, negative reinforcement, shaping, prompting, modeling, and token economy, are frequently applied. In contingency contracting, the teacher serves as the contract manager, providing procedures and explaining the principles to the student. When applying behavior interventions in inclusive learning communities, the teacher should consider utilizing partial participation and fading.

TEST YOUR KNOWLEDGE

Completion of the "Self-Evaluation," "Make the Language Your Own," and "Application Activity" sections will aid readers in understanding and retaining the information presented in this chapter. Answer keys for the "Self-Evaluation" and "Make the Language Your Own" sections are located in the Appendix at the end of the book.

Self-Evaluation

Select the most appropriate response to complete each of the following statements:

1. Issues regarding the design of a behavior intervention plan are
    a. Determined by the teacher
    b. Linear in nature
    c. Complex

2. The simplest way to determine a reinforcer is to
    a. Contact past teachers and parents
    b. Ask the student
    c. Complete a reinforcement menu

3. Public reinforcement
    a. Increases the intensity of the reinforcement
    b. Enhances modeling
    c. Is unwelcome to some students

4. Negative reinforcement is
    a. The addition of an aversive stimulus
    b. The removal of a desired stimulus as a consequence
    c. The removal of an already operating aversive stimulus

5. Shaping is based on the assumption that
    a. Some target behaviors are unlikely to occur without additional help
    b. Successive approximations decrease accuracy
    c. Students need help in learning new behaviors

6. Prompts are
    a. Part of the final task
    b. Hints or cues
    c. Verbal in nature

7. Modeling has a disinhibitory effect when the model
   a. Performs a behavior that is imitated identically
   b. Is punished for a behavior and the student does not exhibit the behavior
   c. Exhibits a previously learned but dormant behavior

8. In using positive reinforcement, the teacher should
   a. Remove the reinforcers when the student exhibits inappropriate behavior
   b. Prefer tangible to social reinforcers
   c. Reinforce the behavior each time it is exhibited in the initial stages of the process

9. In partial participation, the learner
   a. Is taught the full activity
   b. Does not engage in the activity until he or she is ready
   c. Engages in the activity to the best of his or her ability

10. In inclusive environments,
   a. Accommodations are always completely faded
   b. Accommodations may remain in place over extended periods of time
   c. Efforts are made to remediate learners' disabilities

Make the Language Your Own
Match the following terms with their definitions:

1. _____ Intervention data
2. _____ Baseline data
3. _____ Partial participation
4. _____ Contract
5. _____ Principles of reinforcement
6. _____ Modeling
7. _____ Punishment
8. _____ Aversives
9. _____ Positive reinforcement
10. _____ Reinforcer
11. _____ Extinction
12. _____ Prompting
13. _____ Negative reinforcement
14. _____ Shaping
15. _____ Contingency contracting
16. _____ Target behavior
17. _____ Fading
18. _____ Token economy
19. _____ Premack principle

a. An agreement, written or verbal, between two or more parties, individuals, or groups, that stipulates the responsibilities of the parties concerning a specific item or activity
b. Quantitative data collected on the target behavior before a behavior change intervention is implemented
c. The discontinuation or withholding of a reinforcer that has previously been reinforcing a behavior
d. Quantitative data collected on the target behavior during intervention
e. The provision of an individual or group behavior to be imitated or not to be imitated by an individual
f. The specific behavior to be changed as a result of intervention
g. The strengthening of a behavior as a consequence of the removal of an already operating aversive stimulus

h. The systematic, gradual reduction of prompts and supports

i. The engagement of an individual with disabilities in a skill to the best of his or her ability in an age-appropriate, meaningful, natural environment

j. The consequence of a behavior, which may be tangible or social, positive or negative

k. Presentation of a desirable reinforcer after a behavior has been exhibited; the process of reinforcing a target behavior in order to increase the probability that the behavior will recur

l. Noxious and sometimes painful consequences of behavior; undesirable results of behavior that the individual would typically wish to avoid

m. A behavior that has a high rate of occurrence that is used to increase a behavior with a low rate of occurrence

n. A set of rules to be applied in the behavior change process; the rules of learning

o. The process of providing verbal, visual, aural, or manual assistance to a student during the behavior change process to facilitate the completion of a task

p. The addition of an aversive stimulus or the subtraction of a pleasurable stimulus as a consequence of behavior

q. A system of exchange in which the student earns tokens as reinforcers and exchanges them for tangible and social reinforcers

r. The process of contracting so that the student gets to do something that he or she wants to do after completing something that the teacher wants the student to do

s. The systematic, immediate reinforcement of successive approximations of a target behavior until the behavior is established

Application Activity

1. Observe a teacher in an inclusive setting for a 20-minute period. During this time, what behavioral principles does he or she employ? How many times does he or she use each of these principles? Are the principles effective in modifying the students' behavior?

REFERENCES

Axelrod, S. (1983). *Behavior modification for the classroom teacher.* New York: McGraw-Hill.

Bandura, A. (1969). *Principles of behavior modification.* Austin, TX: Holt, Rinehart & Winston.

Baumgart, D., Brown, L., Pumpian, I., Nisbet, J., Ford, A., Sweet, M., Messina, R., & Schroeder, J. (1982). Principle of partial participation and individualized adaptations in educational programs for severely handicapped students. *Journal of The Association for Persons with Severe Handicaps, 8*(3), 71–77.

Clarizio, H.F., & Yelon, S.L. (1967). Learning theory approaches to classroom management: Rationale and intervention techniques. *Journal of Special Education, 1,* 267–274.

Cooper, J.O., Heron, T.E., & Heward, W.L. (1987). *Applied behavior analysis.* Columbus, OH: Merrill.

King-Sears, M.E. (1997). Best academic practices for inclusive classrooms. *Focus on Exceptional Children, 29*(7), 1–22.

Premack, D. (1965). Reinforcement theory. In D. Levine (Ed.), *Nebraska symposium on motivation* (pp. 113–118). Lincoln: University of Nebraska Press.

Savard, C. (1988). Taking part in the dream. In G. Allan Roeher Institute (Ed.), *The pursuit of leisure: Enriching the lives of people who have disabilities* (pp. 39–42). Downsview, Ontario, Canada: G. Allan Roeher Institute.

Schleien, S.J., Ray, M.T., & Green, F.P. (1997). *Community recreation and people with disabilities: Strategies for inclusion* (2nd ed.). Baltimore: Paul H. Brookes Publishing Co.

Shea, T.M., & Bauer, A.M. (1987). *Teaching children and youth with behavior disorders* (2nd ed.). Upper Saddle River, NJ: Prentice-Hall.

Shea, T.M., Whiteside, W.R., Beetner, E.G., & Lindsey, D.L. (1974). *Contingency contracting in the classroom.* Edwardsville: Southern Illinois University Press.

Walker, J.E., & Shea, T.M. (1995). *Behavior management: A practical approach for educators* (6th ed.). Upper Saddle River, NJ: Merrill.

Walker, P. (1990). *Resources on integrated recreation/leisure opportunities for children and teens with developmental disabilities.* Syracuse, NY: Center on Human Policy.

Walker, P., & Edinger, B. (1988, May). The kid from Cabin 17. *Camping Magazine,* 19–21.

Walker, P., & Shoultz, B. (1996). *Community integration report: Supporting children and youth with disabilities in integrated recreation and leisure activities.* Syracuse, NY: Center on Human Policy.

Weigle, K.L. (1997). Positive behavior support as a model for promoting educational inclusion. *Journal of The Association for Persons with Severe Handicaps, 22*(1), 36–48.

Wolery, M., Ault, M.J., & Doyle, P.M. (1992). *Teaching students with moderate to severe disabilities: Use of response prompting strategies.* White Plains, NY: Addison Wesley Longman.

Yeaton, W.H., & Sechrest, L. (1981). Critical dimensions in the choice and maintenance of successful treatment: Strength, integrity, effectiveness. *Journal of Consulting and Clinical Psychology, 49,* 156–167.

Self-Management
and Comprehensive
Intervention Strategies

Self-advocacy, or speaking for yourself, is a big part of living in the community. People with disabilities who live in the community should have the right to make their own decisions just like everyone else.

Michael Kennedy and Patricia Killius,
two individuals with disabilities
who spent much of their lives in institutions
(Olson, 1986, p. 1)

This chapter focuses readers' attention on strategies that are essential to effective student functioning in inclusive classrooms: self-determination, self-management, and empowerment. The opening section of the chapter is a discussion of the importance of self-determination and self-management. As members of the learning community in the inclusive classroom, students and teachers must know who they are, what they do well, and what they need help in doing. The first section concludes with a brief discussion of learned helplessness. Next, the chapter discusses self-management and its component skills, including self-instruction, cognitive behavior modification, self-monitoring, self-recording, and self-reinforcement. This section includes useful vignettes, sample worksheets, and tables to exemplify the strategies presented. The final section of the chapter discusses empowering students to be decision makers.

LEARNING OBJECTIVES

After completing this chapter, readers will be able to

1. Recognize the importance of self-determination and self-management in inclusive classrooms
2. Assist students in developing self-management
3. Empower students as decision makers

KEY WORDS AND PHRASES

cognitive behavior modification—the selective, purposeful combination of various learning principles and procedures to modify thoughts, feelings, and/or behaviors (Harris, 1982)

cognitive framework—teaching tools that help learners transfer and retain content by presenting component information in an organized manner and by linking related information (Boyle & Yeager, 1997)

critical thinking map—a guide that focuses learners' attention on essential components of a problem or issue (e.g., important events, main ideas, other perspectives, conclusions, relevance)

guided notes—outlines containing the main ideas and related concepts of a lecture and including designated spaces for students to complete during lecture

learned helplessness—the perception that an individual's behavior and its outcomes are independent of each other (Weiss, 1981)

self-determination—the ability to define and reach goals based on a foundation of knowing and valuing oneself (Field & Hoffman, 1994)

self-instruction—the use of self-talk to direct personal behavior

self-management—any process that an individual uses to influence his or her behavior (Carter, 1993)

self-monitoring—the process of monitoring and recording personal performance when engaged in a specific task

self-recording—the concrete application of self-monitoring (i.e., the student's noting his or her behavior or work performance on a data sheet)

self-reinforcement—administering reinforcers to oneself on completion or performance of a specific task

story map—a guide that focuses learners' attention on essential story components, that is, environment, problem, goal, action, outcomes

study guide—written information that highlights important points of an academic activity

LEARNING OBJECTIVE 1: To be able to recognize the importance of self-determination and self-management in inclusive classrooms

According to King-Sears (1997), **self-determination** is a foundational component of inclusion. King-Sears applied Field and Hoffman's (1994) model and definition of self-determination in inclusive classrooms: Self-determination is the ability to define and reach goals based on a foundation of knowing and valuing oneself. The Field and Hoffman model is composed of the following five components:

1. Know yourself
2. Value yourself
3. Plan
4. Act
5. Learn

In an inclusive classroom, students and teachers explore who they are, what they do well, and what they need help in doing. Each individual is valued for the unique contribution that he or she makes to the classroom learning community. As participants in the community, students and teachers are actively engaged in planning and acting with the goal of learning.

Self-determination and **self-management** are closely related. King-Sears argued that teaching students to manage their own behavior in itself promotes their self-determination. Self-management systems allow students with disabilities as well as students without identified disabilities to independently accomplish tasks and control their behavior. Students become responsible for their own systems of control. They are not just accommodated but are independent participants in the classroom.

Self-determination is highly valued by individuals with and without disabilities. In The Arc of the United States' (1996) self-determination program, an emphasis is placed on individuals' making choices based on their preferences. Individuals who are self-determined take risks, assume responsibility for their actions, and advocate on behalf of themselves and others. Although its discussion was aimed primarily at individuals with mental retardation, The Arc contended that individuals with disabilities not only have not been provided with the opportunity to become self-determined but also have not had the opportunity to learn the skills and have the daily experiences that will enable them to take more control of and make choices in their lives. Rather, The Arc contended, these individuals experience overprotection, are not included in decisions that affect their lives, and have limited choices among limited options.

A study (Reis, Neu, & McGuire, 1997) of adults with learning disabilities who have achieved success offered additional insights into self-determination, self-management, and self-advocacy. These successful individuals, to facilitate their achievement, took responsibility for using compensatory strategies that included using computers, word processors, books on tape, and self-advocacy. They planned carefully, used time management strategies, and set personal work priorities. In addition, they received large-scale parental support. Their parents monitored their homework, told them they were smart, scheduled conferences, argued with school personnel, and sought information. These successful adults expressed the belief that their capacity for hard work was their greatest asset. In describing the group, Reis and colleagues reported that these individuals

- Exhibited talents outside of the school that often provided them with the belief in their ability to succeed
- Had continued maternal support
- Were determined and stubborn, persevered, and had a strong work ethic
- Developed and used personal plans that included multiple learning strategies and integration of planning and organization
- Had a strong sense of self-awareness and knowledge about how to create the process of academic success through their individual experiences and with the help of parents, educators, and peers

Choice is a key aspect of self-determination. Often referred to as *having our say* (Olson, 1986), self-determination assumes that individuals with disabilities have a voice. Individuals with disabilities may need support in making choices or even in understanding their options. Kennedy and Killius, the individuals whose experiences were recorded by Olson (1986), conceded that individuals with disabilities may not always be able to make decisions for themselves; parents, staff, and friends can support people with disabilities in making choices if they "pay attention to the person" with disabilities (Olson, 1986, p. 2).

Self-determination means different things for learners with disabilities at different times in their lives. Kennedy (1997), describing his own development in terms of self-determination, stated that when living in an institution, self-determination was as basic as getting care such as personal hygiene and three meals per day. As he moved into the community, self-determination became related more to running his own life and directing his personal care assistants, the individuals he employed to support him in completing his self-care tasks and transportation. Similarly, for a second grader with disabilities, self-determination may be as simple as choosing where to sit in the cafeteria. In the upper grades, it may include making choices related to middle school electives or extracurricular activities. In secondary school, self-determination may be related to which types of career education and vocational training to pursue.

The sense of **learned helplessness** (Weiss, 1981) is a perception that an individual's behavior and its outcomes are independent of each other. For example, a student may work hard on a group project, and his or her contribution to the project may be ignored. On future group projects, he or she may be less likely to make an active contribution, sensing that his or her contribution is not important. The student learned that his work and the outcome for the group are not related. Students must be encouraged to try and their efforts must be recognized to avoid their falling into learned helplessness traps such as those represented by the following statements:

"No reason for me to take the spelling test. I always flunk."
"I don't do art—my stuff always looks stupid."

Teachers must work with students to establish their sense of self-awareness. In addition, they must teach students the strategies that allow them to become full participants in activities.

 LEARNING OBJECTIVE 2: To be able to assist students in developing self-management

Self-management is any process that an individual uses to influence his or her behavior (Carter, 1993). Carter discussed several components of self-management, including skills in

- **Self-instruction**, in which the student uses self-talk to direct his or her behavior
- **Self-recording** and **self-monitoring**
- **Self-reinforcement**, in which the student administers himself or herself rewards on performance or completion of a specified task

Although the specific steps for teaching self-management strategies may vary, Carter (1993) recommended some general procedures. These procedures are presented in Table 1 and are further clarified by the worksheet in Figure 1. The procedures are generic and can be applied to various efforts to develop self-management programs with students. The key to effective self-management, however, is to ensure that the student is a collaborator in planning as well as in implementation and evaluation.

Table 1.   Procedures for teaching self-management skills

1.   Identify the behaviors of concern.
2.   Define the behaviors of concern.
3.   Determine how you will collect data on the behavior.
4.   Teach the student how to use the self-management system.
5.   Implement the system.
6.   Evaluate the system.

Source: Carter (1993).

Self-Management Planning Form

Student: _____   Teacher: _____   Date: _____

Target behavior

What is the behavior of concern?	
What replacement behavior should be encouraged?	
Under what conditiions is the behavior unacceptable?	

Data collection

What type of data will be recorded?	
When will the data be recorded?	
What will be used as a data collection form? [Attach]	
How will the student be taught to use the data collection form? How will the student practice?	
How will the reliability of the data be checked?	

Setting goals and contingencies

What is the student's involvement in setting the goal?	
Will the goal be public?	
What will be the reward for meeting the goal?	
How will the student and the teacher review performance?	
When will the plan be modified if the goal is not met?	

Maintenance and generalization

How will the self-recording procedures be faded?	
How will the behavior be generalized to different environments and situations?	

Figure 1. Sample self-management planning form.

Self-management programs may be simple or complex and multidimensional. A self-management program may be implemented as simply as by providing a student with 10 chips and a cup and asking the student to put a chip in the cup each time he or she leaves the work group during a session. In this way, the student can monitor his or her personal behavior by counting the number of chips in the cup at the end of the activity.

Self-Instruction

During self-instruction, a student is actively engaged in his or her own learning. Teachers can support student self-instruction in several ways. The most common self-instruction strategies are **cognitive behavior modification**, **cognitive frameworks**, and study structures. These strategies are discussed in the following subsections.

Cognitive Behavior Modification

Cognitive behavior modification is based on the belief that all of the student's thoughts, feelings, and behaviors are interactive and reciprocal (Harris, 1982). Harris defined *cognitive behavior modification* as "the selective, purposeful combination of principles and procedures from diverse areas into training regimens or interventions, the purpose of which is to instate, modify, or extinguish cognitions, feelings, and/or behaviors" (1982, p. 5).

Lloyd (1980) described several characteristics of cognitive behavior modification programs:

- The student is an active participant in the program.
- The student uses verbalizations and eventually self-talk while using a plan or strategy.
- Monitoring and evaluation are ongoing.
- The process is initiated by an adult but involves the student as a collaborator.

The Think Aloud program (Camp & Bash, 1981) is an example of a general problem-solving strategy that is considered cognitive behavior modification. In this program, the student uses a series of self-talk questions to monitor his or her behavior. When confronted with a problem, the student asks him- or herself the following questions:

1. What am I supposed to do?
2. How can I do it?
3. Am I using my plan?
4. How did I do?

For example, a student may have difficulty with waiting in the lunch line. The teacher may begin the Think Aloud intervention by giving the student support in the following way:

Teacher: Mei Mei, remember! "What am I supposed to do?"
Mei Mei: Wait in line with my hands to myself.
Teacher: "How can I do it?"
Mei Mei: Tell myself, "Keep your hands to yourself," and lock my thumbs behind my back.
Teacher [after a few seconds]: "Are you using your plan?"

Mei Mei: Yes, I'm telling myself, "Keep your hands quiet," and I'm holding my thumbs.

Teacher [as Mei Mei picks up her lunch tray]: How did you do?

Mei Mei: Fine. I followed my plan.

As Mei Mei becomes more comfortable with using her plan, the teacher may fade the external cues, leaving Mei Mei to manage her own behavior after saying, "Mei Mei, remember!"

Cognitive behavior modification programs also have been applied for the management of aggression and anger. Smith, Siegel, O'Connor, and Thomas (1994) offered a detailed procedure for teaching cognitive behavior modification. The steps that they applied to help students learn this self-talk program are presented in Table 2.

Cognitive behavior modification programs are most effective with students who are verbal and can engage in the sequential, verbal self-cuing required. These programs are effective for helping students become more reflective in responding to and managing their impulsivity. Teachers can provide a positive model for students by modeling self-talk throughout the day.

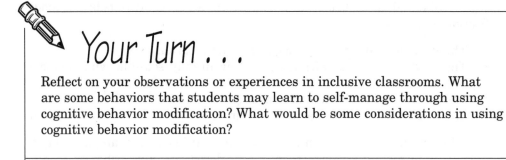

Your Turn . . .

Reflect on your observations or experiences in inclusive classrooms. What are some behaviors that students may learn to self-manage through using cognitive behavior modification? What would be some considerations in using cognitive behavior modification?

Cognitive Frameworks and Study Structures

Cognitive behavior modification strategies such as those discussed in the previous section are used most commonly to help students manage their personal behavior. Other self-instruction techniques may be applied with students for the learning and retention of instructional content and skills. Cognitive frameworks and study structures may help students who require accommodations regarding the content and skills taught in inclusive classrooms. Cognitive frame-

Table 2.   Steps to teaching students to use a cognitive behavior modification program

Day 1:   Private interview with the student, during which the student and teacher discuss a hypothetical situation and the way in which the student typically reacts. Consequences of the student's typical response are discussed, and a rationale for involvement in the program is developed. The student signs an agreement to learn the strategy.

Day 2:   The teacher works with the student in describing the steps and modeling the self-statements. The teacher and student role-play applying the steps.

Day 3:   The teacher works with the student, using verbal rehearsal and practice. The teacher also introduces sheets on which the student will keep track of whether he or she has gone through each step.

Day 4:   Additional practice in going through the steps and collecting data.

Day 5:   Additional scenarios using the strategy and collecting data.

Day 6:   The teacher works with the student to gain his or her commitment to use the strategy outside of the individual sessions. The student is encouraged to make the statements to him- or herself when confronted with an appropriate situation. The teacher and student identify times throughout the school day during which it would be appropriate to apply the plan.

Maintenance: The student continues to take data on his or her use of the plan.

Source: Smith et al. (1994).

works are teaching tools that help learners transfer and retain content by presenting component information in an organized manner and by linking related information (Boyle & Yeager, 1997). These cognitive frameworks may help students learn not only the material at hand but also ways to organize and structure information for future application.

Boyle and Yeager (1997) described three cognitive frameworks to support students in inclusive environments. The first is the **study guide** (i.e., written information that highlights important points in an academic activity). A study guide provides a process for students to follow to enhance their learning and retaining of content area information. Through the study guide, students are presented with content materials and engage the materials in a structured way. Boyle and Yeager (1997) suggested several key components for study guides presented in Table 3.

Next, Boyle and Yeager (1997) suggested the **story map** as a cognitive framework to enhance learning and retaining content information. On a story map, the environment, the problem, the goal, the action, and the outcome of the story may be completed individually by the student, by a small group of students, or by the whole class. Through use of the story map, the critical features of the story are presented. An example of a story map is provided in Table 4.

Table 3.   Components of study guides

Study guides may contain:
- A description of the reading materials
- Objectives and rationale for the unit
- Key vocabulary for understanding the content
- A description of each of the activities that will be used to meet the criteria of the objectives
- Questions, which vary in their comprehension level
- A key or other strategy to allow the students to self-correct
- Multiple written prompts (e.g., "To answer these questions, reread pages 11–15")
- Key words highlighted throughout

Source: Boyle and Yeager (1997).

Table 4.   Story map

Story: *Hansel and Gretel*

The setting: The woods, a witch's cottage

The problem: Hansel and Gretel's parents cannot afford to keep them, so their father leaves them in the woods. They are captured by a witch, who wants to fatten up Hansel to eat him.

The goal: Hansel and Gretel want to return home uneaten and with enough money so that their family can eat.

The action:

- Hansel and Gretel's father walks them into the woods, camps out with them, but leaves them. Although Hansel sprinkled bread crumbs along the way to mark the path, birds ate them, and the children are lost.
- Hansel and Gretel come upon a gingerbread-and-candy cottage. They eat some of the cottage and are captured by the witch who lives there.
- The witch throws Hansel into a cage and makes Gretel do chores. The witch keeps trying to fatten up Hansel.
- After discovering the children are tricking her, the witch decides Hansel is fat enough. Gretel asks the witch to show her how to light the oven, and she pushes the witch into the oven.
- Hansel and Gretel take the witch's jewels and return home.

The story map may be applied on various levels. Some students may use the story map to identify themes and details. Others may use the story map to sequence the basic ideas. By keeping in mind the student's individualized education program (IEP) objectives, the story map may be used to address vocabulary, sequencing, story structure, or identifying themes.

Critical thinking maps are another method for structuring learning. In critical thinking maps, the important points of the content are mapped, with other concepts linked to those points. An example of a critical thinking map is presented in Figure 2. Again, the complexity and number of linkages on the critical thinking map depend on each student's needs.

Guided notes (Lazarus, 1996) may provide support for students with disabilities who are participating in classes that are conducted largely in a lecture format. Guided notes are outlines containing the main ideas and related concepts of a lecture with designated spaces for students to complete during the lecture. The teacher develops guided notes using existing lecture notes. At a minimum, guided notes contain the main ideas to be covered in the lecture. They may also include important phrases, definitions, related issues, and opinions. An example of a guided note worksheet is presented in Figure 3.

Guided notes can be used in a number of ways with students, depending on their individual needs. During lectures, transparencies of completed copies of the guided notes can be used so that students have accurate information and a model for their notes. Lazarus also suggested giving students the guided notes sheets for the readings associated with a unit as well. Holding a 5- or 10-minute supervised review period at the end of the class also provides the teacher with an opportunity to evaluate how students are completing and using their guided notes. Lazarus maintains that guided notes are useful for all students and should be provided for all class members rather than only for students with disabilities.

Self-Recording and Self-Monitoring

Student self-recording is a concrete application of self-monitoring. In self-recording, the student notes his or her behavior or work on a data sheet, graph, or list. In self-monitoring, the student may or may not actually record his or her behavior or activity.

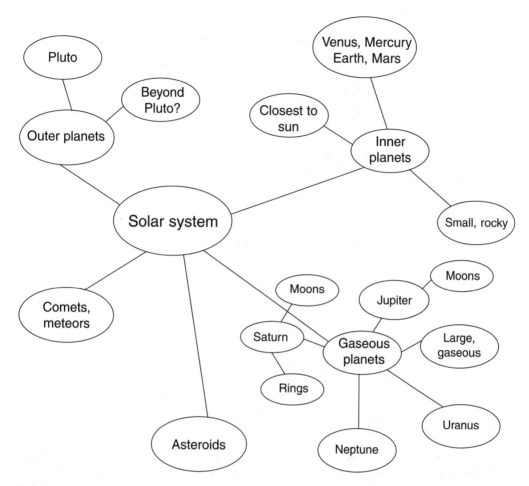

Figure 2.   The solar system critical thinking map.

Student self-recording may help students learn. Clees (1995) used self-recording with students to increase their awareness of various teachers. Students' daily schedules were used to develop recording sheets for each teacher's expectations. Having students self-record whether they were meeting the teachers' expectations was found to be effective in increasing the percentages of teachers' expectations exhibited by the students. Once having reached a higher level of behaviors, students were found to maintain the change. Using such a technique may be useful on several levels. Most important, students become aware that different individuals have different expectations. In addition, by referring to the sheets, students are reminded to shift gears from one teacher to another.

Self-recording can also be applied to academic work. Carr and Punzo (1993) taught students to self-record the number of items that they completed correctly during reading, mathematics, and spelling and to record this information on a graph sheet. They found that students began to observe their own levels of accuracy and productivity and to modify their academic performance. In addition, the students began to engage spontaneously in goal setting, making statements such as, "I'm going to try to get 100% tomorrow."

Guided Note Worksheet

Introduction to unit on the solar system

1. Solar system consists of:
   a. The Sun, our local star
   b. Nine planets
   c. 70+ moons

2. Nine planets fall into three groups
   a. Four small, rocky planets close to the sun
   •
   •
   •
   •

   b. Four large, gaseous planets
   •
   •
   •
   •

3. Outer planet(s): Pluto and beyond

4. Asteroids
   a. What are they?
   b. Where are they?

Figure 3.   Sample guided note worksheet.

Self-recording and self-monitoring may be combined in simple ways. McDougall and Brady (1998) reported the successful use of a multiple-component package to increase fluency in math skills. Each student used two packages. The first included the self-monitoring of attention, during which students heard their own tape-recorded voices, through headphones, asking, "Am I paying attention?" When the students heard the cue, they assessed their behavior and put a check mark by the word "Yes" or "No" on a printed form taped to their desks. The second package included students' self-monitoring of their work completion, with the tape-recorded cue "Am I working quickly?" followed by students' self-assessing and self-recording their behavior on a form taped to the desk. Cues occurred between 50 and 70 seconds apart. The students graphed their data, determined whether their work was improving, and marked how many token points they had earned. Each student maintained a folder to document points earned and exchanged, the types of reinforcers selected, and the dates on which reinforcers were self-administered.

Self-monitoring does not need to involve pencil-and-paper activities. For example, a student who has difficulty in taking turns may be given a card with 10 paper clips on it. If the student interrupts, he or she may be required to remove a paper clip and put it on his or her desk. In this fashion, the student learns to monitor his or her behavior. Putting chips in cans, removing a bead, and adding a clothespin are all ways for students who cannot effectively engage in pencil-and-paper activities to learn to self-monitor their behavior.

Working together, the teacher and the student can graph or record the number of occurrences of the desired behavior.

As students grow older, time management becomes a critical self-management issue. This appears to be especially true of students with disabilities. Manganello (1994) contended that time management problems are greater for individuals with learning disabilities than for other students. He suggested that students with learning disabilities must be taught specific strategies to overcome their time management difficulties. Teachers can model appropriate time management for their students by actively using a calendar in the classroom, wearing and referring to a wristwatch or referring to a clock, being punctual, and making effective transitions. Calendar use can be reinforced by having students use individual weekly calendars to note activities, assignments, co-curricular activities, conferences, and so forth. Encouraging students to check their watches at transition times can reinforce their sense of time. Teachers can help students develop a sense of time by choosing a time interval and asking the students to indicate when they think that amount of time has passed during a lesson or activity. Punctuality should always be reinforced. Many students have difficulty in tracking their time. When students track the amount of time that passes during each activity, they discover that there is adequate time to complete required activities even if they need to make adjustments in their daily routines.

Self-recording or self-management strategies used in the classroom should be as natural as possible. Any time teachers choose to use self-recording or self-monitoring strategies, they must ascertain how intrusive the strategies will be for both individual students and the class. Does the procedure stigmatize the student? Does it involve carrying materials or sheets that are difficult to manage and easily lost? Does it draw negative attention to the student? Does the procedure negatively affect the classroom as a whole?

Your Turn . . .

Consider a student in an inclusive classroom with whom you are familiar. Identify one behavior of that student that would be appropriate for self-recording and/or self-monitoring. Which procedure would you use for self-recording? Would the system be intrusive?

LEARNING OBJECTIVE 3: To be able to empower students as decision makers

Self-advocacy is closely related to self-management. Students, however, need help in developing the skills they need to act as decision makers on their own behalf. Van Reusen, Deshler, and Schumaker (1989) reported that secondary students with learning disabilities can be taught to self-advocate and can make important and relevant contributions to their IEPs. In their study, Van Reusen and colleagues found that students become active participants in their IEPs as a result of preparation in self-advocacy. When students were taught to self-advocate, the likelihood was much greater that their IEP objectives were generated during the IEP conference rather than by professional staff and teachers prior to the IEP conference.

Self-advocacy requires teachers to put students in the center of the communication network surrounding their school program. Battle, Dickens-Wright, and Murphy (1998) suggested that, early in the school year, parents and students should be introduced to the idea that adolescents are able to assume responsibility for communication regarding their own programs and progress. Conferences involve students not only because of students' legal right to participate but also because they have the skills in monitoring and communication needed to assume ownership of their progress.

Battle, Dickens-Wright, and Murphy suggested using portfolios as a management system for monitoring students' growth. Students participate in selecting the work to be included in the portfolio that demonstrates their learning in specific areas. It is recommended that student and teacher discuss the portfolio weekly, with an emphasis on having the student assess his or her progress toward goals in a specific area, monitoring growth through self-comparison, and using self-reflection to adjust their goals.

The Arc of the United States (1996) contended that self-advocacy is essential to improve the quality of life of individuals with disabilities. In their position statement for self-advocacy, The Arc argued that many people in the community still have not accepted the fact that individuals with disabilities must speak, choose, and act for themselves. The Arc's position statement lists the following principles:

1. All children and adults, regardless of the type or level of disabilities, should be supported and encouraged to make decisions throughout their lives.
2. Mentioning the person first, then the disability, promotes these individuals' self-esteem and self-worth.
3. Individuals with disabilities should develop and use their abilities to control their own lives.
4. Individuals with disabilities should be provided information and experiences with choices and their possible consequences.
5. Individuals with disabilities should be treated in a respectful, age-appropriate manner, just as one would treat anyone else. (1996, p. 1)

Self-advocacy requires that students be given the opportunity to express their needs. Teachers must be open to students' suggesting what they need in order to learn more effectively in the classroom. Key to developing self-advocacy is an openness on the part of the teachers and staff. If a student begins a request by saying, "It would help me if . . . ," and the student's request is reasonable, then the teacher should accommodate the student. If the supports are not necessary or helpful, the student will cease to use them on his or her own.

SUMMARY

This chapter addresses the following major concepts:

1. Self-determination is based on a foundation of knowing and valuing oneself.
2. In inclusive classrooms, students and teachers are actively engaged in planning and acting with the goal of learning.
3. Self-management includes self-instruction, self-monitoring, and self-reinforcement.
4. Individuals with disabilities can be taught to self-advocate and make relevant contributions to their IEPs.
5. Self-advocacy requires teachers to put students in the center of the communication network around their school program.

TEST YOUR KNOWLEDGE

Completion of the "Self-Evaluation," "Make the Language Your Own," and "Application Activity" sections will aid readers in understanding and retaining the information presented in this chapter. Answer keys for the "Self-Evaluation" and "Make the Language Your Own" sections are located in the Appendix at the end of the book.

Self-Evaluation

Select the most appropriate response to complete each of the following statements:

1. In inclusive classrooms, each individual is valued for
    a. Demonstrating self-determination
    b. The unique contribution he or she makes
    c. The natural supports he or she provides to individuals with disabilities

2. A student who has difficulty in reading does not attempt his assignment. This is an example of
    a. Choice
    b. Self-determination
    c. Learned helplessness

3. Self-management programs
    a. Are complex and multidimensional
    b. Are as simple or as complex as they are designed to be
    c. Require reading skills

4. Cognitive behavior modification is based on the belief that
    a. Thoughts and feelings are irrelevant in a carefully managed classroom
    b. Thoughts, feelings, and behaviors are interactive
    c. Thoughts, feelings, and behaviors are reciprocal

5. Cognitive behavior modification programs are most effective for
    a. Managing behaviors
    b. Increasing academic skills
    c. Students who are verbal and can engage in sequential, verbal self-cuing

6. Self-recording is
    a. Limited to behavior management
    b. Limited to academic work
    c. Applicable to behavior management and academic work

7. In terms of time management,
    a. Young children should be given responsibilities
    b. Individuals with learning disabilities have greater problems than those who are not identified as having disabilities
    c. Students can acquire the skills through modeling

8. Self-recording or self-management in the classroom should
    a. Emphasize honesty
    b. Emphasize accuracy
    c. Emphasize recording as naturally as possible

9. Conferences should include students because
    a. It is the law
    b. It is often desired by parents
    c. It is the law, and students need to assume ownership of their programs

10. Students can be included as active participants in their IEPs
    a. Simply by attending
    b. Through instruction in self-advocacy
    c. Through discussion with their parents

Make the Language Your Own

Match the following terms with their definitions:

1. _____ Self-management

2. _____ Cognitive framework

3. _____ Cognitive behavior modification

4. _____ Self-determination

5. _____ Self-monitoring

6. _____ Guided notes

7. _____ Story map

8. _____ Self-instruction

9. _____ Critical thinking map

10. _____ Self-recording

11. _____ Learned helplessness

a. A guide that focuses learners' attention on the essential components of a problem or issue (i.e., important events, main idea, other perspectives, conclusions, relevance)

b. Teaching tools that help learners transfer and retain content by presenting component information in an organized manner and by linking related information (Boyle & Yeager, 1997)

c. The perception that an individual's behavior and its outcomes are independent of each other (Weiss, 1981)

12. _____ Study guide

13. _____ Self-reinforcement

d. Administering reinforcers to one-self upon completion or perfor-mance of a specific task

e. Selective purposeful combination of various learning principles and procedures to modify thoughts, feelings, and/or behaviors; the ability to define and reach goals based on a foundation of knowing and valuing oneself (Field & Hoff-man, 1994)

f. Defining and reaching goals based on a foundation of knowing and valuing oneself

g. The use of self-talk to direct per-sonal behavior

h. The process of monitoring and recording personal performance when engaged in a specific task

i. Outlines containing the main ideas and related concepts of a lecture and including designated spaces for students to complete during lecture

j. The concrete application of self-monitoring (e.g., the student notes his or her behavior or work performance on a data sheet)

k. Any process that an individual uses to influence his or her be-havior (Carter, 1993)

l. A guide that focuses learners' at-tention on essential story compo-nents (setting, problem, goal, ac-tion, outcomes)

m. Written information that highlights important points of an academic activity

Application Activity

1. Interview a teacher regarding self-recording. What is his or her opinion of students' monitoring their own behavior? Do they have concerns about ac-curacy? What role does self-recording have in the teacher's evaluation of students' performance or behavior?

REFERENCES

The Arc of the United States. (1996). *Self-advocacy.* Arlington, TX: Author.

Battle, D.A., Dickens-Wright, L.L., & Murphy, S.C. (1998). How to empower adoles-cents: Guidelines for effective self-advocacy. *Teaching Exceptional Children, 30*(3), 28–33.

Boyle, J.R., & Yeager, N. (1997). Blueprints for learning: Using cognitive frameworks for understanding. *Teaching Exceptional Children, 29*(4), 26–32.

Camp, B.W., & Bash, M.S. (1981). *Think aloud: Increasing social and cognitive skills: A problem-solving program for children: Primary level.* Champaign, IL: Research Press.

Carr, S.C., & Punzo, R.P. (1993). The effects of self-monitoring of academic accuracy and productivity on the performance of students with behavioral disorders. *Behavioral Disorders, 18*(4), 241–250.

Carter, J. (1993). Self-management: Education's ultimate goal. *Teaching Exceptional Children, 25*(3), 28–32.

Clees, T.J. (1995). Self-recording of student's daily schedules of teacher's expectancies: Perspectives on reactivity, stimulus control, and generalization. *Exceptionality, 5*(3), 113–129.

Field, S., & Hoffman, A. (1994). Development of a model for self-determination. *Career Development of Exceptional Individuals, 17,* 159–169.

Harris, K.R. (1982). Cognitive-behavior modification: Application with exceptional students. *Focus on Exceptional Children, 15*(82), 1–16.

Kennedy, M. (1997). *Self-determination.* Syracuse, NY: Center on Human Policy, Research and Training Center on Community Integration.

King-Sears, M.E. (1997). Best academic practices for inclusive classrooms. *Focus on Exceptional Children, 29*(7), 1–22.

Lazarus, B. (1996). Flexible skeletons: Guided notes for adolescents with mild disabilities. *Teaching Exceptional Children, 28*(3), 37–40.

Lloyd, J. (1980). Academic instruction and cognitive behavior modification. The need for attack strategy training. *Exceptional Education Quarterly, 1*(1), 53–63.

Manganello, R.E. (1994). Time management instruction for older students with learning disabilities. *Teaching Exceptional Children, 26*(2), 60–62.

McDougall, D., & Brady, M.P. (1998). Initiating and fading self-management interventions to increase math fluency in general education classes. *Exceptional Children, 64*(2), 151–166.

Olson, D. (Producer and Director). (1986). *Self-advocacy: Speaking for yourself.* (Videotape). Syracuse, NY: Center on Human Policy.

Reis, S.M., Neu, T.W., & McGuire, J.M. (1997). Case studies of high-ability students with learning disabilities who have achieved. *Exceptional Children, 63*(4), 463–479.

Smith, S.W., Siegel, E.M., O'Connor, A.M., & Thomas, S.B. (1994). Effects of cognitive-behavioral training on angry behavior and aggression of three elementary aged students. *Behavioral Disorders, 19*(2), 126–135.

Van Reusen, A.K., Deshler, D.D., & Schumaker, J.B. (1989). Effects of a student participation strategy in facilitating the involvement of adolescents with learning disabilities in the individualized education program planning process. *Learning Disabilities: A Multidisciplinary Journal, 1*(2), 23–34.

Weiss, J.R. (1981). Learned helplessness in black and white children identified by their schools as retarded and nonretarded. *Developmental Psychology, 17,* 499–508.

Group Strategies

I was so frustrated when I started teaching in the inclusion program. I was used to giving a direction to the group, and they would do it. There were even fewer students in my new classroom, but I felt like I was herding cats. I had to rethink my whole way of doing things, increasing the students' responsibility for each other, figuring out ways that everyone could respond at the same time, and making everything far more active. We don't just sit much anymore.

Ms. C., a teacher describing her transition to an inclusive, ungraded elementary classroom

Large-group instruction should be used with care in inclusive class-rooms. Logan, Bakeman, and Keefe (1997), in a study of instructional variables and the engagement of learners with severe disabilities or intense needs, contrasted student engagement in whole-class, small-group, one-to-one, and independent work. When whole-class instruction was taking place, there were low levels of student engagement. Small-group and one-to-one instruction were clearly superior to whole-class instruction in obtaining higher levels of engaged behavior of students with a range of disabilities. Logan and associates inferred that the increased engagement in certain environments was related to either the nature of the tasks in these environments or peer modeling.

This chapter describes ways to use groups in inclusive learning communities and discusses group meetings and group problem-solving strategies as well as cooperative learning structures. Conflict resolution and surface management techniques are reviewed. The chapter concludes with ways to use students as instructional agents in inclusive classrooms.

LEARNING OBJECTIVES

After completing this chapter, readers will be able to

1. Use group meetings and group problem-solving strategies in classrooms
2. Implement cooperative learning structures
3. Identify strategies related to conflict resolution
4. Apply surface management techniques
5. Recognize the role of social skills instruction in classrooms
6. Implement peer tutoring and supports in the classroom

KEY WORDS AND PHRASES

class meeting—a meeting conducted in the classroom to teach decision making, social responsibility, and cooperation

conflict—disagreement

cybernetic sessions—a four-phase small-group cooperative learning strategy that involves preplanning, response generation, data synthesis, and final presentation

dyadic learning—students working in pairs to learn

fact storm—a cooperative learning strategy emphasizing consolidating information and using self-monitoring that includes six phases: 1) students, working in pods or small groups, confront a body of text; 2) students begin previewing the assigned body of text, noting key concepts, words, pictures, and other cues; 3) the pods or small groups of students display their initial fact storm sheets to the class, and the teacher may present a minilesson; 4) members of pods are assigned different aspects of the body of text for detailed study; 5) pods of students read for comprehension; and 6) pods of students review answers to questions and modify the fact storm sheet

mediators—neutral individuals who help two or more people to resolve a conflict

numbered heads together—a strategy in which the teacher assigns students to groups, students number off within their groups, the teacher asks a question and tells the students to "put their heads together" to find an answer, and then the teacher calls a number and the student assigned that number within each group presents the group's answer

peer-mediated instruction—instruction strategies such as peer modeling, peer initiation training, peer monitoring, peer networking, and peer tutoring

purposeful access—groups formed around specific characteristics or interests

reciprocal teaching—structured dialogue using prediction, questioning, summarization, and clarification

surface management techniques—classroom management techniques that address superficial behaviors but not long-term issues

three-step interview—a structure in which the teacher asks a question and students talk it over within small groups; students form pairs within groups of four and conduct one-way interviews within pairs and reverse interviewer and interviewee roles, and all students share with the large group information learned during interviews

LEARNING OBJECTIVE 1: To be able to use group meetings and group problem-solving strategies in classrooms

Glasser (1965) first used group meetings during the 1960s as part of his work in reality therapy. In an effort to reduce what he perceived as an overemphasis in schools on competition, Glasser proposed meetings to teach students decision making, social responsibility, and cooperation. The social problem-solving meeting he proposed focused on individual and group problems in the classroom and school.

Morris (1982) proposed a format for goal-setting meetings, a "pow-wow." The goal-setting meeting, which the teacher conducts, is used to help students determine their personal goals. Goal setting is seen as the first step in a student's effort to gain self-control. In the pow-wow, the student is given an opportunity to become aware of his or her behavior, verbalize it, and make a public commitment to change the behavior with the assistance of peers and teachers. The pow-wow is generally scheduled as the first activity of the first day of the school week. Students and teacher sit in a circle, if possible, in the classroom. Each student is invited to present his or her behavior goal for the week. The teacher encourages the students to set a goal that is challenging but realistic. Each student's goal is recorded and posted on a chart. The goal and the student's progress toward it are evaluated at the next week's meeting. Table 1 presents the steps for implementing the pow-wow.

Morris (1982) described several advantages of using the pow-wow. The pow-wow requires each student to determine a personal behavior goal and think

Table 1.   Steps in implementing the pow-wow intervention

1. Seat students in a circle if possible.
2. Explain that during the pow-wow, each member of the group will establish a personal goal to be attained by the next pow-wow.
3. *For first pow-wow only:*
    Starting with student on the teacher's left, teacher makes a statement such as the following to each student in turn:
    > If we had done this before, you would now tell us whether or not you had met your goal, and then we would ask the others if they thought you had met your goal. Since this is the first time we are doing this, you are to set a goal for the next time.

    Explain what goals are, giving examples as needed. (Go to Step 8.)
    For second and following meetings: Have the student on the teacher's left restate his or her goal. (The teacher may read the student's goal if the child does not remember it.)
4. Ask the student on the teacher's left to answer "yes" or "no" as to whether the student's goal was met.
5. Ask each other student whether the student on the teacher's left met his or her goal. (If "no," elicit specific instances. If none are given, then it is assumed that the student met the goal.)
6. After all of the other students have had a chance to respond, ask the student again whether the goal was met.
7. Ask the student to make a new goal.
8. Ask each student in the circle if the goal seems appropriate. (If "no," elicit reasons why not.)
9. Ask the student if he or she wants to keep the goal or change it in light of the others' comments. (If the student wants to change the goal, then he or she may do so. If not, then the goal is kept.)
10. Write the goal on a large sheet of paper next to the student's name.
11. Ask each student for ways to help the student meet the goal.
12. Ask each student to make one positive comment about the student who just finished making the goal.
13. Go to the next student in the circle and repeat Steps 3–12.
14. After the last student is finished, post the goals in clear sight.

about which events bring about certain behaviors. It provides a stimulus to students to become more observant about what is going on around them. When students are asked to indicate whether an individual has attained a goal, they must be able to provide evidence of specific instances to support their opinions; to do so, they must observe others' behavior. Morris maintained that the pow-wow improves the self-image of many students and may be the only time during the day when students have an opportunity to hear positive statements about themselves.

Teachers in inclusive classrooms have modified these **class meeting** strategies to generate solutions to group problems, plan activities, and make decisions that affect the entire group. A typical agenda for this type of group meeting is provided in Table 2. With a clear agenda and a teacher model to emulate, students can eventually take turns leading the group.

Group Problem-Solving Strategies

Reciprocal teaching (Palincsar & Brown, 1988) is perhaps one of the best researched and most widely recognized group problem-solving strategies. Reciprocal teaching is grounded in the belief that listening and reading comprehension can be conceptualized as a problem-solving activity.

Reciprocal teaching assumes the form of a discussion. The members of the group conduct the discussion, with the teacher participating as both a leader

Table 2. Agenda for group meeting

1. Call the meeting to order.
2. Review the classroom rules or routines regarding participating in group discussions (e.g., students should be positive, one person speaks at a time, everyone has a say).
3. Group issues (i.e., issues affecting the group or issues introduced by the teacher, including field trip plans, ideas for new learning centers, events that are coming up) are discussed.
4. Personal business (i.e., personal issues that students want to share) may be discussed.
5. Concerns are presented. (Concerns about situations, events, or interpersonal problems may be discussed. Concerns should be stated as issues, and problem-solving strategies are applied to support the individual presenting the concern.)
6. Each individual makes a positive statement about another student.
7. Meeting is adjourned.

and a respondent. The dialogue is structured to enable the teacher to use any of four strategies to direct the discussion. For each segment of the text discussed, the teacher poses a question to which the group members respond. The participants are then free to pose additional questions generated while they read the material. The teacher summarizes by identifying the essence of the segment that was read. Next, the group comments and elaborates on the teacher's summary. At any time during the reading or discussion, the group is encouraged to note when the content of the text or a point raised in the discussion should be clarified. Finally, the teacher signals that he or she is preparing to move on to the next portion of the text by making and asking for predictions regarding the upcoming content.

Through reciprocal teaching, the teacher models and students practice four problem-solving strategies. First, they use prediction as a technique for organizing in advance the material to be learned. Second, they question and are questioned regarding the material. Third, students and teacher summarize the material, identifying the main points to be remembered. Finally, teacher and students clarify what they have learned, making sure that there is a mutual understanding of the material. These strategies help students anticipate the information to be learned, integrate what is presented in the text with what they know to reconstruct what they know in view of the new information, and monitor for understanding. This strategy is most often applied during reading, social studies, or science, with an emphasis on increasing the students' comprehension. The discussion takes the form of a dialogue such as the following:

Teacher: This section has talked about how plants need sunlight to live. What do you think the next section is going to describe?

Linda: Other things plants need.

Sam: The way plants need water, air, and nutrients.

Teacher: Let's continue to read and see. [Students and teacher read the next section quietly.] What is another thing that plants need?

Mario: Nutrients.

Teacher: And where are the nutrients found?

Yiping: In the soil.

Teacher: Do they have to be in the soil?

Francesca: No, they can be in liquids.

Teacher: Is there a word that describes that unusual way of giving plants nutrients?

Sal: Hydroponic.

Teacher: Great. Let's summarize what we've covered so far.

Steven: Plants needs sunlight, water, nutrients, and air to live. Nutrients can be in the soil or given directly to the plants.

Teacher: That was a clear summary. Does anyone else have anything to add? [Pause. No responses.] Does anyone have any questions before we continue? Anything you'd like me to clarify?

Sylvia: Do plants that get their nutrients some way other than soil turn out different than plants that grow in dirt?

Teacher: What do you think, class?

Steven: The book talks about it like as long as plants get what they need, they'll be fine. So I don't think it makes any difference.

Teacher: Does that clarify the point for you, Sylvia?

Sylvia: Okay. I was just wondering if they look weird or anything. You know, pale or something.

Teacher: Are we ready to go on? [Pause.] What do you think is the next thing that we're going to cover about plants?

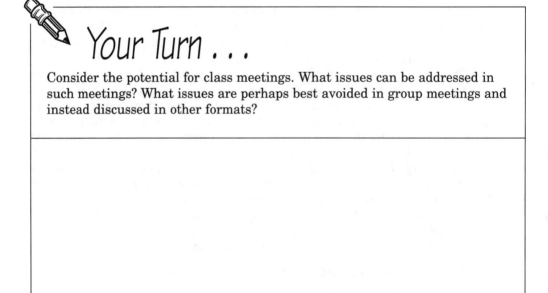

Your Turn . . .

Consider the potential for class meetings. What issues can be addressed in such meetings? What issues are perhaps best avoided in group meetings and instead discussed in other formats?

LEARNING OBJECTIVE 2: To be able to implement cooperative learning structures

One set of structures that is supportive of inclusion is cooperative learning. Kagan (1989) described a structural approach to cooperative learning that is based on the systematic application of content-free ways of organizing social interactions in the classroom. These structures may be used repeatedly with almost any subject matter, at a wide range of grade levels, and at various points in a lesson plan.

One of the most common structures that Kagan described was the whole-class question-and-answer session. In this structure, the teacher asks a question, and students who wish to respond raise their hands. The teacher then calls on one student, and the student states his or her answer. Kagan suggested that rather than employ this competitive structure teachers should use **"numbered heads together."** In the numbered heads together method, the teacher assigns the students to groups. The teacher then has the students number off within their groups. The teacher asks a question and tells the students to "put their heads together" to make sure that everyone on the team knows the answer. The teacher then calls out a number, and students who were assigned that number can raise their hands to respond. In this cooperative structure, all students know the answer. High achievers share answers because they know that their numbers may not be called, and they want their group to do well. Lower achievers listen carefully because they know that their number might be called.

Kagan provided another comparison in his presentation of group discussion versus **three-step interviews.** In group discussions, the teacher poses a question, and students talk it over in groups. In this pattern, students are allowed not to participate. In three-step interviews, students form pairs within teams of four and conduct one-way interviews in pairs. After each interview is completed, the students reverse roles. Each student then takes a turn in the larger group, sharing information learned during the interview. All students must participate, and each individual is accountable.

There are many other cooperative learning structures. Wood (1987) suggested the use of associational dialogue. In associational dialogue, the teacher provides students with a list of key concepts from the material to be discussed. Students are instructed to take notes from their textbooks, class lectures, and discussions on a separate piece of paper. Notes are organized around major concepts within the general topic until the students have several clusters of information. Then the students, working in pairs, have an associational dialogue during which they discuss each concept in their own words. The teacher then elicits and elaborates on responses from the whole class.

Cybernetic sessions (Masztal, 1986) are a high-involvement cooperative learning technique. Cybernetic sessions involve having small groups of participants respond quickly to preplanned questions within a specific time frame. Centered around these thought-provoking questions, the sessions unfold as participants work within several group contexts to produce many answers. Students then collectively evaluate and summarize their product. The following are the four phases of the cybernetic sessions technique:

1. *Preplanning:* The teacher first generates questions to be answered, which are written one per page on large sheets of paper and posted around the room. Questions also may be prepared as a handout to be distributed to each group member.

2. *Response generation:* During the response generation phase, the students move to one of the question areas and form groups. Students letter off within the group (e.g., if there are five questions: A, B, C, D, E), with A being the recorder for the first question, B for the second, and so forth. The students are told that the initial area is their home base. The teacher says, "A is going to read his or her question. You, as a group, will generate a list of answers to A's question. A will write down your responses. You have ____ [e.g., 2, 3, 4] minutes to respond. Please begin." After a few (e.g., 2, 3, 4) minutes, the teacher says, "Stop. B's go to your home bases. Everyone else, go to a base other than your home base or a base where you have already been." When the students arrive at the new location, the teacher says, "B, read your question." After the question is read, members of the group generate answers, which B records. Next the teacher says, "You have ____ [e.g., 2, 3, 4] minutes to respond." This process is repeated until all students have functioned as a group recorder. Each question has been answered and discussed the same number of times as the total number of questions asked.

3. *Data synthesis:* During the data synthesis phase, the teacher directs participants, "Everyone go to home base. Your task is to make one consolidated list of all of the ideas you have generated. You have ____ [e.g., 10, 15, 20] minutes to complete this task."

4. *Final presentation:* In the final presentation, one person from the group presents the question and the listed responses to the total group.

Cybernetic sessions have several advantages. Students must think both divergently and convergently and synthesize information. In addition, they must interact socially and take responsibility for recording answers. Several other cooperative learning structures are described in Table 3.

Cooperative learning structures have been expanded beyond the mastery and team-building structures that Kagan (1989) described. One emerging area is the application of cooperative learning strategies to literacy. Two significant models are cooperative integrated reading and composition (Slavin, Stevens, & Madden, 1988) and cooperative literacy (Klemp, Hon, & Shorr, 1993).

The cooperative integrated reading and composition strategy is comfortable for many teachers and principals because it uses basal-related activities and direct instruction in reading comprehension. In addition, it integrates language arts and writing. Throughout these activities, students work in heterogeneous learning teams. The activities follow a set pattern of teacher presentation, team practice, peer preassessment, additional practice, and testing.

In cooperative integrated reading and composition, students are assigned to pairs or triads within ability-level reading groups. The pairs are assigned to teams composed of partnerships from two different reading groups. Most of the activities are done in pairs with others in the team available for assistance and encouragement. Students work independent of the teacher while the teacher either instructs groups drawn from the various teams or works with individuals. Students follow a weekly schedule of activities. Their partners record each assignment and initial a recording form as the students complete each of the week's tasks. Students' scores on all quizzes, compositions, and book reports are combined to form a team score. Rewards for meeting various

Table 3. Common cooperative learning structures

Structure name	Description
Round robin	Each student shares something with his or her classmates.
Corners	Teacher presents four alternatives; students divide into four groups and move to a corner of the room. Students discuss and then listen to and paraphrase ideas from other groups.
Pairs check	Students work in pairs within groups of four. In pairs, students alternate as one solves a problem while the other coaches. After every two problems, one pair checks to see if they have the same answers as the other pair.
Think-pair share	Students think to themselves about a topic provided by the teacher; they pair up with another student to discuss it, then they share their thoughts with the class.
Team word-webbing	Students write simultaneously on a piece of chart paper, drawing main concepts and supporting elements and bridges.
Co-op	Students work in groups to produce a group product to share with the whole class; each student makes a contribution to the group.
Roundtable	Each student in turn writes one answer as a paper and pencil are passed around the group.
Jigsaw	Each student becomes an expert on one topic by working with members from other teams that are assigned the corresponding topic. Upon returning to the team, each one in turn teaches the group on the expert topic. All students are assessed on all aspects of the topic.

Source: Kagan (1989).

levels of achievement are based on team performance. Several of the activities that may be used in cooperative integrated reading and composition are presented in Table 4.

Cooperative literacy is grounded in the belief that all members of the school community are obliged to increase the literacy and numeracy skills of all other members of the community. Students are grouped in pods that are evaluated as a group for both behavior and performance. Pods are usually a group of four students with two students sitting side-by-side and the other two group members sitting behind them. During group work, desks can be turned 90° so that the four students in the pod are facing each other. Interdependence is emphasized, with the whole group receiving points for attendance, being on time, having needed materials, and demonstrating appropriate behavior. Pod members function as a support group and use a structure called **fact storm** to engage in learning activities.

The *fact storm* is a strategy that emphasizes consolidating information and self-monitoring. Fact storm involves six phases. In the first phase, students are confronted with a body of text. The teacher assigns reading selections, and, in their pods, students formulate a plan for studying the assignment. During the second phase, students begin previewing the assigned text, citing key words, pictures, or other cues that may be of help in comprehending the reading. A member recorder documents the group's responses. In the third phase, each pod displays its initial worksheets to the rest of the class. During the third phase, the teacher may present a minilesson, emphasize key points, or review essential vocabulary that recurs in the individual pod's reports.

In the fourth phase of the fact storm strategy, the individual members of each pod are assigned different aspects of the text for study. Each member con-

Table 4. Cooperative integrated reading and composition activities

Basal activities	Stories are introduced and discussed in teacher-led reading groups for about 20 minutes daily. Teachers set the purpose for the reading, introduce new vocabulary, review old vocabulary, and discuss stories. After stories are introduced, team activities take place, including the following: • *Partner reading:* Students read silently, then take turns reading aloud with their partners, correcting each other's reading. • *Story structure and story writing:* Students are given questions related to the story, respond to the story as a group, and write a few paragraphs on a topic related to the story. • *Words out loud:* Sight-word practice • *Word meaning:* Using the dictionary, paraphrasing, and writing sentences showing the meaning of the words • *Story retelling:* Summarizing the main points to their partners • *Spelling:* Pretesting one another on the spelling list, using a disappearing list strategy; making new lists of missed words for each assessment until the list disappears and they can go back to the full list
Partner checking	Students initial each other's assignment forms. Students complete activities at their own rates, completing the activities earlier if they wish and creating additional time for independent reading.
Testing	At the end of three class periods, students are given a test on the story and are asked to write meaningful sentences for each vocabulary word and to read the word list to the teacher.
Direct instruction in reading comprehension	Students complete worksheets or participate in games.
Integrated language arts and writing	In their teams, students participate in writers' workshops and mini-lessons.
Independent reading	Students read trade books of their choice for at least 20 minutes each evening. Parents initial forms and contribute points to their children's teams. One book report is due every 2 weeks.

Source: Slavin, Stevens, and Madden (1988).

tributes items from his or her segment to a more detailed or more comprehensive study. In the fifth phase, the pod is ready to read for comprehension. At this point in the procedure, the teacher may choose to use a study guide. Finally, in the sixth phase, students review answers to questions and modify their fact storm sheets. At the end of the activity, the fact storm sheets are again displayed, serving as a review for the entire class.

When using cooperative learning, issues around management and classroom procedures emerge. Thompson and Taymans (1996) suggested several strategies for effective cooperative learning classroom procedures. In terms of materials management, they suggested that each team should have a tote tray in which the team's folder, charts, evaluations, and other papers are kept. In addition, teachers may need a sign or a signal to ensure that students hear directions given to the whole group while teams are actively engaged in their work. Thompson and Taymans suggested using standard roles in teams, including the following:

• *Equipment manager:* Retrieves the team tote tray and handles equipment during activities
• *Team leader:* Makes certain that all team members are taking turns and doing what they should be doing

- *Recorder:* Keeps the job chart, team evaluation, and any written material required for that day's activities
- *Reader:* Reads any written material required for the activity
- *Presenter:* Reads the group's decision or describes the group's project to the class
- *Quiet captain:* Reminds the group when members are getting too loud

Your Turn . . .

Many of us had limited experiences with cooperative learning during our schooling. Reflect on your experiences as a student. What will you need to consider as you implement cooperative learning structures?

LEARNING OBJECTIVE 3: To be able to identify strategies related to conflict resolution

Johnson and Johnson (1996) argued that **conflicts** are not only inevitable but desirable if managed constructively. They suggested that conflicts may

- Focus attention on problems that need to be addressed
- Clarify values
- Clarify patterns of behavior that need to be changed
- Help students to further understand each other
- Strengthen relationships by increasing confidence that students can resolve their differences
- Keep relationships clear of irritations and resentments
- Release emotions
- Clarify personal goals, values, and commitments
- Provide insights into new goals

In devising their *Teaching Students to Be Peacemakers* curriculum, Johnson and Johnson (1996) focused on teaching all students to be peacemakers. Their program created a cooperative context in which competition and the need to win are deemphasized. Students are taught to recognize when a conflict is or is not occurring and are provided with a concrete, specific procedure for negotiating agreements. They are taught to employ a peer mediation program and use a concrete, specific mediation procedure. To continuously refine and upgrade students' skills, negotiation and mediation procedures are taught from the first through the twelfth grades.

A key skill in conflict resolution is negotiation. Johnson and Johnson (1995) described several steps in problem-solving negotiations. These steps are presented in Table 5. Johnson and Johnson argued that this procedure must be practiced until it is overlearned. They emphasized that negotiation should become automatic for students; if students must stop and think about what they should do, it may be too late to manage the conflicts constructively.

Peer conflict mediation also has emerged as a management tool for use in schools. A **mediator** is a neutral individual who helps two or more people resolve their conflict, usually by negotiating an agreement (Johnson & Johnson, 1995). Mediation is not arbitration. In arbitration, two individuals submit their problem to a third party, who then makes a binding decision. In mediation, a student mediator stands between two conflicting parties and facilitates their progression through each step of the problem-solving process until a mutual agreement is reached.

Table 5.   Steps in negotiation

Step	Example
The student describes what he or she wants.	I want my turn at the computer.
The student describes how he or she feels.	I'm frustrated because the timer went off, it's my turn, and you won't move from the computer.
The student describes reasons for his or her wants and feelings.	I need to type my report, and you've used up your computer time. I'm frustrated because it's my turn.
The student takes the other's perspective and summarizes his or her understanding of what the other person wants, feels, and reasons for both.	I think you're feeling frustrated too, because you didn't finish your work. But you started by playing a game instead of typing your report, and now you're feeling rushed.
The student invents three optional plans that maximize joint benefits.	Plan A is that you give me my turn right now, and if I don't use all my time you can return to your report. Plan B is that I give you three minutes to finish up, and then it's my turn. Plan C is that we both tell the teacher that we don't have enough time and see if she can help us.
The students choose a plan and shake on it.	Let's agree on Plan B.

Adapted from Johnson and Johnson (1995).

Johnson and Johnson (1995) described four steps in mediation. The mediator

1. Ensures that the students end their hostilities and cool off
2. Ensures that the students are committed to the mediation process and
    a. Agree to solve the problem
    b. Do not engage in name calling
    c. Do not interrupt
    d. Are honest regarding the conflict
    e. Abide by any decision that is agreed to
    f. Keep everything confidential
3. Helps students negotiate successfully by
    a. Having the students jointly define the conflict by asking and re-
        sponding to the following questions: "What happened?", "What do you
        want?", "How do you feel?"
    b. Exchanging reasons for their positions
    c. Reversing perspectives
    d. Suggesting at least three options for resolving the conflict
4. Formalizes the agreement by helping students weigh advantages and dis-
    advantages of the various options, reach an agreement, and sign a media-
    tion report form to establish their commitment to abide by the agreement

Perhaps the most challenging behavior pattern that occurs in the classroom is
direct confrontation. Calvin, Ainge, and Nelson (1997) suggested that there is
a typical pattern that occurs in confrontation. First, the student displays a defiant, challenging, or inappropriate behavior. The teacher then reacts, providing a directive that is in opposition to the student's behavior. The student,
challenged by the directive, does not comply and displays additional inappropriate behavior. The teacher, in return, presents the student with an ultimatum. The student is further challenged by the ultimatum and exhibits additional hostile behavior or more explosive behavior.

The teacher's problem in coping with confrontation is twofold: Defuse the
situation and maintain a sense of order in the classroom. Calvin and associates (1997) suggested several strategies for coping with confrontation. Perhaps the simplest solution is to defuse the initial confrontation by focusing on
the task at hand and attending to the students who are complying. Rather
than draw attention to the behavior, the teacher can then redirect the student
to the task at hand. A choice between the expected behavior and a small negative consequence also can decrease the intensity of the situation.

Calvin and colleagues also suggested that the teacher privately present
an option to the student in the context of violating a rule or an expectation.
The teacher may talk with the student, state the rule or expectation, and request explicitly that the student take care of the problem. For example, if the
student is wearing a T-shirt that has printed on it a rude or inappropriate slo-
gan or design, the teacher can present the options of turning it inside out or
keeping his or her jacket on over the T-shirt.

Key to managing confrontation is to reduce agitation. Calvin and colleagues (1997) presented the following suggestions for reducing agitation:

*   Communicate your concern to the student.
*   Give the student space.

- Give the student choices or options.
- Allow the student to engage in a preferred activity for a brief period of time to help him or her regain focus.
- Move or stand near the student.
- Engage the student in independent activities to provide isolation.
- Use activities and tasks that require movement, such as running an errand or erasing the board.
- Use relaxation activities; ask the student to take a deep breath, put his or her head down, tighten his or her muscles and then relax, or engage in some other tension-relieving activity.

Teachers should plan in advance the procedures that they are going to employ to defuse confrontations. Limits should be established, and steps for maintaining these limits should be communicated and modeled for the students. Information should be communicated to students in a nonconfrontational manner that allows the students to save face. When confronted, teachers should disengage, delay their responses, and then return to the student, redirect him or her, and withdraw. If the confrontation is not defused, then the teacher follows through with options provided to the student.

Conflict management should take place in a climate of support. Embry (1997) suggested that, in many schools, the very conditions that are arranged to avoid conflict increase the opportunities for conflict. He provided several characteristics related to a peaceful school environment. The following are some of these characteristics:

- A common language about belonging and striving toward a greater good is used by students, teachers, administrators, staff, and families (e.g., "We excel," "We are all learners here").
- Students and staff hear, see, and read daily stories about people who are doing good in the world.
- Daily rewards and recognitions are provided using the common language about belonging.
- Group rewards are used frequently.
- Student-created posters, stories, and signs saturate the school and are changed every 1–2 weeks.
- Students, teachers, staff, and families frequently receive and write notes about positive actions.
- Schoolwide lessons focusing on social skills are included as part of the curriculum.
- Students have positions of responsibility and are engaged daily in running the school.
- There are schoolwide solutions or procedures for basic behaviors such as stopping and visiting, paying attention, sitting in groups, and moving from place to place.
- Staff praise positive behavior, and cooperative games and activities are common.

Your Turn . . .

Reflect on your own experiences as a student. Was there an incident in which the teacher directly confronted a student? What was the teacher's response? How did the student react?

LEARNING OBJECTIVE 4: To be able to apply surface management techniques

It is not always necessary for teachers to interfere directly in students' behavior problems in the classroom. Redl (1959) suggested that there are four major behavior management alternatives available to a teacher. A teacher may permit, tolerate, interfere, or prevent behaviors from occurring. For example, a teacher may encounter students who, preparing to leave the gym after physical education, linger by the water fountain. The teacher may permit that behavior, recognizing that perhaps the students are hot, thirsty, and in need of a break during the transition from gym to their next class. The teacher may smile and chat with the students while they are getting their drinks, demonstrating that the behavior is acceptable. The teacher may only tolerate the behavior, however, allowing the students to get drinks while providing nonverbal cues that it is time to move on to the next activity. Such cues may include not smiling, not talking, or giving the students a "teacher look" that makes it clear to the students that the teacher would prefer that they not get drinks from the water fountain and instead move on to the next class or activity. In terms of interference, the teacher could make a specific response to the behavior. For example, the teacher could say, "Let's move along to the classroom. You can get a drink later." Finally, the teacher could prevent the behavior by having the students line up outside the gym in a location where a water fountain is not available and then have them proceed directly to the classroom.

When teachers choose to interfere, they may apply any of a broad number of management techniques. Long, Morse, and Newman (1980) called these

surface management techniques. The following are surface management techniques:

- *Planned ignoring:* The teacher may simply ignore the student's inappropriate behavior. Subsequently, the teacher may choose to reward the student when he or she is exhibiting an appropriate behavior.
- *Signal interference:* The teacher may provide the offending student with a nonverbal gesture or a cue that the behavior is inappropriate. This signal may be a look or a frown or may involve staring, finger tapping, or shifting position. Signals are useful because they generally do not interfere with ongoing activity.
- *Proximity control:* The teacher may move toward or stand near the student who is engaged in problem behavior. In addition to stopping the inappropriate behaviors, proximity may provide the student who is uncomfortable or becoming frustrated with needed support.
- *Interest boosting:* The teacher may encourage the student to continue a task by exhibiting a personal interest in his or her efforts.
- *Tension decontamination through humor:* The teacher may use humor when a situation becomes tense or the student is becoming anxious. Humor may never be directed at a particular child or group.
- *Hurdle helping:* The teacher may provide help to the student before he or she becomes disruptive, thus assisting the student to calm down and reorganize his or her effort.
- *Restructuring the program:* The teacher may modify an activity when students become bored and before they become disruptive. Restructuring may be as simple as taking a break or as drastic as stopping the lesson and doing an alternative activity.
- *Support from routine:* The teacher implements a daily routine that provides structure and security to students.
- *Direct appeal to value areas:* The teacher may appeal to the students' understanding of fairness, authority, and the consequences of their behavior on themselves or on others.
- *Removing seductive objects:* The teacher may remove an object that is distracting or disturbing the student with the understanding that it will be returned at an appropriate time.
- *Antiseptic bouncing:* The teacher may ask the student to go to another place where he or she can presumably calm down or regain self-control. The teacher may ask the student to get a drink of water, take a note to the office, or go to another location in the classroom. The teacher simply communicates to the student that the student needs to withdraw for a short period of time to reorganize him- or herself. It is communicated to the student that the teacher's antiseptic bouncing is imposed to help, not to punish, the student.

The preceding techniques are not applied to address students' long-term or deep psychological problems. Preventive planning, Redl's fourth alternative, is an essential aspect of managing classrooms. As stated and discussed previously, an orderly classroom in which students know and are governed by reasonable rules, procedures, and routines is a strong preventive measure.

Your Turn . . .

Observe a teacher conducting a whole-group lesson. Which surface management techniques does he or she apply? Were these techniques helpful?

**LEARNING OBJECTIVE 5: To be able to recognize the role of social skills
instruction in classrooms**

Belonging is one of the primary goals of inclusion. Schnorr (1997) explored the
issue of belonging in secondary classrooms in which students with severe disabilities and intense needs were included. In her analysis of interview data,
she identified several themes related to belonging in secondary inclusive classrooms. Following are some of the considerations for membership and belonging that emerged:

- Having friends in classes is important to students and is a defining feature
  of the school experience.
- Classes actually are composed of partners and small groups of students.
- There is a priority for new students to get connected; people, not tasks, are
  the route to membership.
- Becoming a member is a process that all students must address and is not
  related to disabilities.
- New students must pursue relationships.
- Similar and shared tasks are important factors in whether students are
  considered to belong.
- Peak times for interpersonal interaction include before and between
  classes, at the beginning of class, during seat work following a group lesson, during breaks and transitions between activities, and during work on
  shared activities.
- Ongoing interactions sustain the student's membership in the group.

Purposeful Access

Inclusive classrooms may have a low incidence of students with certain disabilities. As a result, some students may have few opportunities to interact
with other students who share their challenges, concerns, and questions.
Stainback, Stainback, East, and Sapon-Shevin (1994) suggested the use of
purposeful access groups, that is, groups formed around specific characteristics or issues. In these groups, students can share information, support, and
strategies that enable them to cope more effectively with their challenges
and their environment. Schools can provide the framework necessary for students to develop such groups, just as schools enable students to initiate other
student-centered groups.

School environments require students to interact in specific ways. McGinnis, Goldstein, Sprafkin, and Gershaw (1984) described 13 survival skills that
students need to be successful in the classroom. These skills include listening,
asking for help, saying "thank you," bringing materials to class, following instructions, completing assignments, contributing to discussions, offering to
help adults, asking questions, ignoring distractions, making corrections, finding tasks to occupy their time, and setting goals. Small-group instruction and
role playing may be used so that students can practice these skills.

There are several commercially available programs that provide specific
instruction and activities related to social skills development. Carter and
Sugai (1989) presented several issues to be considered in selecting and utilizing a social skills curriculum or program. Questions to ask when evaluating a
social skills program are presented in Table 6.

 **LEARNING OBJECTIVE 6: To be able to implement peer tutoring and
supports in the classrooms**

Peer tutoring and supports are forms of **peer-mediated instruction**, in
which peers serve as instruction agents or helpers. Utley, Mortweet, and
Greenwood (1997) described several advantages of peer-mediated instruction.
The most evident advantage is that using peers as instructors creates a more
favorable pupil–teacher ratio and increases students' time on task. In addition, with more opportunities to respond, students with and without disabilities have more access to teacher–student discussions, worksheets, workbooks,
written tasks, and projects. Peer-mediated instruction also uses procedures
such as frequent error identification, practice, immediate feedback, and peer
encouragement, all of which have been related to increased learning. In addition, it taps into positive peer group influence and emphasizes cooperation.
Peer-mediated instruction allows students to motivate their peers to contribute their best performance to complete tasks and ensure success.

Peer-mediated instruction employs many practices and strategies that are
known to be necessary to optimize students' performance, such as incidental
peer help, supervision, and direct instruction in subject matter (Greenwood,
Terry, Delquardri, Elliott, & Arreaga-Mayer, 1995). Utley and associates described several components of peer-mediated instruction:

- *Peer modeling,* in which peers serve as exemplars of appropriate, competent behavior

- *Peer initiation training,* in which peers provide opportunities to respond to and support other students in their efforts to learn to establish eye contact, initiate conversation, offer and ask for help, describe ongoing social interactions, and expand the content of speech
- *Peer monitoring,* in which peers provide evaluation and feedback with regard to the student's responses
- *Peer networking,* in which peer support extends across time and environments, providing a positive social environment by creating a support system of friends and socially competent peers
- *Peer tutoring,* in which peers provide one-to-one instruction, increasing students' opportunities to respond
- *Group-oriented contingencies,* in which an individual's rewards are based in whole or in part on the successful performance of the individual and others

This section of the chapter describes several uses of peer-mediated instruction, ranging from simple buddy systems to classwide peer-tutoring systems.

Buddy Systems and Dyadic Learning

Perhaps the simplest way of using students as peer tutors or supports is the buddy system. In the buddy system, students of varying abilities are paired or grouped. The students are responsible for each other's having the appropriate assignments, completing projects, writing down work, keeping materials together for portfolios, or other support activities.

A more structured pattern for the use of buddies is **dyadic learning** (Wood, 1987). In dyadic learning, students work in pairs. Each student reads his or her material silently. Students begin by reading two pages of the text. One partner is the *recaller,* who is responsible for orally summarizing from memory what has been read. The other partner is the *listener* or *facilitator,* who corrects errors, clarifies concepts, and elaborates on materials. The students may take notes, draw, or in any way facilitate their learning. When the students begin the next two pages of the text, they switch roles; that is, the recaller becomes the listener or facilitator and vice versa.

Table 6.   Evaluating social skills programs

---

1. What instruction strategies are used?
    - Is modeling used?
    - Is the student strategically placed in situations in which other students are using the skill(s)?
    - Is there direct instruction of the social skill(s)?
    - Are students reinforced for accurate reports of their practicing the skill(s)?
    - Is there structured rehearsal and practice?
    - Is shaping used?
    - Is the student provided with prompting and coaching?
    - Is there the opportunity for positive practice?
    - Are several methods combined?
2. Are assessment procedures included?
3. Can the program be adapted for individual students?
4. Can the program be used with small groups?
5. Is there any extra cost related to the program? Are additional materials or personnel needed?
6. Are strategies used that encourage maintenance and generalization?

Adapted from Carter and Sugai (1989).

Students as Instruction Agents

Gartner and Lipsky (1990) suggested that using students as instruction agents provides unique opportunities for learning for all students. They suggested the use of classwide tutoring teams, in which students' opportunities to respond and to have their responses affirmed and/or corrected are greatly expanded. Their model for classwide tutoring included:

- Small, heterogeneous (four to five students) learning teams
- Game formats for reviewing weekly instructional content
- Cooperative goal structures among team members
- Systematic, prescribed instruction strategies
- Daily earning of points and public posting of students' performance

Once classwide tutoring teams are developed, they remain together for anywhere from 1 to 8 weeks.

Before actually setting up tutoring teams, Gartner and Lipsky suggested training sessions in which students are told that their job is to help their teammates learn the weekly subject matter presented on practice sheets distributed to the group. Students are shown how to use modeling and how to assist in guided practice. Tutoring sessions last 30 minutes per day and take place two to four times per week. Students take turns acting as tutors, and the remaining teammates are tutees. Tutors use materials and questions and answers that the teacher prepares. The primary role of the tutor is to reflect on each tutee's response so that errors are corrected quickly. The teacher's role, having prepared the tutoring material, is to monitor the process to ensure that the procedures are carried out correctly. Bonus points are awarded to teams for cooperative work habits and correct tutoring behaviors. Individual and team points are recorded, and weekly quizzes are given to evaluate students' achievement.

Group Retelling

Peer group work can be used as an enrichment activity to enhance materials presented in class. Wood (1987) described group retelling as a strategy through which additional resources can be brought into a discussion. In group retelling, students work in pairs or in small groups. Each student reads a different piece of material on the same topic. In the group, the students first silently reread their specific material and then retell it to the whole group in their own words.

SUMMARY

This chapter addresses the following major concepts:

1. Large-group instruction must be used carefully in inclusive classrooms.
2. Teachers in inclusive classrooms can use class meetings to generate solutions to group problems, plan activities, and make decisions that affect the group.
3. Cooperative learning structures are supportive of inclusion.
4. Cooperative learning structures have expanded beyond mastery and team building to literacy development.
5. Conflicts can be used to clarify values and focus attention on problems that must be addressed.

6. Confrontation usually follows a pattern of student defiance, teacher reaction and direction, subsequent student noncompliance, and teacher ultimatums.
7. Teachers should plan in advance the procedures that they are going to employ during confrontations.
8. Teachers need not always intervene in behavioral issues; rather, they may permit, tolerate, interfere with, or prevent behaviors.

TEST YOUR KNOWLEDGE

Completion of the "Self-Evaluation," "Make the Language Your Own," and "Application Activity" sections will aid readers in understanding and retaining the information presented in this chapter. Answer keys for the "Self-Evaluation" and "Make the Language Your Own" sections are located in the Appendix at the end of the book.

Self-Evaluation

Select the most appropriate response to complete each of the following statements:

1. The purpose of pow-wows is to
   a. Negotiate resolutions to conflicts
   b. Help students determine their personal goals
   c. Build the classroom team

2. Reciprocal teaching
   a. Emphasizes role playing
   b. Assumes the form of discussion
   c. Assumes increased empathy on behalf of the students

3. A structural approach to cooperative learning uses
   a. Systematic application of content-free ways of organizing social interaction in the classroom
   b. Systematic application of contingencies for students' participation
   c. Structured dialogue, discussion, and prediction

4. The application of cooperative learning strategies
   a. Provides greater freedom to students
   b. Requires teachers to develop management procedures as the activities develop
   c. Requires teachers to have strategies for materials management in place before using those materials in the classroom

5. Conflicts are
   a. Undesirable in inclusive classrooms
   b. Inevitable
   c. Preventable

6. A key skill in conflict resolution is
   a. Rule application
   b. Subjectivity
   c. Negotiation

7. Mediation may be
    a.   The same as arbitration
    b.   Required by the teacher
    c.   Conducted by a student mediator

8. When engaged in a confrontation with a student, the teacher should
    a.   Rely on peer pressure for compliance
    b.   Provide the student with the appropriate alternative
    c.   Privately present an option to the student

9. When an undesirable behavior occurs, the teacher should
    a.   Interfere with the behavior
    b.   Permit the behavior
    c.   Determine whether to permit, interfere with, tolerate, or prevent the behavior

10. Purposeful access suggests that
    a.   Students be included in all classroom activities
    b.   Students be included in the activities that are consistent with their goals
    c.   Groups be formed for students around specific characteristics or issues

Make the Language Your Own
Match the following terms with their definitions:

1. ＿＿＿ Associational dialogue

2. ＿＿＿ Fact storm

3. ＿＿＿ Cybernetic sessions

4. ＿＿＿ Surface management techniques

5. ＿＿＿ Numbered heads together

6. ＿＿＿ Class meetings

7. ＿＿＿ Purposeful access

8. ＿＿＿ Three-step interview

9. ＿＿＿ Dyadic learning

10. ＿＿＿ Peer-mediated instruction

11. ＿＿＿ Conflict

12. ＿＿＿ Reciprocal learning

13. ＿＿＿ Mediators

a. Neutral individuals who help two or more people resolve a conflict

b. Students working in pairs to learn

c. A four-phase small-group cooperative learning strategy of pre-planning, response generation, data synthesis, and final presentation

d. A cooperative learning structure in which the teacher provides a list of key concepts from materials to be discussed; students take notes from textbooks, lectures, and discussions and organize them around the key concepts; students, in pairs, engage in associational dialogue about the concepts; and the teacher elicits and elaborates on responses from the whole class

e. A meeting conducted in the classroom to teach decision making, social responsibility, and cooperation

f. A six-phase cooperative learning strategy that emphasizes consolidating information and using self-monitoring: 1) Students, working in pods or small groups, confront a body of text; 2) students begin previewing the assigned body of text, noting key concepts, words, pictures, and other cues; 3) pods or small groups display their initial fact storm sheets to class, and the teacher may present a mini-lesson; 4) members of pods or small groups are assigned different aspects of the body of text for detailed study; 5) pods or small groups read for comprehension; and 6) pods or small groups review answers to questions and modify the fact storm sheet

g. Groups formed around specific characteristics or interests

h. A strategy in which the teacher assigns students to groups, students number off within groups, the teacher asks a question and tells the students to put their heads together to find an answer, the teacher calls a number, and the student within each group who was assigned that number presents the group's answer

i. Instruction strategies such as peer modeling, peer initiation training, peer monitoring, peer networking, and peer tutoring

j. Disagreement

k. A structured dialogue using prediction, questioning, summarization, and clarification

l. Classroom management techniques that deal with superficial behaviors and do not address long-term issues

m. A structure in which the teacher asks a question and students talk it over within small groups: Students 1) form pairs within groups of four and conduct one-way interviews within pairs, 2) reverse interviewer and interviewee roles, and 3) share information learned during interviews with the large group

Application Activity

    1.   Identify a teacher who uses cooperative learning strategies in the classroom. Observe an activity in that teacher's classroom. What are some of the management issues that emerge? What procedures or strategies does the teacher employ?

REFERENCES

Calvin, G., Ainge, D., & Nelson, R. (1997). How to defuse confrontation. *Teaching Exceptional Children, 29*(6), 47–51.

Carter, J., & Sugai, G. (1989). Social skills curriculum analysis. *Teaching Exceptional Children, 21*(1), 35–39.

Embry, D.D. (1997). Does your school have a peaceful environment? Using an audit to create a climate for change and resiliency. *Intervention in School and Clinic, 32*(4), 217–222.

Gartner, A., & Lipsky, D.K. (1990). Students as instructional agents. In W. Stainback & S. Stainback (Eds.), *Support networks for inclusive schooling: Interdependent integrated education* (pp. 81–98). Baltimore: Paul H. Brookes Publishing Co.

Glasser, W. (1965). *Reality therapy: A new approach to psychiatry.* New York: Harper-Collins.

Greenwood, C.R., Terry, B., Delquardri, J., Elliott, M., & Arreaga-Mayer, C. (1995). *Class-wide peer tutoring (CWPT): Effective teaching and research review.* Kansas City, KS: Juniper Gardens Children's Project.

Johnson, D.W., & Johnson, R.T. (1995). *Teaching students to be peacemakers.* Edina, MN: Interaction Book Co.

Johnson, D.W., & Johnson, R.T. (1996). Peacemakers: Teaching students to resolve their own and schoolmates' conflicts. *Focus on Exceptional Children, 28*(6), 1–11.

Kagan, S. (1989). The structural approach to cooperative learning. *Educational Leadership, 47*(4), 12–15.

Klemp, R.M., Hon, J.E., & Shorr, A.A. (1993). Cooperative literacy in the middle school: An example of a learning strategy based approach. *Middle School Journal, 24*(3), 19–27.

Logan, K.R., Bakeman, R., & Keefe, E.B. (1997). Effects of instructional variables on engaged behavior of students with disabilities in general education classrooms. *Exceptional Children, 63*(4), 481–497.

Long, N.J., Morse, W.C., & Newman, R.G. (1980). *Conflict in the classroom: The education of emotionally disturbed children* (4th ed.). Belmont, CA: Wadsworth.

Masztal, N.B. (1986). Cybernetic sessions: A high involvement teaching technique. *Reading Research and Instruction, 25*(2), 131–138.

McGinnis, E., Goldstein, R.P., Sprafkin, R.P., & Gershaw, N.J. (1984). *Skillstreaming the elementary school child: A guide for teaching prosocial skills.* Champaign, IL: Research Press.

Morris, S.M. (1982). A classroom group process for behavior change. *Pointer, 26,* 25–28.

Palincsar, A.S., & Brown, A.L. (1988). Teaching and practicing thinking skills to promote comprehension in the context of group problem solving. *Remedial and Special Education, 9*(1), 53–59.

Redl, F. (1959). The concept of the life space interview. *American Journal of Orthopsychiatry, 29,* 1–18.

Schnorr, R. (1997). From enrollment to membership: "Belonging" in middle and high school classes. *Journal of The Association for Persons with Severe Handicaps, 22*(1), 1–13.

Slavin, R.E., Stevens, R.J., & Madden, N.A. (1988). Accommodating student diversity in reading and writing instruction: A cooperative learning approach. *Remedial and Special Education, 9*(1), 60–66.

Stainback, S., Stainback, W., East, K., & Sapon-Shevin, M. (1994). A commentary on inclusion and the development of a positive self-identify by people with disabilities. *Exceptional Children, 60*(6), 486–490.

Thompson, K.L., & Taymans, J.M. (1996). Taking the chaos out of cooperative learning: The three most important components. *Clearing House, 70*(2), 81–84.

Utley, C.A., Mortweet, S.L., & Greenwood, C.R. (1997). Peer-mediated instruction and interventions. *Focus on Exceptional Children, 29*(5), 1–23.

Wood, K.D. (1987). Fostering cooperative learning in middle and secondary classrooms. *Journal of Reading, 32,* 1–18.

13

Individual Strategies

We were all having a hard time trying to figure out what to do about Susan's apparently unpredictable behavior. Then we started charting her "bad mornings," those mornings during which she took at least until 10:00 to settle into the routine. It seemed that they occurred on Thursday. We called her mom and discovered that on Thursdays, rather than having Susan take the yellow bus to school, her mom drove her so that she could go straight to the hairdresser's. Susan slept in longer on Thursdays and didn't get to see her friends on the bus, which she enjoyed. Her mom said she really needed to drive her on Thursdays, but that she would get her up at the usual time instead of letting her sleep in. The result was amazing—Susan needed far less time to "get her motor running" on Thursday mornings. The whole situation convinced me that we need to look closer at setting events.

> *Ms. M., a middle school teacher*
> *in an inclusive classroom*

Problem behaviors are the primary cause of the exclusion of students with severe disabilities from the general education classroom (Reichle, 1990). Even in the most carefully structured classrooms, individual students sometimes demonstrate behaviors that are disruptive to the extent that teacher intervention is necessary. This chapter addresses several individual management strategies. The first section of the chapter is devoted to the design, implementation, and evaluation of comprehensive management interventions. Among those interventions discussed are functional communication training, curricular revision, setting events, and choices. The goal of intervention is also discussed in the first section. The PASSKey assessment intervention model is then presented and exemplified. The next section discusses the implementation of instruction strategies that include the use of mnemonics. The final section is devoted to a detailed discussion of life space interviewing and its implementation.

LEARNING OBJECTIVES

After completing this chapter, readers will be able to

1. Design, implement, and evaluate comprehensive interventions
2. Implement strategy instruction with students
3. Use life space interviewing to support students

KEY WORDS AND PHRASES

comprehensive interventions— interventions that produce rapid, durable, and generalized reduction in problem behaviors while improving the individual's success at school, at home, and in the community (Horner & Carr, 1997)

curricular revision—the reduction of a problem behavior by identifying the features of a task that are aversive and changing the task to minimize those features (Dunlap, Kern-Dunlap, Clark, & Robbins, 1991)

ecological interview—an interview conducted to obtain information on the unique characteristics of the student, the school, or the home and the relationship between the child and the environment

functional communication training—instruction in the use of communication responses that are socially acceptable, have the same effect as the problem behavior being replaced (e.g., helping the student obtain what he or she needs or wants, or helping the student escape from unwanted situations), and are at least as efficient as the problem behavior (Durand & Carr, 1991)

generalization (*or* **transfer of learning**)—process by which a behavior reinforced in the presence of one stimulus is exhibited in the presence of another stimulus (Morris, 1985)

keystone behaviors—behaviors that have the potentially widest range of positive consequences with regard to a group of behaviors and behaviors that occur concurrently (Evans & Meyer, 1985)

life space interview—a here-and-now intervention built around a student's direct life experiences that is imposed to structure an incident in the student's life, which enables the student to solve his or her problems

PASSKey—an assessment intervention model whose components include planned activity, strategic sampling, and keystone behaviors

scaffolded instruction—temporary and adjustable support for the development of new skills

setting events—events in the environment that increase the probability that certain kinds of student–teacher or student–student interactions will occur (Repp & Kirsch, 1990)

strategy instruction—an alternative format for working with students with disabilities that does not focus on helping the students keep up with the day-to-day demands of content learning but redirects their energies toward enabling them to learn strategies by which they can keep up with those demands themselves (King-Sears, 1997)

 LEARNING OBJECTIVE 1: To be able to design, implement, and evaluate comprehensive interventions

Comprehensive interventions are interventions that produce rapid, durable, and generalized reduction in problem behaviors while improving the individual's success at school, at home, and in the community (Horner & Carr, 1997). Horner and Carr suggested that comprehensive interventions

- Address several problem behaviors concurrently
- Are driven by an assessment that identifies the variables that reliably predict and maintain a problem behavior
- Blend several intervention procedures, such as concurrently changing structure, instruction, and consequences
- Are applied throughout the day
- Use procedures that are consistent with the values, skills, and resources of the implementors

Horner and Carr (1997) described four comprehensive intervention strategies that are gaining support in the literature: **functional communication training, curricular revision,** setting-event manipulation, and choice.

Functional Communication Training

In functional communication training, a student is taught to use communication responses that are socially acceptable; have the same effect as the problem behavior being replaced (e.g., helping the student obtain what he or she needs or wants, helping the student escape from unwanted situations); and are at least as efficient as the problem behavior or even easier, faster, or more efficient (Durand & Carr, 1991). In functional communication training, the conditions and situations that provoke and maintain a problem behavior are identified. The intervention always includes teaching new communication skills.

For example, a student may throw a specific work activity off the table in a learning center when that activity is presented for completion. As a result of throwing the activity on the floor, the time allocated for working in the learning center is spent picking up the pieces rather than engaging in the activity. The student's motive for throwing the materials involved in an activity on the floor—avoiding the task—is successful; however, it is not efficient. If the student were able to express "no" or "not now," the same communicative effect—avoiding the activity—might occur and would be far more efficient.

Reichle (1997) described several communicative functions of, or reasons why an individual may produce, a particular utterance or response. The functions of communication may include

- Requesting
- Commenting or providing information
- Rejecting
- Extending social greetings or courtesies

In addition, communicative utterances may serve the purposes of

- Obtaining attention
- Obtaining objects or precipitating events
- Escaping or avoiding attention
- Escaping or avoiding objects or events

In functional communication training, then, the role of the teacher is to overlay new, more productive communication forms on communicative functions that are viewed as inappropriate. The question is not "What are they doing?" but "What are they saying?" In the previous example, the teacher focuses on what the student is trying to communicate by throwing on the floor the materials used in an activity and does not focus simply on the fact that the student does throw the materials on the floor.

Curricular Revision

Curricular revision, another comprehensive intervention, is used when certain instructional tasks appear to promote the problem behavior. Dunlap and colleagues (1991) found that by identifying the features of a task that are aversive and changing the task to minimize those aversive features, the problem behavior can be reduced. For example, a task may be altered by making it shorter, by making the directions clearer, or by increasing the practical outcomes of the task. Dunlap and associates maintained that instruction goals should not be compromised but that efforts should be made to identify which features of the task are aversive, and the task should then be revised.

Setting Events

Setting events also influence problem behaviors. Setting events are events in the environment that increase the probability that certain kinds of student–teacher or student–student interactions will occur (Repp & Kirsch, 1990). Fox and Conroy (1995) gave the example of a teacher's instructions being attended to more closely when a student with attention-deficit/hyperactivity disorder (ADHD) had received his or her medication than on the days on which he or she had not. The setting event (i.e., receiving medication) increases the probability of the behavior (i.e., attending to the teacher).

Sometimes the loss of an activity can increase the aversive features of a task and, as a consequence, increase the likelihood of problem behavior. For example, if the student missed gym, which was a preferred activity, then his or her tolerance for other learning tasks during the day might be reduced. Fox and Conroy (1995) suggested that it may not always be possible or feasible to directly alter some setting events. In those situations, the teacher's goal may be to neutralize them. When the setting events are such that a student may have a more difficult time in attending to or engaging in classroom activities, Fox and Conroy suggested that the teacher increase praise, provide the student with additional time, or increase the student's choices. More specifically, when setting events may be affecting a student's behavior, the teacher may need to give the student "more slack" (reduce or modify demands on the student rather than jeopardizing the relationship with the student).

Choice

Student choice tends to reduce problem behaviors by allowing the student to avoid more aversive situations. When a student chooses an activity, the activity is less likely to evoke problem behaviors than if the teacher had selected and presented the same activity (Dunlap et al., 1991). Horner and Carr (1997) found that the research on choice did not indicate that students should determine all facets of their curriculum, but they did suggest that teaching students with severe disabilities and intense needs to make choices and incorporating choices into daily schedules may be promising behavioral interventions.

In designing comprehensive interventions, there is never only one appropriate intervention for a behavior (Horner & Carr, 1997). Rather, comprehensive interventions should be consistent with the results of functional assessment, recommended practice, and the resources and constraints within the school (Albin, Lucyshyn, Horner, & Flannery, 1996).

What is the goal of intervention? Comprehensive interventions assume that several behaviors are being addressed concurrently and that the teacher would be unable to apply several individual, artificial, intrusive interventions at one time. Consequently, interventions must be naturalistic; that is, they must capitalize on the natural interactions between the student and people in close contact with him or her (Barnett et al., 1997). The focus of the analysis in identifying the goals of the interventions is the situations that are a problem for the student and the actual roles, skills, and interests of both the student and the teacher (Barnett, Ehrhardt, Stollar, & Bauer, 1994).

Barnett and associates (1994) suggested an assessment intervention model called **PASSKey,** which stands for *planned activity, strategic sampling,* and **keystone behaviors.** This model utilizes the early work on **ecological interviews** conducted by Wahler and Cormier (1970), who explored the patterns of problem behavior situations during a day. In PASSKey, an interview discussing each of the aspects of the individual's day and observation is conducted to uncover the planned activities and keystone behaviors within those activities. *Keystone behaviors* are those behaviors that have the potentially widest range of positive consequences with regard to a group of behaviors and behaviors that occur concurrently (Evans & Meyer, 1985). For example, turn taking is a keystone behavior because it affects the student's ability to converse, attend to instruction, play games, and interact with his or her peers.

The PASSKey process begins with a waking day interview and observations. The waking day interview (Wahler & Cormier, 1970) is conducted to identify the problem behaviors and the contexts in which they occur. An example of a waking day interview is presented in Table 1.

Patterns of behavior emerge when the information obtained during the waking day interview is reviewed and analyzed. In the example in Table 1, Paolo appears to have a consistent problem with waiting his turn. This is reflected in his difficulties in following classroom routines, engaging in dialogue, and completing group tasks. That, then, is a keystone behavior. Increasing Paolo's ability to wait his turn will have an impact across environments and will increase his ability to engage in other tasks.

In order to gather additional information and work toward naturalistic supports to change the problem behavior, a directed observation is conducted. There are several ways to record observations, but the most frequently used are 1) antecedent, behavior, and consequences (ABCs); and 2) incident recording. In ABCs, the observer records the antecedent, the behavior, and the consequences of that behavior (see Table 2 for an example). In incident recording, the observer records changes in the student's behaviors or actions as these are related to the time at which they occurred (see Table 3 for an example).

The ABCs and incident recording methods provide several additional insights into Paolo's behavior. He appears to recognize the routine and begins to initiate it. His inability to wait makes it difficult for him to complete the task, however. He follows the teacher's directions and responds when the teacher

Table 1.   Waking day interview for Paolo, Grade 2

Situation	Actions
Arrival	Paolo stands by hooks for a few minutes while other students are putting their book bags away, then drops his bag and wanders around the classroom; must be cued later to put his bag away and get his home folder
Opening activity	Interrupts during meeting; when he brings a required note, he gets up and stands by teacher; waits momentarily, then leaves group
Language arts block	Pushes to get folder or materials; if he is unable to reach his materials quickly, begins to wander; needs to be cued to get into line to get his materials
Recess	Usually begins playing game with other students; if he is not "it" or very active, leaves the group and watches cars rather than playing
Math block	Works well independently; has difficulty working with his group because he wants to be first or loses interest
Lunch	"Messes" in line; teacher usually makes him the line leader and stays with him to avoid incidents
Lunch recess	Same as morning recess
Sustained silent reading	Teacher usually keeps a book for him on her desk so that she can hand it to him immediately upon the beginning of the period to avoid incidents; enjoys being read to by a peer
Social studies block	Difficulty in group; interrupts, grabs materials first; students usually manage his behavior by giving him his materials and tasks first
Science/art block	As in social studies block; concerns about safety because of his grabbing materials and pushing; has difficulty in replacing materials because of his inability to wait; art teacher indicates that she gives him a "personal invitation" to put his materials away first, then asks the other students to put materials away

Table 2.   ABCs for Paolo's behavior upon arrival

Antecedent	Behavior	Consequence
Paolo arrives at school.	Paolo walks into the class-room, walks to Ms. B's desk, and says, "Hi, teacher."	Ms. B: "Hi, Paolo. Put your book bag up and get your home folder."
Ms. B asks Paolo to put materials away.	Paolo walks over to the wall that has the hooks and cub-bies, stands behind the hud-dle of students for 10 sec-onds, then pushes student in front of him.	Student: "Stop pushing, Paolo.
Student: "Stop pushing, Paolo."	Paolo: "I need to put my bag away."	Paolo stands for another 5 seconds, then drops his bag, and goes over to the gerbils.
Paolo drops his bag and goes to the gerbil cage.	Students put away book bags, get home folders, and go to desk clusters.	Paolo stays by the gerbil cage.
Paolo stays by the gerbil cage.	Ms. B: "Paolo, where are you supposed to be?"	Paolo looks at the other stu-dents. Lisa says, "Come on, Paolo, get to your desk."
Lisa cues Paolo.	Paolo comes to desk cluster.	Ms. B: "Great. Everybody seems to be in their clusters. I'm coming around to check home folders."
Ms. B goes around to check home folders and comes to Paolo.	Ms. B: "Paolo, where is your home folder? Didn't you get it out of your bag?"	Paolo goes to book bag on floor, gets out home folder, drops book bag.
Paolo drops book bag.	Ms. B: "Paolo, go back and hang up your book bag."	Lisa: "I'll get it for him, Ms. B."

gives him specific cues. During ABCs and incident recordings, information was gathered regarding the teacher's pattern of behavior. Rather than cope with Paolo's behavior in a proactive way, the teacher tends to react to it and provides Paolo with additional cues. It was also observed that when Paolo failed to complete a routine, often another student would complete it for him. The students appeared to be fairly tolerant of Paolo (e.g., verbally telling him to stop pushing rather than pushing him back), and he reacted to them (e.g., he dropped his bag rather than persist with pushing). Finally, both the ABCs and incident recordings appear to identify a peer (Lisa) who can serve as an intervener with Paolo.

After identifying the behavior that seems to be cutting across environments and current interactions that are occurring around the behavior, the teacher can begin to design ways of addressing the behavior. The most naturalistic and least intrusive intervention is the most likely to be faithfully carried out. Lisa appears to be a potential buddy for Paolo. The teacher may ask Lisa to stand by Paolo when he arrives and cue him to wait, removing his home folder. Having Lisa chat with Paolo while he is waiting may also increase Paolo's ability in conversing and interacting with his peers. After Paolo hangs up his book bag, Lisa could cue him to join her in the desk cluster. By using a natural support such as a peer, the teacher does not need to intervene, and the student has increased positive peer interaction.

At times, more directive strategies may need to be applied. The positive reinforcement strategies described in Chapter 10 may need to be applied. The

Table 3.   Direct observation of Paolo

Time	Event
8:17 A.M.	Paolo walks into classroom, walks to Ms. B's desk, and says, "Hi, teacher." Ms. B: "Hi, Paolo. Put your book bag up and get your home folder."
8:18 A.M.	Paolo walks over to the wall that has the hooks and cubbies, stands behind the huddle of students for 10 seconds, then pushes student in front of him. Student tells Paolo to stop pushing. Paolo says that he needs to put his bag away, stands waiting for another 5 seconds, drops the bag, and goes over to the gerbils. Other students put away book bags, get home folders, and go to desk clusters.
8:24 A.M.	Ms. B: "Paolo, where are you supposed to be?" Paolo looks at other students. Lisa tells Paolo to get to his desk.
8:25 A.M.	Paolo comes to cluster.
8:27 A.M.	Ms. B states that she is going to come around and check folders. When she gets to Paolo, she asks, "Paolo, where is your home folder? Didn't you get it out of your bag?" Paolo goes to book bag on the floor and gets out home folder. Ms. B says, "Paolo, go back and hang up your book bag." Lisa states that she will hang it up for him and does so. Paolo sits in cluster.
8:30 A.M.	End of observation

least intrusive intervention, however, is considered recommended practice. Naturalistic interventions may not be apparent when an observer (e.g., parent, administrator, other teacher) visits the classroom yet may make a significant difference in the way the classroom functions.

LEARNING OBJECTIVE 2: To be able to implement strategy instruction with students

Strategy instruction, or learning strategies, is an alternative format for working with students with disabilities that does not focus on helping students keep up with the day-to-day demands of content learning but redirects their energies toward enabling them to learn strategies by which they can keep up with those demands themselves (King-Sears, 1997).

Dana (1987) argued that students need strategies that they can use on their own and that require little time and effort. Students can develop strategies to assist themselves in both their frame of mind and the skills that they need for reading. By applying a mnemonic, a student can describe the essential aspects of a skill or an activity. Dana provided the example of the "BURP" strategy, which was designed by a group of boys:

B = Breathe and relax
U = Understand what you read
R = Reread if you need to
P = Predict what will happen next

Dana used printed strategies on a bookmark to remind students to ask themselves a series of questions when first confronting and then engaging in a reading task:

- Am I ready to read?
- Am I paying attention?

- Am I understanding what I am reading?
- Did I achieve my purpose?

Each question is designed to cue the student to a specific learning strategy. Another example of a learning strategy is a RAM! bookmark:

- R = Relax
- A = Activate your purpose
- M = Motivate yourself!

Harris and Graham (1993) provided a detailed illustration of the teaching of a learning strategy for writing instruction. First, the teacher meets with the class and offers learning strategies instruction to all of the students in the class and then works with those students who choose to learn the strategy. Next, the teacher discusses story grammar and the various ways in which authors develop or use different story parts. The teacher meets with individual students or with small groups of students to introduce and explain the purpose of self-monitoring strategies and their use in learning. Then students learn to graph their behavior, and the teacher introduces and gives each student the steps of the strategy in the form of a mnemonic. The teacher models the strategy with the students and provides an example. The students memorize the mnemonic and strategy, engage in collaborative practice, and work together to apply self-graphing and self-monitoring. Finally, the students apply the mnemonic independently, with the teacher providing constructive feedback as necessary. Harris and Graham's method for teaching the strategy is presented in Table 4.

Deshler, Ellis, and Lenz (1996) suggested eight stages for the teaching of learning strategies to students:

1. Pretest and obtain the students' commitment to learn the strategy.
2. Present the strategy steps. These steps are usually a mnemonic to help students remember the steps.
3. Model the strategy by talking aloud while performing it.
4. Verbally practice the strategy steps until the students have memorized the steps.
5. Provide controlled practice and feedback with students using the strategy.
6. Provide more difficult practice and feedback with the students using the strategy with grade-level content.
7. Posttest using the same format as was used in the pretest.
8. Generalize the strategy to other environments and situations.

Table 4. Stages of strategy instruction

1. Initial conference with whole class, offering instruction in the strategy
2. Discussion of the content, instruction in self-monitoring and self-graphing
3. Discussion of the strategy itself
4. Modeling application of the strategy
5. Memorization of the strategy and mnemonic
6. Collaborative practice
7. Independent application

Source: Harris and Graham (1993).

According to Deshler and colleagues, through the use of learning strategies, students may require less tutorial or special instruction and may be more fully included with their peers.

Englert, Raphael, Anderson, Anthony, and Stevens (1991) offered another example of the use of learning strategies in inclusive classrooms. In their strategy for writing instruction, they emphasized the role of dialogue in the development of writing, the provision of **scaffolded instruction** (i.e., temporary and adjustable support for the development of new skills), and the transformation of solitary writing into a collaborative activity. Throughout the instruction, they employed self-talk to make the learning strategy more evident to the students. Their POWER strategy resulted in improved overall writing quality for the students' expository texts. POWER is the abbreviation of

P = Plan
O = Organize
W = Write
E = Edit or Editor
R = Revise

Harris and Pressley (1991) argued that generalizing strategies outside of the instruction environment is essential. From their study of the literature of generalization of instruction strategies, they suggested that teachers engage in the following activities in order to promote generalization:

- Involve students in planning their own instruction programs and learning objectives.
- Require students to think or act on their own.
- Remind students of the variety of contexts within which a strategy can be applied.
- Provide opportunities to practice a strategy with many materials, in many situations, and in many environments.

In reinforcement theory, **generalization**—the **transfer of learning**—is the process by which a behavior reinforced in the presence of one stimulus is exhibited in the presence of another stimulus (Morris, 1985; Walker & Shea, 1995).

Vaughn, Bos, and Lund (1986) recommended several practical strategies for teachers wishing to help students develop generalization skills. These recommendations include the following variations:

- The amount, power, and type of reinforcers applied to students, such as fading reinforcers, changing from tangible to social reinforcers, or using reinforcers in different environments
- The instructions given to students, such as using alternative and parallel directions, rewording directions, and using photos and pictures
- The media of the instruction materials used by the students to complete tasks (In the written medium, this can mean varying items such as paper size and color, writing instruments, and inks. The teacher may also use other instructional media, such as films and computers.)
- The response modes that students use to complete tasks (e.g., changing from written to oral responses, using a variety of test question formats)

- The stimulus provided to students (e.g., changing the size, color, and shape of illustrations; using concrete objects)
- Instruction environments (e.g., changing the work location, changing from individual to small-group instruction)
- Instructors (e.g., using aides, peers, parents, other teachers)

Learning strategies and their instruction should be carefully planned, monitored, and evaluated.

LEARNING OBJECTIVE 3: To be able to use life space interviewing to support students

In any classroom, there is the potential for a crisis. A crisis is a disruption in the program that is so intense that it disturbs others (both the students and the teacher) or an event that has had an impact on relationships between students or between students and the teacher. Redl (1966) described the **life space interview** as an intervention for talking with a student or students involved in a crisis. More specifically, the life space interview is a here-and-now intervention built around a student's or students' direct life experiences. It is conducted by a teacher perceived to be significant in the student's life space. The interview is imposed to structure an incident in the student's life to enable the student to solve the problem confronting him or her. The teacher, as interviewer, serves as a facilitator (Walker & Shea, 1995).

Redl (1966) suggested that the interview may be applied for either of two purposes. First, the life space interview may serve as a way in which to explore with the student a consistent behavioral characteristic (i.e., the clinical exploitation of life events). When using the interview for this purpose, the teacher assists the student in increasing his or her conscious awareness of distorted perceptions of existing realities, pathological behavior characteristics, hidden social and moral values and standards, or reactions to the behaviors and pressures of the group. The interviewer and student discuss more personally productive and socially acceptable means of solving problems. This application of the life space interview intervention requires considerable training and experience on the part of the interviewer.

Second, the interviewer may apply the life space interview with a student for the purpose of supplying "emotional first aid" on the spot in times of stress. For this purpose, the interview is used to reduce the student's frustration, support the student in an emotionally charged situation, restore strained student–teacher or student–student relationships, reinforce existing behavioral and social limits and realities, or assist the student in efforts to find solutions to everyday problems of living. Although they originated in residential treatment programs, life space interviews have been found to be effective in school environments (DeMagistras & Imber, 1980; Naslund, 1987).

Life space interviews provide a structure for talking with students. This structure involves the following steps:

1. *An instigating incident:* The teacher clarifies the content, testing for the depth of the issue at hand. By the conclusion of this step, the student

should express his or her responsibility and a potential reason for the action. For example, if Wanda pushed Marcella's chair over because Marcella was smiling at an incorrect answer that Wanda made to a question from the teacher, then Wanda may enter this step by saying, "She was laughing at me." By the end of this step, Wanda would state, "I was angry because Marcella was laughing at me, so I pushed her chair over."

2. *Enhancing a feeling of acceptance and avoiding value judgments:* During this phase of the interview, the teacher communicates to the student that it is acceptable to have feelings but that acting on those feelings in certain ways and under certain circumstances is not acceptable. In addition, the teacher needs to place the decision regarding the appropriateness of the response in the hands of the student rather than make a value judgment type of statement such as, "You know the rules" or "I expect better of you than that." The teacher's question could be phrased as "How do you feel about the decision to push Wanda's chair over because you thought she was laughing at you?"

3. *Exploring the potential for change:* During the third phase of the interview, the teacher helps the student formulate other ways of coping with similar events. The teacher can ask, "What would be a better way to show you're mad and to let me know what's happening?"

4. *Resolution:* During the resolution phase, the teacher and student agree on a way to resolve the situation and how to react in similar situations in the future. In some situations, the teacher and the student may want to develop a contract (see Chapter 10) to show their commitment to the resolution (Fagan, 1981; Morse, 1980).

The previous list is not a rigid series of steps; on occasion during these interviews, some steps are skipped and others are reordered. There are several prerequisite skills that a student must have to be able to engage effectively in a life space interview. Wood and Weller (1981) suggested that the student be aware of self, events, and others; be able to sustain attention; understand the language necessary for such a discussion; recall a sequence of events; be able to produce words or signs of sufficient complexity to represent the event; have a positive relationship with the interviewer; be able to describe personal experiences; and be able to give reasons why events occur.

Brenner (1969) offered several guidelines for people conducting a life space interview:

- Be polite; if the interviewer does not have control of his or her emotions, he or she should not begin the interview.
- Establish eye contact with the student or students being interviewed, that is, talk with—never at—those being interviewed.
- When unsure of the history of the incident, investigate. Do not conduct an interview on the basis of second- or third-person information or rumors.
- Ask appropriate questions to obtain a knowledgeable grasp of the incident, but do not probe areas of unconscious motivation; limit the use of "why" questions.
- Listen to the student and attempt to understand his or her perceptions of the incident.

- Encourage the student to ask questions and respond appropriately.
- When the student is suffering from apparent shame or guilt as a result of the incident, attempt to reduce and minimize these feelings.
- Facilitate the student's efforts to communicate what he or she wishes to say. If the student is having difficulty in this area, provide help.
- Work with care and patience to develop a mutually acceptable plan of action for immediate or future implementation.

Gardner (1990) expressed concern about the amount of academic time lost when life space interviews are used and the focus is on feelings rather than on the behavior that needs to change. Long (1990), however, contended that life space interviews help students see the connection between their behavior and their feelings and to manage the improper expression of those feelings.

SUMMARY

This chapter addresses the following major concepts:

1. Comprehensive interventions address several problem behaviors concurrently, are driven by assessment, are applied throughout the day, and blend several intervention procedures.
2. In functional communication training, the situation that provokes and maintains problem behaviors is identified and new communication skills are taught.
3. By identifying the features of tasks that are aversive and changing the task to minimize those aversive features, problem behaviors can be reduced.
4. Setting events increase the probability that certain kinds of behaviors will occur.
5. Student choice can reduce problem behaviors.
6. Strategy instruction redirects students' energies toward enabling them to learn strategies by which they can keep up with the demands of content area learning.
7. Life space interviewing may be applied to address crises in inclusive classrooms.

TEST YOUR KNOWLEDGE

Completion of the "Self-Evaluation," "Make the Language Your Own," and "Application Activity" sections will aid readers in understanding and retaining the information presented in this chapter. Answer keys for the "Self-Evaluation" and "Make the Language Your Own" sections are located in the Appendix at the end of the book.

Self-Evaluation

Select the most appropriate response to complete each of the following statements:

1. Comprehensive interventions
   a. Identify a single target behavior
   b. Address several problem behaviors concurrently
   c. Utilize a variety of reading materials

2. In functional communication training, the student is taught to use communicative responses that
    a. Are briefer
    b. Are specifically requested
    c. Perform the same function as the problem behavior

3. In functional communication training, the teacher asks him- or herself,
    a. What is this student saying?
    b. What is this student doing?
    c. What are the student's peers doing to support this behavior?

4. In curricular revision,
    a. Instruction goals are not compromised
    b. Instruction goals are reduced, depending on the student's reaction
    c. Instruction goals are adapted through accommodations

5. Setting events
    a. Increase the likelihood of problem behavior
    b. Reduce the aversive aspects of behavior
    c. Are independent of the features of the tasks required

6. In using choice in inclusive classrooms,
    a. Students determine all facets of their curriculum
    b. Choices are provided only to learners with disabilities
    c. Choices are incorporated into daily schedules

7. ABCs suggest that
    a. Antecedents and consequences are important in viewing learners' behavior
    b. Antecedents should be under the control of the teacher
    c. Consequences should be under the control of the teacher

8. Strategies employ
    a. Group mediation
    b. A mnemonic
    c. Natural supports

9. In teaching the generalization of skills, teachers should
    a. Consistently present tasks using the same materials in the same way
    b. Vary instructions given to students
    c. Consistently apply reinforcement as new tasks are learned

10. Life space interviews require that students
    a. Are violent
    b. Get counseling
    c. Have adequate language skills to carry on a discussion

Make the Language Your Own
Match the following terms with their definitions:

1. _____ Setting event

2. _____ Life space interview

3. _____ Keystone behaviors

a. Interventions that produce rapid, durable, and generalized reductions in problem behaviors while improving the individual's suc-

4. _____ Comprehensive interventions

5. _____ Ecological interview

6. _____ Scaffolded instruction

7. _____ Generalization

8. _____ PASSKey

9. _____ Functional communication training

10. _____ Curricular revision

11. _____ Strategy instruction

cess at school, at home, and in the community (Horner & Carr, 1997)

b. Instruction in the use of communication responses that are socially acceptable, have the same effect as the problem behavior being replaced (i.e., helping the student obtain what he or she needs or wants, helping the student escape from unwanted situations), and are at least as efficient as the problem behavior) (Durand & Carr, 1991)

c. An interview conducted to obtain information about the unique characteristics of the student, the school, or the home and the relationship between the child and the environment

d. Reducing a problem behavior by identifying the features of the task that are aversive and changing the task to minimize those features (Dunlap et al., 1991)

e. An alternative format for working with students with disabilities that does not focus on helping the students keep up with the day-to-day demands of content learning but redirects their energies toward enabling them to learn strategies by which they can keep up with those demands themselves (King-Sears, 1997)

f. Behaviors that have the potentially widest range of positive consequences with regard to a group of behaviors and behaviors that occur concurrently (Evans & Meyer, 1985)

g. Process by which a behavior that is reinforced in the presence of one stimulus will be exhibited in the presence of another stimulus (Morris, 1985)

h. An assessment intervention model whose components include planned activity, strategic sampling, and keystone behaviors

      i. Temporary and adjustable support for the development of new skills

      j. Events in the environment that increase the probability that certain kinds of student–teacher or student–student interactions will occur (Repp & Kirsch, 1990)

      k. A here-and-now intervention built around a student's direct life experiences that is imposed to structure an incident in the student's life, which enables the student to solve the problems confronting him or her

Application Activity

1. Using an ABCs chart, observe an interaction sequence between two individuals. Analyze their behavior. Using the chart, does your perception of their behavior change? In what way?

REFERENCES

Albin, R.W., Lucyshyn, J.M., Horner, R.H., & Flannery, K.B. (1996). Contextual fit for behavioral support plans: A model for "goodness of fit." In L.K. Koegel, R.L. Koegel, & G. Dunlap (Eds.), *Positive behavioral support: Including people with difficult behavior in the community* (pp. 81–98). Baltimore: Paul H. Brookes Publishing Co.

Barnett, D.W., Ehrhardt, K.E., Stollar, S., & Bauer, A.M. (1994). PASSKey: A model for naturalistic assessment and intervention design. *Topics in Early Childhood Special Education, 14,* 350–373.

Barnett, D.W., Lentz, F.E., Bauer, A.M., Macmann, G., Stollar, S., & Ehrhardt, K.E. (1997). Ecological foundations of early intervention: Planned activities and strategic sampling. *Journal of Special Education, 30,* 471–490.

Brenner, M.B. (1969). Life space interviewing in the school setting. In H. Dupont (Ed.), *Educating emotionally disturbed children: Readings* (pp. 287–301). Austin, TX: Holt, Rinehart & Winston.

Dana, C. (1987). Strategy families for disabled readers. *Journal of Reading, 32*(1), 30–35.

DeMagistras, R.J., & Imber, S.C. (1980). The effects of life space interviewing on the academic and social performance of behavior disordered children. *Behavioral Disorders, 6,* 12–25.

Deshler, D.D., Ellis, E.S., & Lenz, B.K. (1996). *Teaching adolescents with learning disabilities: Strategies and methods* (2nd ed.). Denver: Love Publishing Co.

Dunlap, G., Kern-Dunlap, L.K., Clark, S., & Robbins, F.R. (1991). Functional assessment, curricular revision, and severe behavior problems. *Journal of Applied Behavior Analysis, 24,* 387–397.

Durand, V.M., & Carr, E.G. (1991). Functional communication training to reduce challenging behavior: Maintenance and application in new settings. *Journal of Applied Behavior Analysis, 24,* 251–264.

Englert, C.S., Raphael, T.E., Anderson, L.M., Anthony, H.M., & Stevens, D.D. (1991). Making strategies and self-talk visible: Writing instruction in regular and special education classrooms. *American Educational Research Journal, 28,* 337–372.

Evans, I.M., & Meyer, L.H. (1985). *An educative approach to behavior problems: A practical decision model for interventions with severely handicapped learners.* Baltimore: Paul H. Brookes Publishing Co.

Fagan, S.A. (1981). Conducting an LSI: A process model. *Pointer, 25*(2), 9–11.

Fox, J., & Conroy, M. (1995). Setting events and behavioral disorders of children and youth: An interbehavioral field analysis for research and practice. *Journal of Emotional and Behavioral Disorders, 3*(3), 130–140.

Gardner, R. (1990). Life space interviewing: It can be effective, but don't. . . . *Behavioral Disorders, 15,* 111–119.

Harris, K., & Pressley, M. (1991). The nature of cognitive strategy instruction: Interactive strategy construction. *Exceptional Children, 57*(5), 392–404.

Harris, K.R., & Graham, S. (1993). Cognitive strategy instruction and whole language: A case study. *Remedial and Special Education, 14*(4), 30–34.

Horner, R.H., & Carr, E.G. (1997). Behavioral support for students with severe disabilities: Functional assessment and comprehensive intervention. *Journal of Special Education, 31*(1), 84–104.

King-Sears, M.E. (1997). Best academic practices for inclusive classrooms. *Focus on Exceptional Children, 19*(7), 1–22.

Long, N.J. (1990). Comments on Ralph Gardner's article "Life space interviewing: It can be effective, but don't. . . ." *Behavioral Disorders, 15,* 119–125.

Morris, R.J. (1985). *Behavior modification with exceptional children: Principles and practices.* Glenview, IL: Scott Foresman–Addison Wesley.

Morse, W.C. (1980). Worksheet on life space interviewing for teachers. In N.J. Long, W.C. Morse, & R.G. Newman (Eds.), *Conflict in the classroom: The education of emotionally disturbed children* (4th ed., pp. 267–271). Belmont, CA: Wadsworth.

Naslund, S.R. (1987). Life space interviewing: A psycho educational interviewing model for teaching pupil insights and measuring program effectiveness. *Pointer, 32*(2), 12–15.

Redl, F. (1966). The life space interview: Strategy and techniques. In F. Redl, *When we deal with children: Selected writings* (pp. 35–67). New York: Free Press.

Reichle, J. (1990). *National working conference on positive approaches to the management of excess behavior: Final report and recommendations.* Minneapolis: University of Minnesota, Institute on Community Integration.

Reichle, J. (1997). Communication intervention with persons who have severe disabilities. *Journal of Special Education, 31*(1), 110–134.

Repp, A.C., & Kirsch, K.G. (1990). A taxonomic approach to the nonaversive treatment of maladaptive behavior of persons with developmental disabilities. In A.C. Repp & N.N. Singh (Eds.), *Perspectives on the use of nonaversive and aversive interventions for persons with developmental disabilities* (pp. 331–348). Sycamore, IL: Sycamore Publishing Co.

Vaughn, S., Bos, C.S., & Lund, K.A. (1986). . . . But they can do it in my room: Strategies for promoting generalization. *Teaching Exceptional Children, 18*(3), 176–180.

Wahler, R.G., & Cormier, W.H. (1970). The ecological interview: The first step in outpatient child behavior therapy. *Journal of Behavior Therapy and Experimental Psychiatry, 1,* 279–289.

Walker, J.E., & Shea, T.M. (1995). *Behavior management: A practical approach for educators* (6th ed.). Upper Saddle River, NJ: Merrill.

Wood, M.M., & Weller, D. (1981). How come it's different with some children? A developmental approach to life space interviewing. *Pointer, 25*(2), 61–66.

Moving Toward Inclusion

I wasn't sure what my fourth-grade social studies class was going to do with Layla. I had visited with her when she was in the primary school building, and she rocked her whole body and bit on the back of her hand so much that she had a callous. She was only 10, but she was pretty large physically. Her teacher came with her and just answered everything the students asked. They asked, "Why does she rock like that?" The teacher replied that Layla found it calming. "What's wrong with her hand?" "She chews on it when she gets excited." Then came my first surprise, instead of the "Yuck" and "Gross" I thought we would hear, one of the students said, "How can we help her not hurt herself like that?"

Ms. W., a fourth-grade teacher

The assumption stated at the beginning of this book is that learners with disabilities, the focus of the book, are educated in inclusive classrooms. *Inclusion* is defined as the philosophy that all students, regardless of disability, are a vital and integral part of the general education system and that special needs services addressing the individualized education program (IEP) goals and objectives of students with disabilities are rendered in the general education classroom. Although this assumption is made for purposes of the organization of and presentation and discussion, in this book, the authors are not naïve enough to believe or even to suggest that all learners with disabilities are served in inclusive classrooms. Consequently, it must be recognized that students with disabilities periodically move among various restrictive environments and from restrictive to inclusive environments. As a result, the challenges of transition, that is, the movement from one system or service to another, must be confronted.

This chapter presents several strategies and services for the transition into inclusive classrooms. The first section of the chapter presents strategies to facilitate inclusion that focus on instruction. The second section focuses on strategies to facilitate the social transition of students into inclusive classrooms. The third section discusses the supports that students need during the transition to inclusive classrooms. The final section discusses challenges that are unique to the inclusion of students with severe disabilities and intense educational needs.

LEARNING OBJECTIVES

After completing this chapter, readers will be able to

1. Recognize ways to help learners make the transition into inclusive classrooms with regard to instruction
2. Develop ways to help learners make the social transition into inclusive classrooms
3. Identify supports for learners in the transition into inclusive classrooms
4. Identify challenges that are unique to including learners with severe disabilities and intense educational needs

KEY WORDS AND PHRASES

audiologists—licensed individuals with expertise in hearing testing and amplification

challenging behaviors—behaviors that are seen by those around the individual as dangerous, disgusting, or disruptive

communication specialists—professionals with expertise in communication, including speech and language; social interaction; communication devices; and counseling parents, learners, and teachers regarding communication development and disorders

conversation book—a book that provides numerous ideas for discussion

educational interpreter—an individual, usually licensed by the state or by a national organization, who provides American Sign Language (ASL) interpretation for individuals who are deaf or hard of hearing

inclusion—the philosophy that all students, regardless of disability, are a vital and integral part of the general education system; IEP goals and objectives of students with disabilities are rendered in the general education classroom

inclusive—a sense of belonging, a just opportunity for children with disabilities, an important choice for parents (Erwin & Soodak, 1995)

instructional assistant—a teacher's aide, who is usually provided training by the employing district or organization and who provides direct support to individuals

Personal Futures Planning—a strategy for forming a vision with an individual in order to help that individual develop appropriate short- and long-term goals

occupational therapists—licensed individuals with expertise in sensory factors and independent functioning

physical therapists—licensed individuals with expertise in sensorimotor, gross motor, and mobility skills

setting events—events in the environment that increase the probability that certain kinds of student–teacher or student–student interactions will occur (Repp & Kirsch, 1990)

transition—the movement from one system or service to another

vision specialists—individuals with expertise in vision and instructional and technological supports for students with vision impairments

LEARNING OBJECTIVE 1: To be able to recognize ways to help learners make the transition into inclusive classrooms with regard to instruction

Moving learners into more **inclusive** classrooms requires teamwork. As the roles of general and special educators are blended, developing an awareness of the perspectives of the general educator with regard to serving learners with disabilities in their classrooms is essential. Schumm and Vaughn (1992) reported that general education teachers were willing to serve students with disabilities in their classrooms as long as these students did not exhibit emotional or behavior problems. General educators were willing to make adaptations for these students while they were taking tests or working on instructional assignments. The teachers were unlikely, however, to spend significant time planning for or making adaptations to the current curriculum or tests (i.e., preplanning) or constructing new objectives based on students' performance (i.e., postplanning).

General educators identified budgetary factors, accountability, access to equipment and materials, and the physical environment of the classroom and the school as barriers to planning for students with disabilities. General education teachers cited class size, lack of professional preparation in special education and disabilities, problems with students with behavior and emotional problems, and limited instruction time as factors that inhibit planning for students with disabilities. Schumm and Vaughn (1992) reported that elementary education teachers were more likely to make adaptations in preplanning, interactive planning, and postplanning than were middle school and high school teachers.

To analyze and problem solve how the needs of students with disabilities can be met in inclusive classrooms, Williams and Fox (1996) suggested using matrices. Although they assumed that one of the decisions to be made is whether the student with disabilities will actually participate in the general education activity, parts of their process may be helpful. They suggested developing a matrix down one side of which are listed the general education activities that take place in the classroom. Across the bottom of the matrix are listed the student's IEP priorities, goals, and objectives and noninstructional needs or accommodations (e.g., medication, hearing aid checks, braille materials). Williams and Fox suggested that, after filling in the information on their matrix and reviewing a series of questions about the student, the general education teacher can determine whether and how the student will participate in the activity. The following questions developed by Williams and Fox for use with their matrix can be used to determine how students can participate rather than whether they can participate:

- Will the student's critical concerns and needs be addressed through the activity?
- Will the student be responsible for the same content as other students or a subset of the content? for similar but adapted content? an overlapping activity? for practicing problem-solving or communication skills during the activity?
- Will the student need accommodations to engage in the activity?
- Which of the student's priority skill areas can be addressed through the activity?

Salend and Viglianti (1982) were pioneers in developing formats to identify the dimensions of classrooms that may be significant in the **transition** to inclusive classrooms. Their work was based not on observation of the student to be transitioned into the inclusive classroom but on observation of the classroom itself. The areas that they observed to be important to effective **inclusion** are summarized in Table 1.

 LEARNING OBJECTIVE 2: To be able to develop ways to help learners make the social transition into inclusive classrooms

A primary goal of inclusive learning environments is that students feel connected (i.e., a part of the classroom's social system). Jorgensen and Rudy (1990) suggested that students are connected and truly belong to an inclusive learning environment when they

- Have real friends, not just buddies or peer tutors
- Interact with their peers after school and on weekends and holidays
- Receive telephone calls at home from friends
- Are chosen by others to be on their team
- Send and receive notes from other students in school
- Are named as a friend by other students

Table 1. Variables to be observed in classroom to support transition

Aspect of the classroom	Variables to be observed
Instructional materials and support personnel	Books • Titles of books, series, study guides • Reading level of books used • Supplementary materials used Media • Television, videocassette recorder • Slides, overheads • Audiotapes • Computers Support personnel • Instructional assistants • Volunteers • Peers
Presentation of subject matter	Teaching strategies • Lecture • Use of chalkboard • Use of groups • Use of individualized learning centers • Expectations regarding language • Expectations regarding vocabulary
Response modes	Learner responses • Notetaking • Copying from chalkboard • Reading aloud • Level of directions requiring response • Requesting assistance
Evaluation strategies	Learner evaluation • Frequency with which teacher evaluates learners • Nature of tests, quizzes, or exams used • Nature of homework • Frequency and nature of special projects
Management	Management system • Implicit and explicit rules • Consequences • Reinforcement patterns • Routines
Social interactions	Student norms • Student dress • Student appearance (e.g., hair, jewelry, nails, accessories) • Outside interests (e.g., music activities) • Tolerance
Potential physical barriers	Accessibility and movement • Accessibility of classroom • Accessibility of materials • Movement within classroom

Source: Salend and Viglianti (1982).

In her description of one learner's natural supports, Jorgensen (1992) indicated that it is essential that a learner's support person(s) make a concerted effort to facilitate that learner's support and interaction with others. She urged that the general education teacher spend as much time interacting with the learner with disabilities as with other students in the classroom. In addition, to avoid having other students talk through a support person(s) to the learner with disabilities, the support person(s) must keep as much distance as possible between him- or herself and the learner whom they are supporting. For example, when people wish to interact with a learner with disabilities, they frequently are heard to ask the learner's support person (e.g., "Is it okay to speak with _____ ?" "Can _____ go for a walk?"). The individual must be encouraged to speak directly to the learner with disabilities (e.g., "Hi, _____! Want to go for a walk?" "Do you want to study the math assignment?"). In interactions about a person with disabilities, speaking about the person with disabilities in the third person is common. Support staff should consistently redirect any questions and comments from others away from themselves and to the learner with a disability.

Jorgensen (1992) questioned whether students without identified disabilities should be concerned or embarrassed by the attention that the student with a disability receives from support personnel. She suggested developing a "least intrusive supports first" plan to encourage others to socially interact with learners with disabilities. She suggested that helping others and cooperating with others should be an expectation of everyone in the classroom and that students should not be singled out to receive special assistance. In addition, when

Your Turn . . .

Reflect on your participation with friends and classmates during elementary school. What were the activities in which you and your friends engaged? What supports would be needed in these activities for an individual with disabilities?

planning lessons in which some students will need assistance, the activity could be structured so that students provide the needed help to each other.

In some situations, especially when inclusion is new to a school or a class, interaction between learners with and without identified disabilities must be specifically structured. Hunt, Farron-Davis, Wrenn, Hirose-Hatae, and Goetz (1997) described a specific intervention to increase the social interactions of individuals with and without identified disabilities. First, a "partner of the day" system was implemented. Next, **conversation books** (i.e., books that provide numerous ideas for discussion) were developed, and a conversational turn-taking structure was taught to all of the students. In addition, the education staff were provided with professional development training that introduced them to strategies to be used to promote student interaction. The strategies included the following:

1. *Providing information during weekly class meetings:* During weekly class meetings, ongoing information about using conversation books and how to be a partner for the day is provided. In addition, the weekly class meetings serve as a forum for activities and discussions to increase students' awareness of diversity in general.
2. *Identifying various media designed to facilitate interaction and utilizing interactive computer activities, education materials, toys, games, and conversation books:* Students are taught to use specific interaction structures that allow for the turn taking and chaining necessary for exchanging messages.
3. *Providing teachers with interaction facilitation strategies:* The partner system is implemented to ensure that interactive media are available. A "get in and get out" approach is taught in which the teacher arranges the interactive activity, prompts interaction, and then backs away, returning only when additional support is needed.
4. *Instructing students with disabilities to self-monitor:* The student learns to identify his or her partner for the day and sit with him or her in class. In addition, the student is encouraged to go to lunch and recess with his or her partner and without the support person. The student is encouraged to take and use the conversation book during these times.

LEARNING OBJECTIVE 3: To be able to identify supports for learners in the transition to inclusive classrooms

One of the issues that is most often resolved through the courts is the provision of related services and similar supports for learners with disabilities (Osborne, 1984). Several of the court cases that addressed the provision of related services are summarized in Table 2.

Because most related-services personnel are trained to provide direct services, it is sometimes difficult for them to shift to more collaborative, inclusive ways of delivering their services (Rainforth & York-Barr, 1997). Giangreco (1990) identified two outcome roles for related-services personnel. First, these personnel may develop adaptations and/or equipment to facilitate the functioning and participation of learners with disabilities. Second, related-services personnel may facilitate the development of the functional skills and activities

Table 2. Court cases addressing related services and supports

Barnett by Barnett v. Fairfax County School Board (1991)	A student with hearing loss who was progressing well in an inclusive classroom requested cued speech interpreter services at his home school. The school district maintained cued speech interpreter services at a centrally located facility. The court held that the district was not required to duplicate the service at a school near the student's home.
Board of Education v. Rowley (1982)	The Supreme Court ruled that a New York school board was not required to provide a sign language interpreter to a deaf student; the child was advancing through school and was deemed not to be entitled to an interpreter, despite evidence that an interpreter would allow her to better meet her potential.
Board of Education v. Holland (E.D. Cal. 1992)	A federal district court agreed with the parents of a student with disabilities that a school district should enroll the student in a general education classroom with supplementary aids and services instead of in a special education classroom.
Ellison v. Board of Education (1993)	A New York court ruled that the provision of a special full-time nurse to perform tracheotomy suctioning and catheterization was not a related service.
Irving Independent School District v. Tatro (1984)	The U.S. Supreme Court held that a school district was required to provide catheterization services for a student with disabilities while she attended school.
Cefalu v. East Baton Rouge School Board (M.D. La. 1995)	A federal district court held that a school district was required by the Individuals with Disabilities Education Act (IDEA) of 1990 (PL 101-476) and accompanying regulations to provide a sign language interpreter for a private school student in its jurisdiction.
Chris D. v. Montgomery City Board of Education (M.D. Ala. 1990)	A federal district court granted the parents' request to adopt the outside consultant's individualized education program, which called for parent counseling, noting that parent counseling is a related service if it is needed to allow a student to benefit from his or her education.
Zobrest v. Catalina Foothills School District (1993)	The U.S. Supreme Court held that the provision of a sign language interpreter was a service under IDEA.

Source: Data Research (1997).

of learners with disabilities. In addition to these outcome roles, Giangreco described enabling roles for related-services personnel to support students in their efforts to attain educational outcomes (i.e., IEP goals and objectives). In enabling roles, related-services personnel may engage in consultation, remove or modify barriers to participation, intervene to prevent a loss of skills, or provide resources and support to families.

Related-services personnel can contribute from their unique perspective and area of expertise to support the inclusion of learners with disabilities. The following are some of these professionals and their areas of expertise:

- **Occupational therapists** have expertise in sensory factors related to posture and movement, muscle tone, range of motion, self-care, adaptive equipment, and adaptive devices, as well as in interventions to improve independent functioning skills and to prevent further loss of function.

- **Physical therapists** have expertise in sensorimotor factors related to posture and movement, muscle tone, range of motion, strength, endurance, flexibility, and mobility.
- **Communication specialists** have expertise in communication, including speech and language; social interaction; communication devices; and counseling parents, learners, and teachers regarding communication development and disorders.
- **Audiologists** have expertise in hearing testing and amplification, language, auditory and speechreading training, and hearing devices.
- **Vision specialists** have expertise in vision and training procedures to enhance vision, braille, and adaptive devices for individuals with visual impairments (Campbell & Banevich, 1986; Regulations for the Education for All Handicapped Children Act, 1977).

Other related-services personnel who provide direct and indirect services to learners with disabilities and their families include psychiatrists; psychologists and counselors; adaptive physical education and recreation specialists; medical and school health professionals; and social services personnel, including social workers and case workers. Each of these related-services professionals can contribute from their areas of expertise to the well-being of the learner with disabilities and his or her family.

There are two support individuals who spend a great deal of time in the classroom interacting with the learner with disabilities and his or her peers and teacher. These individuals, the **educational interpreter** and the **instructional assistant,** are described in the following subsections.

Educational Interpreter

An educational interpreter may be involved in a classroom to work with students who are deaf and hard of hearing. Because of the diversity of students who are deaf or hard of hearing, the student, the teacher, and the interpreter must have clear guidelines related to their functions and their interactions with these students. Salend and Longo (1994) suggested that the following questions be used in developing these guidelines:

- What communication method will be used?
- Will the interpreter voice for the student?
- What is the interpreter's role with regard to the student's peers?
- What will the interpreter's activities be during transition times?
- How will the interpreter preserve confidentiality with regard to the student?

The teacher and the interpreter should come to a consensus on their roles with regard to the student. In general, the teacher has the responsibility for instruction, and the interpreter serves in a support role. For example, the teacher is responsible for presenting a lesson, correcting students' work, and providing further explanation as necessary to learners. The teacher provides the interpreter with an orientation to the curriculum and any curriculum guides, textbooks, or materials that may help the interpreter understand and function effectively in the classroom with the learner. Describing class routines, projects, and long-term assignments provides an important context for the interpreter. Other important factors designed to facilitate working with an educational interpreter are provided in Table 3.

Instructional Assistants

Instructional assistants often are used to facilitate the transition of learners with disabilities into inclusive classrooms. Giangreco, Edelman, Luiselli, and MacFarland (1997) found that instructional assistants tend to remain in close proximity to their assigned students (i.e., being in physical contact with the student, sitting immediately next to the student, accompanying the student everywhere). They reported several problems that may result from the close proximity of the instructional assistant and the learner. First, when the instructional assistant was in close proximity to the student, the general educator sometimes assumed less ownership of and responsibility for the student. At times, the teacher completed his or her typical instruction activities with the other students in the classroom and left the instructional assistant to figure out how to engage the student with disabilities in the activity. On such occasions, the instructional assistant frequently separated the student with disabilities from his or her classmates and worked independently with that student. When instructional assistants were in close proximity to their assigned student, they tended to allow the child to remain dependent on them. Giangreco and colleagues found that instructional assistants may affect the student's peer interactions, stigmatize the student, or intimidate the student's peers. Giangreco and colleagues also reported problems with the instructional assistants' teaching methods. An additional drawback is that the instructional assistant may distract the other students in the classroom.

Giangreco and colleagues made several recommendations that may contribute to the more appropriate use of instructional assistants. First, instructional assistants should be hired for classrooms rather than for individual students. By hiring instruction assistants for classrooms, the instructional assistant's time and job responsibilities may be more equitably distributed to benefit a variety of students. In addition, the teacher and the student's parents should agree on when the student needs the close proximity of an adult and when the natural support of peers may be adequate. The role of the teacher as the instructional leader in the classroom should be clarified; the classroom teacher's responsibility is to direct the activities of the classroom, including the activities of the instructional assistants. Students with disabilities should be physically, instructionally, and interactionally included in activities that the teacher plans for the class.

Table 3. Working with educational interpreters

- Provide the interpreter with a list of key terms.
- Monitor the position of the interpreter in the classroom. Typically, the interpreter should be slightly in front of the student without blocking his or her view in a glare-free, well-lit location with a solid-colored background.
- Remember the time delay that is associated with interpreting.
- Talk to the student, not to the interpreter.
- Be aware that the use of media (video- and audiocassettes) may be problematic; provide the interpreter with a script or provide closed captioning.

Source: Salend and Longo (1994).

LEARNING OBJECTIVE 4: To be able to identify challenges that are unique to including learners with severe disabilities and intense educational needs

Perhaps the greatest challenges in the implementation of inclusion are presented by learners with severe disabilities or intense educational needs. These issues, as they relate to parents, teachers, and instruction, are discussed in the following subsections.

Parents

Parents have been actively engaged in the inclusion of learners with severe disabilities or intense educational needs in general education classrooms since the late 1970s (Erwin & Soodak, 1995). Parents have expressed the belief that *inclusive* means a sense of belonging, a just opportunity for their children, and an important choice for parents (Erwin & Soodak, 1995). In interviews, parents of learners with severe disabilities suggested that they were key players in the inclusive programs of their children. Parents serve as an important source of evaluation information about inclusive placement for learners with severe disabilities or intense educational needs.

In a study by Ryndak, Downing, Jacqueline, and Morrison (1995), all parents reported growth in the speech, language, and communication skills of their children following their children's placement in inclusive classrooms. Parents reported that their children made friends and that their exhibition of appropriate social behaviors increased. Parents argued that their children were accepted by their peers. Parents of children without identified disabilities reported that their children were comfortable in interacting with their peers with disabilities, that having opportunities to interact with classmates with disabilities had a positive impact on their children's social and emotional growth, that their children had positive feelings about having classmates with disabilities, and that having a classmate with disabilities did not interfere with their children's education (Giangreco, Edelman, Cloninger, & Dennis, 1993).

Teachers

The inclusion of learners with severe disabilities or intense educational needs is perhaps most effective as a part of districtwide reform (Alessi, 1991). Perceiving inclusion as part of a reform movement, particularly the move to outcomes-based education, should be grounded in a vision-based decision process. Alessi contended that there should be a consensus on a set of values that incorporate a belief in inclusive education. In a description of change within a system, Alessi found that the following policy changes occurred. The roles and responsibilities of the educational staff shifted to allow individuals to function outside traditional roles to more adequately support all students. Class sizes were reduced when learners with severe disabilities or intense educational needs were included. All students and teachers had opportunities for daily contact with students with disabilities. The parallel curriculum pull-out model was replaced by a curricular adaptation model that promoted instructional inclusion.

As learners move into inclusive classrooms, the roles of the teachers shift. In their discussion of the means and meaning of inclusion, Janney and Snell (1997) suggested that teachers devise an inclusion agreement that stipulates the modifications that will and will not be made for learners. One of the bases of the inclusion agreement they suggested dealt with teacher role modification. In inclusive classrooms, the learner with disabilities belongs to the general education teacher, who receives assistance from the special education teacher and instructional or support assistant. The role of the general education teacher is that of teacher, with the special educator becoming the helper. Learners are treated as students in the general education classroom rather than as special cases.

Teachers have described the inclusion of a learner with severe disabilities or intense educational needs as an experience that transforms their professional practice. In a study of general education teachers whose classes included a student with severe disabilities or intense educational needs, Giangreco, Dennis, Cloninger, Edelman, and Schattman (1993) reported that teachers increased their ownership and involvement with the student, became more willing to interact with the student, and became more competent in working with the student, and that teachers changed their attitudes about learners with disabilities based on these experiences. Teachers reported several positive results from inclusion, including increased self-reflection, an increased awareness of the importance of their roles as positive models for the other students, an increased level of confidence, and a sense of pride. The teachers reported that it was helpful to have a shared framework and goals for including the student with disabilities in the general classroom routine; the presence of another person on whom they could rely; and teamwork, which provided them with technical, evaluation, and moral supports.

Hunt and Goetz (1997) concluded that the following six guidelines emerged from their review of the research on inclusive educational outcomes:

1. Parental involvement is an essential part of effective inclusion.
2. Students can make positive academic and learning growth in inclusive classrooms.
3. Students with severe disabilities and intense educational needs experience acceptance and friendships in inclusive classrooms.
4. Students without disabilities benefit from functioning in inclusive classrooms.
5. Collaborative efforts among school personnel are essential to achieving successful inclusive schools.
6. Curricular adaptations are a vital component in effective inclusion efforts.

Instruction

Browder (1997) contended that the three greatest concerns of teachers working with learners with severe disabilities or intense educational needs are what to teach, where to teach, and how to teach. Research concerning what to teach typically has focused on life skills instruction (Nietupski, Hamre-Nietupski, Curtin, & Shrikanth, 1997). Browder concluded that because of that emphasis, little research is available for teachers in making curricular decisions. Rather, Browder argued, assessment models provide the greatest insight into what to teach.

Ecological assessment models have provided direction for teachers struggling with what to teach learners with severe disabilities and intense educational needs. Models such as the PASSKey model (see Chapter 13) present ways to identify the needs of learners with severe disabilities and intense educational needs. Browder (1997) argued that a key component of what to teach with regard to curriculum selection is the preferences of the student and the student's family.

With learners with severe disabilities or intense educational needs, the student's preferred method of communication may be a challenge in itself. In these situations, interviewing individuals who are significant in the student's life may be necessary (Green et al., 1988). Reichle (1997) explored the issue of communication further, suggesting that communication may, in fact, be enhanced by naturally occurring options and choices. In addition, individuals with severe disabilities and intense educational needs may not have repair strategies; that is, they may not have an effective way of indicating that a misunderstanding has occurred.

Families also may have strong feelings about what to teach their children. Hamre-Nietupski, Nietupski, and Strathe (1992) provided families with a listing of curriculum areas, including social, functional academics, and life skills instruction. Having the family set priorities was useful in determining how much emphasis to give the general education curriculum, life skills instruction, and socialization.

One way to develop answers to what to teach is person-centered planning, or **Personal Futures Planning** (Mount & Zwernik, 1988). These approaches share five valued accomplishments in an individual's life. The following are some of these accomplishments:

1. Being a part of community life, doing typical things with typical people
2. Developing and maintaining friendships and satisfying relationships
3. Making choices in everyday life
4. Living with dignity while fulfilling a respected role in the community
5. Having a plan for lifelong learning and continuing to develop competence (Kincaid, 1996)

Making Action Plans (MAPS) (Pearpoint, Forest, & O'Brien, 1996) is a structured procedure for determining what to teach that is grounded in Personal Futures Planning. Personal Futures Planning recognizes that the individual with a disability and his or her family have a voice about the services that they want and need. MAPS is structured around seven questions:

1. Who is the learner?
2. What are the learner's strengths, gifts, and abilities?
3. What are the learner's needs?
4. What is the learner's history?
5. What is the dream vision for the learner?
6. What is the nightmare—the least desirable outcome—for the learner?
7. What would be the learner's ideal day at school, and what must be done to make that day happen?

Through using MAPS, a clearer vision of the goals and objectives for the learner emerges. These goals can then be viewed in terms of the learner's education environment. For example, if the dream for the learner is that he or she work in a supported employment environment, the language and interaction skills that he or she needs for that environment would be an emphasis of what to teach.

Even though the answer to the question of where to teach appears to have a simple answer within the inclusive classroom perspective, concern exists among those responsible for the learner with severe disabilities and intense educational needs. If students are being educated with their age peers, when will they learn the skills needed to function in the community? At what point does the classroom cease to be the future environment for which students are preparing? Horner and Carr (1997) suggested that, given the need to consider academic skills, life skills, and social priorities, where to teach is a significant issue. Research has not yet provided any indication of the amount of time that must be invested in instruction in school and in the community to meet the student's need to benefit from general education and yet make the transition to adult living (Browder, 1997).

Providing a functional curriculum in school as well as community-based instruction needed by students with multiple disabilities makes scheduling difficult. Adequate staff coverage may be difficult to obtain to provide instruction as well as to promote social integration. Hamre-Nietupski, McDonald, and Nietupski (1992) suggested strategies to meet these challenges, which are presented in Table 4.

There is a growing research base related to how to teach learners with severe disabilities and intense educational needs. Providing instruction to students with severe disabilities and intense instructional needs in the general education environment remains a challenge, however. Wolery and Schuster (1997) suggested that strategies can be selected based on whether the outcome for instruction is the student's interaction with the environment or the student's acquisition of a specific behavior. In addition, the way in which peers and general education teachers view instruction procedures must be considered.

Janney and Snell (1997) described two kinds of modifications that must occur in the transition into inclusive classrooms. First, there are modifications to classroom routines. Classroom routines and the physical environment are modified to keep learners with disabilities situated near their peers in similar environments. Students with severe disabilities or intense educational needs may need help to stay with the group, such as with the help of a teacher or assistant walking with the student or pushing his or her wheelchair. The timing and location of activities may need to be modified, with additional time provided between transitions. Second, modifications also may be made to instructional activities. Although the topical connections with the class' learning activities remained, the degree of participation of learners with severe disabilities or intense educational needs varied. In addition, students may be engaged in

- *Academic adaptations,* in which students are expected to achieve the active academic and social participation goals of the class lesson with some support directed toward their individualized learning goals
- *Social participation strategies,* in which students maintain connections to the group through social participation but do not have goals related to active academic participation
- *Parallel activities,* in which instruction occurs in the classroom and generally near classmates yet separate from the classroom group (In parallel activities, there is topical similarity to the class lesson, but social participation is minimized. There is a different activity, with a similar lesson topic, designed and delivered by special educators.)

Table 4. Challenges and strategies

Providing a functional curriculum in general education classrooms	• Use peers to provide partial assistance. • Identify down times in the school day during which functional skill instruction can be provided without disrupting the school's routine. • Provide parallel instruction in functional skills while peers participate in their academic work.
Providing community-based instruction	• Bring the community to the classroom. • Ask small groups of students without disabilities to accompany a peer with disabilities on a rotating basis.
Scheduling staff coverage	• General and special educators determine cooperatively when support is most needed. • Empower general education teachers to assume greater instructional responsibility for students with disabilities. • Determine how and when students without disabilities might serve in a supporting role. • Reduce class size.
Promoting social integration	• Promote the use of neighborhood schools so that social interaction after school is more convenient. • Administrators should set the tone for inclusion. • Arrange after-school social opportunities. • Treat students with disabilities as typically as possible. • Pair students with disabilities with students who do not have disabilities.

For example, in a fourth-grade classroom that serves students with severe disabilities or intense educational needs, academic adaptations may be in place during science. During the science lesson, all of the students are investigating gravity by dropping balls of various sizes from the table or by rolling them down inclines. In social participation strategies, the student with severe disabilities or intense educational needs may be seated with the group during silent sustained reading but may be looking at conversation books or other materials. In parallel activities, the instructional assistant or special educator may work with a small group of learners with severe disabilities or intense educational needs on grouping objects by using a grid while the teacher is working on multiplication with the remainder of the class.

Challenging Behaviors

Teachers often are concerned about the **challenging behaviors** presented by learners with severe or multiple disabilities. Risley (1996) described behaviors as challenging when they are seen as dangerous, disgusting, or disruptive by those who live and work with the student. One difficulty, Risley suggested, is that teachers, peers, and staff members almost always respond immediately to actions that are dangerous, disgusting, or disruptive. The very behaviors that are found to be so difficult, then, may be sustained by the reactions of the very people for whom they are a problem. In order to address this problem, Risley suggested common-sense contingency management. Common-sense contingency management addresses the long-range outcomes and quality of life for everyone. Risley suggested that teachers, parents, and peers focus on the positive and increase prosocial behavior by

- Analyzing the context and function of challenging behaviors
- Rescheduling with the student in order to avoid contexts that are recognized as problematic
- Increasing the level of engagement so that the challenging behaviors are crowded out and providing more frequent social, material, and symbolic consequences
- Teaching acceptable, functionally equivalent social and communicative behaviors that work as well as or better than the challenging behavior
- Enhancing the level of the individual's engagement rather than putting the student in time-out

The emphasis of these strategies, again, is the quality of life of all people in the instructional environment. Risley's suggestions are not easy to implement; rather, they involve the whole community as well as the whole school. Risley suggested that a team that publicly attests its commitment to the student has taken the first step toward working proactively with behaviors. In addition, Risley argued that the interventions must take place in the individual's life space. In addition, an intervention that is based on environmental analysis should be implemented at a time when the student is receptive to influence and is practicing prosocial behavior. Through coaching and contingency management, the primary gains of the challenging behaviors can be decreased. For example, if a student kicks the table when presented with a task he or she does not prefer, the primary gain of this challenging behavior is to have the task removed. With coaching and contingency management, however, the behavior may be eliminated.

Through accelerating development (i.e., by deliberately developing the depth and complexity of a person's knowledge and behavior), challenging behaviors decrease. Acting positively decreases the student's opportunities to act negatively. Plans must be made for the student's real life. Risley argued that the most powerful, durable, and inexpensive level of behavioral intervention is the strategy of arranging a life for a person and coaching him or her to live that life.

Another emerging trend in addressing the challenging behaviors of individuals with severe disabilities is an emphasis on antecedent variables (i.e., what happens before the challenging behavior occurs). "What happens before" includes context variables, or **setting events** (Carr, Reeve, & Magito-McLaughlin, 1996). Michael (1982) suggested that setting events alter the reinforcing or aversive properties of stimuli. For example, if the student did not have breakfast, his or her hunger might increase his or her crankiness and his or her potential for having a tantrum. Carr and colleagues described three categories of setting events: duration events, behavioral histories, and physiological conditions. *Duration events* include the presence or absence of certain people or things. For example, when a specific staff member is present, a student may be less likely to engage in a self-injurious behavior, such as head banging.

Another example is that the uncommon absence of a parent before the student comes to school may set off the student's day in a negative manner.

Behavioral history refers to the relationship of one behavior to another. For example, sometimes a problematic task that has been known to trigger aggression from a student can be embedded among other tasks. Carr and colleagues gave the example of cleanup as a problematic task that might trigger a student's aggressive episode. They suggested that if the problematic task is removed from or presented last in the series of requests to which the student is asked to respond, then the challenging behavior will not occur.

Physiological conditions are the third category of setting events. *Physiological conditions* are factors such as physical illness, hunger, thirst, medication, or other events that have a biological basis. For example, strenuous physical activity may reduce behaviors such as self-injury (Baumeister & MacLean, 1984). Teachers should be aware of the potential of setting events. Setting events reflect the incredible complexity of human behavior and the detailed level of analysis that is sometimes required in order to develop an intervention to change the behavior. Challenging behavior may be anticipated and, at times, prevented by rearranging setting events in the environment rather than by direct intervention.

SUMMARY

This chapter addresses the following major concepts:

1. Moving learners into more inclusive classrooms requires teamwork, analysis of the situation, and problem solving.
2. A primary goal of inclusive learning environments is that students feel connected and a part of the classroom's social system.
3. Interactions between individuals with and without identified disabilities may sometimes need to be specifically structured.
4. Related-services personnel can contribute their expertise to support the inclusion of learners with disabilities.
5. Specific planning and preparation are often required when including learners with intense educational needs or severe disabilities.

TEST YOUR KNOWLEDGE

Completion of the "Self-Evaluation," "Make the Language Your Own," and "Application Activities" sections will aid readers in understanding and retaining the information presented in this chapter. Answer keys for the "Self-Evaluation" and "Make the Language Your Own" sections are located in the Appendix at the end of the book.

Self-Evaluation

Select the most appropriate response to complete each of the following statements:

1. In identifying the dimensions of classrooms involved in moving toward inclusive environments,
    a. The student is observed carefully
    b. The setting is observed carefully
    c. The parents are involved thoroughly

2. Students are truly connected when they
    a. Have instructional assistants or educational interpreters to support them
    b. Have real friends
    c. Are included in all activities through partial participation

3. In planning social interactions for learners with disabilities, it is best to
    a. Make sure that adequate supports are in place
    b. Provide the least intrusive supports first
    c. Assign a buddy

4. Occupational therapists are most concerned with
    a. Gross motor skills
    b. Mobility
    c. Self-help and independent functioning skills

5. Educational interpreters should
    a. Tutor the student when he or she is experiencing difficulties
    b. Communicate directly with the teacher regarding his or her concerns about the student's ability to participate
    c. Arrive at a consensus with the teacher and the student regarding their roles

6. Instructional assistants may
    a. Reduce the general educator's sense of ownership of the student
    b. Successfully remove the student from the group when the class' activities are too challenging
    c. Design and implement alternative activities independently

7. Parents of learners with severe disabilities served in inclusive classrooms have reported that their children
    a. Made friends
    b. Did not receive adequate related services
    c. Were physically unsafe in school because of mobility issues

8. In inclusive classrooms, the learner with disabilities is considered a student of
    a. The general education teacher
    b. The special educator
    c. Both general and special educators

9. What to teach
    a. Is a simple decision related to the general education curriculum
    b. Must be related to maintaining the student in the inclusive classroom
    c. Must be related to long-term and short-term goals

10. Setting events
    a. Are easily analyzed in the classroom
    b. May not be within the control of the teacher
    c. Are irrelevant because of the cognitive level of students with severe disabilities or intense educational needs

Make the Language Your Own
Match the following terms with their definitions:

1. _____ Challenging behaviors
2. _____ Occupational therapist
3. _____ Physical therapist
4. _____ Inclusion
5. _____ Setting events
6. _____ Audiologist
7. _____ Educational interpreter
8. _____ Conversation book
9. _____ Transition
10. _____ Vision specialist
11. _____ Inclusive
12. _____ Instructional assistant
13. _____ Personal Futures Planning

a. A licensed individual with expertise in hearing testing and amplification

b. Philosophy that all students, regardless of ability, are a vital and integral part of the general education system; education program goals and objectives of students with disabilities are rendered in the general education classroom

c. Behaviors that are seen by those around the individual as dangerous, disgusting, or disruptive

d. Licensed individuals with expertise in sensorimotor, gross motor, and mobility skills

e. Factors in the individual's life space that alter the reinforcing power of stimuli

f. An individual, usually licensed by the state or by a national organization, who provides ASL interpretation for individuals who are deaf or hard of hearing

g. Licensed individuals with expertise in sensory factors and independent functioning

h. The movement from one system to another

i. A book that provides numerous ideas for discussion

j. An individual with expertise in vision and instructional and technological supports for students with vision impairments

k. A sense of belonging, a just opportunity for children with disabilities, an important choice for parents (Erwin & Soodak, 1995)

l. A teacher's aide, usually provided training by the employing district or organization, who provides direct support to individuals

m. A strategy for forming a vision for an individual in order to develop appropriate short- and long-term goals

Application Activities

1. Interview a teacher who is involved in an inclusive classroom. What were his or her concerns before beginning work in the classroom? What are his or her feelings now?
2. Interview the parent of a student in an inclusive classroom. How does he or she perceive that being in an inclusive classroom has influenced his or her child?

REFERENCES

Alessi, F. (1991, April). ODDM: The gentle bulldozer. *Quality Outcomes Driven Education,* 11–18.

Barnett by Barnett v. Fairfax County School Board, 927 F.2d 146 (4th Cir. 1991), cert. denied, 112 S. Ct. 175, 116 L.Ed.2d 138 (1991).

Baumeister, A.A., & MacLean, W.E. (1984). Deceleration of self-injurious and stereotypic responding by exercise. *Applied Research in Mental Retardation, 5,* 385–393.

Board of Education v. Holland, 786 F. Supp. 874 (E.D. Cal. 1992).

Board of Education v. Rowley, 458 U.S. 176, 102 S. Ct. 3034, 73 L.Ed.2d 690 (1982).

Browder, D.M. (1997). Educating students with severe disabilities: Enhancing the conversation between research and practice. *Journal of Special Education, 31*(1), 137–144.

Campbell, P.H., & Banevich, C. (1986). *The integrated programming team: An approach for coordinating multiple discipline professionals in programs for students with severe and multiple handicaps.* Akron, OH: Children's Hospital Family Child Learning Center, Integrated Services Project.

Carr, E.G., Reeve, C.E., & Magito-McLaughlin, D. (1996). Contextual influences on problem behavior in people with developmental disabilities. In L.K. Koegel, R.L. Koegel, & G. Dunlap (Eds.), *Positive behavioral support: Including people with difficult behavior in the community* (pp. 403–424). Baltimore: Paul H. Brookes Publishing Co.

Cefalu v. East Baton Rouge School Board, 907 F. Supp. 966 (M.D. La. 1995).

Chris D. v. Montgomery City Board of Education, 753 F. Supp. 922 (M.D. Ala. 1990).

Ellison v. Board of Education, 597 N.Y.S.2d 483, 189 A.D.2d 518 (App. Div. 3d Dept. 1993).

Erwin, E.J., & Soodak, L.C. (1995). I never knew I could stand up to the system: Families' perspectives on pursuing inclusive education. *Journal of The Association for Persons with Severe Handicaps, 20,* 136–146.

Giangreco, M.F. (1990). Making related service decisions for students with severe disabilities: Roles, criteria, and authority. *Journal of The Association of Persons with Severe Handicaps, 15*(1), 22–31.

Giangreco, M.F., Dennis, R., Cloninger, C., Edelman, S.W., & Schattman, R. (1993). "I've counted Jon": Transformational experiences of teachers educating students with disabilities. *Exceptional Children, 59,* 359–372.

Giangreco, M.F., Edelman, S.W., Cloninger, C., & Dennis, R. (1993). My child has a classmate with severe disabilities: What parents of nondisabled children think about full inclusion. *Developmental Disabilities Bulletin, 21*(1), 77–91.

Giangreco, M.F., Edelman, S.W., Luiselli, T., & MacFarland, S. (1997). Helping or hovering? Effects of instructional assistant proximity on students with disabilities. *Exceptional Children, 64*(1), 7–18.

Green, C.W., Reid, D.H., White, L.K., Halforn, R.C., Brittain, D.P., & Gardner, S.M. (1988). Identifying reinforcers for persons with profound handicaps: Staff opinion versus systematic assessment of preferences. *Journal of Applied Behavior Analysis, 21,* 31–43.

Hamre-Nietupski, S., McDonald, J., & Nietupski, J. (1992). Integrating elementary students with multiple disabilities into supported regular classes. *Teaching Exceptional Children, 24*(3), 6–9.

Hamre-Nietupski, S., Nietupski, J., & Strathe, M. (1992). Functional life skills, academic skills, and friendship's social relationship development: What do parents of students with moderate/severe/profound disabilities value? *Journal of The Association for Persons with Severe Handicaps, 17,* 53–58.

Horner, R.H., & Carr, E.G. (1997). Behavioral support for students with severe disabilities: Functional assessment and comprehensive intervention. *Journal of Special Education, 31*(1), 84–104.

Hunt, P., Farron-Davis, F., Wrenn, M., Hirose-Hatae, A., & Goetz, L. (1997). Promoting interactive partnerships in inclusive educational settings. *Journal of The Association for Persons with Severe Handicaps, 22*(3), 127–137.

Hunt, P., & Goetz, L. (1997). Research on inclusive educational programs, practices, and outcomes for students with severe disabilities. *Journal of Special Education, 31*(1), 3–29.

Irving Independent School District v. Tatro, 486 U.S. 883, 104 S. Ct. 3371, 82 L.Ed.2d 664 (1984).

Janney, R.E., & Snell, M.E. (1997). How teachers include students with moderate and severe disabilities in elementary classes: The means and meaning of inclusion. *Journal of The Association for Persons with Severe Handicaps, 22*(3), 159–169.

Jorgensen, C.M. (1992). Natural supports in inclusive schools: Curricular and teaching strategies. In J. Nisbet (Ed.), *Natural supports in school, at work, and in the community for people with severe disabilities* (pp. 179–215). Baltimore: Paul H. Brookes Publishing Co.

Jorgensen, C.M., & Rudy, C. (1990). *INSTEPP project student inclusion checklist.* Durham: University of New Hampshire, Institute on Disability.

Kincaid, D. (1996). Person-centered planning. In L.K. Koegel, R.L. Koegel, & G. Dunlap (Eds.), *Positive behavioral support: Including people with difficult behavior in the community* (pp. 439–466). Baltimore: Paul H. Brookes Publishing Co.

Michael, J. (1982). Distinguishing between discriminant and motivational functions of stimuli. *Journal of the Experimental Analysis of Behavior, 37,* 149–155.

Mount, B., & Zwernik, K. (1988). *It's never too early, it's never too late: A booklet about Personal Futures Planning* (Pub. No. 421-88-109). St. Paul, MN: Governor's Planning Council on Developmental Disabilities.

Nietupski, J., Hamre-Nietupski, S., Curtin, S., & Shrikanth, K. (1997). A review of curricular research in severe disabilities from 1976 to 1995 in six selected journals. *Journal of Special Education, 31*(1), 36–56.

Osborne, A.G. (1984). How the courts have interpreted the related services mandate. *Exceptional Children, 51*(3), 249–252.

Pearpoint, J., Forest, M., & O'Brien, J. (1996). MAPs, Circles of Friends, and PATH: Powerful tools to help build caring communities. In S. Stainback & W. Stainback (Eds.), *Inclusion: A guide for educators* (pp. 67–86). Baltimore: Paul H. Brookes Publishing Co.

Rainforth, B., & York-Barr, J. (1997). *Collaborative teams for students with severe disabilities: Integrating therapy and educational services* (2nd ed.). Baltimore: Paul H. Brookes Publishing Co.

Regulations for the Education for All Handicapped Children Act, 34 C.F.R. § 121.550 (1977).

Reichle, J. (1997). Communication intervention with persons who have severe disabilities. *Journal of Special Education, 31*(1), 110–134.

Repp, A.C., & Kirsch, K.G. (1990). A taxonomic approach to the nonaversive treatment of maladaptive behavior of persons with developmental disabilities. In A.C. Repp & N.N. Singh (Eds.), *Perspectives on the use of nonaversive and aversive interventions for persons with developmental disabilities* (pp. 331–348). Sycamore, IL: Sycamore Publishing Co.

Risley, T. (1996). Get a life! Positive behavioral intervention for challenging behavior through life arrangement and life coaching. In L.K. Koegel, R.L. Koegel, & G. Dunlap (Eds.), *Positive behavioral support: Including people with difficult behavior in the community* (pp. 425–438). Baltimore: Paul H. Brookes Publishing Co.

Ryndak, D.L., Downing, J.E., Jacqueline, L.R., & Morrison, A.P. (1995). Parents' perceptions after inclusion of their children with moderate or severe disabilities. *Journal of The Association for Persons with Severe Handicaps, 20,* 147–157.

Salend, S.J., & Longo, M. (1994). The roles of education interpreter in mainstreaming. *Teaching Exceptional Children, 26*(4), 22–29.

Salend, S.J., & Viglianti, D. (1982). Preparing secondary students for the mainstream. *Teaching Exceptional Children, 14,* 137–140.

Schumm, J.S., & Vaughn, S. (1992). Planning for mainstreamed special education students: Perceptions of general classroom teachers. *Exceptionality, 3,* 81–98.

Williams, W., & Fox, T.J. (1996). Planning for inclusion: A practical process. *Teaching Exceptional Children, 28*(3), 6–13.

Wolery, M., & Schuster, J.W. (1997). Instructional methods with students who have significant disabilities. *Journal of Special Education, 31*(1), 61–79.

Zobrest v. Catalina Foothills School District, 509 U.S. 1, 113 S. Ct. 2462 (1993).

Voices from Inclusive Learning Communities

Karen Matuszek, Linda Phillips,
Jan Rich, Regina H. Sapona, and Mary Ulrich

When speaking with teachers and administrators, the authors some-
times are the focus of disagreements about why inclusive learning
environments cannot work. We are accused of being dreamers, locked
away in our ivory towers, though we have been teachers ourselves,
have worked in schools, and have engaged in action research for
many years.

This chapter adds three sets of voices from inclusive learning communities to support arguments presented in this book that inclusive environments not only should work but can work. These voices are as diverse as their sources: a teacher and a university faculty member who engaged in action research in an elementary school on the outskirts of a metropolitan area, a parent in a suburban school district, and a special educator and principal of an inner-city high school. This chapter provides a platform for their voices, their stories, and their views on inclusion. One is a description of an inclusive environment, one is a letter from a parent to her son, and the third is a description of the journey undertaken by a high school in making the commitment to serve all students. As readers review these narratives, it is hoped that they will recognize within each narrative the challenges presented in inclusive learning communities and celebrate the strength of those who work in those communities daily.

AN INTERACTIVE LEARNING COMMUNITY
By Regina H. Sapona and Linda Phillips

Walk into Room 104 in a particular northern Kentucky elementary school, and you will be amazed at the many communicative interactions taking place. Enter at 8:15 A.M., and you will find learners signing a marker board to indicate their presence at school and whether they are buying lunch that day. You will note that there is only one more space (out of five) on the sharing-time sign-up sheet and that two students are negotiating for that opening. Look to the left, and you will see shelves of books. Nonfiction books are organized by topic, and fiction books are arranged alphabetically by author. Above the shelves, at the student's eye level, crates filled with books by authors previously studied are labeled with the authors' names (e.g., Eric Carle, Steven Kellogg, Lois Ehlert, Frank Asch). Look to the right, and you will see a chalkboard flanked by calendar activities. Since this is the 175th day of the school year, you will see various ways to write 175 (tally marks; Roman numerals; sticks in bags to indicate hundreds, tens, and ones). To the left of the sign-in board are posted five classroom rules; underneath the rules is a pocket chart filled with colored cards. The chart is labeled "How is your day going?" After signing in, learners either go to the classroom's game center to play for a few minutes or to find something to read from the shelves.

As you enter the room, you will hear lots of conversation. At various times throughout the day, you will notice excitement and interest among the learners as they engage in various projects. During calendar time (8:30 A.M.), the students develop questions, collect data, and organize a graph titled "What is your favorite dinosaur?" During mathematics time, the students draw life-size posters of dinosaurs (incorporating the skills of measuring, estimating, comparing, and recording), graph the approximate length and height of the dinosaur, and write on the graph. At 9:30 A.M., the students divide into three groups: One group will read with a teacher a book with a dinosaur as a character, the second group will read poetry with the other teacher, and the third group will read a big book with a teacher. At 11:45 A.M., one teacher begins theme time by reading to the class about scientists who study dinosaurs, a topic chosen in response to questions raised during the previous day's class discussion. Learners working in research groups study one type of dinosaur and prepare presentations as well as drawings and paintings to share their knowledge with others. At 1:50 P.M., during writing workshop, the students continue to work on their stories. Later in the week, they will write a position paper on why they think dinosaurs became extinct.

You, the visitor, might be taken on a tour of the learning environment by one of the students. You will notice the pride that the student takes in conducting the tour as he or she notes the various learning centers, areas for special kinds of work and activities, and sharing and celebrating of the accomplishments of all of the students. As the tour continues, you will discover a community of learners engaged in activities that encourage interaction and cooperative learning. The children read aloud to each other and help each other as they engage in interesting projects. As a visitor, you might ask yourself, "Where are the learners who have special needs?"

Designing the Learning Community

Establishing classroom communities and learning environments that support all learners regardless of individual needs is one of the goals of the teaching partnership in this school. In the learning community described previously, teams of teachers implement several kinds of partnerships for inclusion ranging from full inclusion for learners who differ from their peers in their interactions and behaviors to partial inclusion for learners who differ from their peers in their learning rates and styles.

With the support of the principal, a special educator and a general educator designed a learning environment that was structured to promote the academic and behavioral needs of 24 learners, 5 of whom the school district had identified as having emotional or behavior disorders. The two teachers shared their classroom space and worked with an instructional assistant assigned to the special education class. Thus, three adults were available to support instruction in the classroom.

In this example, a special education teacher implemented the initial work of inclusion with two general education teachers who were willing to share their classrooms. She was assigned to teach a group of learners identified as having emotional or behavior disorders. The previous year, the special educator took some of the students in her special education unit to several general education classrooms, where they participated in mathematics instruction connected to various classroom themes. Initially, the special educator did not share in the instruction but provided support for students. Over the course of the year, she assisted the general education teachers by gathering resources and gently suggesting, for example, "I wouldn't mind explaining that part of the lesson," or "Could we get together for planning, and maybe you could do the introductory part of that activity and I could do the second part of it?"

The special education teacher noticed her students' frustration when they missed discussions about a particular theme that the general education students were studying:

> When we arrived in the class we hadn't heard any of the literature, we hadn't done any research about the topic, we hadn't been thinking about the topic, . . . and suddenly we were doing an extended mathematics project that needed a lot of language and knowledge about a topic that we hadn't been studying. That was the impetus to try to fully include the learners with disabilities into the general education community.

The following year, the special education teacher and a general education teacher decided to blend their classrooms and teach the learners together as a team. The principal encouraged each teacher to keep her classroom so that there would be a place for learners to go if they needed time to talk or to solve a crisis.

The teachers began by talking about what they liked most about their classroom environment and the routines that they found most effective with their students and then blended their ideas into a learning community composed of the best of both classroom learning environments. One classroom became the center room (including areas such as a science center and a mathematics center); the other classroom had desks and tables where small-group instruction was conducted. Each teacher used both rooms, depending on the activity in which the class was engaged; both taught and assumed responsibility for instruction with an instructional assistant assigned to the special education unit.

Although the teachers managed learners in different ways, they thought about learners in a similar way. The teachers enjoyed observing learners and evaluating their development. They became excited over learners' accomplishments and valued their diverse learning styles. Over the year, the teachers shared ideas and learned from each other. One learned new ideas about instruction, and the other became more skilled in handling behavior issues. For example, the special education teacher encouraged the general education teachers to handle behavior issues by making explicit suggestions: "Here's an idea. If he starts doing _____ , you might try saying _____ ," and "I suggest that you keep your voice at a low level." Some of the explicit modeling focused on tone of voice, waiting time between an incident and the teacher's response, and following through on what has been said and on consequences.

This collaborative team designed a learning environment that encouraged and invited all learners to develop academic as well as social and communication skills. There were no specific elements that could be singled out as contributing to the success of the learners. The next section discusses several factors of the learning environment that appear to support an inclusive program.

Authentic Tasks and Predictable Routines

The teachers in this learning environment used themes to organize instruction in reading, writing, mathematics, and various content areas such as social studies and science. Students engage in a wide variety of reading (reading stations, big book, author study, and poetry), D.E.A.R. (Drop Everything and Read) time, literature study groups in which learners select books to read in small groups and complete a project about the books to share what they have learned, and reading research associated with themes (e.g., the dinosaur research projects). The students are in a classroom environment in which they are immersed in print and in which all kinds of reading materials are available. One is amazed at the variety of writing that students generate, including stories, journals, learning logs, reading logs, and science projects.

How does engaging learners in authentic tasks such as reading literature and writing stories in a workshop format support the development of all learners, including those identified as having emotional or behavior problems? In this learning community, the students often worked in small groups, capitalizing on the strengths of all members of the group. If all learners are actively engaged in the learning tasks, there is little opportunity for behavior problems to emerge as a result of material that is too boring or too difficult. Learners select the topics for their research, write in their journals about the topics that they choose, generate ideas for stories to write about, and edit with their colleagues' input (i.e., students share their writing before publishing it). During literature study groups, learners choose from among several trade books or children's literature at their instruction level that the teacher has selected. By working in groups, children learn the communication and social skills necessary for sharing ideas, getting along with others, compromising, and negotiating projects.

The students know the routines and schedule of events as well as topics of study for the classroom. Guidelines for the writing workshop, tasks during center time, and routines for tasks as mundane as signing up for share time make the classroom environment predictable and therefore comfortable for students. The multi-age nature of the classroom means that some students are experts and can assist others by modeling the kinds of routines and behaviors expected during the school day (from lining up for recess to moving from center to center during theme time).

Instruction in Communication Skills Is
Embedded and Practiced Throughout the Day

The learners who differ from their peers in their interactions and behaviors often take part in social skills instruction that is out of context. In the learning environment under discussion, instruction in social skills is embedded throughout the school day. There are natural, contextual opportunities for learners to learn and practice social skills such as turn taking, seeking clarification, negotiation, and listening to ideas as groups engage in project design and completion. There are specific times for addressing classroom dilemmas: Any child may suggest a particular issue for discussion during classroom meeting time. Problems range from pushing in line, saying "bad" words, not putting materials away, or erasing a name from the share time list. The classroom meeting is led by a student and is composed of a specific routine that includes a description of the problem, a discussion, the generation of solutions, and the recording of results. The social and pragmatic skills needed to participate in any kind of group discussion are practiced throughout the school day as multiple opportunities for group work occur.

Proactive Total Class Behavior Management System with
Therapeutic Interventions for Critical Emotional and Behavioral Moments

Rather than the teachers' instituting a classroom management system for only those learners identified as having emotional or behavior problems, the entire class participates in the management system. This allows all learners to celebrate their terrific days or weeks by contributing to a class celebration for good behavior. Rules are posted, and the consequences of violating those rules are clearly defined (see Table 1).

Table 1. Posted rules and signal cue cards

Classroom rules
I will follow directions.
I will wait my turn to speak.
I will speak nicely to others.
I will keep my hands and feet to myself.
I will help take care of our classroom things.

Signal cue cards and their meanings

Green card:	Terrific job! Keep it up!
Blue card:	Warning: Get back on track.
Yellow card:	Slow down and solve your problems.
Red card:	Not such a good day, lots of problems.

There are times when learners have trouble expressing themselves, such as when someone brushes against them during recess or when they are frustrated with another child during cooperative learning activities. The two teachers and the instructional assistant have learned to recognize indicators of frustration prior to full-blown behavior outbursts. When necessary, a learner leaves the classroom with the teacher to talk through the problem, puzzling through alternatives to the behavior. The teacher might ask the student to describe two ways in which he or she might have solved the problem differently. The teacher talks with the learner, modeling how to express feelings, think about alternatives to behavior, or just sit quietly with the learner as he or she calms down. In this partnership, there is one special education teacher, one general education teacher, and an instructional assistant, all of whom at some point assist learners during critical moments.

Genuine Choices: Academic and Behavioral

How often does a learner have a choice in what he or she studies in the typical classroom? Learning to select topics for writing, books to read, and specific research topics is an integral part of this classroom learning environment. The excitement is evident as learners share their discoveries and ideas. For example, during D.E.A.R. time, learners select specific books to read. When a learner who is reluctant to read gets to select a book to browse through or read and sees an entire class of students reading interesting fiction or nonfiction books, there is an increased likelihood of encouraging that learner's interest in reading.

The learners are also involved in making choices about their behavior. The students are encouraged to solve their own problems as often as they can by using a three-step problem-solving strategy:

1. Tell the person in a nice but strong voice to stop, and tell the person which behavior you want them to stop.
2. If the person keeps bothering you, get away from the person.
3. If the person follows you or starts a new problem, ask an adult to help you.

If the situation gets to Step 3, then the adult works with the learners to talk through the problem. For example, one day, some learners expressed their irritation with a student who was whistling during group work time. Several children got annoyed and expressed displeasure. This gave the teacher an excellent opportunity to support learners as they applied the problem-solving strategy by first asking them to tell the offending student to stop whistling in a gentle but firm voice. She said to the learner who was whistling, "Look, you're with friends around this table, and they are really aggravated with the way you are whistling. They have asked you to stop. It's really making them mad, and they are not going to want to be in this group with you." The whistling student was then faced with a choice. In contrast to having the teacher intervene by removing the learner causing the disruption, the learner must stop whistling to remain a member of the group.

In other instances, the teacher might model how to tell someone that you are annoyed by his or her behavior, providing an opportunity for learners to learn to share their feelings in an appropriate manner. Each learner is given a choice of complying with the group's decision or leaving the group until he or she is ready to rejoin the group. The power of the peer group often leads the learner to stop whistling immediately. The next day, the learner might tell the teacher, "I'm not going to whistle today! I won't bother anybody with my whistling!" One of the things the teachers try to teach the learners in problem solving is to speak up when they do not like something and get some help if what they do not like is not changing. In this case, the learners in the group spoke up and said that they did not want the whistling, so it was the other child's responsibility to do what the group asked him to do. Such types of learning opportunities were endless!

Thus, the multiple opportunities for making genuine choices in both academic and behavioral realms support the development of the academic and social skills of all learners. The learners have a chance to assume leadership positions during classroom meetings and to lead the group during share time and in writing workshop, which allows them to run a group meeting. By assuming leadership, all learners have a better understanding of how to behave in a manner that allows share time to proceed smoothly.

Celebrations

Celebrations of learning occur frequently in the inclusive learning environment. When learners finish their stories and publish their books, their writing is shared with the class and placed in a display of classroom authors. Projects are posted and displayed in the hallways for all of the members of the school community to see. Videotapes of literature study projects are made and shared with parents.

Celebrations of good work occurs, not just the celebration of finished projects. One typical celebration occurred when learners were celebrating their writing. When a learner who was typically a reluctant writer had a particularly productive day, he was asked to share his writing with the others in the class. The teacher publicly praised him for what he had done. This public praise seemed to be a great source of encouragement for the reluctant writer.

Encouragement comes from other learners. Keith struggled with writing—he did not like to write and would engage in a lot of disruptive behaviors to avoid writing. Some days were more difficult than others, so on days when Keith was really trying to do his work and trying to participate, other learners around him would praise him spontaneously, "Keith, you're working hard today!" The students working with him whispered to him and encouraged him.

Finally, celebrations for good behavior occur in the form of videotapes associated with themes and playing games that most children play. All learners contribute to earning the celebration by placing pieces of popcorn in a large jar when they demonstrate positive behavior. When the popcorn in the jar reaches a designated level, the class has a party. Learners support each other's behavior, hoping that each child has a successful day.

An Inclusive Learning Environment Supports Diversity

This inclusive classroom learning environment encourages diversity and choice, which allows learners to approach learning and demonstrate their knowledge in different ways. For example, after studying the growth of trees, the teacher decided to have learners draw a tree on a piece of 8½- by 11-inch paper with cutouts from various colors of construction paper and label the parts of the tree (trunk, branches, and roots). Around the room, learners cut out branches of green paper and trunks of brown paper. At one table, however, a learner was ripping pieces of green paper into tiny, confetti-size pieces. Another learner had rolled up a piece of brown construction paper and put it in his mouth as if it were a horn. A third learner had cut out long, green pieces of paper. In some learning environments, the teacher might interpret these behaviors as being off task or as not complying with directions. These learners took longer to get started and longer to finish the project but did finish making their trees.

Imagine the teacher's surprise to see and hear three diverse approaches to the tree assignment as the learners shared their projects with the class. The learner who seemed to be making confetti created a tree with a textured trunk: That learner used small pieces of paper to create the bark of the trunk. The second learner, who had appeared to be playing with a horn made of rolled brown paper, made a three-dimensional tree trunk with a squirrel looking out of a hole in the trunk. The third student created a perfectly labeled palm tree with the long, green pieces of paper he had cut for branches. Thus, what appeared to be students' taking too much time to start their projects were actually learners who completed the task differently from others. Contrast that situation to the use of a worksheet that requires learners to label the parts of the tree. Think about the teacher who might not tolerate the variety of ways in which students may share their knowledge in the tree study. Active involvement of learners and the genuine choices they are encouraged to make contribute to a learning environment that is supportive of all learners, especially those learners who differ from their peers in their interactions and behaviors.

UPON GRADUATION

By Mary Ulrich

Parents often have been the instigators of more inclusive learning communities for their children. In the following letter to her son Aaron, a young adult with autism, Mary Ulrich describes the efforts made and the collaboration that occurred in maintaining Aaron in inclusive learning communities.

Dear Aaron,

Today is a special day for both of us. Today you will graduate from high school. In the speeches, they say that the measure of success is not what you achieve but the number of obstacles you have overcome. The last 22 years have been a journey filled with more than a few obstacles. You are a success, and we are all very proud.

Our culture celebrates this ritual of graduation as a transformational experience from childhood to adulthood, from dependence to independence. But dearest, like everything else in your life, you are rewriting the book on what *childhood, adulthood, dependence,* and *independence* mean. You thought for all these years that you were the student, but in reality you have been the teacher for all who would care to listen and learn. I cannot speak for you or for others, but I can tell you of my transformational experiences as your mother and co-traveler.

When your dad and I brought you home from the hospital, you had balloons over your crib to help your eye tracking, bells on your wrist, and bright blue booties on your feet to encourage movement. You were nursed, cuddled, exercised, sung to, and loved as the most precious baby on earth. Yet, despite the best advice of the Brazeltons, the Whites, and all the other experts of the world, at 9 months of age you could not reach for objects or raise your stomach off the carpet, and you cried incessantly. Although the pediatric neurologist could find nothing wrong with you physically, he told us that your mental development was far below typical and that you would always be in special schools. We made a trip to the National Institutes of Health in Rockville, Maryland. We began weekly regimens of occupational and physical therapy. What is ironic is that the speech-language/communication therapy, which is probably what you needed most, was never even suggested, because your chart carried the label of *mental retardation.* We tried vitamins, special diets, standing you on your head, swinging you in nets, and reading everything about anything anyone would recommend. It seemed impossible that our precious baby had some mysterious problem that Modern Medicine could not even identify, much less cure. Aaron, you were just so beautiful, so wonderful, we just did not want you ever to have to suffer anything. Your dad and I wondered what kind of a life you and your new brother, Tommy, would have—would you know any happiness, have any friends, enjoy a camping trip to the mountains, ride a bike, grow to be independent and make a contribution to society?

Even though your dad and I are teachers, we did not have a clue about what the neurologist meant by "special schools." Did he really think we would send you and Tommy to a school that was not "special"? Your dad and I also did not know anything about people with disabilities. In our 25 or so years of living in our neighborhood—going to school, church, the grocery store, and being part of our community—we had never had a single firsthand experience with a person with a significant challenge. We were naïve.

We also did not know that a federal law called Education for All Handicapped Children Act of 1975 (PL 94-142) was just being implemented and that this single piece of legislation would be as important to us as the Emancipation Proclamation was to the slaves. This law was the difference between our neurologist's worldview of specialness (i.e., charity and pity for those less fortunate) and a different paradigm based on the philosophy that individuals with disabilities are citizens with the right to an education in the least restrictive environment. It seems, dear Aaron, that you could not have picked a better time to be born.

Your right to an education began at age 5 years. So, almost on your fifth birthday, we filed a lawsuit on your behalf so that you could go to school with your brother, Tommy, and the neighborhood children. Remember Neill Roncker, your friend, who was also in a U.S. Supreme Court suit with our school district over the same issue? It took almost 3 years of battle, but when we won, Aaron, you were the first person with a significant disability to enter the public school system. Large school districts do not like to lose, however, and our school district was not child centered. Besides, we had this little problem that Dad worked for the same school district in which we wanted you to attend school. Fortunately, Dad had tenure, but the specialness paradigm was just too embedded in our community. So, we searched the five-county area around our community and learned that you and your brother could attend the same school if we moved into one specific subdivision in one specific school district. After we moved, Dad drove the 20 miles back to the old neighborhood to work each day. It seems outrageous, but such is discrimination. The name of the new school district, *Lakota*, derived its name from a Native American word meaning "coming together as one."

On your graduation day 13 years later, the old school district still has segregated schools and classes. Your developmental twins, 21-year-old students with developmental disabilities, are still stacking colored rings while you're working half a day in the local police station as a custodian's assistant and, together with a job coach, half a day in the community with other adults with disabilities. Yea, Aaron!

Not that the new school district or new county board were perfect—not by any means. We certainly had our difficulties. But they grew with us. They made the effort.

Remember when the big yellow school bus came to our street, and you and Tommy got on together to go to the neighborhood school? No police escort, no angry mob—you just sat at the front of the bus and went to school with the other children from our neighborhood. What a moment! After all the lawsuits and numerous meetings with 25 professionals telling us that integration was folly—just by moving to a different district, you just got on the bus and rode to school. That was a transformational moment for me. As the bus pulled away, I cried and cried that such a simple event was possible. If our vision was for you to be assimilated into our society, and if the other students were to learn tolerance, then this simple act of inclusion on the bus was a giant step. Later, when the bus drivers formed a union to try to get you off the bus, the director of special education came to the rescue. The bus drivers were trained. Some drivers quit, but others became your good buddies. They began to understand that discrimination, whether because of race, religion, or disabilities, is wrong. For the next 13 years, we would run into boys and girls, young women and young men, in the grocery store or at the mall who would come up and say, "Hi, Aaron!" and when asked how they knew you, they would frequently reply, "Aaron rides on my bus," and they would give you a "high five."

There was a wonderful gymnastics teacher who allowed you into the after-school gymnastics class "as long as you didn't take away from the other students." We had to choose between a physical therapy session and the gym class, and we made the right choice. I was your assistant in the beginning, but later your special education teacher took over. It seems she was a cheerleader and gymnast in high school and really enjoyed getting to know other kids in the school.

This led us to Jessica, a 9-year-old general education student, who observed that when there was music with a steady beat during gym class, you were able to walk easier and faster. Her father, who happened to be the music teacher at our school, was then asked by his daughter at the dinner table to allow you to play in the school band. So, the next week, Jessica not only stopped by your classroom to insist you go to band but also stopped by our house one afternoon and wanted to take you for a walk around the neighborhood. Aaron, you and Jessica made it only about 10 houses down the street, but when you came back, Jessica said, "Aaron is such a good listener. I was telling him all my problems, and he stopped and gave me a hug and said, 'Ahhh.' " Well, there was much celebrating in our house that night and every time thereafter that Jessica came to visit. The fact that you did not talk with words was a plus for Jessica.

Aaron, you and your dad and Tommy went on many Cub Scout and Boy Scout outings. The troop was sponsored first by the elementary school and later by a local church. Andy, Bobby, Todd, and, of course, Tommy figured out ways you could participate in the Klondike Sled Pull; the winter sleepout; and the highlight of the year, summer camp at Woodland Trails. In the middle of the week at each summer camp, the boys were to rise before sunrise, paddle canoes across the lake, and cook breakfast on an island. In order to ride in the canoes, you have to pass the swimming proficiency test. Aaron, you have always been a pretty good swimmer, but it was impossible for you to do all the different strokes for even the beginner's certificate. The scout director knew that you would be wearing a life jacket and that your father and brother would be with you. What they decided was that if you could do some sort of an independent float without a life jacket for 10 minutes, then it would be safe for you to join the canoe trip. The scouts went into action.

They surrounded the deep end of the pool, and you were set adrift. Each time you would head toward the pool wall, one of the scouts would "shoo" you back into the deep water. It was probably the longest 10 minutes in Woodland Trails history, but Aaron—with the help of all the other scouts—you passed the swim test. You participated in the canoe trip, and, during the awards ceremony at the end of the week, you received a "Special Beginners" swimming badge to shouts and a standing ovation. That was another transformational moment for me because my old definition of *independent* was replaced with a new concept called *interdependence*. With a few modifications, some accommodations, and a little support, safety rules were upheld and scout laws were not deemed sacred; these boys did not just recite but honored a code that says, "A scout is trustworthy, loyal, helpful, friendly, courteous, kind, obedient, cheerful, thrifty, brave, clean, and reverent." Years later, when Todd and Bobby became Eagle Scouts, they talked about how they helped you achieve your swimming badge, and they asked you to light a candle in their court of honor ceremony.

Because many of the same kids were in band and scouts, at the spring chorus recital at the junior high school, instead of wondering why you and your teacher would stand in the front row of the chorus and not sing a word, their parents came up to Tom and me and said, "It's great that Aaron got to sing in the chorus. I noticed that he swayed to the music and one time clapped." The finale was a rendition of "That's What Friends Are For" (Warwick, John, Knight, & Wonder, 1985). Indeed! That's what friends are for!

In all your years in school, being on the cross-country team was the seminal experience. Because the Special Olympics track team was practicing at the other end of the playing field, the coach pointed in their direction and, when we declined, asked if Aaron or I were going out for the cross-country team. (I was not, since I was obviously not 13 and did not own a purple spandex jogging suit—which all the little 13-year-old girls were wearing.) I thought it was obvious that you were to be the one on the team, and I was to be your support person. There were about a million details for the coach to be concerned with, so he had one of the students lead the warmups. Aaron, you were probably laughing inside as we just joined in the exercises as best we could, because you were in the general education gym class; the rest of the kids were comfortable and hardly noticed you. As we were told to jog around the tennis court, the coach watched and then asked, as we went past, "Can Aaron run?" I remember that I calmly said "No" and kept going. The next practice, the coach called me over and said that he had spoken to the adapted physical education teacher (also the coach of the Special Olympics), and she said not only that Aaron could not run but also that he had to sit down on the floor to cross over from the carpet to the linoleum. I said that was true, and then we just continued on our laps around the tennis courts. Of course, one of our laps was three laps for the other kids, but we got in a routine of encouraging and saying hello by name to all the runners who passed us.

The coach, Mr. Seiple, taught science at the high school and was a lovely person. He just did not want anyone hurt, and he could not imagine why you or I were there. (Plus, I'm sure he got an earful from the adapted physical education teacher.) The wonderful thing about cross-country is that each school has one select team, and everyone else runs in the open division to beat their individual times. Several times, Tommy ran fast enough to be on the select team; but 90% of the time he, Andy, Bobby, Renuka, Elaine, and the majority of the rest of the group ran independently.

Since all of the 13-year-old students needed rides, the parents of the team members in our neighborhood were more than a little thankful that I was willing to drive every day. I loved to look in the back seat and see Aaron squished between three other kids. Gradually, you and I became accepted members of the team.

I remember the offhand questions as the runners would lap us. Renuka once asked why you bit your hand when we went down a hill. She slowed her pace for the answer that Aaron has balance problems and that going down the hill is especially hard for him. "Oh" was her response, and she ran on. Tommy told me that, in one race in which he lost his shoe on a tree root and finished the race with one bare foot, when his foot really hurt, he remembered how the beat of music helped Aaron. He started singing and that strategy helped him finish the race.

There is a rule in our state that you are not allowed to have a coach or a co-runner. So, our family decided that we would save that fight for another day, and Aaron and Dad ran the prerace practice run. Then Aaron and I would stand at the head of the trail and shout encouragement and the runner's names as they ran past us. It sounded like an old church chant as "Go, Todd!" and "Go, Tommy!" echoed down the sidelines. Because none of the other parents knew the kids' names, this was a contribution that we could make to the cross-country team community. So, Aaron, even though you never ran an official race, we partially participated in everything. You lost 10 pounds, slept better at night, and could walk up to 3 miles at a time. You rode the team bus, got a team uniform, and you and Tommy were both in the cross-country team photograph for the yearbook. At the award ceremony, you both got school letters that were proudly worn through all of high school. More than one co-athlete told us that when they would get really tired, they would pass you and be inspired to keep on.

Each happy story is a golden nugget that I keep close to my heart. Your Personal Futures Plan (Mount & Zwernik, 1988), or dream plan, hopes that each day you will get a hug, a song, a tickle, and opportunities to sweat and learn new things. Your dad, your brother, and I hope that you will be surrounded by people who love you—that people will see your gifts, strengths, and talents. We hope you have lots of choices in each activity and varied environments. Now we smile at our earlier concerns because we know that you can have happiness, friends, camping trips to the mountains, and go for rides on a tandem bicycle and a motorbike. We know that you will be interdependent—a much healthier condition than being independent—and that you will continue to make contributions to society.

Through the last 22 years, your lifetime, our society has gone from legal isolation and segregation, to integration and mainstreaming, to inclusion and full rights and citizenship for persons with disabilities. I have gone through the personal transformations of being oblivious, to being a mother, to being an advocate, to wishing I could be just a regular citizen who cares about all devalued people. I no longer beg for opportunities to mainstream "if it doesn't bother the others." Now we just assume that you will be allowed to participate. We do not try to "fix" you but rather try to fix the environment with accommodations and adaptations. You are a great kid just the way you are. Working on this new vision, this new worldview, has consumed the years. Because of you, dearest Aaron, I am a different person than I might have been. You have been and continue to be an incredible teacher. Perhaps that is your greatest gift and contribution to society.

Today all of the 600 graduates in our district are also making the transformation from childhood to adulthood, from dependence to independence. They are not just more computer literate than their parents, these graduates are starting from a different place with different transformational experiences than their parents. They are not oblivious about people with disabilities. They at least have some reference point, some beginning history. As they are creating their visions of the future, some of those future visions have deep roots in past experiences—experiences from observations and the interactions of their parents, teachers, bus drivers, school administrators, scout leaders, coaches, and peers. Remember Renuka? She is Lakota's class valedictorian and is attending premed school at the University of Virginia. Andy is going to the University of New Mexico and wants to become a priest. Bobby is going into engineering at the University of Cincinnati. Lauren is getting married and wants to start a family. Amanda is in nursing school. Lamont is on a football scholarship at the University of Kentucky. Your brother Tom is going into elementary education at Morehead State in Kentucky.

Aaron, you have touched each of their lives, just as they have touched ours. Their vision and power are interrelated and intertwined with yours. Their future and worldview are also interrelated and intertwined with yours, for they are the next generation of taxpayers, parents, leaders, friends, and neighbors of people with disabilities. For us, school surely means "coming together as one."

Love,
Mom

AT THE TABLE

By Karen Matuszek and Jan Rich

Private schools as well as public schools struggle to meet the challenges of inclusion. In private schools, the commitment to a particular set of values is often inseparable from the commitment to inclusion. In these environments, mission and service provide additional support for inclusion. The following vignette describes the development of one Catholic secondary school in the inner city as an inclusive learning community for individuals from diverse ethnic, cultural, linguistic, ability, and disability groups.

Learners with disabilities have long been served in elementary school special education programs in our archdiocese. Secondary schools, however, were viewed as too much of a challenge for learners with disabilities. After many years of recognizing the need for such a program in a Catholic environment and much research and observation of similar programs locally and across the state of Ohio, Purcell Marian High School announced in February 1993 the creation of a program for learners with disabilities.

In the fall of 1993, eight students were admitted to what was primarily a self-contained program. Objectives for each student were written in academic areas with an emphasis on functional life skills. The plan was to base the curriculum on the strengths and weaknesses of the students in the program. Work experiences for the students would be provided initially through volunteer activities in the community, then in a work–study program in our school, and later in work environments in the community.

From this segregated beginning, an inclusive learning community grew. In 5 years, the program has graduated seven students: five to the world of work and two to university programs for individuals with disabilities. The program serves 30 students, who attend general education classes with support, receive individualized programming, and participate in elective classes open to all students.

The transition from a more traditional Catholic high school to an inclusive learning community began with a new mission statement:

> Influenced by the charisma of William Chaminade and Elizabeth Seton, Purcell Marian High School is Catholic, coeducational, multiracial, and urban. As Jesus came to invite all to the table, Purcell Marian embraces and promotes inclusiveness in all areas by accepting diverse academic levels, faith traditions, and socioeconomic backgrounds. We actively commit ourselves to innovative education of the whole person. By our words and actions, our faculty and staff strive to be an example in the classroom of what we want our graduates to be: respectful of others, thirsting for knowledge, and equipped with tools and a foundation necessary for a life of learning and service. (Purcell Marian High School, 1995)

Helen Keller was once asked, "What could be worse than not being able to see?" Her reply was, "Being able to see and having no vision" (1904, p. 341). Our mission statement and encouragement of school administrators helped us both see and have a vision for the program. We followed an eight-step process to design and develop the program.

Our first step was to make a commitment to serve students with disabilities. This was the easy step. It was followed by an intense effort to educate faculty and staff. Our summer in-service days were provided by the special education regional resource center, a local university, and special educators. We talked about fears and the challenges ahead. Techniques were suggested that would help all of us be successful educators of all teenagers, including teenagers with disabilities.

Our third step was to introduce students to the school. We supplied the faculty with biographies of all entering students, describing their learning characteristics, strengths, weaknesses, and pertinent medical concerns. We then introduced our school to the students. Students were invited to spend a full day in classes during the spring prior to their year of entry. In addition, students attended a back-to-school pizza party with student council representatives and some teachers the day before school started. At that time, they toured the school, got locker assignments, purchased plan books, and got a head start on being freshmen.

Our fourth step is ongoing. We continually work on a curriculum that is both academic and functional in nature. We are constantly changing course offerings to better meet students' needs. Courses include Independent Living, Career Explorations, Leisure Activities, and Study Skills. In addition, special education faculty are in almost daily contact with the general education faculty. Different approaches are offered, and a checklist of techniques to support students' inclusion is provided. A full-time instructional assistant helps implement accommodations. The general education teachers are asked to evaluate each student's progress at least twice quarterly.

The seventh step is to make sure that the students take advantage of every opportunity to become involved in extracurricular activities. Two students with disabilities have been elected to the student council, and two play in the band. Three have had speaking parts in the school play. The athletics program has been extremely supportive: two students have played freshman and varsity football, one has been on the wrestling reserve team, another has played freshman volleyball and softball, and another played freshman basketball and baseball. Students have served as managers of the men's varsity basketball team, and two have been managers of women's sports teams. Two students served as peer ministers and went into freshman religion classes to tell their stories to upperclassmen. One student was featured in *The Cincinnati Enquirer* as a "hometown hero" for her volunteer work.

Our eighth step is to celebrate success. The job of supporting students in an inclusive learning environment is not an easy one. We know that most Catholic secondary schools have chosen not to serve students with disabilities, for a variety of reasons. We are not afraid to pat ourselves on the back occasionally and share our stories with each other and with others.

We were not surprised by statements that general education religion teachers made regarding their teaching inclusive classes. One stated, "Nothing had prepared me for the magic of working daily in an inclusive classroom." Another stated, "One of the perks of teaching at Purcell Marian has been the opportunity to be an inclusive teacher. The program has added an entirely new element to our school's diversity." Yet another said, "We are very blessed with the ability to bring any teenager into this school building, and make him or her feel special, loved, and appreciated." Finally, one remarked, "The more exposure my students [without identified disabilities] have to students of varying abilities, the more they come to some significant conclusions about the dignity of all people."

The impact of students with disabilities on faculty teaching general education classes was both surprising and affirming. One general education faculty person stated, "Being an inclusive teacher has proved to be one of the highlights of my 21-year teaching career." Another stated, "I know of no other situation where caring and concern for others is so crucial as that of the inclusion of students with special needs. I am convinced that when students, and teachers for that matter, are faced with this challenge, they rise to it. And, in many cases, they exceed it." General education teachers tell of the impact that inclusion has had on their students. One said, "If someone had told me 5 years ago that teenagers could be so compassionate and so understanding, I would have never believed it. I have witnessed the most unlikely teens go out of their way to befriend or help the special students. It has been amazing to see what wonderful qualities inclusion has brought out of my general education students."

As we say in our mission statement, "as Jesus came to invite all to the table," Purcell Marian embraces and promotes inclusiveness in all areas. This means we believe not only that everyone should have access to a Catholic education but also that the education should take place within a faith community, not within a group defined by academic ability, race, gender, or socioeconomic level. The diversity found in the world is found in our school, and our students are well prepared by it. Our students learn to navigate a racially charged society together rather than simply learning about one another. We are a coeducational institution—our students work, play, and pray together as whole human beings. They see one another not as distractions but as partners. Some of us are poor, some are wealthy, and most are hard-working members of the middle class. All learn that poverty and wealth have little to do with talent, hard work, and compassion. Our students learn that people are not their disabilities. They have witnessed incredible struggles back from traumatic brain injuries. They have seen extraordinary musical talent coexist with profound developmental disabilities. They have cheered their classmates' athletic success. They have learned that the worst disabilities are those we choose: ignorance and intolerance.

SUMMARY

The voices expressed in this chapter provide examples of three different movements toward inclusion. In the first, teachers began to collaborate, forging change. In the second, a parent began the momentum to maintain her son in inclusive environments. In the third, a school made a commitment to diversity and change. Learning is ongoing in all environments. The goal of an inclusive learning community places us all in the role of lifelong learners, striving for equity for all of our students. The authors of this book hope that you will be adding your voice to those expressed here.

REFERENCES

Education for All Handicapped Children Act of 1975, PL 94-142, 20 U.S.C. §§ 1400 *et seq.*

Keller, H. (1904). *The story of my life.* New York: Doubleday.

Mount, B., & Zwernik, K. (1988). *It's never too early, it's never too late: A booklet about Personal Futures Planning* (Pub. No. 421-88-109). St. Paul, MN: Governor's Planning Council on Developmental Disabilities.

Purcell Marian High School. (1995). *Mission statement.* Cincinnati, OH: Author.

Warwick, D., with John, E., Knight, G., & Wonder, S. (1985). That's what friends are for. On D. Warwick, *Friends* [Recording]. New York: BMG/Arista Records.

Appendix: Answer Keys for "Self-Evaluation" and "Make the Language Your Own" Sections

CHAPTER 1

Self-Evaluation
1. B
2. B
3. B
4. A
5. B
6. B
7. C
8. C
9. C
10. A

Make the Language Your Own
1. A
2. D
3. M
4. E
5. I
6. L
7. C
8. K
9. B
10. F
11. N
12. P
13. G
14. J
15. H
16. O

CHAPTER 2

Self-Evaluation
1. C
2. B
3. A
4. C
5. A
6. B
7. A
8. B
9. C
10. A

Make the Language Your Own
1. K
2. B
3. A
4. C
5. E
6. J
7. D

8. H
9. F
10. G
11. I

CHAPTER 3

Self-Evaluation
1. B
2. B
3. B
4. A
5. B
6. C
7. C
8. B

Make the Language Your Own
1. F
2. B
3. H
4. G
5. D
6. E
7. C
8. A

CHAPTER 4

Self-Evaluation
1. B
2. B
3. B
4. A
5. B
6. C
7. A
8. C
9. B
10. B

**Make the Language
Your Own**
1. D
2. B
3. I
4. H
5. J
6. E
7. F
8. A
9. C
10. G

CHAPTER 5

Self-Evaluation
1. B
2. A
3. B
4. A
5. B
6. C
7. B
8. C
9. B
10. A

**Make the Language
Your Own**
1. C
2. A
3. F
4. E
5. B
6. D
7. G

CHAPTER 6

Self-Evaluation
1. A
2. B
3. B
4. A
5. B
6. A
7. B
8. C
9. B
10. C

**Make the Language
Your Own**
1. E
2. C
3. F
4. G
5. A
6. B
7. D

CHAPTER 7

Self-Evaluation
1. B
2. B
3. B
4. B
5. B
6. B
7. C
8. A
9. B
10. B

**Make the Language
Your Own**
1. B
2. E
3. J
4. I
5. D
6. A
7. H
8. C
9. F
10. G

CHAPTER 8

Self-Evaluation
1. C
2. B
3. B
4. A
5. B
6. A
7. B
8. C
9. C
10. C

**Make the Language
Your Own**
1. G
2. C
3. B
4. D
5. I
6. E
7. A
8. F
9. H
10. J
11. K

CHAPTER 9

Self-Evaluation
1. C
2. A
3. B
4. B
5. B
6. C
7. C
8. B
9. C
10. B

**Make the Language
Your Own**
1. C
2. D
3. E
4. A
5. B

CHAPTER 10

Self-Evaluation
1. C
2. B
3. C
4. C
5. A
6. B
7. B
8. C
9. C
10. B

Make the Language Your Own
1. D
2. B
3. I
4. A
5. N
6. E
7. P
8. L
9. K
10. J
11. C
12. O
13. G
14. S
15. R
16. F
17. H
18. Q
19. M

CHAPTER 11

Self-Evaluation
1. B
2. C
3. B
4. C
5. C
6. C
7. B
8. C
9. C
10. B

Make the Language Your Own
1. K
2. B
3. E
4. F
5. H
6. I
7. L
8. G
9. A
10. J
11. C
12. M
13. D

CHAPTER 12

Self-Evaluation
1. B
2. B
3. A
4. C
5. B
6. C
7. C
8. C
9. C
10. C

Make the Language Your Own
1. D
2. F
3. C
4. L
5. H
6. E
7. G
8. M
9. B
10. I
11. J
12. K
13. A

CHAPTER 13

Self-Evaluation
1. B
2. C
3. A
4. A
5. C
6. C
7. A
8. B
9. B
10. C

Make the Language Your Own
1. J
2. K
3. F
4. A
5. C
6. I
7. G
8. H
9. B
10. D
11. E

CHAPTER 14

Self-Evaluation
1. B
2. B
3. B
4. C
5. C
6. A
7. A
8. C
9. C
10. B

Make the Language Your Own
1. C
2. G
3. D
4. B
5. E
6. A
7. F
8. J
9. H
10. J
11. K
12. L
13. M

Index

Page numbers followed by "f" indicate figures; those followed by "t" indicate tables.